St. Paul's Epistle to the Romans

A DEVOTIONAL COMMENTARY

By the

REV. W. H. GRIFFITH THOMAS, D.D.

Professor of Old Testament Literature and Exegesis
Wycliffe College, Toronto
Formerly Principal of Wycliffe Hall, Oxford

Author of
"A Devotional Commentary on Genesis,"
"The Apostle Peter," etc.

WM. B. EERDMANS PUBLISHING COMPANY
Grand Rapids 1947 Michigan

ST. PAUL'S EPISTLE TO THE ROMANS
By Rev. W. H. Griffith Thomas, D.D.

Set up and Printed, April, 1946
Second printing, June, 1947

PRINTED IN THE UNITED STATES OF AMERICA

CONTENTS

CONTENTS — Continued

CONTENTS — Continued

CONTENTS — Continued

CONTENTS — Continued

NOTE

It is hoped that this work adheres as closely as possible to the aim of the series of which it forms a part—to provide a Devotional Commentary. To this end the exposition has been kept subordinate to the spiritual purpose, and difficult passages which usually demand great length of space have necessarily been dwelt on only so far as was required for the elucidation of the spiritual messages. Conditions of space, and, still more, the desire to lead the reader to do as much as possible for himself, have made this book largely one of outlines and suggestions. Devotional meditation can never be done by one for another; all that is possible is to provide suggestions. It must be "My meditation of Him," and no one else's, if it is to be "sweet," and if the soul is to "be glad in the Lord" (Psalm civ. 34, A.V.). As it is "the heart that makes the theologian," so it is the heart that must penetrate most deeply into the secrets of this doctrinal, theological, and yet always personal Epistle. The Apostle's own spiritual experience is the main key to his meaning, and those who enter into similar experiences of the profound truths here recorded will possess the best clue to the interpretation.

A list of the Commentaries and other works consulted and used in the preparation of this book is appended, and the quotations and references will show the extent of my indebtedness. But special mention must be here made of the great and valued help derived from a series of papers by my friend, the Rev. C. G. Moore, which appeared in the *Life of Faith* in the years 1894 and 1895. His careful scholarship, exegetical insight, and spiritual experience have done much to shed light upon several dark places in the Epistle, and I have freely availed myself of my friend's invaluable guidance.

St. Paul's Epistle to the Romans

1

INTRODUCTION

On taking up this book, one of the most important in the New Testament, there are several preliminary inquiries to be made, the answers to which will enable us to understand the Epistle much more clearly. It is of course impossible in our space, and indeed unnecessary for the specific purposes of this Devotional Commentary, to do much more than make suggestions, referring readers to general Commentaries for fuller information. The following points should receive attention:—

I. *The Writer.*—There is no question as to this Epistle being written by St Paul. "The letter is so characteristic of Paul's genius that to doubt its authenticity is to confess that we have not, and cannot have, any knowledge of the Apostolic age at all" (Garvie, *Century Bible*, Introduction). Romans is at once a revelation of the man, his teaching, and his work, and when studied from the purely personal standpoint is full of fascinating interest. A knowledge of the life of the Apostle is an important factor in the due appreciation of his writings, and this is especially true of the Epistle to the Romans. It may be said that we should be less in danger of misunderstanding the Apostle's teaching if we knew more of the essential features of his career. Three factors must carefully be noted.

His antecedents formed quite a striking combination. His Jewish birth, his Hebrew language, his Roman citizenship, his Jewish training, and his Greek culture, all helped to make him the man he was. As Principal David Brown has put it:—

> "His natural characteristics, so far as they can be gathered from his life and writings, seem to have been a masterful and versatile intellect, capable alike of profound thought and close reasoning; a rare combina-

tion of masculine courage and womanly tenderness; a combination, too, of impetuous zeal, sound discretion, and indomitable perseverance; in character straightforward and honest, and in the discharge of duty, as he understood it" (*Romans*, Introduction, p. 5).

Then came his conversion. Pharisaism did not satisfy him, and contact with Jesus Christ necessarily brought about a revolution which thenceforward affected everything in his nature and life.

Then followed his thirty years of Christian life and apostleship, of which some twenty years had been spent before Romans was written. Through the whole of this time the Apostle's personal contact with Christ was the source of all that was deepest in his theology. Whatever he may have derived from Pharisaism, or mere controversy, or even the Old Testament, Christ was the soul of the man, and influenced with transforming, uplifting, and inspiring power the thoughts of his mind and the feelings of his heart. His profound experiences and his strenuous service constituted the finest preparation for the writing of his Epistles.

A sketch of the Apostle's life in relation to his writings appears in all the important Commentaries on the Epistle, but there are three books of brief compass that may be specially recommended as in every way full of suggestion for study: *The Life of St. Paul*, by Dr. Stalker; *The Epistles of St. Paul*, by Dr. G. G. Findlay; *Epochs in the Life of St. Paul*, by Dr. A. T. Robertson.

II. *The Date and Place of Writing.*—Bishop Lightfoot says that "the date of this Epistle is fixed with more absolute certainty, and within narrower limits than that of any other of St. Paul's Epistles" (Smith's *Dictionary of the Bible*, Second Edition). Certain names point clearly to Corinth as the place whence this Epistle was written. Thus Phoebe (ch. xvi. 1, 2), Gaius (ch. xvi. 23; 1 Cor. i. 14), Erastus (ch. xvi. 23), are all connected with Corinth, while Timothy (ch. xvi. 21) was with St Paul at this time (Acts xix. 22; 1 Cor. xvi. 10). The Epistle was probably written when the Apostle was at Corinth, as recorded in Acts xx. 3, while on his way to Jerusalem with contributions for the poor Christians there (Acts xx. 22; 1 Cor. xvi. 4; 2 Cor. viii. 1, 2). According to the older chronology the date was probably the spring of the year 58, when St Paul had been a believer twenty years, though more recent chronological scholarship suggests the year 55 or 56 (C. H. Turner, Hastings' *Bible Dictionary*). The Epistle was thus written some eight or ten years before his death.

III. *The Occasion and Circumstances of Writing.*—Rome had a natural fascination for St. Paul, as a Roman citizen and as the Apostle to the Gentiles. He had long purposed to visit the metropolis (ch. i. 9-13; xv. 22-29), but had been unavoidably hindered. So he sends this Epistle to explain his absence, to pave the way for his coming, and to supply meanwhile the lack of personal teaching. Other Epistles of his were addressed to Churches founded by him, or to those closely associated with him and his disciples, but here he writes to a Church already experiencing a Christian life which had not originated through his instrumentality. He was on his way to Jerusalem bearing contributions from Gentile Churches to Judæan Christians, and he intended afterwards to travel westwards to Spain (ch. xv. 28), and to take Rome on his way thither.

IV. *The Destination.*—How and when the Church in Rome was founded is entirely unknown. It would seem clear that no Apostle had been there (ch. xv. 20), and the fact that the Christians in Rome were able to enter fully into the Pauline Gospel of this Epistle perhaps indicates that the Church was not founded more than ten years before the Apostle wrote, and therefore not, as is sometimes imagined, shortly after the Day of Pentecost. The door of faith was not opened to the Gentiles for several years after Pentecost. But in any case the close and frequent communication between Palestine and Rome through Asia Minor and Greece would easily give the opportunity for Christianity to reach the metropolis of the Empire.

The Church seems to have been composed partly of Jews and partly of Gentiles, though pretty certainly with Gentile predominance. The names in ch. xvi. are mostly Gentile, and the way in which the Apostle speaks from time to time (ch. i. 13-15; xv. 15, 16) also suggests a strong, prominent Gentile influence. But the constant reference to Jewish questions clearly shows that there must either have been a strong Jewish element, or else that the Gentiles were thoroughly conversant with Jewish teaching. In several chapters it is evident that the readers were well acquainted with the Old Testament, and there is no trace of antagonism between Jew and Gentile, for the Apostle's argument turns now to one side and now to the other. As evidence is available for both Jewish and Gentile elements, it has been suggested, with great probability, that the Church was largely composed of Jewish proselytes. This fact would certainly account for the manifest unity between both sections which is assumed and clearly implied in the Epistle.

V. *The Character.*—Romans is one of the few Epistles written to a Church with which the Apostle had had no personal dealing, either as founder or visitor. Consequently it is as much a treatise as a letter, and, indeed, some authorities consider that, apart from the personal introduction and closing verses, it might have been addressed to any Church. Perhaps this goes too far, but the contrast between Romans and the personal character of Epistles like those to Corinth, Galatia, and Philippi is very striking.

As the result of recent discoveries of papyri in Egypt and elsewhere, Deissmann distinguishes between literary and non-literary documents, and argues strongly in favor of St. Paul's Epistles being all non-literary, that is, letters, not epistles. While therefore he thinks that at first we might be in doubt whether Romans is a letter or an epistle, he comes to the conclusion that it is not an epistle addressed to all the world, or even to Christendom, containing a compendium of the Apostle's teaching, but a long letter written to pave the way for his visit to the Roman Christians (*Light from the Ancient East,* p. 231). We shall probably be nearer the truth if we regard Romans as at once a personal letter and a theological treatise. Godet calls it "a treatise contained in a letter," and the versatility of St. Paul would easily lead to a combination of both elements. The Apostle was a man whose theology was thoroughly saturated with his spiritual experience, and this twofold point of view is pre-eminently seen in Romans. As Sanday and Headlam well say, "A man of St Paul's ability, sitting down to write a letter on matters of weight, would be likely to have several influences present to his mind at once, and his language would be moulded now by one, and now by another (Introduction to *Romans,* p. xl.).

Then, again, as we have now been made familiar through the writings of Sir William Ramsay, "St Paul had early grasped the importance of the Roman Empire as a vehicle for the dissemination of the Gospel" (Robertson, Hastings' *Bible Dictionary*, Art. on "Romans," p. 299). So that it was no accident which addressed this letter to the great metropolis, for it was peculiarly appropriate to all the existing circumstances of the Apostle's life.

VI. *The Purpose.—St.* Paul at the date of writing Romans was just closing his work in Asia Minor, and the time seemed to have come to review and discuss the general position in view of his completed tasks and the circumstances awaiting him in Jerusalem. He was naturally, and rightly, desirous of winning the sympathy of the Roman Christians for his Gospel, and for his plans in furtherance of it. He wished to obtain their support for the operations contemplated by him, and so he writes this comprehensive letter, stating fully his position. It is scarcely possible to omit a further consideration; he evidently looked forward to serious difficulties, and even dangers, in Jerusalem, and this might therefore easily be his last Epistle.

One crisis in his strenuous life was just over, but another was now upon him. The problem of the Gentile reception of the Gospel had necessarily forced the Doctrine of Justification into prominence, and that had been definitely settled in connection with the Churches of Galatia. But now the question of Jewish unbelief was coming to the front. The relation of the Gospel to the Jews and the Gentiles respectively was pressing upon the Apostle. To the Gentile he had preached a free, full, and universal message, and yet there was the enigma of Jewish unbelief and rejection facing him and his fellow-Christians. How was it that in spite of everything the Jews were still rejecting Jesus Christ? St Paul could not, and had no wish to, ignore the Jew, and now he takes up the great question of the relation of the Jew to Christ and His salvation. He points out that the Gospel is for the Jew "first," and yet "also to the Greek," and that though the Jew is now outside the Gospel owing to his rejection of it, there is a future for him which is divinely certain and assured. He desired to show Gentile believers in Rome and elsewhere that his Gospel did not ignore the Jew, but, on the contrary, regarded him as either occupying a definite place in the Christian Church, or else as constituting a large unbelieving section outside it. Sanday and Headlam thus clearly and convincingly state the problem which faced the Apostle after his victory over the Judaisers in Galatia:—

> "This battle had been fought and won. But it left behind a question which was intellectually more troublesome—a question brought home by the actual effect of the preaching of Christianity, very largely welcomed and eagerly embraced by Gentiles, but as a rule spurned and rejected by the Jews—how it could be that Israel, the chosen recipient of the promises of the Old Testament, should be excluded from the benefit now that those promises came to be fulfilled. Clearly this question belongs to the later reflective stage of the controversy relating to Jew and Gentile. The active contending for Gentile liberties would come first, the philosophic or theological assignment of the due place of Jew and Gentile in the Divine scheme would naturally come afterwards. This more advanced stage has now been reached; the Apostle has made up his mind on the whole series of questions at issue; and he takes the opportunity of writing to the Romans at the very centre of the Empire, to lay down calmly and deliberately the conclusions to which he has come" (Introduction to *Romans*, p. xliii.).

In view of these important considerations, it will be readily seen that chs. ix.-xi., which deal specially with the subject of the Jew, are an integral and necessary part of the Epistle, and in our judgment no view of the Apostle's purpose in writing Romans can possibly be right which ignores or minimizes the importance of this section, which is essential to the true understanding of his attitude. In some respects the closing verses of ch. xi. are the culminating point of the Epistle. God's attitude to both divisions of mankind, Jew and Gentile, is there stated with special reference to the future salvation of both. Indeed, the entire Epistle is full of "the Jewish Question," as may be seen from the earliest reference in ch. i. 2 and a careful study of the allusions in chs. ii., iii., iv., xiv., and xv.

The peculiar position of the Apostle at the time of writing, as he reviews the past and anticipates the future, enables us to understand the absence of controversy in this Epistle, the conciliatory attitude, and the didactic and apologetic elements which are all found combined herein. Both of the great doctrinal sections, chs. i.-viii. and ix.-xi. are absolutely essential to the full understanding of the

Apostle's purpose, and there is no necessary contradiction between the various elements of the apologetic and didactic which are found in Romans, for, as Dr. Denney says, these are not by any means mutually exclusive. Dr. Barmby (*Pulpit Commentary*, p. x.) remarks that this Epistle is,

> "in its ultimate drift, a setting forth of what we may call the philosophy of the gospel, showing how it meets human needs, and satisfies human yearnings, and is the true solution of the problems of existence, and the remedy for the present mystery of sin. And so it is meant for philosophers as well as for simple souls; and it is sent, therefore, in the first place, to Rome, in the hope that it may reach even the most cultured there, and through them commend itself to earnest thinkers generally."

Dr. Elder Cumming some years ago (*Life of Faith*, September 19, 1894) made a suggestive contribution to the consideration of the purpose of Romans. He thought that we have in it the record of the personal mental history of the Apostle, in which, after his conversion, he worked his way from the old Jewish standpoint to his standpoint under the Gospel. In writing he takes himself as a representative of all his fellow-countrymen who had accepted Christ, and putting his own process of thought into general terms, makes it applicable to all. As he went along, working from principle to principle in his own case, he discovered that the Gentiles also had had to face the same problems, and to go through with necessary modifications the same process. Hence, Dr. Cumming argues, the entire Epistle bristles with personal allusions which we can read between the lines. For the same reason the Apostle is never really out of sight of Jewish questions, and so as the light into which he himself came was clear and cloudless, he endeavours to lead all his readers into the same. Dr. Cumming points out that it is not without weight that in the closing chapter we have more information given about the family and relatives of St. Paul than in all other places put together. In Rome itself there were three kinsmen, who had been converted to Christ while he himself was still a persecutor (vs. 7, 11), and in Corinth there were three other kinsmen who joined him in greeting relatives and others in Rome. So the man Paul "really pervades the whole Epistle; going back over the road he once trod so slowly and carefully, and taking us with him as our guide."

We believe this suggestion is a very fruitful one, and may well prove the unifying factor to bring together various elements in the Epistle which, if considered by themselves, do not satisfy the requirements of the situation. The contents of the Epistle seem to fit this view, which opens the door to a number of difficult places, especially the references to Sin, Righteousness, Union with Christ, the fight with self and the law, the references to "Abraham our father," and the touching personal mention of Israel and his brethren according to the flesh. When thus considered we can the more readily understand the fulness and depth of meaning of the Apostle's significant phrase, "My Gospel," for Romans then reveals to us what the Apostle himself had received, what he was proclaiming, and what he wished to commend to Jew and Gentile everywhere as "the power of God unto salvation to every one that believeth."

VII. *The Integrity.*—The only question that arises here is with reference to the last two chapters, which present some curious phenomena of text in the manuscripts, and have therefore been regarded by some scholars as either mutilated or misplaced. But all the great manuscripts present these chapters in the ordinary connection with one slight exception in regard to the closing doxology. Those who desire to have a general outline of the critical problems connected with this subject, will find it useful to look at the Introduction to Romans in the *Cambridge Bible for Schools*, by the Bishop of Durham (p. 27).

II

SUGGESTIONS FOR STUDY

CHRYSOSTOM had this Epistle read to him once a week. Luther speaks of it as "the chief book of the New Testament." Coleridge calls it "the profoundest book in existence." Melanchthon, in order to become thoroughly acquainted, copied it twice with his own hand, and it was the book which he lectured on most frequently. Godet remarks that "in studying the Epistle to the Romans we feel ourselves at every word face to face with the unfathomable." These testimonies indicate at once the importance of the study and the need of all possible guidance.

I. *Reasons for Study.*

1. The *Intellectual* Value is very great. Romans is concerned with a number of the deepest problems of Christian thought, which are well worthy of all the attention we can bestow upon them. Then, again, the logical arrangement of the Epistle is another reason for intellectual effort. Indeed, it is not too much to say that a study of Romans will provide a mental gymnastic of the finest type. As Dr. Garvie rightly remarks (introduction, p. 35), "the logical method of the Epistle will repay study," for St. Paul uses various forms of argument that necessarily appeal to the thoughtful mind (see Garvie, pp. 36, 37). Dr. David Brown's fine testimony is well worth quoting:—

> "Its texture is so firm, its every vein so full, its very fibres and ligatures so fine and yet strong, that it requires not only to be again and again surveyed as a whole, and mastered in its primary ideas, but to be dissected in detail, and with unwearying patience studied in its minutest features, before we can be said to have done it justice. Not only every sentence teems with thought, but every clause; while in some places every

word may be said either to suggest some weighty thought, or to indicate some deep emotion" (*Romans* p. xviii.).

2. The *Historical* Value is equally real. The Epistle is largely occupied with the great thoughts of Christianity and the world of St. Paul's day, and in many respects it is an expression of Pauline Christianity. Two books of interest, covering the substance of the first eight chapters, have both been entitled *The Gospel according to St. Paul* (Dr. Oswald Dykes and Dr. W. B. Du Bose). Not the least important element of this historical aspect is the witness the Epistle gives to the relation of St. Paul to our Lord, for herein we have depicted the Christ of St. Paul in relation to the Christ of the Gospels. It has often been pointed out that the modern cry "Back to Christ" does not, and cannot mean "Away from St. Paul." The Apostle's recent experience of the Christ of heaven, as recorded in this Epistle, amply justifies and vindicates the Evangelist's accounts of Christ on earth. In Romans, too, we have brought before us one, if not two, of the great controversies of the Apostle's life, and as these controversies occupied a large part of his career, we can see at once the historical value of the Epistle. And then, again, we have in Romans what Sir William Ramsay has rightly called St. Paul's "Philosophy of History." The universalism of the Epistle, too, is noteworthy, and its world-wide view naturally and necessarily commends it to the consideration of all serious historical students.

3. The *Theological* Value must not be overlooked. While it does not contain a complete statement of Christian doctrine, since there is no special emphasis on Christology, as is Colossians and Ephesians, and no teaching about Eschatology, as in Corinthians and Thessalonians, yet it deals with a number of great theological principles in a thoroughly comprehensive way, and no one can ponder what is here said on such subjects as Sin, Righteousness, Grace, Law, Justice, and Love, without being made conscious of the profound theological importance of the Epistle. There is a remarkable care shown in the presentation of the truth, and an equally remarkable balance of statement, and all this goes to show that the thorough study of the Epistle is really a theological education in itself. And lest we

should be repelled by the thought of theology as something abstract, remote from life, and unpractical, it must be noticed that the theology of Romans is always based on the exegesis of the Apostle's words. Nothing in its way is more striking than the fact that the theology which deals with some of the profoundest truths of the Christian religion comes directly out of the grammatical and accurate interpretation of the Apostle's teaching. The more it is studied from the theological standpoint, the more it will be seen that it is of the very highest value for Christian doctrine.

4. The *Spiritual* Value of the Epistle follows as a necessary consequence. In it will be found some of the prime secrets of the spiritual life. Its first great truth is the reality, extent, and awfulness of sin. This leads necessarily to its teaching on Redemption, with its spiritual results in the reconciliation of the soul to God, its deliverance from sin, and its renovation by the Holy Spirit. Holiness is the very centre of the Epistle (chs. vi.-viii.), and may be described in a word as God dwelling in the heart. But this indwelling presence of God for holiness, on the one hand, comes from the reception of the atonement of Christ through faith (chs. iii.-v.), and, on the other hand, expresses itself in loyalty, love, and obedience (chs. xii.-xv.), and the more the spiritual life is allowed to ponder the Apostle's words the stronger will be its fibre and force. As Luther said of this Epistle:—

> "It is the true masterpiece of the New Testament, and the very purest Gospel, which is well worthy and deserving that a Christian man should not only learn it by heart, word for word, but also that he should daily deal with it as the daily bread of men's souls. For it can never be too much or too well read or studied; and the more it is handled the more precious it becomes, and the better it tastes."

And as a modern writer (Dr. Beet) has aptly put it:—

> "A careful study of the words and arguments of this Epistle will enrich greatly the student's own spiritual life. And this spiritual enrichment will shed important light on the meaning of the Apostle's words. For it will enable us to see the matters about which he writes from his own point of view" (*St. Paul's Epistle to the Romans,* p. 27).

5. The *Practical* Value of the Epistle must also be carefully observed. Godet goes as far as to say that "the probability is that every great spiritual revival in the Church will be connected as

effect and cause with a deeper understanding of this book" (*Commentary on Romans,* vol. i. p. 1). There is much in the past history of the Church which goes to support this statement. Certainly the main factor in the great Reformation Movement in the sixteenth century was the teaching of this Epistle and the companion one to Galatians, while in the Evangelical Revival of the eighteenth century and the various Evangelistic Movements of the nineteenth, the truths of Romans have been at the very heart of the situation. Dr. David Brown points this out in saying that,

> "While all Scripture has stamped its impress indelibly on the Christian world, perhaps it is scarcely too much to say, that—apart from the Gospels—for all the *precision* and the *strength* which it possesses, and much of the *spirituality* and the *fire* which characterise it, the faith of Christendom in its best periods has been more indebted to this Epistle than to any other portion of the living oracles" (*Romans,* Introduction, p. 18).

This may be said without the slightest qualification, and certainly without the faintest fear of contradiction; that a Christian life nourished on the Epistle to the Romans will never lack the three great requisites of clear preception, strong conviction, and definite usefulness.

II. *The Methods of Study.*

1. The Epistle should be studied with all possible intellectual attention and concentration. It is worthy of all the consideration we can give to it. It is important that the whole Epistle should be read right through in the Revised Version, at one sitting, and that this should be done if possible day by day for a month. It will not take long, and the advantage will soon be seen to be immense. Failing the possibility of doing this, one of the great sections of the Epistle should certainly be read over and over again in order that we may become thoroughly habituated to its general lines of thought. At first there is no need to try to study it deeply, but simply to read it through with care and attention as we would an ordinary article in a newspaper, or a chapter in a book. Gradually the mind will become accustomed to its teaching and gain a general impression of its contents and meaning.

2. It should be studied with earnest prayer and personal trust. Intellectual attention alone is insufficient. The Epistle should be regarded as a personal letter to ourselves. Its deepest secrets will only be revealed to the heart that is willing to submit to its teaching and translate it into action. "Access to the inmost sanctuary of Holy Scripture is granted only to those who come to worship" (*St. Paul's Epistle to the Romans*, by J. A. Beet, p. 27).

3. It should be studied with an earnest endeavour to grasp its leading ideas. The early chapters teach the profound truth that man has always failed to manifest righteousness in his life, and the Epistle deals with this universal failure and brings before us the message of a new Divine righteousness for guilty man. Thus, the leading ideas may perhaps be summarized as Sin, Guilt, Propitiation, Righteousness, Faith, the Holy Spirit, Consecration; and these indicate in turn man's need of righteousness, and his responsibility for it, and then the ground, the means, the effect, and the proof of that Divine righteousness which is provided by God in Christ.

4. It should be studied with special reference to its great theme, as stated in ch. i. 16, 17. In these two verses there are seven terms which go through the entire Epistle and affect every part of it: God, Gospel, Power, Salvation, Righteousness, Faith, Life. So that the theme of Romans is man's reinstatement in righteousness by the provision found in the Gospel of Jesus Christ. Salvation is provided and made possible for sinful man by a righteousness which is not his own. Like the warp and woof of a piece of cloth, these great thoughts are the very substance of the Epistle.

5. It should be studied with all available helps. The character of this Epistle is such that the aids of scholarship and of spiritual insight are particularly valuable and welcome. Of the many books written on Romans it is impossible to refer to more than a few. For all ordinary purposes the two books by the Bishop of Durham will be ample. As a foundation his detailed Commentary in the *Cambridge Bible for Schools* should be used, and side by side with it his larger work in the *Expositor's Bible.* The latter book is one of the choicest works of scholarly, intellectual, and spiritual exposition, and if only one volume can be obtained this certainly

should be the one adopted. *The Century Bible,* by Garvie, is also full of suggestion, and if read with constant discrimination will be found very useful, though in the present writer's judgment it is occasionally too free in regard to Apostolic authority and inspiration. The little volume by Dr. David Brown in the "Handbooks for Bible Classes" is also extremely valuable, and well merits the testimony of a leading American scholar who said that it was a "perfect book of its kind."

Larger works, involving for full appreciation a knowledge of Greek, are the Commentaries by Dr. Denney, Dr. J. Brown, Dean Vaughan, Dr. Beet, Dr. Gifford, Drs. Sanday and Headlam, and Dr. Godet. Each has its own particular excellence, though for general scholarly use that by Dr. Gifford is perhaps the most serviceable. My own indebtedness to it is constant, for it was the basis and guide of my earliest work in student days. It certainly merits the fine testimony given to it by Drs. Sanday and Headlam, that it is "on the whole the best, as it is the most judicious, of all English Commentaries on the Epistle." A list of the books used in the preparation of this present work will be found in the Bibliography. A further list is provided in the article on Romans in Hastings' *Bible Dictionary,* by the Bishop of Exeter, Dr. Robertson.

The value of several Commentaries to the present writer is that they specially emphasize and bring out particular points. Thus Dr. John Brown is peculiarly helpful on the meaning of Faith in Romans iv.; Dr. Forbes is illuminating on the word "righteousness"; Haldane is very clear on "imputed righteousness"; while some of the other works like *Curae Romanae,* by Walford, which are little known, frequently shed light on passages which other writers fail to elucidate. Dr. Denney, in the *Expositor's Greek Testament,* shows such remarkable insight into Pauline thought and experience that the obvious limitation of his space is much to be regretted.

In connection with Romans it is very important to remember that the older Commentaries should not be overlooked or despised. With many of the books of the New Testament the more modern the Commentary the better, but with Romans this is not necessarily the case, and among the older Commentators it is safe to say that Calvin, Hodge, Haldane, and Chalmers will never be superseded.

Dr. Alexander Whyte once said that whenever a new book on Romans comes out and is sent to him by its publisher for consideration, he at once turns to the comments on chapter vii., and according to the view taken of that important section he decides on the value of the entire work. While this may perhaps be too sweeping and severe a test, it is certain that the treatment of ch. vii. is a good criterion of the value of a Commentary on Romans, and we will venture to say that while every commentator endeavours to face the great questions involved in that chapter, there are comparatively few who seem to take into consideration *all* the elements necessary for its complete elucidation. The present writer has found two works of particular value in shedding light on ch. vii.: *Romans 7—What does it Teach?* by Laicus (S. W. Partridge & Co.) and *The Wretched Man and His Deliverance* by Philip Mauro.

Last but not least, one of the very best helps to the study of Romans (especially of chaps. i.-viii.) will be found in the little volume by the Rev. W. H. T. Gairdner of Cairo, entitled *Helps to the Study of the Epistle to the Romans* (Student Christian Movement). Its small size and its terse comments may perhaps lead some people to overlook the fact that it is based on a close and continuous study of the greatest authorities.

III

THE ANALYSIS

It is essential to take a general view of the Epistle before proceeding to the study of details, for it has a logical sequence and a completeness of treatment which make it imperative for us to try to grasp and appreciate the Apostle's leading ideas. By concentrating attention primarily on separate verses, or even small sections, we are in danger of failing to understand the Epistle in its entirety. We do not see the wood for the trees.

Like most of the Apostle's writings, the Epistle consists of three parts; a personal introduction (ch. i. 1-15); the substance (ch. i. 16—xv. 13); a personal conclusion (ch. xv. 14—xvi. 27)

I. *Introduction* (ch. i. 1-15).

1. *A Salutation* (vers. 1-7). He writes as the Apostle of the Gentiles, and on the strength of this official position he greets them with a somewhat elaborate address in justification of his writing the Epistle.

2. *Expression of personal feelings* (vers. 8-15). His thanksgivings for them show his deep interest. He wishes to see them and to impart some spiritual gift. He explains why he has not been able to visit Rome, and also states his obligation to preach the Gospel to all men.

3. *The Theme* of the Epistle (vers. 16, 17). From the personal reference the Apostle naturally passes to the object of writing. He is ready to preach the Gospel even in Rome, inasmuch as he is not

[1]This plan, while following the generally accepted outline of the Epistle, is greatly indebted to Bishop Lightfoot's fine analysis (*Notes on the Epistles of St. Paul,* p. 239), together with the analyses found in the works by Professor Godet, Dr. Beet, Dr. J. Brown, Bishop Handley Moule, Dr. Campbell Morgan, and the Rev. C. Neil.

ashamed of it. It is God's power for the salvation of everyone through faith, because it reveals God's righteousness. Thus out of the purely personal expressions he leads his readers up to his theme, which occupies the main body of the Epistle.

II. *The Epistle* (ch. i. 16—xv. 13).

A. The Gospel is God's power unto salvation through faith, for in it is revealed God's righteousness as opposed to the righteousness of the law (ch. i. 16—viii. 39).

1. *God's righteousness needed and unattained by all because of the Divine wrath against sin* (ch. i. 18—iii. 20).

(*a*) In relation to the heathen (ch. i. 18-32).

The wrath of God falls on impiety and unrighteousness. The Gentile world could, and ought to have seen God through His works in nature. They refused to see Him, and so they suffered His righteous punishment and fell into idolatry. This led to impurity and shamelessness, and they not only practised these things, but even took a keen delight in those who did so.

(*b*) In relation to the Jew (ch. ii. 1—iii. 20).

The Jews condemn Gentiles, and yet they do the same things and equally need God's righteousness. God is absolutely impartial and there will be no exemption for the Jew. As he has a priority of knowledge so also he will have a priority of condemnation. This Divine impartiality is shown in the distribution of final awards based on personal character and the standard of knowledge possessed. The Jew has God's law and proudly boasts of his privileges; yet he violates the law and in regard to spiritual religion is no better than the heathen (ch. ii.) Although the Jews had great privileges, nevertheless there is no excuse for them and no possibility of their being preferred before the Gentiles. They stand condemned by their own Scriptures, and by the utter powerlessness of the law of works to justify them before God (ch. iii. 1-20).

2. *God's Righteousness provided and received* (ch. iii. 21—iv. 25).

(*a*) Provided by the atoning sacrifice of Christ (ch. iii. 21-26).

To meet this failure of Jew and Gentile a remedy has been provided in God's righteousness through faith in Jesus Christ, offered to all, "to the Jew first and also to the Greek." Whatever may have been the past sins of the world, God's perfect righteousness of character is now demonstrated beyond all question in the gift of His Son as the Propitiation for Sin.

(*b*) Received by faith (ch. iii. 27—iv. 25).

This method of salvation through faith does not destroy God's requirement of law in its proper place; on the contrary, law is confirmed and established in and through Christ (ch. iii. 27-31).

Abraham is a striking illustration of this very principle of righteousness received through faith. It was because he believed in God that he became righteous. The language of the Psalms supports this position, and it is yet more evident from the fact that Abraham was still uncircumcised when he was declared to be justified through faith. So that neither through circumcision nor through law, but by faith, Abraham was justified, and this constituted him "the father of the faithful," for the record concerning him was written for our sakes as well, since we believe on Him Who raised up our Lord from the dead (ch. iv.).

3. *God's Righteousness a power for the believer's present and future as opposed to the powerlessness of the law* (ch. v. 1—viii. 39).

(*a*) In relation to Sanctification (ch. v. 1—viii, 17).

There are several spiritual results of this great blessing of righteousness through faith (ch. v. 1-11), and the greatest of all is that the foundation is laid in the gift of Jesus Christ as the Second Adam, the Lord from heaven. As sin brought death through the first Adam, so righteousness brings life through the Second Adam, and notwithstanding that where sin abounds grace superabounds (ch. v. 12-21).

But abundance of grace does not mean continuance in sin, which would be an utter contradiction of our position in Christ. The acceptance of Him in His atoning sacrifice implies and involves a spiritual union in all that He did for us in death, burial, and resurrection. When this is clearly understood we realize that sin is no longer to be a tyrant over us, since we are not under law but under grace (ch. vi. 1-14).

"Under grace" means, therefore, that the despotism of sin is altogether impossible. The former slavery to sin is over, and now the believer in Christ is a slave to righteousness: the end of his former bondage was death; the end of his present slavery is life eternal (ch. vi. 15-23).

But what is the meaning of "Ye are not under law?" The obligation of the law is always cancelled by death. A wife is free to marry again when her husband dies. So, we in our unregenerate state were in union with sin, but now this "old man," or unregenerate self, has been crucified with Christ, and our true self is set free to be united with Christ Jesus and thereby enabled to bring forth fruit to His praise and to serve in newness of spirit (ch. vii. 1-6).

Yet this does not for a moment mean that God's law itself is sinful, quite the opposite, for the Divine law reveals and convicts the conscience of sin. Law is intended to make us conscious of sin, and the more we contemplate God's law on the one side and our own powers on the other, the more we become aware of our utter powerlessness to fulfil the Divine requirements. This powerlessness when considered alone leads to despair by reason of the bondage of sin, until the soul bursts out with longings for deliverance and the joyous confession that Christ alone can deliver (ch. vii. 7-25).

When the believer becomes joyfully conscious that there is now no condemnation to those who are in Christ Jesus, he enters fully into the blessings provided through His atoning sacrifice. God has delivered us in Christ from sin and death, and we have been transferred from the dominion of the flesh to the dominion of the Spirit. Not only is this true in regard to sin, but also in regard to death, for the same Spirit that quickens our spirits for present living will make our mortal bodies alive in the Resurrection Day (ch. viii. 1-11).

We are therefore under an obligation to live to the Spirit, being led by Him, and thereby realizing our sonship and heirship (ch. viii. 12-17).

(*b*) In relation to preservation (ch. viii. 18-39).

With such spiritual possessions present afflictions are utterly insignificant and powerless to lead us astray, for the Spirit helps our infirmities and enables us to live in Christ and for Him (ch. viii. 18-27).

The present possession of the Spirit is also an earnest of our coming glory, for notwithstanding all the tribulations of the present, everything is working together for good, and God who commenced the work of grace will not allow it to be interrupted, and will take care that it issues in final glory. If He is with us no one can be against us, or lay anything to our charge. There is no condemnation, and no separation from the love of God in Christ (ch. viii. 28-39).

B. The Gospel of God's Righteousness in Relation to Israel (ch. ix. 1—xi. 36).

1. *Israel's Rejection in Relation to God's Sovereignty* (ch. ix.).

But what about the Jews? The Apostle has great sorrow on their behalf. Yet God's word is absolutely true and cannot possibly fail of accomplishment. Even the Old Testament made a distinction between the spiritual and the natural Israel, and salvation is not a matter of human preference but of God's decision. Pharaoh's case shows that God was absolutely righteous and at the same time absolutely free. The gathering in of the Gentiles as well as the remnant of Israel was actually foretold by the prophets.

2. *Israel's Rejection in Relation to their own Responsibility* (ch. x.).

The true explanation of Israel's failure is Israel's disobedience. While the Gentiles have attained unto righteousness, Israel has failed to obtain it because of a determination to seek it in their own way rather than God's. Righteousness comes through faith, based upon Christ's Death and Ascension, as seen in the Old Testament itself. Jews and Gentiles are entirely on a level here, and the Gospel must be preached to all. If the Jews will not listen and heed the message, it is their own fault and sin. Even this was anticipated by their own Scripture, and the Gentiles, it was predicted, should stir Israel to emulation by their acceptance of God's mercy.

3. *Israel's Rejection in Relation to their future Restoration* (ch. xi.).

But God has not forgotten His people. As it was in former days, so it is now; the faithful are few and the unbelieving many. But the failure of the Jews has been a blessing to the Gentiles, and in turn this reception of the Gospel by the Gentiles will influence the Jews and lead to their salvation. God's ultimate purpose is one of mercy for all.

C. The Gospel of God's Righteousness as manifested in Daily Life (ch. xiii. 1—xv. 13).

I. *Christian life in relation to the Christian body* (ch. xii.).

All these mercies of God in the provision of righteousness in Christ are intended to lead to consecration of life and service, and the first and most natural expression of this life of righteousness will be among our fellow-Christians. Humility and love will necessarily characterize our attitude.

2. *Christian life in relation to the State* (ch. xiii.).

The Christian is a citizen as well as a member of a Church, and this demands obedience to the temporal powers, the payment of everything that is due, and the fulfilment of the law of love in the light of the great and imminent event of the Lord's Coming.

3. *Christian life in relation to Special Duties* (ch. xiv. 1—xv. 13).

There are particular duties under special circumstances as well as the more general life of the believer. We are to respect the consciences of our fellow-Christians, since some are more scrupulous than others in regard to the observance of days and the eating of special meats. Those who are strong are to be tender, those who are weak are to be careful. We are not to please ourselves, but, following the example of Christ, to please our neighbors, living in such harmony that we may glorify God and rejoice with thankfulness that all, both Jews and Gentiles, have been brought within the circle of the Christian fold.

Thus these three great sections (ch. i. 16—viii. 39; ix. 1—xi. 36; xii. 1—xv. 13), forming the substance of the Epistle, have to do respectively with doctrine, dispensation, and duty. Each should be thoroughly mastered in turn, and its relation to the entire Epistle clearly grasped.

III. *Conclusion* (ch. xv. 14—xvi. 27).

1. *Expression of Personal Feeling* (ch. xv. 14-33).

The Apostle explains his motive in writing the letter (vers. 14-21); tells them his plans for the immediate future, and his hopes of coming to them (vers. 22-33).

2. *Salutations* (ch. xvi. 1-24).

He introduces the bearer of the letter; salutes a number of the Roman Christians (vers. 1-16); utters a warning against divisions and other offences and promises victory over Satan (vers. 17-20); and then sends greetings from a number of his companions (vers. 21-24).

3. *Ascription* (ch. xvi. 25-27).

In the closing doxology the Apostle introduces once again, but with significant additions, the theme of the Gospel as the power of God to the salvation of all (cf. ch. i. 16).

It will be seen that these three closing sections answer almost exactly to the three sections of the introduction, giving the Apostle's personal statements and greetings together with a closing ascription of praise.

This outline should be compared with those found in the various commentaries, and any necessary modifications or corrections made. Once again, let it be said that it is essential to study the Epistle as a whole first of all, and to obtain an idea of its general character, its main lines of thought, and its chief doctrinal teaching. The knowledge of details will be all the easier to acquire when we have made ourselves acquainted with the general drift. Not only so, but in studying any section it will be well to refer back to this or some similar outline, and thus to see the place of that particular section in the plan.

From the definite analysis it will be seen that, following the Apostle's words, the theme of the Epistle can be thus stated: the Gospel is God's righteousness for sinful man (ch. i. 16, 17).

This word "righteousness" should receive the closest possible attention, for it is the essential characteristic of the Gospel as brought forward in this Epistle, that it reveals, not God's love, or mercy, or grace, but His *righteousness.* Righteousness when applied to God means (1) His personal righteousness, that is, His own character, and (2) His gift of righteousness bestowed on man. Cf. ch. iii. 26, "That He might be *just*" (personal) "and the *justifier*" (bestowed). We must never forget that the term "righteousness" is much wider than justification, though this is of course, included. Righteousness really covers all that is necessary to reinstate a sinner as right with God, and therefore includes his position, his character, his privileges, and his prospects. It embraces the past, present, and future, and means "the state of being right."

The "righteousness of God" is the keynote of the Epistle, and from beginning to end the entire letter is built up on this thought. Study carefully the following analysis, which can be expanded almost indefinitely.

(*a*) Righteousness needed by sinful men (ch. i. 17—iii. 20).
(*b*) Righteousness provided by God (ch. iii. 21-26).
(*c*) Righteousness received through faith (ch. iii. 27—iv. 25).
(*d*) Righteousness experienced in the soul (ch. v. 1—viii. 17).
(*e*) Righteousness guaranteed as a permanent blessing (ch. vii. 18-39).
(f) Righteousness rejected by the Jewish nation (ch. ix.-xi.).
(*g*) Righteousness manifested in practical life (ch. xii.-xvi.).

IV

THE WRITER

ROM. i. 1, 5

1. Paul, a servant of Jesus Christ, called *to be* an apostle, separated unto the gospel of God,
5. By whom we have received grace and apostleship, for obedience to the faith among all nations, for *his* name.

IN every Epistle St. Paul's opening words are at once characteristic of the man and appropriate to the occasion. In writing to Rome he is addressing those to whom he is personally unknown, and he naturally desires to win their confidence and goodwill, and to predispose them to listen to his message. With keen spiritual sensitiveness, and with a wonderful blending of dignity and graciousness, he endeavours to get at once into close touch with the Roman Christians. Nothing in himself, if he could possibly help it, should hinder the reception of his message in the great metropolis. It was essential, too, that he should present proper credentials, as he was not known to the Roman Christians.

A stateliness and a fulness mark the Apostle's opening words, which are peculiarly appropriate to the great themes of the Epistle, as well as to the representatives of Christ in the greatest city of the world. This is seen especially in the fact that the first six verses consist of only one sentence, and that verses 1 and 7 are closely connected, with verses 2-6 as a parenthesis. The Apostle gives a fourfold description of himself.

I. *A Slave of Jesus Christ.*—This was a favorite designation of St. Paul. He regarded himself as the purchased possession of his Lord and Master. The two ideas of property and service are suggested. There was no serfdom or servility, and yet there was an absolute loyalty in the consciousness of absolute possession. The bond-servant owned nothing, and was nothing, apart from his master. His time, his strength, everything belonged altogether to another. There was nothing nobler to St. Paul than to be a slave of the Lord Jesus. He desired to be nothing, to do nothing, to own nothing apart from Him. If this title is not a reality, it is an utter mockery. If it is real, it always brings blessedness; if it is unreal, it must bring shame, for to be called a slave of Jesus Christ and yet to remain enslaved to self is the depth of moral degradation.

The title "Jesus Christ" should be noted at the outset. It is no matter of indifference to observe the way in which the Apostle varies the expressions between "Jesus Christ" and "Christ Jesus" and "the Lord Jesus Christ." There is a different emphasis on each of these forms (see this especially in Eph. i.). The changes are remarkable for their variety and frequency. When "Jesus" comes first it emphasizes Him who was Man and was also the divinely anointed One. When "Christ" comes first it is the divinely anointed One Who became the Man.

II. *A Called Apostle.*—This means that it was not by his own commission that he did his work. His Apostleship came from none other than Jesus Christ his Lord (1 Cor. i. 1; Gal. i. 1; Heb. v. 4, 5). An Apostle is one who is sent forth, a missionary, and this reference to his commission is of great importance. The history of the Apostle in the Acts and elsewhere tells us of his threefold call. He was called from his birth (Gal. i. 15); at his conversion (Acts ix. 15); and then specifically to his work through the Church at Antioch (Acts xiii. 2). These were his credentials; there was no human merit, and he occupied no mere human position.

III. *Separated unto the Gospel of God.*—Here the Apostle further describes his position. As a servant of Jesus Christ, commissioned as an Apostle, he had a specific work to do. To this he had been "separated" (Gal. i. 15; Acts xiii. 2). Concentration thus follows consecration and commission. The one and only purpose of his life was devotion to the Gospel of God, and it is only by concentration of aim and effort that the purpose of God concerning us will be realized.

IV. *Received Grace and Apostleship* (ver. 5). This describes the Apostle's equipment for his task. "Grace and Apostleship," or, as we may perhaps venture to render it, "Apostolic grace." Grace was always characteristic of the Apostle's life and mission. J. N. Darby's comment is both true and forcible:—

> "The Apostle's mission was not only his service; the being trusted with it was at the same time the personal grace and favour of Him whose testimony he bore . . . . There was grace and favour in the commission itself, and it is important to remember it. It gives character to the mission and to its execution. An angel performs a providential mission; a Moses details a law in the spirit of the law; a Jonah, a John the Baptist, preaches repentance, withdraws from the grace that appeared to falsify his threatenings against the wicked Gentiles, or in the wilderness lays the axe to the root of the unfruitful trees in God's garden. But by Jesus, Paul, the bearer of the glad tidings of God, receives grace and apostleship. He carries, by grace and as grace, the message of grace to men wherever they may be" (*Synopsis of the Books of the Bible,* Vol. iv. p. 116).

These verses are full of thoughts on service which should come home to the heart of every believer in Christ. Let us consider some of the aspects of the work to which Christians are called.

1. *The Divine Source.*—"Through whom we have received," etc. It was from the Risen Christ, his Saviour and Lord, that St. Paul derived his position and authority as a worker. It is from the same Divine Source that we must ever receive our call to labor in the Master's vineyard.

2. *The Divine Commission.*—The words "Apostle" and "Apostleship" in these two verses lay emphasis on the thought of *mission.* We must be sent if we would serve aright. "How shall they preach unless they be sent?" As the Lord Himself was the sent of God (John ix. 7), even so He sent His disciples (John xx. 21), and He still sends all who do Him service. The unique Apostleship differs only in degree from the commission of the humblest worker in the Kingdom of Christ.

3. *The Divine Equipment.*—"Grace and Apostleship." It is well that this is associated with the high thoughts of source and commission, for it reminds us of the provision made to carry out the work to which the servant is called and appointed. How full of encouragement for every true-hearted worker to remember that

God never commands and commissions without providing grace to obey.

4. *The Divine Purpose.*—"For obedience to the faith." This phrase occurring here, and at the close of the Epistle (Rom. xvi. 26), is very significant, and the combination of faith and obedience is particularly noteworthy. Faith always implies submission and surrender, which in turn express themselves in loyal and glad obedience. This, beyond everything, is the purpose of all our service for Christ; to bring men into line with this great principle of obedience to the faith, and faithful obedience. Lives are to be based on trust, and proved by activity. Our hearts surrender to the Gospel of Christ and thereby receive power to obey it and manifest the "obedience of faith."

5. *The Universal Range.*—"Among all nations." Here the great Apostle strikes his characteristic note of universality. There is no limit to the purpose of the Gospel and there can be no limit to the sphere of our service. "All nations" are included in the great redemption and must necessarily be involved in the great proclamation. Happy for us if our Christian life ever keeps in the forefront this world-wide range of the activities of the Gospel.

6. *The Supreme Motive.*—"For His Name." It was "on behalf of His Name" that the Apostle was commissioned to do his work. That the name of Jesus Christ might be honored among men, the Apostle was summoned and equipped to serve God as the Apostle to the Gentiles. The "Name" in Scripture is always the revealed character, and when the Apostle speaks of it here it may be said to include both the motive and the theme of his work. It was "the Name that is above every name" that he delighted to proclaim, and it was because of this Name, because of what it was to him in his own personal experience, that he did so.

> "How sweet the Name of Jesus sounds
> In a believer's ear."

7. *The Personal Acceptance.*—"By Whom we have *received* grace and apostleship." The word rendered "received" may with equal literalness and accuracy be rendered "taken," for it implies at once a Divine gift and a human acceptance. This call, com-

mission, and equipment was no compulsory service, but the glad, joyous welcome acceptance of the position God desired him to occupy. Not compelled, but impelled—this must ever be the true attitude of the soul to God as it contemplates service in His vineyard. And when the hand of faith is stretched out to "receive," there comes abundance of grace for every need; authority and ability are combined for the service of God.

V

THE SUBJECT

Rom. i. 1, 2-4

1. . . . The gospel of God.
2. (Which he had promised afore by his prophets in the holy scriptures,)
3. Concerning his son Jesus Christ our Lord, which was made of the seed of David according to the flesh;
4. And declared *to be* the Son of God with power, according to the spirit of holiness, by the resurrection from the dead.

The Apostle soon passes away from himself to his message, about which there is much to be noted that is full of the deepest interest.

I. *The General Subject.*—His message is "the Gospel of God." "Gospel" is a favorite word of the great worker. "Good news" was what he rejoiced to possess and proclaim. Some one has truly said that the Gospel is "good news" not "good advice," and it was this inspiring thought of the glad tidings that the Apostle delighted in for himself and for his hearers. "Good news from God." This seems to mean "Good news of which God is the Author," though perhaps we might also include, for it is certainly true, "Good news of God" as the subject or message. It is very striking how in one chapter of his Epistles (1 Thess. ii.) the Apostle several times describes his message as "The Gospel of God." This thought is fundamental, for if the Gospel does not come from above it is not "good news" at all.

II. *The Scriptural Anticipation.*—The Apostle at once calls attention to the Old Covenant. "Which He promised afore through His prophets in the Holy Scriptures." He is particularly anxious to show that his Gospel is no novelty, that it is closely related to the past, that it is no afterthought either of his Master or of himself. The promise of the coming Messiah and His salvation is found in every part of the Old Testament, and it is the feature that makes those Scriptures unique. Here, too, we are enabled to see the Apostle's view of the Old Testament. It consists of "holy writings"; it comes from God; and was mediated "through His prophets." For the Apostle the Old Testament has an abiding authority, and it would be well if we were always to have the same estimate of the writings of the Ancient Covenant. This Messianic element, which is the warp and woof of the Old Testament, gives it its abiding value and permanent validity for the Christian Church. It is a fact so familiar as to be overlooked far too frequently, and yet the apologetic evidential value of the Old Testament is a very striking and convincing argument when it is properly stated and realized.

> "Is there not something remarkable in the way and extent of the applicability of the spirit and the letter of the Old Testament to the New, even where the connection is only application and not genuine interpretation? What other whole history and literature is so applicable to a single fact or event which nevertheless so completely transcends, while fulfilling its meaning?" (Du Bose, *The Gospel according to St Paul*, p. 24).

III. *The Special Theme.*—Now the Apostle proceeds to dilate upon the theme of the Gospel, the Person of Jesus Christ; and no less than seven aspects of His Person and Work are brought before us in the simplest possible way in this introductory statement. The very simplicity gives the statement a profound significance.

1. His Divine Sonship. "Concerning His Son." This is the foundation of God's revelation in Christ. He gave His Son. "He spared not His own Son." He has spoken to us in His Son. The unique Sonship of Jesus Christ is one of the fundamental truths of the Christian religion.

2. His official Name and Title. "Jesus Christ." The combination of these two words "Jesus" and "Christ" is once more seen. "Jesus" refers to the human Person Who lived on earth. "Christ" is the Divine Person, anointed by the Holy Spirit for His redemptive work.

3. His Lordship. "Our Lord." Here again we have the Person of Christ brought before us in relation to His position in the universe and in the Christian Church. He is "the Lord," and there can be none higher than He.

4. His Human Life. "Born of the seed of David, according to the flesh." It is quite clear from this statement that the Apostle believed Jesus Christ of Nazareth to be of David's line, and we cannot for a moment doubt that any flaw in the line of descent would have been quickly detected and revealed by the inveterate hosility of the Jews (John vii. 42; Heb. vii. 14).

5. His Resurrection. "The resurrection from the dead." This statement naturally follows the one concerning His birth, and together they give us the two facts of the Incarnation and Resurrection on which Christianity rests. The same combination of David's seed and the Resurrection as part of St. Paul's Gospel is seen in 2 Tim. ii. 8. But the Gospel, as preached by St. Paul, really started from the Resurrection rather than the Incarnation (Acts xvii. 32; xxiv. 15-21; xxvi. 23). From the Resurrection it was easy to proceed to the earthly life and its supernatural beginning in the Virgin-Birth.

6. His designation to be the Son of God and Fount of Power. "Who was declared to be the Son of God with power." This second reference to our Lord's Sonship should be carefully observed. He was already Son before He came into the world, but the Resurrection designated Him Son of God in a special sense. The word rendered "declared to be" should be translated "designated," "ordained," "appointed." The resurrection was not a demonstration but a designation, and the precise point of the designation is found in the words "with power." Hitherto He had been in Himself "Son of God," but now through the Resurrection He was Son of God with the possession of power that He was ready to bestow upon all who should receive Him. Thus by resurrection He was made available for all.

7. His Divine Nature. "According to the spirit of holiness." The contrast here between "according to the flesh" and "according to the spirit," shows that we are to understand the phrase "spirit, of holiness," not as referring to the Holy Spirit, but to the spiritual nature of Him Who was human as well as divine. On the one side He was of the seed of David, and on the other He was the Eternal Son of God.

These seven fundamental facts concerning the Person and work of Jesus Christ should be carefully noted. Their agreement with the statements of the Apostles' Creed, as now held by the Church Universal, is close and striking. Sometimes men discuss "What is Christianity?" and seek to discover what they call "primitive Christianity." Here it is, quite evidently set before us. These profound truths about our Lord were believed and obeyed as early as thirty years after His death and resurrection. Nothing could well be more primitive than this.

As we ponder these verses we can readily understand how fully and heartily the Apostle Paul believed that his message was one of "good news." Let us dwell upon some aspects of the Gospel as here presented.

1. *It has a Divine Source.*—It comes from God; it speaks of God; it contains God's message; it tells of God's gift; it provides God's guarantee; it is the Gospel of God from first to last.

2. *It agrees with the Old Testament.*—The Gospel in the Old Testament is a fruitful theme, whether we think of the prophet, or the priest, or the king. "Christ is all." The earnest, humble, thoughtful soul will ever take a delight in pondering the Old Testament teaching in type, history, parable, and prophecy, to find therein the footsteps of the Messiah.

3. *It has a Divine Saviour.*—Jesus Christ is the Son of God, and nothing short of Deity would suffice for our salvation. As Bishop Moule so aptly says: "A Saviour not quite God would mean a broken bridge on the farther side." Here is our rock foundation. "God was in Christ, reconciling the world to Himself."

4. *It has a Human Saviour.*—This is as necessary as the other. Jacob's ladder was "set up on the earth," and if man is to be saved he must be saved by One Who is Man as well as God. Let us bind this closely to our hearts. Jesus Christ is "bone of our bone, and flesh of our flesh." He was "touched with the feeling of our infirmities." He was "Perfect Man" for our redemption.

5. *It has a Risen Saviour.*—The Resurrection is the divine proof that the work of Christ is complete, and by it Jesus Christ was designated to be our Divine Redeemer. "The Church of Christ is

built on an empty tomb," and in the Resurrection our salvation finds its full assurance.

6. *Its Practical Effects.*—Thus early does the Apostle strike his keynote of "power," for this beyond all else is the characteristic of the Gospel. Christ possesses power and bestows it on His people, and herein is the secret of all that is worth knowing and possessing in Christianity.

7. *Its Personal Requirements.*—"Jesus Christ our Lord." It is only as we realize and recognize the Lordship of Jesus Christ that we find Him to be "Son of God with power." Submission and surrender are essential to the full reception and enjoyment of the Gospel of God in Christ.

VI

THE READERS

Rom. i. 6, 7.

6. Among whom are ye also the called of Jesus Christ:
7. To all that be in Rome, beloved of God, called *to be* saints: Grace to you and peace from God our Father, and the Lord Jesus Christ.

THE Apostle now turns to the Christians in Rome. They also were included in the "called ones," and as such are addressed in significant terms.

I. *A Fourfold Description.*—They are "the called of Jesus Christ," or "called to be Jesus Christ's." The term "called" as used in the Gospels and Epistles has a very distinct difference. In the Gospels it always means simply the invitation of God, but in the Epistles it invariably implies both the invitation and its acceptance by us.

They are "beloved of God," as in Christ. What an inspiration to realize that they were the objects of God's love because they belonged to Jesus Christ. God delights to call us His beloved ones, and as we contemplate this love which finds and takes us just as we are and loves us with an everlasting love, we should rest and rejoice in His love and take it home to our own souls for comfort, encouragement, and peace. "Who loved *me* and gave Himself for *me*."

They are "called saints," or, "called to be saints." This means that they were "commissioned saints," just as the Apostle himself had been called and commissioned to be an Apostle (ver. 1). Even here, in ordinary saintship, there must be a call from God, and no one can intrude upon this heritage any more than upon the Apostleship. The term "saint" invariably means "consecrated," that is, "separated," "dedicated," "belonging to God." They were not called because they were saints, but they were saints because they were called. It is a mistake to think that a "saint" means one who is specially holy, for the word never applies to spiritual condition or state, but always and only to spiritual position which is ours from the moment of conversion. Of course the fact of our possession by God carries with it the absolute necessity of what we call holiness. We are dedicated and consecrated for the purpose of being true, pure, genuine, as followers of our Master. Since God is Love, holiness which is the very nature of God must be love also. Du Bose makes the following important distinctions:—

> "The Greek *virtue* is an ideal, rather aesthetic than ethical, of highest and most beautiful *manhood.* The Hebrew *righteousness* carries with it primarily the conception of conformity to an outward law, with them the highest and most universal law, the law of God. The *holiness* of Christianity is an inward spirit, the Spirit of God, the divine nature" (*The Gospel according to St. Paul,* p. 41).

They are described as "in Rome." Let us mark carefully this twofold aspect of the believer. He is beloved of God, he belongs to Christ, he is commissioned to be a dedicated one, and all this in the great Roman metropolis. What an honor all this was for those who were surrounded by heathenism. There were many sorts of Christians in Rome; high and low, rich and poor, yet these titles belonged to them all. "In Rome"; "In Christ." Here is the twofold environment of the Christian, and whatever may be the problems, the difficulties, the sorrows, the trials, the temptations of our "Rome" today let us never forget that we are "in Christ."

II. *The Twofold Greeting.*—"Grace to you and peace from God our Father, and the Lord Jesus Christ." Mark the blending of the Greek and Hebrew salutations. The Greek invariably greeted his friends with a word which was almost exactly identical with "grace," while the Hebrew salutation was invariably "peace." These two sum up the whole of the Gospel. Grace is the cause and Peace is the effect. Grace as opposed to debt, Favor as opposed to wrath; while Peace is the result of the attitude and action of Divine grace. There is perhaps no word so characteristic of the Gospel as the term "grace." "By grace are ye saved." "The Gospel of the grace of God." "The grace of God that bringeth salvation."

Both these blessings come direct from God our Father and the Lord Jesus Christ. Let us note carefully the close association of Christ with the Father in this salutation. No human being could possibly be associated in this way. The equality of both as the source of grace clearly implies the Deity of our Lord.

As we review these opening verses we cannot but be impressed with the truth of the following statement made by Drs. Sanday and Headlam:—

> "It is impossible not to be struck by the definiteness and maturity of the theological teaching contained in them. It is remarkable enough, and characteristic of this primitive Christian literature, especially of the Epistles of St. Paul, that a mere salutation should contain so much weighty teaching of any kind; but it is still more remarkable when we think what that teaching is and the early date at which it was penned. There are no less than five distinct groups of ideas, all expressed with deliberate emphasis and precision: (1) a complete set of ideas as to the commission and authority of an Apostle; (2) a complete set of ideas as to the status in the sight of God of a Christian community; (3) a clear apprehension of the relation of the new order of things to the old; (4) a clear assertion of what we should call summarily the Divinity of Christ, which St. Paul regarded both in the light of its relation to the expectations of his countrymen, and also in its transcendental reality, as revealed by or inferred from the words and acts of Christ Himself; (5) a somewhat advanced stage in the discrimination of distinct Persons in the God-head" (*International Critical Commentary on Romans*, p. 17).

The salutation is indeed "remarkable for its developed theology" (Garvie, p. 81).

Looking back over all these opening verses, our attention is naturally drawn to the following:—

1. *The titles of Christ.*—"Jesus Christ"; "His Son"; "Son of God"; "Jesus Christ our Lord." The fulness of this description is all the more impressive because of its naturalness and simplicity, and the absence of all endeavour to pile up statements about Jesus Christ. Each title carries its own meaning and makes its own impression on mind and heart. He is the human Jesus; He is the Anointed Messiah; He is the unique Son of God; and as such He is the Lord and Master of us all.

2. *The titles of Christians.*—What a variety of descriptions we have here. "Bondslave"; "Called"; "Beloved"; "Saints." These titles cover the whole of the believer's life, including what God is to us and what we are to be to God. Let us see that we live out to the full their solemn yet precious meaning.

3. *The idea of Holiness* is very prominent in these verses. The Scriptures are called "holy"; the Divine nature of Jesus Christ is called "the Spirit of holiness"; and both the Apostle and the Roman Christians are described as "holy," or "saints." Holy writings; a holy Saviour, and a holy people. Let each one of us never forget that when he says "I believe," it also involves "I belong."

4. *The picture of the Apostle* in these opening verses must not be overlooked. Godet's comment is to the point:—

> "It is impossible not to admire the prudence and delicacy which St. Paul shows in the discharge of his task towards this church. To justify his procedure, he goes back on his apostleship; to justify his apostleship to them as Gentiles, he goes back to the transformation which the resurrection wrought in Christ's person, when from being Jewish Messiah it made Him *Lord* in the absolute sense of the word. Like a true pastor, instead of lording it over the conscience of his flock, he seeks to associate it with his own" (*Commentary on Romans,* vol. i. p. 141).

Let us also ponder these suggestive words of Dr. Beet:—

> "Notice the beauty and symmetry of Paul's opening sentence. It is a crystal arch spanning the gulf between the Jew of Tarsus and the Christians at Rome. Paul begins by giving his name: he rises to the dignity of his office, and then to the Gospel he proclaims. From the Gospel he ascends to its great subject-matter, to Him Who is Son of David and Son of God. From this summit of his arch he passes on to the apostleship again, and to the nations for whose good he received it. Among these nations he finds the Christians at Rome. He began to build by laying down his own claims; he finished by acknowledging theirs. The gulf is spanned. Across the waters of national separation Paul has flung an arch whose firmly knit segments are living truths, and whose Keystone is the incarnate Son of God. Over this arch he hastens with words of greeting from his Father and their Father, from his Master and their Master" (*St. Paul's Epistle to the Romans,* p. 38).

As we ponder his wonderful words shall we not pray afresh for grace to follow St. Paul even as he followed Christ?

VII

PERSONAL INTEREST

Rom. i. 8-15.

8. First, I thank my God through Jesus Christ for you all, that your faith is spoken of throughout the whole world.
9. For God is my witness, whom I serve with my spirit in the gospel of his Son, that without ceasing I make mention of you always in my prayers;
10. Making request, if by any means now at length I might have a prosperous journey by the will of God to come unto you.
11. For I long to see you, that I may impart unto you some spiritual gift, to the end ye may be established;
12. That is, that I may be comforted together with you by the mutual faith both of you and me.
13. Now I would not have you ignorant, brethren, that often-times I purposed to come unto you, (but was let hitherto,) that I might have some fruit among you also, even as among other Gentiles.
14. I am debtor both to the Greeks, and to the Barbarians; both to the wise, and to the unwise.
15. So, as much as in me is, I am ready to preach the gospel to you that are at Rome also.

In order to ensure acceptance for his message and to lead up to his theme, St. Paul proceeds to express his deep personal interest in the Christians in Rome. The position was one of great delicacy. He was a stranger, and must have been heard of from time to time as a dangerous person. How then was he to introduce himself as the Apostle to the Gentiles? As the one specially commissioned by divine grace to labor in Gentile lands, he had a natural interest in the progress of Christianity in Rome, and added to this, his intense sympathy with everything connected with the spread of the Gospel, to say nothing of his Roman citizenship, would make him particularly desirous that Christianity should flourish in the great metropolis, and spread thence on all sides.

The frankness with which he reveals his feelings in these verses suggests the motives that led him to write the Epistle. The Gospel had long reached Rome by other messengers, and groups of believers had been gathered together in different parts of the city. These simple, earnest souls had doubtless received with intense joy the "good news" of divine grace, but they were still in need of such Christian instruction as the great Apostle alone was qualified to give. Perhaps, therefore, this was the real motive which led him to write this letter, as a preparation for his own coming there. He wished to confirm the faith of the young Church and to place the Christian life on stronger foundations. And he does this by proclaiming his own special Gospel which circumstances had hitherto prevented him from delivering by word of mouth. It is well pointed out that we today have reason to be thankful that the Apostle was prevented from going sooner to Rome, since it is to this delay that we owe this wonderful Epistle.

The entire section is full of the Apostle's personal characteristics, and as we look at them one by one we shall see revealed some of the essential elements of a true Christian life.

I. *Thanksgiving* (ver. 8).—He commences, as usual, with thanksgiving on their behalf, the special point being that their life in Christ was well known throughout the Christian world. The fact of a Church witnessing in the great metropolis was doubtless a cause of joy to believers in other places (see also 1 Thess. i. 8-10). We note also the wide diffusion of Christianity by that time (*cf.* Col. i. 6). It is sometimes thought that by opening with the term "First," the Apostle intended to add "Second," but that the construction was interrupted. It may well be, however, that the "First" was only intended to refer to the prominent place thanksgiving occupied in his mind. He uses the phrase "My God," but it is very seldom that he employs this personal, appropriating pronoun (1 Cor. i. 4; 2 Cor. xii. 21; Phil. i. 3; iv. 19; Philemon 4; *cf.* Rom. ii. 16, "My Gospel."). Luther speaks of Christianity as the religion of possessive pronouns. Anyone can say "God," but only a Christian can say "My God."

How characteristic this attitude of thankfulness was in the life of St. Paul. It should mark every healthy, vigorous, Christian life. "Think and thank" must ever be our motto.

II. *Interest* (ver. 8).—He thanks Gods for them "all," making no distinction whatever, and the cause of his thankfulness is that their faith "is being announced throughout the whole world." The communications between place and place had brought him word of the Christian life of these believers in Rome, and at once a great interest is kindled in his soul. He had never seen these Christians, but he had heard of them and had long been praying on their behalf.

This is another true mark of the Christian life, preventing us from being self-centered, and enabling us to rejoice in all tidings of the grace of God in other lives.

III. *Sincerity* (ver. 9). The Apostle now makes a solemn appeal to God. "God is my witness, Whom I serve with my spirit." Probably the Christians had been expecting him earlier, and were wondering why, as he had come so comparatively near as Corinth (Acts xviii. 1-18), he had never reached Rome. Twenty years had elapsed since his conversion, and although most of that time had been spent in work among the Gentiles, he had not yet come. He now explains the reason, calling "God to witness" that he was speaking the truth. Man may observe our use of bodily organs and efforts, but only God can see whether we are truly "serving in our *spirit.*" Sincerity of heart and conscience is one of the prime necessities of a healthy Christian life.

IV. *Service* (ver. 9).—"Whom I serve with my spirit in the Gospel." The word rendered "serve" was originally used of the labor of a workman for hire, but in the Greek of the Old Testament, as also in the New, it is found associated with a service of worship, thus suggesting that all true labor for Christ is sacred. Service in "the spirit" should also be carefully noticed. It is as real as service with the body, and often far more exacting. Service is one of the essential elements of all true Christianity. No Christian life can possibly be lived aright apart from work for God. If service was "in the Gospel of His Son." This is another aspect of a son, then a servant, and service is the proof of our sonship. His that Gospel which, as in verse 1, is called "the Gospel of God," and in verse 16 (A.V.) "the Gospel of Christ."

V. *Prayer* (vers. 9, 10).—Intercessory prayer was a prominent feature in the life of the Apostle, and without ceasing he prayed for the Christians of the various Churches. He prayed for those in Rome with special reference to his own coming. Nothing was excluded from his prayers, for he does not hesitate to ask God to open the way by His providential circumstances for a journey to them. "If now at last I may be prospered by the will of God to come unto you." As he says elsewhere, "In *everything* by prayer . . . . let your requests be made known." What a study are the prayers of St. Paul! As Godet truly says, "Paul thinks of those times of intimate intercourse which he has daily with his God in the exercise of his ministry; for it is at His feet, as it were, that he discharges this task." It has also been well remarked that Paul, while reaching multitudes by his preaching, certainly reached far more by his prayers, for "prayer moves the Arm that moves the world."

> "Preaching is a rare gift—prayer is a rarer one. Preaching, like a sword, is a weapon to use at close quarters; those far off cannot be reached by it. Prayer, like a breechloader, has longer range, and under some circumstances is even more effective" (Wenham, *Romans*, p. 7).

Prayer is one of the most definite and genuine proofs of sincere Christian affection. Faith tends to call into play the joys of family love, and intercession is the supreme expression of that love as it pours itself out to God on behalf of others. Bishop Gore's words aptly confirm this:—

> "It was a remark of General Gordon's that it makes a great difference in our feeling towards a stranger if before we meet him we have prayed for him. And we may with equal truth say that it makes a great difference in the feelings of others towards us if they have reason to believe that we have prayed for them. St. Paul therefore gives himself this advantage" (*The Epistle to the Romans*, vol. i. p. 54).

VI. *Submission* (ver. 10).—His prayer for a prosperous journey is conditioned "by the will of God." Here is another of the profound secrets of the Apostle's life, and of ours also. The will of God must be supreme. As he wrote the words he was doubtless conscious of the risks he ran in journeying to Jerusalem (ch. xv.

30f.). What force there is in this phrase, "by the will of God," when we remember the circumstances under which he came to Rome. How different "the will of God" was for him from what he expected it to be. "Thy will be done." "Teach me to do Thy will." "My meat is to do the will of Him that sent Me." Only as we are subject to the will of God can we understand what life really means. "In His will is our peace" (Dante).

VII. *Fellowship* (vers. 11, 12).—The Apostle expresses his intense longing to see the Christians in Rome, and this earnest desire for fellowship and communion with other believers is very striking both here and elsewhere. "I am homesick for you" (Moule). Surely this is a very striking phrase. "It is the manly expression of Christian affection" (Maclaren).

He wanted both to be and to obtain a blessing, to give and to get. The exquisitely beautiful way in which he corrects his statement about imparting a spiritual gift is particularly worthy of note. As an Apostle of Jesus Christ he wished to bestow upon them some gift that would establish them in their faith; but the words are hardly off his pen before he turns them into the suggestion that he himself wished to receive as well as to give. "That is, that I with you may be comforted in you, each of us by the other's faith, both yours and mine." It was "the concurrent encouragement" for which he looked—not merely for comfort and consolation in the modern sense, but for that strength and courage which banishes weakness and depression, and enables the soul to go forward with alacrity in the pathway of God's will.

Strength and comfort are invariably to be found in Christian fellowship. So it has ever been, so it ever will be, and the more fellowship with our fellow-Christians we have, and the more we realize the full force of the terms "brethren" and "brotherhood," the stronger our life will be. Every Christian has received spiritual blessing in order to impart it, and if we cannot impart we may well question whether we have ever received. Calvin truly said, "In Christ's Church no one is so poor as not to be able to confer upon us some important benefit; but our pride hinders us from reaping these mutual advantages." Let us never fail to make the very most of fellowship with those who are in Christ.

VIII. *Eagerness* (ver. 13).—He then proceeds with some explanations which it was necessary that they should have. He tells them of the hindrances which had prevented his coming earlier. He had not only wished to come, but had actually tried, and the supreme reason why he wished to be with them was found in his obligation to preach everywhere in the Gentile world: "that I might have some fruit in you also, even as in the rest of the Gentiles." How modestly the Apostle describes his hopes: "some fruit." This was the explanation of his intense desire. He wished to have spiritual fruit among them, just as he had elsewhere. Ever the eager soul-winner, the Apostle constantly craved and looked out for fresh opportunities. Is this a mark of our life?

IX. *Indebtedness* (ver. 14).—The Apostle was conscious of a spiritual obligation. Christ had done so much for him that he must endeavour to repay the debt. "I am debtor both to the Greeks, and to the Barbarians: both to the wise, and to the foolish." Thus to two races, civilized and uncivilized, and to two capacities of men, intelligent and ignorant, the Apostle realized his indebtedness, and consequently he wished to pay his debts. Whether men were to be divided by nationality or culture mattered not to him, so long as he could repay the incalculable obligation that he felt to his Lord and Master. As a steward of the Gospel (1 Cor. iv. 1; ix. 16, 17) he wished to discharge every duty to the utmost and fulfil every obligation. This sense of obligation lies at the root of all genuine service. The man who in heart and conscience realizes that "I am debtor," is the one who will do most and best work for Christ.

X. *Readiness* (ver. 15).—"So, as much as in me is, I am ready to preach the gospel to you also that are in Rome." The hindrance was not in him, for so far as he was concerned he was perfectly ready to come to the Imperial City and proclaim the Divine Gospel. He was not afraid of Rome, and nothing even in that great place could prevent him. Its language, its culture, its glories, its sins, were as nothing, because he knew his message and his Master. At the outbreak of the Indian Mutiny, Lord Clyde, then known as Sir Colin Campbell, when asked how long it would take him to get ready to start for India, is said to have replied, "I am ready now" (quoted by C. Neil, *Romans*, p. 20). These two confessions, "I am debtor," "I am ready," are at the very heart of all true work of God. We *owe* men the Gospel which we have received and enjoy, and everything in life demands that we should pay our debt, and place ourselves in readiness to obey the Master's call.

As we review these fifteen verses, what a revelation they give of the heart of the great Apostle.

1. *The Ambassador* (vers. 1-7).—Here St. Paul speaks in his official capacity, as an ambassador for Christ, representing his Master, and "every word increases the writer's claim upon the attention of his readers" (J. A. Beet, *St. Paul's Epistle to the Romans*, p. 38). As a called Apostle, as occupied with a theme which fills the old Scriptures, and is embodied in the Divine and Human Son of God, St. Paul can speak with authority. He himself, too, is called to be the Apostle to all the Gentiles, and this divine commission enables him to speak with a right and a force that no one could question. This is the attitude of every true servant of Christ, even though he cannot occupy the high position of a great Apostle. As the Master "spake with authority," so must the servant, if he would do his Master's will. Men expect authoritativeness from the messengers of the Gospel. "We are ambassadors for Christ."

2. *The Fellow-Christian* (vers. 8-15). What a contrast is found in this section. In the former verses—

> "Our spirits bowed before one who stood so high in the service of so great a Master. But now the ambassador of Christ comes to us as one like ourselves. Across the waters which roll between him and us, we hear a brother's voice and see a brother's face" (J. A. Beet, *St. Paul's Epistle to the Romans*, p. 47).

And so not merely and only as a called Apostle, and as a representative of Christ does he address them, but as one who had long loved them, rejoiced over them, and prayed for them; as one who sought for them and for himself all possible spiritual blessings in close fellowship with Christ; and as one who ever regarded himself as their debtor. When a man takes up this attitude to his fellow-Christians he will attract them by his love and win them to himself and his cause. This must ever be the spirit of our approach to our brethren when we desire to serve them in Christ and minister to them the Gospel.

VIII

THE THEME

ROM. i. 16, 17.

16. For I am not ashamed of the gospel of Christ: for it is the power of God unto salvation to every one that believeth; to the Jew first, and also to the Greek.

17. For therein is the righteousness of God revealed from faith to faith: as it is written, The just shall live by faith.

FROM the mention of the Gospel and his desire to preach it in Rome the Apostle naturally leads up to the theme of the Epistle. The transition is made by the phrase, "I am not ashamed," in which he endeavors to remove any idea of fear from the intense eagerness that he has expressed. These two verses should be carefully studied, for they contain practically all the leading thoughts of the entire Epistle.

I. *The Source of the Gospel.*—"God." As in verse 1 and elsewhere, the greatest possible stress is laid upon the fact that the Gospel did not emanate from man, but from God (*cf.* 1 Thess. ii. 2, 8, 12, 13). The various words associated with "of God" in chapters i.-iii. are very significant.

II. *The Nature of the Gospel.*—"The power of God." "Power" is a characteristic word of St. Paul. In verse 4 he has already taught us that by the resurrection our Lord was designated "Son of God," for the purpose of bestowing power on us. All through his Epistles the Apostle lays stress upon the "power of Christ." Christianity is the great moral and spiritual *dynamic,* and this, as contrasted with other religions, is one of its unique characteristics. It is not merely an ideal, or an ethic, though it possesses both, but in addition and primarily it is a dynamic which enables us to realize the ideal and reproduce the ethic. Nothing short of the power of God can suffice to make even one Christian. God's gift of Christ as the Atonement, His love, His grace, His Spirit, are all needed to transform the sinner into the believer.

III. *The Purpose of the Gospel*—"Unto salvation." "Salvation" is another of the great words of the Apostle and of the entire New Testament. What does it mean? It includes deliverance and equipment, and implies "safety" to the fullest possible extent. Salvation is threefold, in relation to the past, the present, and the future. As to the past, the Christian can say, I was saved; as to the present, I am being saved; as to the future, I shall be saved. Salvation is from the penalty, the power, and the presence of sin. It includes Justification, Sanctification, Glorification. The Gospel deals with all three aspects, because it is "unto salvation."

IV. *The Scope of the Gospel.*—"To everyone . . . to the Jew first, and also to the Greek." This reference to "the Jew first" should be carefully noted, for it is characteristic of the Epistle (ch. ii. 9, 10), and yet we must always remember that it invariably means precedence, not preference. Universality is the keynote of Christianity. As there is a world-wide need and a world-wide opportunity, so there is a world-wide provision. All nations, ranks, and capacities are included in its scope and intention. Salvation is for everyone, from every sin, at every time, in every place, under every circumstance. No other religion has ever proved its adaptation to the whole world.

V. *The Reception of the Gospel.*—"Everyone that believeth." This is the one condition. The Gospel requires appropriation. Faith believes the message, rests on the Atonement, and receives the grace. "By grace are ye saved through faith." The emphasis on faith shows that it is the simple condition of confidence in God that brings about our salvation; and yet there is no efficacy in faith apart from its Object, and no merit in believing. Faith is the acknowledgment of our own inability, and of Another's ability. Faith includes intellectual perception and spiritual reception, the assent of the mind and the consent of the heart. As Godet finely puts it:—

"Faith, in Paul's sense, is something extremely simple, such that it does not in the least impair the *freeness* of salvation. God says: I give thee: the heart answers: I accept; such is faith. The act is thus a receptivity, but an active receptivity. It brings nothing, but it takes what God gives; as was admirably said by a poor Bechuana: 'It is the hand of the heart'" (*Commentary on the Romans*, vol. i. p. 152).

VI. *The Efficacy of the Gospel.*—"For therein is the righteousness of God revealed." The reason why the Gospel is God's power is that it reveals, provides, and bestows God's righteousness. "The righteousness of God" means that consistency with His own revealed character whereby He receives sinful man on the ground of the work of Christ. On the one simple condition of trust God will reinstate man in righteousness. As we lost our position through unbelief or lack of faith (Gen. iii.), so when we return to trust once again, God receives us back into fellowship with Himself.

Righteousness always means "conformity to right," and it is the dominant theme of this whole Epistle. It comes before us still more fully in ch. iii. 21-26, but the first mention of it here should be carefully noted. When we compare the phrase, "the righteousness of God," with similar phrases, "the bread of God," "the gift of God," we recognize at once that righteousness is that which God *is*, *has*, and *gives*, and it is in the Gospel that "the righteousness of God is being revealed" in continuous operation. This righteousness of God is often put in contrast with man's own righteousness of our own endeavour and provision; and in all ages the great controversy has been whether men will endeavor to establish their own righteousness, or submit to God's; whether they will endeavor to put themselves right, or let Him do it for them. Never, therefore, must verse 16, in which the Gospel is described as God's power, be separated from verse 17, in which it is said to reveal God's righteousness. It is the righteousness that God *is* in Himself, and *provides* in Christ, that makes the Gospel the divine power unto salvation.

VII. *The Outcome of the Gospel.*—"The just shall *live* by faith." Life is therefore the result of the reception of the Gospel. This is the positive side of which "salvation" is the negative, and life is "by faith." The Apostle speaks of righteousness being continually revealed "from faith to faith"; that is, it is received by faith; it continually depends upon faith; it produces faith; and it ends with faith. The phrase "from faith to faith" must be taken as a whole and not separated into two parts. Similar expressions are found elsewhere which shed light upon its meaning here (Ps. lxxxiv. 7; 2 Cor. ii. 16; iii. 18). Faith is the great principle of righteousness all along the life from the beginning to the close. We are justified by faith, sanctified by faith, and every moment we live by faith. Works have no part in this life. The emphasis on "live," as covering the entire life of the believer, clearly shows the width and fulness of the meaning of "the righteousness of God." It is far more than justification, and while, of course, including this, it embraces everything necessary to replace man in the position, character, and sphere of a righteous person.

The quotation from Habakkuk ii. 4, "The just shall live by faith," should be noticed. It is used three times in the New Testament, and on each occasion with a different emphasis. In Rom. i. 17 the emphasis is upon "righteousness" as contrasted with unrighteousness. In Gal. iii. 11 the emphasis is on "faith" as contrasted with works. In Heb. x. 38 the emphasis is on "live," showing that faith is the great principle and power of true life. It may almost be said that this phrase from Habakkuk sums up the entire Epistle and may suggest the outline of it.

(*a*) ch. i. 17—iii. 20, "the righteous."
(b) ch. iii. 21—iv. 25, "by faith."
(*c*) ch. v. 1—xvi. 26, "shall live."

Righteousness, Faith, Life are the three great truths of the Epistle to the Romans.

Another view of these verses is worthy of consideration for comparison with the foregoing:—

> "Paul justifies his confidence in his message by indicating his conception of (1) its character, 'the power of God'; (2) its contents, 'the righteousness of God'; (3) its claim, 'faith'; (4) its comprehensiveness, 'Jew and Greek'; (5) its consequence, 'salvation,' 'life'; and (6) its confirmation in Scripture" (Garvie, *Romans*, p. 90).

1. *He was not ashamed.*

As we review these verses and the fundamental realities stated by the Apostle we can readily understand why he said, "I am not ashamed of the Gospel." Perhaps some whom he knew were ashamed, and possibly he himself had been so before his conversion (see Matheson, *Spiritual Development of St. Paul,* pp. 33, 37). But there was no need to blush for the power of God, for in that Gospel was the only way in which God could justify Himself to man, and by which man could become right with God. There was no need for shame, and, indeed, every reason for the opposite. Power is always honorable, and divine power ought to be especially so. The Gospel of a divine righteousness was the very thing that men needed, and it was accessible to all. And yet even then there were strong reasons which tempted men to be ashamed. Jewish opposition, the fact of a crucified Master, the insignificant position of many of the followers of Christ, the abhorrence with which the fundamental Christian doctrines were held by Jewish and Greek culture, might easily have led weak natures to feel ashamed (1 Cor. i. 21).

2. *We must not be ashamed.*

The same temptation is found today. Sometimes there is the danger of *intellectual* shame; the fear that the Gospel has not that virility of thought and essential philosophy which will commend it to masculine minds. There is also the danger of *social* shame, for it is still true that "not many wise, not many noble, not many mighty are called." The fact that Christianity has always moved upwards from the lowest strata of society is a stumbling-block in the eyes of the socially proud, and is only too apt to make them ashamed of being regarded among those who "profess and call themselves Christians." Deepest of all is the possibility of *moral* shame. The offence of the Cross has not yet ceased, and the fact that the acceptance of the Gospel often demands severance from old ways, old habits, old tendencies, and even old friends, puts a strain upon certain temperaments which is almost too hard for them to bear. Herein lies the solemn possibility of being ashamed of Christ and His Gospel; and yet the Master's words ring out as clearly as ever —"Whosoever therefore shall be ashamed of Me and My words in this adulterous and sinful generation; of him also shall the Son of Man be ashamed, when He cometh in the glory of His Father with the holy angels" (Mark viii. 28). Be it ours so to ponder, appropriate, and prize the Gospel, that, like the Apostle, we may never be ashamed of it. When a Christian man has by blessed experience such a conception of the Gospel as that which enables him to justify the ways of God to men, and to bring before men the one and only secret of true life in relation to the past, present, and future, he is filled with a divine courage and boldness in proclaiming a power so Divine, so blessed, so perfect, and so permanent. Our testimony may, and often will lead to hardship, and even persecution, but by the grace of God we shall be able to say with the Apostle, "Nevertheless I am not ashamed: for I know Whom I have believed, and am persuaded that He is able to keep that which I have committed unto Him against that day" (2 Tim. i. 12).

IX

HUMAN SIN

Rom. i. 18-23.

18. For the wrath of God is revealed from heaven against all ungodliness and unrighteousness of men, who hold the truth in unrighteousness;
19. Because that which may be known of God is manifest in them; for God hath shewed *it* unto them.
20. For the invisible things of him from the creation of the world are clearly seen, being understood by the things that are made, *even* his eternal power and Godhead; so that they are without excuse:
21. Because that, when they knew God, they glorified *him* not as God, neither were thankful; but became vain in their imaginations, and their foolish heart was darkened.
22. Professing themselves to be wise, they became fools,
23. And changed the glory of the uncorruptible God into an image made like to corruptible man, and to birds, and fourfooted beasts, and creeping things.

The discussion commences here. The Apostle has set forth his theme that the Gospel is God's power unto salvation because it reveals the Divine righteousness to be received through faith. Now he vindicates this statement. Why is righteousness necessary? Because we have none of our own. Salvation must mean righteousness because of God's attitude of righteous wrath against all unrighteousness. The Gospel is always unwelcome to human nature because of its attitude to sin, and this at once shows the need of dealing with the great human, universal fact. The unrighteousness of the Gentiles is first depicted (ch. i. 18-32), then that of the Jews (ch. ii. 1-iii. 8). Then this universal unrighteousness is confirmed from the Old Testament Scriptures (ch. iii. 9-20). So the Apostle prepares the way for the great statement in ch. iii. 21-31, of God's way of righteousness by faith, not by works. Canon Liddon clearly and pointedly puts the teaching of this section:—

(a) Whosoever sins incurs the judgment of God and so needs His righteousness (ch. ii. 1-16).

(b) The heathen, although taught by nature and conscience (ch. i. 18-32), and the Jews, although under the Mosaic law (ch. ii. 17-iii. 8.), have sinned by falling short of their respective standards of righteousness.

(c) Therefore, as the Old Testament had said in effect, all the world becomes guilty before God (ch. iii. 19), and needs His righteousness (ch. iii. 9-20).

We are therefore to be occupied with the proofs of Gentile unrighteousness (ch. i. 18-32), and when the passage is carefully analyzed, it is seen to fall into two main divisions, of which the first is now to be considered.

I. *Divine Wrath* (ver. 18).—God's wrath is being revealed against unrighteousness. We observe the contrast of this Divine revelation with that of the righteousness of ver. 17. Righteousness and wrath are correlatives, and both are in a way revealed in the Gospel, wrath being the alternative of righteousness. Christ is either Savior or Judge (Acts xvii. 31). Since God's righteousness is revealed by faith, it follows that the correlative truth, the wrath of God, is revealed likewise. It is a present revelation to conscience and in history. This may be called the Christian philosophy of history. It is humanity viewed in broad outline from the standpoint of Divine righteousness. The doom of impenitent unrighteousness is absolutely certain, because of the revelation of God's wrath against all unrighteousness. While of course we carefully omit all thought of personal anger from this idea of Divine wrath, we must never forget that it is the judicial personal attitude of God in relation to sin.

This wrath is revealed against "all ungodliness and unrighteousness of men." These are the two expressions of evil; impiety against God and injustice against man. Thus humanity is at once a religious and a moral failure.

These ungodly and unrighteous men are described as those "who hold the truth in unrighteousness." The word translated "hold" means literally "holding down," and is so rendered in the English Revised version. It suggests that they possess the truth and *suppress* it by their unrighteous living. Lightfoot favors the view that the word means simply "grasp," and speaks of their holding and possessing the truth, and all the while living in unrighteousness. Yet another rendering is that of the American Standard Version; "who hinder the truth in unrighteousness." However we express it, we note the deliberate, definite, and wilful opposition to truth shown in unrighteous lives, which thereby inevitably and naturally incur the righteous wrath of God.

II. *Adequate Opportunity* (vers. 19, 20).—This is the way in which the unrighteous first hold and then hinder and suppress the truth in unrighteousness. The opportunity had come to them of knowing God through nature and conscience. "That which is known of God is manifest in them, for God manifested it unto them. For the invisible things of Him since the creation of the world are clearly seen." There is thus no valid reason for ignorance of God, for that which is a matter of knowledge concerning God has been manifested in them by conscience and through nature (Acts xiii. 38; xiv. 17; xxviii. 28). And this revelation of God in nature is really much more than the mere fact of creation, for "the invisible things of Him *since* the creation of the world are clearly seen," thus implying His acts of providence as well as of creation. As Denney well says, "There is that within man which so catches the meaning of all that is without as to issue in an instinctive knowledge of God."

"That they may be without excuse." This opportunity of knowing God through His works was sufficient, and unrighteousness is inexcusable. There is no self-defence. Man may not see much by nature, but what he does see he is able to see clearly, if only he will give heed.

III. *Sinful Declension* (ver. 21).—Indifference to God soon makes its inevitable progress downwards. "Knowing God, they glorified Him not as God, neither gave thanks, but became vain in their reasons, and their senseless heart was broken." The outcome of indifference to known truth was false notions and worthless speculations about God, followed by the disappearance of the idea of God from their minds. The absence of truth is quickly and inevitably succeeded by the presence of positive error. When God is not in the mind vanity soon fills up the void, and darkness suffuses the senseless heart.

IV. *Culpable Foolishness* (ver. 22).—Pride of wisdom resulted from this attitude to God, and yet in reality practical folly was the essential truth of their condition. "Professing themselves to be wise, they became fools." Whenever human wisdom sets itself against God, the result is soon seen in human foolishness.

V. *Utter Degradation* (ver. 23).—The outcome of all this indifference, neglect, wilfulness, and folly, was idolatry in the form of fetichism. Conceit invariably leads to idolatry. Man must have something to worship, and having set aside the worship of the true God he changes "the glory of the incorruptible God for the likeness of an image of corruptible man, and of birds, and of fourfooted beasts, and of creeping things."

The lessons of this solemn and even terrible passage are obvious and familiar, but they need constant reiteration.

1. *Divine Revelation is Sufficient.*—There is no excuse for sin, for man has always had the opportunity of knowing God and doing His will according to the light of nature and conscience. "Without excuse" is the Divine decision, based on the fact of a Divine revelation (ver. 19).

2. *Human Sin is Deliberate.*—From the very first, sin has been a matter of will, and therefore of wilfulness. No one can say, "I could not help it." Light brings responsibility, and the responsibility is in exact proportion to the light. Even neglect is wilful, especially as it invariably leads unchecked to rejection. "What must I do to be lost"? "Nothing." If we neglect so great salvation we shall inevitably drift further (Heb. ii. 1, 2). Moral responsibility is one of the foundation facts of the universe, and it is simply impossible to make any excuse, to say nothing of giving a reason for wrongdoing.

3. *Human Development is downwards.*—Idolatry was not primary, for man at the first was a worshipper of God. He has not developed upwards from the lowest forms of idolatry to the worship of the One True God. His progress has been exactly the opposite. Primeval revelation was monotheistic, and idolatry was neither primitive nor antediluvian. In Scripture the earliest records of idolatry are associated with Rachel, and also found in Joshua

xxiv. 2. We must be careful not to confuse the present savage with primitive man. The terms "primitive" and "savage" are not identical. Sir William Ramsay points out how true to life is the Apostle's teaching in this section.

> "For my own part, I confess that my experience and reading show nothing to confirm the modern assumptions in religious history, and a great deal to confirm Paul. Wherever evidence exists, with the rarest exceptions, the history of religion among men is a history of degeneration . . . . Is it not the fact of human history that man, standing alone, degenerates; and that he progresses only where there is in him so much sympathy with and devotion to the Divine life as to keep the social body pure and sweet and healthy?" (*The Cities of St. Paul*, p. 17).

Instead of growing better in things religious, man has ever been growing worse. This truth which is clearly taught in Scripture is confirmed by scientific research. Sin from the very outset, and all through the centuries, has been the cause of intellectual, social, and moral degration in the individual, and in the human race as a whole. Professor Huxley has these striking words:—

> "The theory of evolution encourages no millennial anticipations. If, for millions of years, our globe has taken the upward road, yet, sometime, the summit will be reached, and the downward route will be commenced" (quoted by Bishop Gore, *The Epistle to the Romans*, p. 79).

We are therefore justified by Scripture and by scientific facts in regarding this section as giving a true philosophy of religion, for "if heathenism is not an apostasy, Christianity is not a restoration" (Philippi, *Romans*, p. 51.[1] As we contemplate this downward development, is it not a call to keep our hearts close to the revelation of God in Christ, lest we should degenerate and wander from Him? Divine revelation is the mirror in which we see ourselves as we really are, and test our life by God's own standard of truth.

4. *Evil is Progressive.*—At first we see neglect. Man, knowing God, did not trouble to acknowledge Him, or to thank Him. From this came emptiness of mind and senselessness of heart, followed by a pride which was essentially foolishness, with its outcome in gross idolatry. We shall see in the next section (vers. 24-28) how

[1]Ramsay's *Cities of St. Paul*, pp. 10-30. The subject may be further studied in Orr's *Christian View of God and the World*, p. 212 ff.; with notes E. and F.; Godet, *The Epistle to the Romans*, p. 176.

from idolatry sensuality necessarily came. Heathenism has almost always been associated with impurity and uncleanness. When the head goes wrong the heart soon follows. Idolatry is the parent of immorality, because there is no safeguard against impurity and no guarantee of holiness. Godlessness, folly, and shame invariably go together. Neglect of God and indifference to Him lead to empty, useless speculation, followed by the practical disappearance of God from the mind, and culminating in fetichism, in which the idea of God is changed for something unutterably base. Man thereby demonstrates that he needs a god of some sort after all. Canon Liddon well says that "All religious truth which is not acted on is on its way to forefeiture." We cannot help observing the three stages of evil in the Epistle to the Hebrews. Neglect came first (ch. ii.); then followed rejection (ch. vi.); and last of all came scorn and contempt of sacred things (ch. x.). Our safeguard lies in remembering the truth; "Resist beginnings."

X

DIVINE CONDEMNATION

Rom. i. 24-32.

24. Wherefore God also gave them up to uncleanness through the lusts of their own hearts, to dishonour their own bodies between themselves:
25. Who changed the truth of God into a lie, and worshipped and served the creature more than the Creator, who is blessed for ever. Amen.
26. For this cause God gave them up unto vile affections; for even their women did change the natural use into that which is against nature:
27. And likewise also the men, leaving the natural use of the woman, burned in their lust one toward another; men with men working that which is unseemly, and receiving in themselves that recompence of their error which was meet.
28. And even as they did not like to retain God in *their* knowledge, God gave them over to a reprobate mind, to do those things which are not convenient;
29. Being filled with all unrighteousness, fornication, wickedness, covetousness, maliciousness; full of envy, murder, debate, deceit, malignity; whispers,
30. Backbiters, haters of God, despiteful, proud, boasters, inventors of evil things, disobedient to parents,
31. Without understanding, covenant-breakers, without natural affection, implacable, unmerciful:
32. Who knowing the judgment of God, that they which commit such things are worthy of death, not only do the same, but have pleasure in them that do them.

The argument of this entire section (ch. i. 18-32), as we have already seen, shows that the rejection of divine light must necessarily incur the divine wrath. "This is the condemnation, that light is come into the world, and men loved darkness rather than light, because their deeds were evil." Now in these closing verses we have the awful picture of the certain progress towards doom of those who cleave to unrighteousness. There is absolutely no hope for them, but only a "certain fearful expectation of judgment" (Heb. x. 27).

I. *Divine Discipline* (ver. 24).—Mark the phrase. "God gave them up," which also occurs with solemn iteration in verses 26 and 28. "Wherefore God gave them up." We have a similar phrase in Psalm lxxxi. 12: "So I gave them up unto their own hearts' lust"; and Acts vii. 42: "God turned, and gave them up to serve the host of heaven." It is a law of nature (which means, it is a law of God) that there is a connection between one act and another; an effect thus becomes a cause in the chain of human action. As Browning says, we pay the price of lies by being compelled to "lie on still."

II. *Terrible Impurity* (ver. 24).—This is the first stage of the divine judgment, and indicates what is well known to follow from the wrong thoughts of God which mark the earlier section. Idolatry is invariably associated with sensuality.

III. *Gross Idolatry* (ver. 25).—Here again we see the connection between false worship and false living. "They exchanged the truth of God for a lie, and worshipped and served the creature more than the Creator, who is blessed for ever. Amen."

IV. *Unnatural Vice* (vers. 26, 27).—This is a still lower depth of evil, and again we have the solemn word, "God gave them up." Such sensual degradation reveals the awful lengths to which sin leads human life.

V. *Complete Depravity* (vers. 28-32).—Once again we are reminded of the divine action: "God gave them up," and this time the lowest depths of all are sounded in the description of a reprobate mind, that is, "a man in which the definite distinctions between right and wrong are confused and lost" (Denney).

(*a*) The depravity is first of all described in general terms; "To do those things which are not fitting." Evil is always unbecoming, unsuitable, "not convenient."

(*b*) Then follow twenty-one illustrations of "things which are not fitting." It is somewhat difficult to classify this list. Dr. David Brown says:—

> "It will be evident to the Greek reader that the *order* in which they are placed follows associations sometimes of *sound* and sometimes of *sense*. Not without reason, therefore, does Fritsche recommend the student not to spend his time and ingenuity in arranging into distinct classes words whose meaning, and vices whose characteristics, differ only by a shade from each other" (*Romans*, p. 22).

On the other hand several authorities are in favor of some classification. Thus we are told that the first four comprehend general descriptions of evil, but with special reference to property. Then come eight words which speak of a disregard of proper relationships. These in turn are followed by three words descriptive of general depravity of character, and last of all there are six words expressive of unprincipled worthlessness of life. It will be seen that in any case the list refers to sins of inward disposition and outward act, to sins of thought, word, and deed, to wrong against self and against neighbor, as well as against God.

With this list we ought to compare others in St. Paul's Epistles. In 2 Cor. xii. 20, there are eight sins against love; in Gal. v. 19, there are seventeen works of the flesh; in Eph. v. 3, six subjects are mentioned; in 1 Tim. i. 9, fourteen kinds of sinners are depicted, and in 2 Tim. iii. 2-5, nineteen sorts are brought before us.

(*c*) The culminating point is seen in verse 32, which sums up verse 18, and restates the judgment of God against unrighteousness. "Who knowing the ordinance of God, that they that practise such things are worthy of death, not only do the same, but consent with them that practise them." Knowledge of evil does not necessarily deter men from it, and this shows that it is only with very careful qualification that we can say, "Knowledge is power." Indeed, very often knowledge is *not* power, for to know is by no means the same as to do.

Thus generally and without any mention of the Gentiles by name, the Apostle has depicted the prominent features of the heathen world.

As we look back over this passage we cannot help seeing some of the most solemn truths that can occupy the attention of man.

I. *The Awful Possibility of Sin.*—We observe that sin starts from the neglect of light, which in turn leads to the rejection of light, followed by madness, idolatry, vice, manifold evil, and a malignant badness that takes a positive satisfaction in wrong-doing (ver. 32). Perhaps our hearts are tempted to say that although this was possible in the old heathen world, it is now quite beyond the bounds of probability in a professedly Christian land. Let us not be too sure of this. The words of the Psalmist are still true, "Who can understand his errors?" The possibilities of evil in the human heart apart from divine grace are as real as they ever were, and no one who knows the plague of his own heart will ever dare to say that even these depths of evil are impossible, apart from the restraining influences of the grace of God. Let us take heed to these wise and solemn words of Bishop Moule:—

> "Nor was it lightly, or as a piece of pious rhetoric, that the saintliest of the chiefs of our Reformation, seeing a murderer carried off to die, exclaimed that there went John Bradford but for the grace of God. It is just when a man is nearest God for himself that he sees what, but for God, he would be; what, taken apart from God, he is, potentially if not in act. And it is in just a mood that, reading this paragraph of the great Epistle, he will smite upon his breast, and say, 'God be merciful to me the sinner' (Luke xviii. 13)" (*Romans*, p. 54).

2. *The Definite Responsibility for Sin.*—There is nothing clearer in this passage than the truth that a measure of divine aid invariably accompanies divine light in the conscience. The people who are described here are shown to be responsible, for unless God had made Himself known in nature and in conscience the entire passage would be meaningless. Even the Mosaic dispensation of law was not wholly and absolutely legal in the sense of being without some provision of divine mercy and graciousness, and neither was the Gentile world entirely bereft of that light from which moral responsibility necessarily flows. Whatever may be the light, however small, the responsibility is in exact proportion, and no one need do wrong if only he heeds the light and welcomes the help provided by God.

3. *The Absolute Inevitableness of Punishment.*—As certain as cause and effect, so is it with sin and punishment. There is no possibility of escape from condemnation for those who persistently continue in unrighteousness. This is a truth that needs constant emphasis and frequent repetition today. God's righteous action against sin is certain, inevitable, universal. "From Thy wrath, and from everlasting damnation, Good Lord, deliver us."

XI

PRINCIPLES OF JUDGMENT

Rom. ii. 1-16

1. Therefore thou art inexcusable, O man, whosoever thou art that judgest: for wherein thou judgest another, thou condemnest thyself; for thou that judgest doest the same things.

2. But we are sure that the judgment of God is according to truth against them which commit such things.

3. And thinkest thou this, O man, that judgest them which do such things, and doest the same, that thou shalt escape the judgment of God?

4. Or despisest thou the riches of his goodness and forbearance and longsuffering; not knowing that the goodness of God leadeth thee to repentance?

5. But after thy hardness and impentitent heart treasurest up unto thyself wrath against the day of wrath and revelation of the righteous judgment of God;

6. Who will render to every man according to his deeds:

7. To them who by patient continuance in well doing seek for glory and honor and immortality, eternal life:

8. But unto them that are contentious, and do not obey the truth, but obey unrighteousness, indignation and wrath.

9. Tribulation and anguish, upon every soul of man that doeth evil, of the Jew first, and also of the Gentile;

10. But glory, honor, and peace, to every man that worketh good, to the Jew first, and also to the Gentile:

11. For there is no respect of persons with God.

12. For as many as have sinned without law shall also perish without law: and as many as have sinned in the law shall be judged by the law;

13. (For not the hearers of the law *are* just before God, but the doers of the law shall be justified.

14. For when the Gentiles, which have not the law, do by nature the things contained in the law, these, having not the law are a law unto themselves:

15. Which shew the work of the law written in their hearts, their conscience also bearing witness, and *their* thoughts the mean while accusing or else excusing one another;)

16. In the day when God shall judge the secrets of men by Jesus Christ according to my gospel.

ALL through this section it is important to keep in mind the general purpose of ch. i. 18—iii. 20. It is not to prove that all men are sinners, but, taking this for granted, to unfold the awful significance of it, in order to bring home to hearts and consciences the terrible results of sin in the certainty of God's judgment on unrighteousness. In ch. i. the Gentiles were referred to without being actually named. There was no need to do this, for the picture would be quickly recognized by all. But these features would not be regarded as applicable to some, and yet these very people in their selfrighteousness were in equal need of conviction of sin. This is done in the early verses of ch. ii. by a special application to one particular individual, "thou" (not "they"). It is generally thought that the Jew is in the Apostle's mind in these verses, although he is not mentioned definitely at the outset. While this is probable, it must not be forgotten that the same spirit of self-righteousness may actuate a Gentile as well. But assuredly it was the Jew more than anyone else who would be liable to this spirit of pride. He would not contemplate the possibility of himself and his fellow-countrymen being subject to condemnation, and it would not be at all easy to convince him of sin, for his self-righteousness and formalism were so strong that he would not feel the need of the Gospel of Christ. Consequently, although the Jew is not named until verse 17, it is more than likely that he is in the Apostle's mind from the outset, and that the purpose of the present section is to show the failure of the Jew as thoroughly as possible and so lead to the conviction of sin. As in ch. i. men are described as "holding down" or "hindering" the truth in unrighteousness by sinning, so in ch. ii. they are shown to be proclaiming the truth in unrighteousness by judging. The spiritual pride of the Jews was doubtless a great stumbling-block to young converts. The position and influence of God's ancient people would impress thoughtful Christians, and make them wonder why they did not accept Christ.

The entire section should be closely analyzed and studied, for it is not without difficulties. The following points of its structure ought to be carefully noted. After verse 1 which gives the introductory practical rebuke to self-righteousness, verse 2 lays down the *first* principle of divine judgment, which is then implied and applied in verses 2-5. Then verse 6 lays down the *second* principle, which is dealt with in verses 7-10. And then verse 11 lays down the *third* principle, which is treated in verses 11-15. Lastly, verse 16 lays down the *fourth* principle, and sums up the whole by referring everything to Christ and His Gospel.

I. *The Rebuke* (ver. 1).—Observe how this appeal is linked with the former statement in ch. i. 18-32 ("Therefore"). The Jews, too, have sinned against light, but before the Apostle can convict them he must remove their arrogance and show that they have no superiority, and that God has one standard for all. If therefore, the man assents to Gentile condemnation he thereby really condemns himself. The man, whether Jew or Gentile, who was apt to judge the Gentiles because of the state of affairs recorded in ch. i. 18-32, was equally guilty himself in other directions, and was therefore "without excuse," since he was practising the same things. This is the case of the man who hides his own guilt by his judgment of others. The Apostle thus appeals to his conscience by pointing out that if he can judge another he can be judged himself, for judging others will not bring escape from God's judgment. Such a man, therefore, cannot plead ignorance.

II. *The First Principle of Judgment* (ver. 2).—God's judgment will be according to truth and therefore absolutely impartial. "We know that the judgment of God is according to truth against them that practice such things."

III. *The Impossibility of Escape* (ver. 3).—"And reckonest thou this, O man, who judgest them that practise such things, and doest the same that thou shalt escape the judgment of God?" The Jew will not be able to claim any exemption because of his national and religious privileges. He of all men will not escape. It has been pointed out that there are four chances of escape to the man who offends against human laws: (1) that his offence shall not be known; (2) that he may escape beyond the bounds of jurisdiction; (3) that there may be some failure in the legal process after arrest; (4) that he may escape from prison and hide himself from the officers of the law (Govett, *Righteousness of God*, p. 20). But, of course, not one of these things will avail with man in regard to the divine judgment. "With Him there is no lack of knowledge, or power, or will to perform what He says."

But there may be another thought in the man's mind (vers. 4, 5). "Or despisest thou the riches of His goodness . . . but . . . treasurest up for thyself wrath?" The divine attitude towards the Jew had repentance for its object, but if it were despised it would only lead to a still deeper condemnation. "The blackest sin is not righteousness violated, but mercy despised." "If you do not trust your own powers of reason, it follows that you must despise the lavish mercy of God" (Lightfoot). And if a man does this he fails to perceive that God's goodness is intended to lead him to repentance, and instead he is piling a treasure of wrath, storing it against the day of judgment. Mark this description of God in His "goodness, and forbearance, and long-suffering." In spite of His judgment against evil He is always long-suffering to the evil-doer. And yet the sinner is here depicted as despising grace, ignoring goodness, and thereby accumulating punishment. Surely the wealth of God's grace is not to be contemptuously treated.

IV. *The Second Principle of Judgment* (ver. 6). God's dealings with mankind are always based upon absolute justice, whether as to punishment or reward. "Who will render to every man according to his works" (See Prov. xxiv. 12). This great and far-reaching principle was intended by the Apostle to come home with unerring force against every form of self-righteousness.

V. *The Reality of Meaning* (ver. 7-10). In these verses only two classes of men are recognized, and only two sorts of deeds allowed. This definite contrast should ever be insisted on. There is no middle pathway; men are either on one side or the other. Those whose character is described as patient in well-doing, and whose pursuit is "glory, and honor and immortality," will be rewarded with eternal life. But those whose character is "factious," whose "pursuit is obedience to unrighteousness" will find as the result, "wrath and indignation." Nothing could well be more assuredly defined than this contrast between the characters, pursuits, and rewards of well-doing and evil-doing (vers. 7, 8). The same contrast is once again seen in a further description. "Tribulation and anguish are to come upon every soul of man that worketh evil, of the Jew first and also of the Greek"; while, on the other hand, "glory, and honor, and peace to every man that worketh good, to the Jew first and also to the Greek." Let us note carefully, as we proceed, every allusion to the Jew, especially "the Jew first," for these references form one of the key-notes to the Epistle, as chapters ix.—xi. will show. As the Jew has already been described as possessing priority in salvation (ch. i. 16), so this priority is now recognized even with reference to judgment in relation to good and evil (vers. 9, 10). It is also full of meaning and profound significance that neither here nor elsewhere in Scripture is the future of the wicked ever called by the term "life"; a striking change of expression is seen to this effect in our Lord's words (John v. 28, 29).

VI. *The Third Principle of Judgment* (ver. 11). "There is no respect of persons with God." This great truth is very prominent in the Old Testament (Deut. x. 17), and seems to have made a profound impression upon almost every writer of the New Testament (Acts x. 34; Eph. vi. 9; Col. iii. 25; Jas. ii. 9; 1 Pet. i. 17). God has no favorites, and it was essential that the Jew above all men should understand this simple but searching truth.

VII. *The Universality of Application* (vers. 12-15).—While there is but one principle of divine judgment for all (ver. 11), yet the standards of judgment will necessarily be different for Jew and Gentile. The standard for the Jew will be the law of Moses, but the standard for the Gentile will be the law of conscience. The Apostle means by "sin without the law" and "perish without the law," that they will perish by unfaithfulness to a law which they possess, namely, the law of nature; not to a law of which they have never heard, namely, the law of Moses. Thus character will be the test in both cases. Denney draws out very clearly the meaning of this important though difficult passage:—

> "There is a triple proof that Gentiles, who are regarded as not having law, are a law to themselves. (1) The appeal to their conduct: as interpreted by the Apostle, their conduct evinces, at least in some, the possession of a law written on the heart; (2) the action of conscience: it joins its testimony, though it be only an inward one, to the outward testi-

mony, borne by their conduct; and (3) their thoughts. Their thoughts bear witness to the existence of a law in them, inasmuch as in their mutual intercourse these thoughts are busy bringing accusations, or, in rarer cases, putting forward defences, *i.e.* in any case, exercising moral functions which imply the recognition of a law" (*Expositor's Greek Testament, Romans*, p. 598).[1]

VIII. *The Fourth Principle of Judgment* (ver. 16).—The Apostle closes this statement about the divine judgment by showing that both Jews and Gentiles will be brought face to face with Christ and the Gospel in the ultimate judgment. "In the day when God shall judge the secrets of men according to my Gospel by Jesus Christ."

Reviewing these verses, it will be seen that the questions of reward and punishment are here isolated from the main subjects of the Epistle; namely, man's justification by the righteous grace of God, which will come before us in its proper place later. This section, therefore, deals with judgment, not with justification; with the completion, not with the commencement of life. The Apostle is simply concerned with the great fact that righteousness leads to life and unrighteousness to death. He is dealing with the results, not the process; the goal, not the way. The teaching of verse 13 as to the judicial verdict of God is no contradiction of the ordinary meaning of justification so characteristic of St. Paul. He was not at all likely to contradict what he was about to say in ch. iii. 19, and teach salvation by law. The entire passage from verse 6-16 is a general statement of the divine principles of judgment, made in order to destroy the refuge of lies. Subordinate passages must always be interpreted in the light of leading truths, and one of the essential truths of this Epistle is that "by the works of the law shall no flesh be justified" (ch. iii. 20). When, therefore, the Apostle shows in ch. ii. 13 that "the doers of the law shall be justified," it must be carefully interpreted in the light of the former text, and it will then be seen to refer to the general principle of judgment. The Apostle does not stay here to show how we may obtain that righteousness which is needed (namely, in the Gospel), and thereby avoid the unrighteousness. What he now says is, that no one can

[1]For a consideration of the meaning of St. Paul's use of terms "law" and "the law" in this Epistle, see Garvie, *Century Bible*, p. 106, and D. Brown, *Handbook for Bible Classes*, p. 30.

be saved eventually apart from doing good, the power to do which comes, as will be shown in its proper place, through the Gospel. Eternal life can be viewed, either as a present position for the believer, or as the future issue or goal of a consecrated life in Christ. It is not the mode of salvation, but the principle of judgment that the Apostle here deals with; not the ground of justification, but the standard; not that on account of which we are saved, but that according to which we are to be judged. Denney points out that the law that "God will render to everyone according to his works" is "valid within the sphere of redemption as well as independent of it," and that Paul had "no feeling that it contradicted his doctrine of justification by faith . . . . the truth which he is insisting upon is equally true whether men are under the law or under grace."

Yet even here there is a hint that the reward implies faith in one who tries for it, and that the wrath is due to the absence of faith and the presence of unbelief in those who obey not the truth. Moreover, everything is ultimately related to the Gospel in verse 16. As Dr. Campbell Morgan forcibly puts it:

> "Thus, at the very beginning of this letter, the master-theme of which is salvation by faith, we have an overwhelming and unanswerable indictment of that particular heresy to which an improper emphasis of the doctrine is liable to give rise. Nothing can be clearer than the Apostle's teaching that works will be the final test of judgment. Faith which does not produce these is declared to be useless . . . Godliness as privileged relationship is of no value except as it produces actual righteousness. . . The basis of judgment is to be the actual condition of man, whether he has lived without the law or under the law; but he is to be judged finally by Jesus Christ. That is to say, the final test of character and of conduct is to be that of man's attitude to the Saviour" (*Romans,* pp. 27-29).

And to quote Godet:

> "Justification by faith alone applies to the time of *entrance* into salvation through the free Pardon of sin, but not to the time of judgment. When God of free grace receives the sinner at the time of his conversion, He asks nothing of him except faith; but from that moment the believer enters on a wholly new responsibility; God demands from him, as the recipient of grace, the fruits of grace . . . . The reason is that faith is not the dismal prerogative of being able to sin with impunity; it is, on the contrary, the means of overcoming sin, and acting holily; and if this life-fruit is not produced, it is dead, and will be declared vain" (Romans, vol. i. p. 196).

In these verses the Apostle deals with some tremendous certainties to which we do well to give heed.

1. *The Certainty of Judgment.*—Nothing is more absolutely assured than that every man will be judged hereafter. The thought of this should lend solemnity to every part of our life.

2. *The Universality of Judgment.*—No one will be able to escape; everybody will be included; "To the Jew first and also to the Greek." This, again, is one of the fundamental principles of our very existence.

3. *The Principles of Judgment.*—Mark once again the four principles of judgment here laid down. "According to truth" (ver. 2). "According to every man's work" (ver. 6). According to absolute impartiality (ver. 11). According to the Gospel of Christ (ver. 16).

4. *The Results of Judgment.*—The rewards will be generous and eternal. The doom will be certain and terrible.

These truths should be pressed home on every man's conscience. They show that there is no possibility of self-deception in the matter of the ultimate issues of right and wrong, and they are intended to lead, and, if properly applied, will undoubtedly lead, to conviction of sin and repentance before God (ver. 4).

XII

PERILS OF SELF-RIGHTEOUSNESS

Rom. ii. 17-24

17. Behold, thou art called a Jew, and restest in the law, and makest thy boast of God.

18. And knowest *his* will, and approvest the things that are more excellent, being instructed out of the law;

19. And art confident that thou thyself art a guide of the blind, a light of them which are in darkness.

20. An instructor of the foolish, a teacher of babes, which hast the form of knowledge and of the truth in the law.

21. Thou therefore which teachest another, teachest thou not thyself? thou that preachest a man should not steal, dost thou steal?

22. Thou that sayest a man should not commit adultery, dost thou commit adultery? thou that abhorrest idols, dost thou commit sacrilege?

23. Thou that makest thy boast of the law, through breaking the law dishonourest thou God?

24. For the name of God is blasphemed among the Gentiles through you, as it is written.

After laying down the four principles of divine judgment the Apostle makes a direct appeal to the Jew to prove to him the profound significance of his unrighteousness. Whatever question there may be about the precise reference to the Jew in verses 1-16, there can be none here, since he is specifically named. He is clearly taught that special privileges cannot shield him from the judgment of God if he continues to obey unrighteousness. This section brings the argument of verses 1-16 to a head. The Jews made much of having a law, but in practice they were no better than the Gentiles. The law which was thought of so highly is seen to have its first application to themselves. There is to be no deviation for Israel from the principle laid down in verse 11: "There is no respect of persons with God."

In ch. i. 18-32, St. Paul has shown that the Gentiles are liable to judgment because of their unrighteousness. In ch. ii. 1-16, the self-righteous, whether Jews or Gentiles, are taught the same lesson, and now in the present section comes the proof beyond all question that the Jew had failed to keep the law, as to which he was continually making his boast. The one thought running through the whole paragraph is the position of the Jew in the sight of God. He had greater light, and his pride and self-sufficiency were not only useless, but positively dangerous, heightening his condemnation and leading to God's name being dishonored among the Gentiles.

I. *The Jewish Claim* (ver. 17).—"If thou bearest the name of a Jew." The term "Jew" is first found in 2 Kings xvi. 6, and was evidently a name of which the owner was particularly proud. The Apostle is about to show him that with all his boast of an honored name, he had failed to attain to righteousness, though all the while possessing the divine law.

II. *The Claims to Jewish Privileges* (vers. 17-18).—Five claims to personal privileges on the part of the Jew are here recorded. "Restest upon the law"; "gloriest in God"; "knowest His will"; "approvest the things that are excellent"; "being instructed out of the law." Each of these formed a part of that ground of boasting which enabled the Jew to feel that he possessed privileges which no one else had. No doubt this was all true. He did "repose on a law"; he did "boast in God"; he did "know the divine will"; he was able to "distinguish things that differ," or "approve things that were excellent," and he was undoubtedly "instructed out of the law." We must never allow his boasting to make us forget that there was a difference constituted by God Himself between the Jew and others, but this was no warrant for wrapping himself in a robe of self-righteousness and despising others.

III. *The Claims to Jewish Superiority* (vers. 19, 20).—Five more claims are here recorded. The Jew was confident as to himself, that he was "a guide of the blind," "a light to them that are in darkness," "a corrector of the foolish," "a teacher of babes," "having in the law the form of knowledge and of the truth." Once again, we may fully allow that the Jew when he realized his position and fulfilled the divine will, was able to guide, teach, and direct those who did not, like him, possess the divine truth in the law. But all this was utterly spoiled by the overweening pride and self-sufficiency which made all instruction of others intolerable through the teacher's self-righteousness.

IV. *The Claims to Superiority Refuted* (vers. 21, 22).—In an inverse order the Apostle deals with this self-righteous boasting. The man who claims to teach others is asked why he does not teach himself; the man who preaches against stealing is asked whether he himself is a thief; the man who urges that others should not commit adultery is asked if he is guilty of this sin; and the lowest deep of all is pointed out when the man that abhors idols is virtually charged with robbing temples. Avarice was a Jewish sin, and it seems clear that sacrilege and temple robbing were popularly associated with the Jews (Acts xix. 37). Thus, with unerring force and definiteness the Apostle drives home the truth against this self-righteousness.

At this point it is worth comparing the charges made against the Gentiles in ch. i. 21-31 with these against the Jews in ch. ii. 21, 22. The following diagram will make it clear:—

GENTILES	JEWS
(1) Ungodliness (Sins against God), ch. i. 21-23.	(1) Ungodliness (Sins against God), ch. ii. 22.
(2) Intemperance (Sins against self), ch. i. 24-27.	(2) Intemperance (Sins against self) ch. ii. 22.
(3) Unrighteousness (Sins against man), ch. i. 21-32.	(3) Unrighteousness (Sins against man), ch. ii. 21.

V. *The Claims of Privileges Refuted* (ver. 23).—The Apostle is not content with indicating the outward and visible proofs of Jewish evil. He will go further and show that the man who glories in the law (see ver. 17) is really through his trangression of that law dishonoring the very God Whose name he bore. There is nothing more solemn or awful than the case of a man who, in mind and speech, is ever boastful and glorying in religion, and yet through his evil life is bringing discredit on the very religion he professes. If a man is to glory at all, he must glory in a personal experience of God in all His reality of goodness and righteousness (Jer. ix. 23-24).

VI. *The Climax of Refutation* (ver. 24).—Here the Apostle goes to the very heart of the Jewish trouble by charging them, of all men, with being the cause of awful blasphemy among the Gentiles. "For the Name of God is blashemed among the Gentiles because of you, even as it is written." It is as though the heathen were saying, "Like God, like people; what a Divinity the patron of this odius race must be" (Denney). The way in which the sentence closes with the words, "As it is written," is very striking. The Apostle refers to Isaiah lii. 5, and instead of actually quoting the words, the emphatic reference is really a challenge; "as if he had said, let him impugn this who dare contest the Word of God" (Denney).

The section is full of solemn, searching, and even startling lessons for those who profess the Name of Christ and work in His vineyard. Let us look at it specially in relation to all who are called upon to do the work of Christian teachers. The description of the Jew in these verses is that of a man who knew the truth and professed to teach it to others.

1. *The Teacher's Relation to God.*—The five statements in verses 17, 18 are all true of the Christian teacher. He "reposes on a law"; "boasts in God"; "knows His will"; "discerns things that differ"; and is "instructed out of the law." These are the secrets of real teaching power and should be cultivated and developed if we would "make full proof of our ministry."

2. *The Teacher's Relation to Others.*—The fivefold description in verses 19-20 suggest what a teacher ought to be—a guide, a light, a corrector, and instructor, one possessing the embodiment of knowledge and truth. Only as these are true of the teacher can he be effective in his instruction of others.

3. *The Teacher's Foundation.*—Let us note carefully the emphasis on "the law" (vers. 17, 18, 20). What the law was to the Jew, the Word of God is to the Christian teacher. It must ever be the secret of all true instruction. The man whose sermons and lessons are based on the Word of God is the only one who can be regarded

in the full sense of the term as a Christian teacher.

4. *The Teacher's Responsibility* (vers. 21-23).—Our life must be in accord with our teaching, or else the teaching will be absolutely useless: "Thou must thyself be true, if thou the truth wouldst teach."

5. *The Teacher's Danger.*—This is especially and almost constantly the peril of censoriousness. The spirit of carping, fault-finding, judging, is one of the most serious dangers of the teacher. He thinks he knows more than his hearers (and as a rule he does), and so is tempted to look down upon others, and to complain if they do not reach the proper standard. In all ages of the Church the peril of censoriousness in the teacher has been one of the most sad and solemn facts.

6. *The Teacher's Sin* (ver. 24).—Inconsistency dishonors God, and leads people to reject and even blaspheme Christianity. How awful are the results of inconsistent living in the case of Christian preachers and teachers! As Dr. Beet says:—

> "Men around think less of God because this man lives among them and calls himself a disciple of God. It were more for His glory, and therefore for the good of those who know this man, if he were a professed heathen."

And Nathaniel Hawthorne aptly remarks:—

> "Let us reflect that the highest path is pointed out by the pure ideal of those who look up to us, and who, if we tread less softly, may never look so high again.

XIII

OUTWARD AND INWARD

ROM. ii. 25-29

25. For circumcision verily profiteth, if thou keep the law: but if thou be a breaker of the law, thy circumcision is made uncircumcision.
26. Therefore if the uncircumcision keep the righteousness of the law, shall not his uncircumcision be counted for circumcision?
27. And shall not uncircumcision which is by nature, if it fulfil the law, judge thee, who by the letter and circumcision dost transgress the law?
28. For he is not a Jew, which is one outwardly; neither *is that* circumcision, which is outward in the flesh:
29. But he *is* a Jew, which is one inwardly; and circumicision *is that* of the heart, in the spirit, *and* not in the letter; whose praise *is* not of men, but of God.

THE Apostle now confirms his contention that there is no respect of persons with God, by showing that the Jewish ordinance of circumcision is absolutely useless apart from personal righteousness, and that the Gentile who has no opportunity of sharing the ordinance may be morally superior to the Jew who has the privilege. Circumcision constituted another plea by the Jews for "preferential treatment," and the Apostle shows the groundlessness of the contention.

I. *Obligation without Obedience* (vers. 25-27).—The covenant of circumcision without a corresponding expression of what the covenant means is shown to be an impossible method of righteousness. "Circumcision indeed profiteth if thou be a doer of the law; but if thou be a transgressor of the law thy circumcision has become uncircumcision." This word "become" is a striking and bold utterance. It means "become *ipso facto*," and the Jew with his vaunted circumcision is seen to have been reduced to a level of the despised Gentile.

Not only so, but the Gentile is told that, if only he observes the ordinance of the law, his uncircumcision shall be reckoned for circumcision, and thereby the Gentile will judge the Jew who, notwithstanding all his circumcision, is a transgressor of the very law he possesses and claims to hold. Thus, the Apostle turns the tables on Jewish pride and exclusiveness, for if there was one thing beyond all others the Jew prided himself on, it was the possession of the sign of the covenant between him and his God. Even in the Old Testament there were not a few references to the absolute necessity of circumcision of heart (Deut. x. 16; xxx. 6; Jer. ix. 26; Ezek. xliv. 7).

This phrase, "reckoned for" (ver. 26), should be specially noted and remembered. It is one of the important expressions of the Epistle, and will come before us later on in connection with faith and righteousness. It means to "put down in the account with reference to." We see the application of it in this verse to circumcision; that God will under certain circumstances put down uncircumcision in the account for circumcision, and circumcision as uncircumcision. Other meanings, as in ch. iv. 5, will be seen in due course.

II. *Religion without Reality* (vers. 28, 29).—Here the two ideas of the Jew (vers. 17-24) and circumcision (vers. 25-27) are summed up, and a contrast is instituted between the Jew "outwardly" and the Jew "inwardly." This distinction is very significant and emphatic, and is found in different parts of Scripture. It is the substance of Isaiah's doctrine of "the godly remnant," as contrasted with the nation at large. The Psalmist refers to the spiritual meaning of sacrifice, and the constant allusions to God's holiness in the Psalter point the same lesson (Psa. i. 13, 14; li. 16, 17). The New Testament draws the same conclusion between Jew and Jew (Luke i. 6; John i. 47; vii. 47-49; Rom. ix. 6 ff.; Phil. iii. 3).

The Apostle shows that the possession of the name of "Jew" was of no real avail, that circumcision is "that of the heart, in the spirit and not in the letter," and that the real meaning of "Jew," which is "praise" ("Judah"), has reference to the praise "not of man, but of God."

This contrast between spirit and letter (ver. 29) must be carefully observed. It is not a contrast between the letter and spirit of Holy Scripture, but between a written law (letter) and an unwritten law (spirit). See 2 Cor. iii. 4. We might have expected a contrast between "spirit" and "flesh," but this is not the point in the Apostle's mind. "Spirit and letter are not the elements in which, but the powers by which, the circumcision is conceived to be effected" (Denney). The old covenant had written documents, but the new covenant is primarily a matter of the heart. St. Paul means that heart-circumcision is produced by the Spirit of God and not by the letter of the written law.

Dr. David Brown (*Romans*, p. 29) calls attention to "the three deep foundations on which all religion reposes, of which two come in the first chapter—the *Physics* and the *Metaphysics* of Natural Theology (ch. i. 19, 20); and the third in this chapter, the *Ethics* of Natural Theology. The testimony of these two passages is to the theologian invaluable, while in the breast of every teachable Christian it wakens such echoes as are inexpressible, impressive, and solemn."

The Apostle is still occupied with the dangers associated with religious profession, and to "all who profess and call themselves Christians" the passage is full of searching meaning.

1. *The Peril of Presumption.* — Nothing is easier than self-righteousness and self-deception in religion. It is well-nigh impossible to enjoy outward privileges without presuming on them as the Jews did. The greater the knowledge, the greater the danger of being content with a merely nominal Christianity. It is one of the most solemn truths that without any real change of heart we may know a great deal of Christian truth, may even be occupied with Christian work, and closely associated with Christian people, knowing with great familiarity religious phraseology and living largely in a Christian atmosphere, and yet all the while may be without the new life that comes from the Spirit of God. The danger of such a position is far greater than that of wilful and deliberate sin. Our Lord was constantly warning His hearers against such presumption. "Many will say to Me in that day, Lord, Lord, have we

not phophesied in Thy Name? and in Thy Name have cast out devils? and in Thy Name done many wonderful works? And then will I profess unto them, I never knew you: depart from Me, ye that work iniquity" (Matt. vii. 22, 23). "Then shall ye begin to say, We have eaten and drunk in Thy presence, and Thou hast taught in our streets. But He shall say, I tell you, I know you not whence ye are: depart from Me, all ye workers of iniquity" (Luke xiii. 26, 27). The greater the privilege the greater the peril. The higher the delight the more imperative the duty. Let us ever pray the Psalmist's prayer; "Keep back Thy servant from presumptuous sins."

2. *The Peril of Formalism.*—The lesson about circumcision reveals the great principle that "the ritual seal and the spiritual reality are separable" (Bishop Moule). Circumcision was a seal, and a seal only, and "what is the value of a seal when torn off from that which it is intended to certify-" (Stifler). If we substitute Baptism and the Lord's Supper for circumcision in this passage, we see at once the solemn application it has for us today. There is a constant danger of identifying the outward sign with the inward spiritual meaning, and of thinking that the reception of the one is a guarantee of the other. St. Paul here teaches us the very opposite. While we must ever insist with all clearness and firmness on obedience to the ordinances of God, we must never fail to remember that the ordinances themselves, apart from genuine spiritual dispositions in the recipients, never convey or guarantee the reception of grace. Ordinances are "visible signs to which are annexed promises." Faith lays hold of the promise and the signs are the pledges of God's fulfillment of them, but if there be no faith in the Divine promise, there is nothing left for the ordinance to seal.

XIV

OBJECTIONS MET

Rom. iii. 1-8.

1. What advantage then hath the Jew? or what profit *is there* of circumcision?
2. Much every way chiefly, because that unto them were committed the oracles of God.
3. For what if some did not believe? shall their unbelief make the faith of God without effect?
4. God forbid; yea, let God be true, but every man a liar; as it is written, That thou mightest be justified in thy sayings, and mightest overcome when thou art judged.
5. But if our unrighteousness commend the righteousness of God, what shall we say? *Is* God unrighteous who taketh vengeance? (I speak as a man).
6. God forbid: for then how shall God judge the world?
7. For if the truth of God hath more abounded through my lie unto his glory; why yet am I also judged as a sinner?
8. And not *rather,* (as we be slanderously reported, and as some affirm that we say,) Let us do evil, that good may come? whose damnation is just.

The Apostle has now really closed his first section, showing the need of righteousness by Gentiles and Jews. But instead of at once summing up the discussion, as he does in ch. iii. 9-20, he perceives the necessity of making a digression to meet an objection. The plain speaking in ch. ii. about the Jew, is supposed to be met by a Jewish objector who argues that if these things be true, and the Jew is put practically on a spiritual level with the Gentile, it is impossible to see where any advantage accrues to the Jew, or what is the explanation of the fact that God Himself has made a distinction between Jew and Gentile. Does not all that the Apostle has been saying prove too much? Was not Judaism from God, with its clear-cut distinctions between circumcised and uncircumcised? The objections may well have been his own opinions before conversion, and like other Jews he might have thought that the Gospel of Jesus Christ really disparaged the Jewish position.

Here is a question which never again quite passes out of sight, though the complete answer is not given until chs. ix.-xi. It is the question whether in laying such stress on righteousness and Divine impartiality, and in apparently making nothing of Jewish privileges, the Apostle is not really charging God with breach of faith with the people of the old covenant? Was not Paul's contention that God's judgment will be "without respect of persons" absolutely opposed to the Jewish position and privilege? Later on, as we shall see, he will make it abundantly clear that Jewish perversion and unfaithfulness, not himself, still less God, have all along been responsible for the difficulties now being raised.

Is not the Apostolic teaching, therefore, obliterating distinctions made by God Himself (ver. 1)? The discussion of this and of other objections will be found in the present section (vers. 2-8). The general sense of the passage will become clear if it is given careful examination, but its abruptness and conciseness tend to make its meaning difficult unless closely studied. There seem to be four objections stated or implied, and then answered in turn.

I. *Objection* (ver. 1) "What advantage then hath the Jew, or what is the profit of circumcision?" Here we have two deep questions of the Epistle. The subject of Jewish superiority is now discussed only quite briefly, and merely so far as is necessary to consider the argument in relation to Jewish sin, and to show that it cannot set aside the argument of ch. ii. The subject is taken up more fully in chs. ix.-xi. We shall see later on still other instances of this characteristic method of St. Paul in just touching upon a subject, then dismissing it for a time and dealing with it subsequently in full. Meanwhile the twofold question of this verse should be considered. The first part, "What advantage then hath the Jew?" is answered in vers. 2-8; the second part, "What is the profit of circumcision?" is dealt with in ch. iv. These two parts of one great question thus take up the two subjects of ch. ii. 28, 29. The Jew naturally argued that according to St. Paul's teaching there was no use whatever in the old covenant, that God's faithfulness is really impugned if He is supposed to have given advantage to Jews under the old covenant when He was really giving none, and that if judgment is to be based on character only, the Jews are no better off than others.

II. *Answer* (ver. 2).—The objector is at once told that there is a great advantage accruing to the Jew. "Much every way"; first of all that they were entrusted with the oracles of God. These privileges, though they cannot screen sinners from Divine judgment, or prove a substitute for Divine righteousness, are nevertheless of real and great worth. In the first place, the Jews possessed God's living oracles, the Old Testament Scriptures (Heb. v. 12; 1 Pet. iv. 11). And these include not merely God's law, but His special and peculiar promises to Israel. This emphasis on the Jewish position in regard to the possession of the Old Testament is very important, and shows what will become clearer when we look at ch. xi., that Israel was never intended to be absorbed into the Gentile Church of Christ. Judaism is "no mere relic of a dead past, but still has advantages which will one day be made clear."

III. *Objection* (ver. 3).—But now comes another question. In view of this possession of Divine oracles, what about the fact that some of the Jews were lacking in faith? Does their lack of faith destroy the validity of these oracles and make of none effect the faithfulness of Him Who gave them? This is how the Jewish objector meets the Apostle, by implying that the mere possession of the Scriptures was nothing in the face of Jewish unbelief.

IV. *Answer* (ver. 4).—St. Paul meets this suggestion with his customary expression of positive horror at the very thought. "God forbid." "Perish the very idea." Although these oracles were not believed in by the nation, they nevertheless retained their Divine power and authority unimpaired, and would yet find their complete fulfilment; and even if some of the Jews have failed to realize their advantages, it has been due to their unfaithfulness and not to any fault of God's nature. If every man on earth were proved to be false, God's truth would still remain true, as is expressed in Psa. li. 4, "That thou mightest be declared righteous in the judgment of mankind." Man's very unfaithfulness, so far from destroying

God's faithfulness, will really make the latter more prominent and glorify God all the more.

V. *Objection* (ver. 5).—But now a very real difficulty occurs, based upon the last statement of the Apostle. If man's unfaithfulness and sin bring about greater glory to God, how can He justly punish man for it? Would He not be unrighteous in inflicting punishment? Why not let man sin more and more in order to bring still greater glory to Himself? Surely if God uses sin to glorify Himself, He ought not to punish the sinner. Thus, the Apostle faces one of the acutest problems of his ministry. Evidently his teaching had been charged with giving an excuse for sinning. Salvation by grace was said to have an immoral tendency, as we shall see again in ch. vi. i. This (by the way) shows quite evidently the meaning of the Pauline doctrine of righteousness without works, for against no other teaching could such a charge be made:—

"Nothing shows more clearly the true meaning of 'salvation by grace' than the charge of 'immoral tendency' brought against it. Had it meant salvation conditioned on any good dispositions wrought in us, or works done by us, even through Divine assistance, it is impossible to see how any encouragement to do evil that good may come could have been charged against such teaching. But if his doctrine was that 'righteousness without works' is imputed to the ungodly who believe in Jesus, it is easy to see how a handle might be made of this to make it appear as an encouragement to 'sin that grace may abound.' And the undoubted fact that in all time the latter doctrine *has been so charged and the former never,* abundantly confirms this" (D. Brown, *Romans,* p. 33).

VI. *Answer* (ver. 6).—Once again the Apostle repels the idea with scorn. The very thought calls for instant and total condemnation. "God forbid." Such an idea would for ever prevent God from judging the world at all. We thus see the force of Bishop Gore's remarks that the Apostle "will not argue with one who reasons at the expense of his conscience":—

"This is an important principle. When the intellect is acting purely, it must be free, and must be dealt with seriously on its own ground. But the conscience must be followed first of all. Its light is clearer than the light of intellect, and must be left supreme. Whatever be the bewilderment of my intellect, I am self-condemned, God-condemned, if I play false to the moral light. And arguments to the contrary, however clever-sounding or philosophical, are in fact sophistry. There is, we must confess, a good deal of such sophistry today in the use of arguments drawn from the current philosophy of necessitarianism and the idea of heredity" (*The Epistle to the Romans*, p. 119).

VII. *Objection* (vers. 7, 8).—Last of all, and following immediately on the former point, the Apostle meets an objection by using himself as an illustration. "If the truth of God through my lie abounded unto His glory, why am I, Paul, myself still judged as a sinner, and why not . . . let us do evil that good may come?" If judgment could be evaded by sinning to the glory of God, Paul and other Christians might naturally act on the principle which slander was imputing to them, that of doing evil that good might result. If a Jew is not to be judged on this account, neither can a Gentile, for any heathen might reasonably urge the same plea, and say, Why am I thus judged as a sinner? Thus, there would be an end to all thought of the present injustice and inequalities caused by sin ever being put right. Sin is evil in itself, quite apart from its consequences. If it should be said that David's sins served moral purposes in the end, it may be at once replied that this was only due to God's marvelous and over-ruling grace. The sin itself, if left alone, would never have accomplished this end. It is impossible and intolerable, therefore, to think of doing evil that good may come. Sin never can be a necessity for man, or for God. Evil is not to be done for the sake of good, nor had the Apostle himself ever said so, though there were some who dared slanderously to report him as teaching this doctrine which he here repels with scorn and horror. On the contrary, he urges that those who teach such a doctrine are justly condemned. "Whose damnation is just." Thus, he does not attempt refutation of the evil sophistries which evil man invents, but simply places one evident truth against another. As Denney says:—

"The doctrine that righteousness is a gift of God, not to be won by works of law, but by faith in Jesus Christ, can always be misrepresented as immoral, "sin the more, it will only the more magnify grace.' Paul does not stoop to discuss it. The judgment that comes on those who by such perversions of reason and conscience seek to evade all judgment is just. This is all he has to say" (*Expositor's Greek Testament*, p. 605).

And so after these objections the Apostle is once again back at the point at which he started in chapter ii. 1, that the Jew in his self-righteousness stands self-condemned, and is "without excuse."

1. *Some Divine Realities.*—Several points associated with God are brought into prominence in this section, and call for constant consideration and practical application.

(*a*) The Oracles of God (ver. 2). This phrase refers to the Old Testament, and is a significant and suggestive description of the Word of God (cf. Heb. v. 12; 1 Pet. iv. 11). Oracles in heathen religions were dim, mysterious, and ambiguous, but the Bible as the divine oracle is the clear revelation of God's character and the definite declaration of His will for man. Is this the way in which we regard it today?

(*b*) The Faithfulness of God (ver. 3). Here we have one of the great fundamental realities of Holy Scripture, teaching us that God is ever true to His Word, both as to promises and to threatenings. This faithfulness is maintained in spite of human sin and unfaithfulness. The unchangeable faithfulness of God is the bed-rock of revelation and Christianity. "He abideth faithful, He cannot deny Himself."

(*c*) The Righteousness of God (ver. 5). This is one of the main phrases of the Epistle. In the present passage it means God's absolute rectitude, with no deviation from the path of perfect truth and right. God's character is at once our warning and our inspiration.

(*d*) The Judgment of God (ver. 6). This expresses one of the great facts of life, the certainty of justice, the universality of the divine judgment.

(*e*) The Truth of God (ver. 7). The expression suggests the reality of the divine character as opposed to everything unreal and shadowy. It also teaches us the absolute accuracy and correctness of the divine will as opposed to human error and untruth.

(*f*) The Glory of God (ver. 7). This term brings before us here and elsewhere in the Epistle the one supreme object for which all creation was brought into being—to glorify God and manifest Him.

2. *Some Human Responsibilities.*—The passage lays equal stress on man's side in the following particulars:—

(*a*) We are entrusted with the Oracles of God (ver. 2). If this was true of the Jew with regard to the Old Testament, much more it is true of Christians with regard to the whole Bible. Its possession is a sacred, solemn, and serious trust, calling for earnest study, genuine faith, practical obedience, and world-wide circulation.

(*b*) We are in danger of Unbelief (ver. 3). Faith is the only adequate, and indeed the only possible, answer that we can make to God's revelation of Himself. Hence we can see the awful results of unbelief; it severs our connection with God, and makes His word of none effect so far as our spiritual life is concerned. We cannot ponder too deeply or too often the barrier, the baseness, and the banefulness of unbelief.

(*c*) We are liable to abuse God's Mercy (ver. 8). The temptation to do evil that good may come is almost inherent in human life, and certainly has been allowed in many quarters. Great crimes have been justified by representing the advantages accruing from them. This whole idea is repugnant to Christian truth, for it is impossible to make sin other than sin. God's over-ruling mercy can bring about good as the result of evil, but this is an effect directly opposite to that which is natural to sin. It is absolutely false to say there is a "soul of goodness in things evil"; there is not, for evil is evil through and through, and never can be anything else. The end does not justify the means. We must beware of such phrases as "white lie," and "pious fraud." If it be a "lie," it is not "white." If it be "white," it is not a "lie." If it be a "fraud," it cannot be "pious." If it be "pious," it cannot be a "fraud."

(*d*) We are certain of the Divine Judgment vers. 6, 8). This is perhaps the most solemn responsibility of all. If there be no such thing as sin there cannot be any judgment, but with sin as an awful fact judgment is absolutely certain. Man is accountable to God for wrong-doing, and this accountability abides quite apart from any over-ruling providence which may use the consequences of evil for some good purpose. It is one of the foundation facts of the universe that man is personally responsible for his actions.

XV

THE VERDICT OF SCRIPTURE

Rom. iii. 9-20.

9. What then? are we better *than they?* No, in no wise: for we have before proved both Jews and Gentiles, that they are all under sin;
10. As it is written, There is none righteous, no, not one:
11. There is none that understandeth, there is none that seeketh after God.
12. They are all gone out of the way, they are together become unprofitable; there is none that doeth good, no, not one.
13. Their throat *is* an open sepulchre; with their tongues they have used deceit; the poison of asps *is* under their lips:
14. Whose mouth *is* full of cursing and bitterness:
15. Their feet *are* swift to shed blood:
16. Destruction and misery *are* in their ways:
17. And the way of peace have they not known:
18. There is no fear of God before their eyes.
19. Now we know that what things soever the law saith, it saith to them who are under the law: that every mouth may be stopped, and all the world may become guilty before God.
20. Therefore by the deeds of the law there shall no flesh be justified in his sight: for by the law *is* the knowledge of sin.

The whole question of universal unrighteousness has been considered in regard to the Gentile and also the Jew. Now comes the summing up and the confirmation of the Apostle's position in the light of the Old Testament. He has stated his position, and charged both Jew and Gentile with unrighteousness, and now he proves from the Scriptures of the Jews themselves the truth of what he has been saying. Thus, verse 9 really continues chapter ii., after the digression of chapter iii. 1-8, by completing the proof of man's universal unrighteousness, and his liability to divine judgment. Righteousness cannot possibly be by works, because from the facts of life (as already seen), and from the Word of God (which is now to be brought forward), every mouth is stopped from claiming justification by law or works.

I: *The Definite Charge* (ver. 9).—He looks back over the entire section from ch. i. 18-iii. 8, and asks how the matter stands? But the precise meaning of his question is doubtful, for authorities differ as to the translation of the word. We must look at the main interpretations given. The question is as to who are referred to by "Are we?"

(1) The Authorized Version and many authorities think the word alludes to the Jews, and accordingly render by "Are we better than they?" that is, "Are we Jews better than the Gentiles?" Bishop Moule favors this view by translating, "Are we superior?" that is, in the light of the privileges mentioned in verses 1-8. The American Standard Version adopts this view. If this is the translation, then the meaning is, "Do we shelter ourselves behind our special privileges, and think to escape God's judgment? Have we any advantage?"

(2) The Revised Version and several authorities favor the rendering, "Are we worse than they?" Thus, Lightfoot translates, "Are we excelled?" "Have the Gentiles any advantage over us?" This would mean that in the light of verse 2 the Gentiles are at a disadvantage, the Apostle's answer being, "By no means"; that is to say, "Are we Jews surpassed by the Gentiles?" "Have they the advantage over us?" "Have the positions been reversed?" to which the Apostle replies with definiteness, "Not at all."

(3) Other authorities translate the words, "Are we making excuses for ourselves?" "Have we Jews any defense to put forward?" That is, in view of the fact that the Jews were the people who had the oracles of God.

(4) But it is perhaps best to understand the Apostle as having both parties, Jews and Gentiles, in view, for it seems impossible to introduce at this point any idea of superiority. In the preceding section (ch. i. 18-iii. 8) he has shown the guilt of both and set aside all excuses until there is none left. And now he asks, "Have we Jews and Gentiles any excuse?" Then he goes on to reply, "No, in no wise," giving as his reason that he has previously laid to the

charge both of Jews and Gentiles the fact that they are all under sin. In respect of the need of righteousness, both Jews and Gentiles are in the same condition. Observe carefully that it is not, as the A.V., "proved," for he is about to do this from Scripture. He has charged them with being "under sin." This phrase is very striking; "Not merely sinners, but under the empire of sin" (Liddon). It occurs again with equal force in ch. vi. 14; vii. 14; Gal. iii. 22. This is the first occurrence of the word "sin" out of nearly fifty places in ch. i.-viii. The various New Testament words for sin are deeply significant. The most familiar and frequent of them means "missing the mark"; another means "overstepping a boundary"; another, falling instead of standing; another, being ignorant instead of knowing; another, diminishing what should be rendered in full; another, disobeying a voice; another, disregarding a command; another, wilfully careless. These are but a few of the various aspects of sinning suggested by the etymology of the terms used.

II. *The Universal Proof.* (vers. 10-18).—In these verses the Apostle brings forward his proof that "all are under sin," that is, both Jews and Gentiles, thereby furnishing an answer to his question of verse 9. Selections are made from the Psalms, the Prophets, and Proverbs. The following arrangement of the verses should be carefully studied, for it affords a completeness of view which is apt to be overlooked if we take the passages verse by verse.

1. Sin in Human Character (vers. 10-12). (a) Negative (vers. 10, 11). The general state of mankind is described as "none righteous, no, not one" (Psa. xiv. 1-3); and then come the two proofs in detail; "There is none that understandeth, there is none that seeketh after God." (b) Positive (ver. 12). All have declined from the divine pathway, all have become utterly unprofitable and useless, and the summary description is that "there is none that doeth good, no, not so much as one." Thus, in this section the term "righteous" (v. 10) seems to be inclusive of everything else, and the rest of the particulars following it may be regarded as so many characteristics making up the total idea.

2. Sin in Human Conduct (vers. 13-17). (a) In word (vers. 13, 14). Specific sins of the tongue are mentioned. Corrupting; "Their

throat is an open sepulchre" (Psa. v. 9). Deceitful; "with their tongues have they used deceit." Uncharitable; "the poison of asps is under their lips" (Psa. cxl. 3). Blasphemous; "whose mouth is full of cursing and bitterness" (Psa. x 7). (b) In deed vers. 15-17). Murderous; "their feet are swift to shed blood" (Isa. lix. 7, 8). Oppressive; "destruction and misery are in their ways." Quarrelsome; "and the way of peace have they not known."

3. The Cause of it all (ver. 18). This is the source and explanation of the preceding description of sin. "There is no fear of God before their eyes" (Psa. xxxvi. 1).

A reference to the contexts of these passages will show that the Apostle does not mean to charge every individual Jew and Gentile with these sins, any more than he does in ch. i. 18-32 all the Gentiles, or ch. ii. all the Jews. The reference is of course to classes and tendencies of sin whether among Jews or Gentiles. The Jewish boast of superiority having been already removed, the way was made open for individuals to apply the truth to their own consciences. From time to time we meet with people full of moral excellences, like the rich young ruler, and we are tempted to think that such words as are here used by the Apostle would be utter mockery; but we must never forget that no charm of attitude towards men can ever take the place of thorough righteousness towards God. It is only too possible for a man's behavior to be admirable everywhere except at home, where his coldness and indifference are a grief and an offense. In the same way our best behavior towards man cannot set aside our attitude of self-righteousness and indifference towards God. When we look within our own hearts we see the possibilities of evil, just as when we read the story of the rich young man we come at last to the point where that good person was not good—his unwillingness to surrender to Christ; thereby showing an unregenerated heart in spite of all his excellences. We are condemned in the sight of God for what we are rather than for what we do. It has been often pointed out that the morality of a Christless heart may be beautiful, but it will not last, since the soul is full of evil seed. Many a social restraint may keep this seed from springing up, but nevertheless it is there, and liable to come forth under proper conditions.

It should also be observed that the Apostle is not here proving what is called "original sin," but the truth of universal sinfulness. He shows that Scripture points in the direction of those facts of life which he has been alleging in the former section. As Maclaren remarks, "Paul does not mean to bring all varieties of character down to one dead level, but he does mean to assert that none is free from the taint" (*Expositions of Scripture, Romans,* p. 48). And Godet writes similarly:—

> "The Apostle in drawing this picture, which is only a grouping together of strokes of the pencil, made by the hands of psalmists and prophets, does not certainly mean that each of those characteristics is found equally developed in every man. Some, even the most of them, may remain latent in many men; but they all exist in germ in the selfishness and natural pride of the *ego,* and the least circumstance may cause them to pass into the active state, when the fear of God does not govern the heart. Such is the *cause* of the divine condemnation which is suspended over the human race" (*Romans,* vol. i, p. 239).

III. *The Specific Application* (vers. 19, 20).—This proof from Scripture is now applied specifically to the Jew, lest he should say that the reference was to the heathen and not to himself. That the Jews are included is evident from the fact that Scripture must necessarily be addressed to Jews, and these Scriptures show that among the chosen people all sorts of sin abounded. Jewish privileges, therefore, do not, and cannot, save from sin, or provide any exemption from the divine judgment. The Apostle shows that the law is intended for those who are under the law, in order that men may be silenced and made to feel their guilt. "Now we know that what things soever the law saith, it saith to them who are under the law: that every mouth may be stopped, and all the world may be brought under the judgment of God." "We know" is the Apostle's way of stating an obvious truth which commends itself to him and his readers (ch. ii. 2; vii. 14; viii. 22, 28).

It is noteworthy, by the way, that the Psalms, Prophets and Proverbs, from which all these quotations are made, are here described as "the law." This is a significant indication of the Apostle's view of the authority of the Old Testament.

In ver. 20 the "Therefore" of the A.V. is incorrect. It should be "because." "Because by the works of the law shall no flesh be justified in His sight." The Apostle is not drawing his conclusion, but seeking to destroy the last argument of the Jew. Justification must be by something other than works, for law only reveals, it cannot redeem. "Through the law cometh the knowledge of sin." He shows that all the world is guilty before God, because by the deeds of the law no flesh can be justified. Duty cannot be done perfectly, as God requires, and thus righteousness is neither attained nor attainable. "Works of law" is a phrase used here for the first time (ch. iii. 28; ix. 32). It means such works as man can do by law, and only in his own strength. This would apply to those Jews who were endeavoring to win righteousness by works (ch. x. 3; Phil. iii. 6). This is the supreme question; the true relation of man to his God. Can we provide an adequate righteousness ourselves? Or must we obtain one from God? God's purpose in giving to us this Epistle is to convict us of the impossibility of the former position, in order to show the possibility of the latter.

"We have an invincible conviction that all righteousness in us must be derived from Him; if it were not so, we should be separated from God by an impassable gulf in precisely those regions of our life in which we believe that we are nearest to Him . . . In the Godhead, according to the Christian doctrine of the Trinity, there are the roots and springs of all created Righteousness." (Dr. R. W. Dale, *Christian Doctrine*).

The special lessons of this passage may be summed up in the one word; conviction.

1. *Conviction of Sins from the Experiences of Human Life.*—(ch. i. 18-iii. 8). In this long section the Apostle calls attention to the facts of every-day experience, in order to show the wrong-doing and unrighteousness of the Jew and Gentile. There is nothing in its way more significant of life at the present time than the absence of a sense of sin. Sir Oliver Lodge has recently told us that men are not now troubling themselves about their sins. As Bishop Gore remarks—

"We are apt to regard sin as it appears in the world at large as a result of ignorance, or social conditions—as in one way or another a form of misfortune. And so viewing it in the world, we view it in ourselves. We make excuses for ourselves. We have largely lost the sense that sin is wilfulness; that it is an inexcusable offence against God; that it does, and necessarily does, bring us under God's indignation; that necessarily, because God is what He is, the consequences of sin in this life, and much more beyond this life, are inconceivably terrible. It is this sense of sin that St. Paul must help to restore in us (*The Epistle to the Romans,* p. 126).

2. *Conviction of Sin from the Word of God* (ch. iii. 9-18).—This looks at the subject from another point of view, and deals with the root (sin) rather than with the fruit (sins). It shows that the sins which are wrong in human life stand absolutely condemned by reason of the wrong principle revealed by the Word of God.

3. *Conviction of Responsibility for Sin and Sins* (ch. iii. 19).—"That every mouth may be stopped" clearly shows that man has no excuse, whether about sin or sins, and that he is responsible for wrong in character and conduct.

4. *Conviction of Guilt before God* (ch. iii. 19).—"All the world may be brought under the judgment of God." This is the standard by which man is to be tested in reference to sin.

5. *Conviction of Human Helplessness with Regard to Righteousness* (ch. iii. 20).—"By the works of the law shall no flesh be justified." It has been aptly said that "one might as well attempt to cross the river on a millstone as to get into heaven by works of law" (Stifler). Dr. Denney says:—

"Under no system of statutes, the Mosaic or any other, will flesh ever succeed in finding acceptance with God. Let mortal man, clothed in works of law, present himself before the Most High, and His verdict must always be: Unrighteous" (*Expositor's Greek Testament, Romans,* p. 608).

Similarly Dr. Du Bose,—

"No man who knows what righteousness is will come into God's presence with a claim of his own to it. And if he does, so far from the claim being recognised, it will be regarded as the one disqualification for the reality to which it pretends" (*The Gospel according to St. Paul,* p. 71).

How true all this is man's own heart will testify!

Could my tears for ever flow,
"Could my zeal no respite know
All for sin could not atone,
Thou must save, and Thou alone."

6. *Conviction of the Absolute Necessity of a Perfect Righteousness before God* (ch. iii. 20).—Bruce considers that St. Paul's object in this entire section is, not simply to prove that both Gentiles and Jews are great sinners, but to show that they are such in spite of all in their religions that tended to help them. The Apostle thus pronounces a verdict, not merely on man, but on systems, and means to suggest that both Paganism and Judaism are failures. The Gentiles had light, but would not use it; the Jews had more light, and are still more blameworthy, and stand condemned by their own Scriptures. Thus, step by step, St. Paul shuts out every other channel of resource, in order to lead men to see their need of God's provision of righteousness. Lightfoot remarks that "Law is the great educator of the moral conscience. Restraint is necessary in order to develop the conception of duty. . . . The law says, 'Do not, or thou shalt die.' Thus, the character of the law is negative: of the Gospel, positive." It is the great and glorious purpose of God that His people shall have a righteousness which does not depend upon the uncertain weakness of their own heart, but on the infinite strength of Him Who is made righteousness unto them, and in Whom they become God's righteousness. We must continually press home upon human hearts and consciences the absolute impossibility of works of righteousness of our own, and the absolute necessity of accepting that divinely provided righteousness which may become ours in Christ Jesus, and of which the Apostle is now to speak in fulness of thought and language. With Dr. David Brown we therefore observe, before advancing further with the argument,

> "How broad and deep the Apostle lays the foundations of his great doctrine of Justification by Free Grace—in the disorder of man's whole nature, the consequent universality of human guilt, the condemnation of the whole world, by reason of the breach of divine law, and the impossibility of justification before God by obedience to that violated law. Only when these humiliating conclusions are accepted and felt, are we in a condition to appreciate and embrace the Grace of the Gospel, next to be opened up" (*Romans*, p. 35).

XVI

RIGHTEOUSNESS BY FAITH

Rom. iii. 21-26.

21. But now the righteousness of God without the law manifested, being witnessed by the law and the prophets;
22. Even the righteousness of God *which is* by faith of Jesus Christ unto all and upon all them that believe: for there is no difference:
23. For all have sinned, and come short of the glory of God
24. Being justified freely by his grace through the redemption that is in Christ Jesus:
25. Whom God hath set forth *to be* a propitiation through faith in his blood, to declare his righteousness for the remission of sins that are past, through the forbearance of God;
26. To declare, *I say,* at this time his righteousness: that he might be just, and the justifier of him which believeth in Jesus.

As the present section constitutes the very center of the Apostle's teaching, it is essential (before proceeding to consider it) to survey the entire preceding part (ch. i. 18-iii. 20), for ch. iii. 21 goes back to ch. i. 17, and ch. i. 18-iii. 20 shows the necessity of the righteousness of ch. i. 17 now to be treated. The Apostle commenced by stating that the Gospel revealed God's provision for man's righteousness, and that this was to be ours through faith (ch. i. 17)). He then addressed himself to the facts of human life and experience, dealing first with the Gentiles (ch. i.), and then with the Jews (ch. ii.), in order to prove that a Divine Righteousness was absolutely essential because of man's pressing need through sin. He showed that it is only the righteous who can live, and that to this end salvation must mean righteousness, because of God's character and revealed will. Any salvation for man must therefore be able to restore him to righteousness, since only righteousness avails with God. Then the Apostle destroyed the excuses of those, whether Jews or Gentiles, who were persisting in unrighteousness and thinking to escape the judgment of God, and as he drew the discussion to a close he showed that this righteousness was utterly impossible through any effort of man's own, and that in the light of Scripture teaching all men have become guilty before God.

Thus the way has been prepared for the exposition of the theme of the verses now before us, that of righteousness by faith. The first division of the Epistle, therefore, forms a kind of negative argument for the present one; for since man has no help in himself, and none in the law, there is nothing left to him but a humble trust in the righteousness of God.

This twofold statement of the need of righteousness, and of righteousness by faith, prepares the way for ch. iii. 21-31, in which two great facts are revealed and emphasized. (*a*) Righteousness by faith is vindicated (vers. 21-26); (*b*) righteousness by faith is explained and safeguarded (vers. 27-31). The first of these great facts is dealt with from ch. iv. 1-v. 21, and the second in chs. vi.-viii.

Thus, a reference to the analysis of the Epistle will show that this subject of the righteousness of God extends to the close of ch. viii., and deals with it in relation, first, to justification, then to sanctification, and lastly to glorification.

Now we must concentrate attention upon the passage before us (ch. iii. 21-26). It is one of the pivots of the Epistle, indeed it may be almost called its very heart, and it therefore demands the minutest attention. It reveals quite a number of the essential characteristics and varied aspects of that salvation which is here described as the Righteousness of God.

I. *The Need of Righteousness* must first of all be understood.—It means "rightness," that is, "the state of being right." Sometimes the word refers to God's character, as in ch. iii. 5, when it means either His righteousness as vindicating Himself, or His character as inflicting retribution on sin (ch. ii 5). In other cases the term "righteousness" applies to man, and has reference to his rightness, or state of being right with God. It means conformity in every respect to the divine law. When thus understood it is a very inclusive term, covering remission of sins, reinstatement in a true position and relation to God, renewal of inward character, and re-establishment in outward conduct. This wide meaning is demanded by the fact that sin is at once a debt, a disease, and a departure. The debt requires to be paid, and this may be called justification. The disease requires to be healed, and this may be called sanctification. The departure requires to be corrected, and this may be called consecration. These varied aspects are not all, and always, included in every passage where the word occurs. Sometimes the emphasis is on justification, as in ch. iii. 21—v. 21; sometimes on sanctification, as in ch. vi.-viii.; and sometimes on consecration, as in chs. xii.-xvi. Each passage where the word occurs must be carefully examined for the precise aspect of righteousness intended.

II. *The Meaning of the Phrase, "Righteousness of God,"* must also be noticed.—We may render it as "Righteousness of God," or as "God's Righteousness" (ver. 21). In every case God is to be regarded in some sense as the Source. But we may distinguish two separate though connected ideas in the use of the term. In some cases it means the righteousness which He Himself has and shows, that is, the perfect consistency with all that He Himself is. In other cases it is a righteousness which He provides for man in Christ, so that the phrase, "Righteousness of God," may refer either to His *character* or to His *gift*. We have already had the former in ch. iii. 5, and the latter in ch. i. 17. In our present section, in vers. 21, 22, it certainly refers to the righteousness which He provides and offers. In verse 25 it refers to the righteousness which He Himself has, and then in verse 26 both ideas are united.

III. *The Manifestation* of the Divine Righteousness is strongly emphasized. "The righteousness of God hath been manifested" ver. 21). The word suggests a revelation undiscoverable by man, an unveiling of God, and a divine action that has permanent results. The word "manifested" is used elsewhere of the unveiling of God in connection with the Incarnation and work of Christ (1 Tim. iii. 16; 2 Tim. i. 10; 1 Pet. i. 20; 1 John i. 2). The thought of manifestation calls special attention to the essentially divine source of this righteousness, and the impossibility of its coming from man.

IV. *The Circumstances* of the Unveiling of this Divine Righteousness must not be overlooked.—"But now" (ver. 21), that is, "as things are at the present time" (see ver. 26). The term may have either a logical or a temporal meaning. St. Paul may be contrasting two states of law and grace, as stated in vers. 20 and 21; or he may be referring to the two periods of time before and after the coming of Christ. There seems no valid reason why both ideas should not be included, making the phrase "But now" apply argumentatively and also chronologically. "But now"—after thousands of years of trial under every posible condition, after every endeavor made on behalf of Israel, after centuries of divine waiting and patience. All time, as Denney says, is divided for St. Paul into "Now" and "Then." Thus, the Apostle returns to the theme of ch. i. 16, 17, and amplifies it. In the interval he had shown the need; Now he is revealing the provision. In contrast to earlier periods in the world's history he is about to depict what has happened in "the fulness of time." For ages men had been sinning and learning the impossibility of putting away their own sin. "But now," at length, Christ came, and the two states of mankind, under the Law and under the Gospel, correspond with two periods of time (Acts xvii. 30; Gal. iii. 23, 25; iv. 1-5; 1 Tim. ii. 6; Tit. i. 3). The Apostle seems fond of this phrase, "But now" (Rom. xvi. 25, 26; Eph. ii. 12, 13; Col. i. 26).

V. *The Relation to Law* of this Divine Righteousness is a special point of importance. "But now apart from the law" (ver. 21). God's righteousness is independent of law as a condition of man becoming righteous. By the term "law" is to be understood any effort of self to work for, or to merit righteousness, so that "apart from the law" means "apart from any human obedience as a condition of attainment." Law forbids disobedience and requires obedience, but it cannot provide the power needed to prevent the one or guarantee the other. "The looking-glass may show us the smeared face, but for cleansing we go to the laver, not to the glass."

VI. *The Scriptural Attestation* of this Divine Righteousness is emphasized by the Apostle.—"Witnessed by the law and the prophets" (ver. 21). By this we are to understand the testimony of the Old Testament to the righteousness of God provided in Christ. While God's righteousness is not legal, it is yet in perfect harmony with the Old Testament Scripture. The Gospel was no afterthought, but was foreshadowed and foretold. This is the special teaching of the first Gospel and the Epistle to the Hebrews, but it is also noted by other writers of the New Testament (John v. 39, 46; 1 Pet. i. 10, 11).

VII. *The Appropriation* of this Divine Righteousness is clearly taught.—"The righteousness of God through faith" (ver. 22). This righteousness is to be accepted by man through simple faith in Jesus Christ. It is thus to be received as a gift, not awarded as a merit. Faith is always the opposite of works. Righteousness by works would mean that we *attain* it; righteousness by faith means that we *obtain* it. There is no virtue or merit in faith, for it finds all its value in the Object, the One in Whom we believe. Faith thus implies acceptance, reliance, dependence, confidence, all of which are opposed to self-effort, self-reliance, self-confidence.

VIII. *The Scope* of this Divine Righteousness needs attention.—"Unto all them that believe" (ver. 22). God's gift of righteousness is intended for all men who are willing to believe. The scope of His purpose is universal; it includes the entire human race, and none are outside His loving intention. "Oh, that all the world might know, At the Cross there's room."

IX. *The Need* of this Divine Righteousness is only too clear.—"There is no distinction, for all have sinned, and are falling short of the glory of God" (vers. 22, 23). Thus, God's gift meets a universal necessity. There is no difference among men in regard to sin, that is, in the fact that they are sinners, though there are many differences in the degree of sins. Even in a prison the inmates differ, and yet all alike are criminals, condemned by the law for particular offenses. "All have sinned, and are continually coming short of the glory of God." "The glory of God" is the divine standard for human life, and in one passage at least the word implies a consciousness of coming short (Luke xv. 14).

> "*There is no difference.* Once, perhaps, you resented that word, if you paused to note it. Now you take all its import home. Whatever otherwise your 'difference' may be from the most disgraceful and notorious breakers of the Law of God, you know now that there is none in *this* respect—that you are as hopelessly, whether or not as distantly, remote as they are from '*the glory of God*.' His moral 'glory,' the inexorable perfectness of His character, with its inherent demand that you must perfectly correspond to Him, in order so to be at peace with Him—you are indeed '*short of*' this. The harlot, the liar, the murderer, are short of it; but so are you. Perhaps they stand at the bottom of a mine, and you on the crest of an Alp; but you are as little able to touch the stars as they" (Moule, "Romans," *Expositor's Bible*, p. 97).

In this simple but significant fact of universal need, we have the one great justification for the Gospel.

X. *The Bestowal* of this Divine Righteousness.—It is bestowed personally by God upon man. "Being justified" (ver. 24). Thus, it is a divine act, not a human attainment. Let us be quite clear as to the meaning of this word "justified." To justify means to declare, or pronounce righteous. We have already seen that this is the meaning in ch. ii. 13 and ch. iii. 4 (see also Matt. xi. 19; Luke vii. 29; 1 Tim. iii. 16). It must be clearly distinguished from "to make righteous," which is to sanctify, and although the two ideas are inseparable in Christian experience, they must always be distinguished in our thought of these things. To justify is to regard as righteous, to restore to the status of one who is righteous. It does not mean merely to forgive and to remove the condemnation of sin, but also, and still more, to regard as right, as though the sinner had never sinned. It includes the removal of his guilt as well as of his condemnation. This is the great difference between a human tribunal and the divine judgment. A king of his royal clemency can pardon, but he cannot reinstate the criminal in the position of one who has not broken the law. God does both, and this is the meaning of Justification. Pardon concerns the past only, and cannot possibly deal with a man's future relation to the law; but God deals with both, and the two together are Justification.

XI. *The Spring* of this Divine Righteousness.—"By His grace" (ver. 24). This divine righteousness is absolutely unmerited and spontaneous. God's grace is the one sole reason and spring of it. Nothing in man elicited it; only divine grace prompted it. Grace in the New Testament always means spontaneous, unmerited divine favor. "By grace are ye saved," and a consciousness of grace will always enable us to "pour contempt on all our pride."

XII. *The Method* of this Divine Righteousness.—"Being justified freely" (ver. 24). God's righteousness is free and gratuitous in its offer to men. The word rendered "freely" is translated in Latin versions of the New Testament by "gratis," and this is the exact meaning of the term. The righteousness comes to us "gratis." "Whosoever will, let him take the water of life gratis" (Rev. xxii. 17). "Gratis ye have received, gratis give" (Matt. x. 8). Sometimes the thought of salvation as a gift, "salvation for nothing," is objected to as "too cheap." We shall see what it cost God to provide it.

XIII. *The Ground* of this Divine Righteousness.—"Through the redemption that is in Christ Jesus" (ver. 24). God's righteousness has been wrought by means of redemption. Its meritorious cause is the redeeming work of Christ. Redemption means complete deliverance by a price paid, and the deliverance includes the penalty, the power, and the presence of sin. It was Christ's death on the Cross that wrought this redemption.

XIV. *The Method* of this Divine Righteousness.—"Whom God set forth to be a propitiation" (ver. 25). The redemption which wrought the righteousness was expressed in a propitiation. Let us mark this word carefully, for it is one of the great words of the Bible. It indicates what is often overlooked, the divine aspect of the Atonement. "Whom *God* set forth." Propitiation always means "something that causes, or enables someone to act mercifully or forgivingly." Deissmann (*Bible Studies,* p. 30) translates the word "means of propitiation," and the Greek papyri, of which we are hearing so much in the present day, clearly teach that the word has reference to an appeasal of divine wrath. When we remove from the idea everything that is unworthy of God's character, we are still face to face with the obvious fact that a propitiation always and necessarily implies someone who propitiates and someone who is propitiated. Even the publican realized this when he prayed, "God, be propitious to me, the sinner." God requires the propitiation by reason of His justice, and He provides it by reason of His mercy. He is at once the One Who propitiates and the One Who is propitiated. What His justice demanded, His love provided, and in view of God's own provision of the Lord Jesus Christ as the propitiation we are able to say with the Apostle, "We have an Advocate with the Father, Jesus Christ the Righteous, and He is the propitiation for our sins" (1 John ii. 1, 2).

XV. *The Efficacy* of this Divine Righteousness.—"Propitiation through faith in His blood" (ver. 25). God's gift of righteousness finds its efficacy in the blood of Him Who died on Calvary. Blood shed always means death, and never merely the consecration of life. The Lord Jesus Christ was our Savior by means of His death, and by nothing short of it. It was because our Lord was Divine that His sacrifice was efficacious. The blood shed on Calvary was the blood of the Son of God, and it is, in Hooker's great phrase, "the infinite worth of the Son of God" which gave efficacy to that death as a propitiation for our redemption.

> "Paul does not merely point to Jesus Christ as Saviour, but to His death as the saving power. We are to have faith in Jesus Christ (ver. 22). But that is not a complete statement. It must be faith in His propitiation, if it is to bring us into living contact with His redemption. A Gospel which says much of Christ, but little of His Cross, or which dilates on the beauty of His life, but stammers when it begins to speak of the sacrifice in His death, is not Paul's Gospel, and it will have little power to deal with the universal sickness of sin" (Maclaren, *Expositions of Scripture*, "Romans," p. 50).

XVI. *The Immediate Object* of this Divine Righteousness.—"To show His righteousness because of the passing over of the sins done aforetime, in the forbearance of God" (ver. 25). The R.V. of this verse should be read, as the A.V. entirely fails to give the true idea. The immediate object of the manifestation of God's righteousness was its relation to sins overlooked up to that time. The world was thinking that God had permanently passed over and ignored human sin. Calvary was His answer, showing that He was not indifferent to it, but only taking His own time and way of manifesting His righteousness. The verse, therefore, teaches the utter impossibility of God overlooking human sin. "Christ died . . . to rescue the righteousness of God from a misunderstanding" (Stifler). Or as Godet puts this important truth:—

> "For four thousand years the spectacle presented by mankind to the whole moral universe (*cf.* 1 Cor. iv. 9) was, so to speak, a continual scandal. With the exception of some great examples of judgments, divine righteousness seemed to be asleep; one might even have asked if it existed. Men sinned here below, and yet they lived. They sinned on, and yet reached in safety a hoary old age! . . . Where were *the wages of sin?* It was this relative impunity which rendered a solemn manifestation of righteousness necessary" (*Romans,* vol. i. p. 261).

The incompleteness of the divine attitude to sin is also seen in the Old Testament ritual, which clearly taught that the problem of righteousness could not be solved except in God's own time and way. "In those sacrifices there is a remembrance again made of sins every year, for it is not possible that the blood of bulls and of goats should take away sins" (Heb. x. 3, 4). Under the old covenant sinners were forgiven, but their sins were not absolutely taken away. But when Christ came there was a complete removal of everything that hindered the divine forgiveness.

> "God gave proof (ch. i. 24-27) of His anger against sin by now and then inflicting punishment on the Gentiles and on Israel. But He did not inflict the full penalty: else the whole race would have perished. He did not forgive, but to a large extent He *passed over,* the sins of men. Now for a king to overlook crime, to forbear to punish, or even to delay punishment, is unjust. And God's character was lowered in the eyes of some by His forbearance, which they misinterpreted to be an indication that they will escape punishment. God gave Christ to die *in order to demonstrate His justice* in view of a tolerance of past sins which seemed to obscure it" (Beet, *St. Paul's Epistle to the Romans,* p. 118).

Thus, the Cross of Christ not only justifies men to God, but justifies God to men, for it cleared the divine character from all appearances of indifference to sin in the ages before Christ came.

XVII. *The Ultimate Purpose* of this Divine Righteousness.—"That He might Himself be just and the Justifier of him that believeth" (ver. 26). The supreme end and aim of God's righteousness was thus twofold: a demonstration of His character ("that He might be just"), and a complete provision for man's life ("and the Justifier"). Thus, God's righteousness meets every need and satisfies every claim. In relation to Himself it vindicates His faithfulness to His own word, and demonstrates His righteous retribution on sin. In relation to man, it provides a perfect justification and a complete sanctification, whereby he is enabled once more to be right with God. Herein lies the deep and precious meaning of the two statements of St. John; "God is light," and "God is love." If God were Light alone, nobody could be saved. If God were Love alone, in the modern sense, there would be the danger of forgetting His righteousness. But in the Cross He is revealed as both Light and Love. All His attributes are blended, united, and correlated. "Mercy and truth are met together, righteousness and peace have kissed each other" (Ps. lxxxv. 10).

> "Glorious paradox! 'Just in punishing,' and 'merciful in pardoning,' men can understand; but 'just in justifying' the guilty, startles them. But the propitiation through faith in Christ's blood resolves the paradox, and harmonizes the seemingly discordant elements. For in that 'God hath made Him to be sin for us Who knew no sin,' *justice* has full satisfaction; and in that 'we are made the righteousness of God in Him,' *mercy* has all her desire" (David Brown, *Romans,* p. 37).

XVIII. *The Human Channel* of this Divine Righteousness.—"By faith . . . them that believe" (ver. 22); "Through faith in His blood" (ver. 25); "Him which believeth in Jesus" (ver. 26). From first to last this divine righteousness is a matter of simple trust in God. We observe the emphasis laid on faith all through the section. Thus, as the Apostle had already said (ch. i. 17), "The righteous shall live by faith." For justification, for sanctification, for everything, the Christian life is a life of faith. Faith hears, understands, assents, accepts, appropriates, applies, trusts, and appreciates the righteousness of God in Christ.

As we ponder this passage with all possible care and minuteness, and dwell upon the various aspects of its wonderful teaching, we cannot help noticing two things.

1. *The Very Heart of the Divine Gospel.*—St. Paul here tells us that the unique feature of the Gospel of Christ is not its revelation of the divine mercy, or pity, or love, or grace, though all these are true, but its revelation of the divine *righteousness.* As has been well pointed out, the difficulty was not so much how to get men to God (for mercy could do that), but how to get God to men. The problem was how a just God could rightly pronounce a sinner just (Stifler, *in loc.*).

> "When, therefore, in the Scriptures God is represented as sacrificially suffering in behalf of the guilty, we must conclude He does truly propitiate Himself. There is, then a *penal element* which He Himself bears, inasmuch as He expresses His grace in such a way as consistently to forgive and cure sin. He can justify the ungodly, while Himself remaining just. God's self-propitiation is a propitiation which holiness *exacts* and clemency *provides*" (Dr. H. C. Mabie, *The Divine Reason of the Cross,* p. 59).

Christ thus died for two reasons: to rescue the righteousness of God from all possible misunderstanding, and at the same time to provide for and secure the righteousness of man. And so, in the light of this passage we may say without any fear of being misunderstood, "Jesus Christ died for man and also for God." The Cross demonstrates God's own righteousness, while it also at the same time provides and offers His gift of righteousness to all who are willing to receive it. This is what St. Paul described as "my Gospel," and it is the Gospel at its very heart.

2. *The Very Heart of the Believer's Experience.*—When we receive and preach this Gospel of God's righteousness in Christ we are receiving and proclaiming the essence of Christianity, Redemption and Righteousness. Herein is the "good news" of the Gospel. The sense of guilt bears us down and compels us to cry out in anguish. Amendment of life is seen to be of no avail, and all efforts towards improvement are intolerable. Prayer seems to have no effect. What, then, is the poor, weary, helpless, disheartened sinner to do? Just at this point comes in the "good news" of God's provision of a perfect righteousness in Christ. The conscience rests on it, the heart receives it, and there is peace. Morison and Godet appropriately call attention to an experience of the poet Cowper in connection with this passage. It was a time when he was brought

to the very verge of despair. He had walked up and down in his room a long while, profoundly agitated. At last he seated himself near his window, and seeing a Bible there, he opened it to seek if possible some consolation and strength.

> "'The passage which met my eye,' says he, 'was the twenty-fifth verse of the third chapter of Romans. On reading it I immediately received power to believe. The rays of the Sun of Righteousness fell on me in all their fulness; I saw the complete sufficiency of the expiation which Christ had wrought for my pardon and entire justification. In an instant I believed, and received the peace of the Gospel.' 'If,' adds he, 'the arm of the Almighty had not supported me, I believe I should have been overwhelmed with gratitude and joy; my eyes filled with tears; transports choked my utterance. I could only look to heaven in silent fear, overflowing with love and wonder.' But it is better to describe the work of the Holy Spirit in his own words: 'It was *the joy* which is *unspeakable and full of glory*'" (1 Pet. i. 8) (*Life of Cowper*, by Taylor; quoted by Godet, *Romans*, vol. i. p. 252).

This agrees with what Dr. Dale well describes as "a wonderful experience." No one who has not passed through it can imagine its blessedness. It is an experience that seems impossible until it is actually known, and then the reality of it becomes one of the great certainties of life.

> "When I discover that I am forgiven I shall condemn my sin—condemn it, perhaps, more sternly than ever. I see that it was inexcusable; I abhor it as I may never have abhorred it before; I may feel as I had never felt, that it justly provoked the divine indignation and wrath; but when I approach God through Christ as the Propitiation for my sin, the guilt of it crushes me no longer; God is at peace with me; I have perfect rest in His love. It is not merely at the commencement of the Christian life that the death of Christ has this wonderful power. Its power endures. Day after day, year after year, when we are troubled by the consciousness of moral failure and of ill desert, we find in the death of Christ for our sin, power to trust in the divine mercy, and to implore the divine forgiveness with an absolute confidence that we shall receive it" (Dale, *Christian Doctrine*).

XVII

INFERENCES DRAWN

ROM. iii. 27-31.

27. Where *is* boasting then? It is excluded. By what law? of works? Nay: but by the law of faith.
28. Therefore we conclude that a man is justified by faith without the deeds of the law.
29. *Is he* the God of the Jews only? *is he* not also of the Gentiles? Yes, of the Gentiles also:
30. Seeing *it is* one God, which shall justify the circumcision by faith, and uncircumcision through faith.
31. Do we then make void the law through faith? God forbid: yea, we establish the law.

THE Apostle has now fully expounded his great theme of righteousness by faith, but he has not yet done with objections, especially from the Jewish side. The greatest and most virulent opposition his doctrine encountered was from the self-righteousness of the Pharisees. The Jew claimed that his God was the only true one, his religion the only right one, and his Scripture the only authoritative one. We can see all this in his boast in ch. ii. 17-20, and in the strictness of the letter his boast was right; but unfortunately he misread his Scriptures, he misconceived his religion, and he misunderstood his God. The false religion of the Gentiles was much more easily dealt with by the Apostolic teaching than the perverted religion of contemporary Judaism. So St. Paul now turns to deal with some of the Jewish objections to his doctrine of righteousness by faith. He has already pointed out that the Old Testament witnessed to that doctrine (ver. 21), and now he proceeds to assert the truth of his contention. The general theme of the passage is that God's righteousness is necessarily independent of law, or, in other words, independent of everything that is merely human, self-righteous, and meritorious. Both the law (in the sense of the Old Testament in general) and the Gospel are shown to be against works, and righteousness by faith to be perfectly consonant with the Monotheism of the Old Testament. Let us follow closely the course of the Apostle's thought.

I. *Righteousness by Faith excludes Boasting* (vers. 27, 28).—What, then, has become of the boasting of the Jew (as in ch. ii. 17)? It does not exist. It is excluded once for all, *ipso facto.* In vers. 9-20 the Apostle has already stopped the mouths of all by his testimony from Scripture, and the method of righteousness by faith best agrees with the view of the Old Testament there mentioned. Like the law, righteousness also brings to silence the boasting of men. Salvation for the Jew is the same as for the Gentile, the terms being identical. But by what law or principle is boasting excluded? Not by a law, or principle of works, but by one of faith. The Gospel is never called a "law" by itself, except with some qualifying word which takes away the literal meaning of the term (*cf.* ch. viii. 2; Jas. i. 25; ii. 12). Works give an occasion for boasting. If a man fulfils the letter of the law he has a right to demand salvation as his due, but there is no credit or merit in the act of believing, for trust in another is absolutely incompatible with self-righteousness and dependence on our own powers. The very fact that we are dependent on another shows that we thereby cease to depend upon ourselves. Further, faith has no power or virtue apart from its *Object.* Faith in God is the essence of Christian trust, and this faith, the Apostle says, is a law, or principle, or rule of procedure like any other, though it is a new and different law or principle from that of works. Nevertheless, it is an essential principle of human life, without which there can be no salvation. And so St. Paul reckons that "a man is justified by faith apart from works of law." This is the reason why all boasting is necessarily excluded, and thus the Apostle strikes effectively at the root of Jewish prejudice, pride, and self-sufficiency.

II. *Righteousness by Faith is equally suited to all* (vers. 29, 30).—Here comes in another side of the Jewish boasting. He thought that God was his God only, but as a simple fact God was the God of the Gentiles also. There are not two Gods, and "seeing that God is one, it is impossible for Him to have two different methods of saving mankind." Thus the Apostle argues for the exclusiveness of his doctrine of righteousness by faith as the only true and possible doctrine, and the only true and possible way of salvation. The unity of God comprises all in its embrace of essential oneness, and out of this fundamental truth of divine unity comes the Pauline doctrine of righteousness by faith for all. "In its universality and sameness for all men it is consistent with (as indeed it flows from) the unity of God. There can be no step-children in the family of God" (Denney). If, therefore, God and faith are involved in salvation, God must necessarily be the God of the Gentiles as well as of the Jews, since it is one God who saves both in the same way. It is impossible to allow any special claims of the Jew to appear in the Gospel. Justification by works would make a manifest distinction between Jew and Gentile, which the Apostle has already refused to allow. Righteousness through faith, therefore, is the only doctrine which properly harmonizes with the Old Testament view of God. God is one Who will justify the Jews from the starting-point of faith, not of works; and will justify the Gentiles through the instrumentality of faith, not by the yoke of the law.

III. *Righteousness by Faith establishes Law* (ver. 31).—Two things have now been settled by these inferences drawn by the Apostle. All boasting has been excluded, and the unity of God is seen to be the basis of universal righteousness by faith. But now comes yet one more question, and that a very serious and difficult one. If the Apostle excludes works and the Old Testament prescribes them, does not this doctrine of faith evacuate the Old Testament of its meaning, and does it not make law void, and lead to disregard of it? Does it not open the door to license of living? To this the Apostle replies that it certainly does not, but that, on the contrary, the Gospel puts law on a proper basis and establishes it on its true foundation as a revelation of God's will.

But the statement, "we establish the law," is difficult, because of great doubt as to the true interpretation of the idea. We must therefore look carefully at the various uses of the term "law," and try to discover the right interpretation of the Apostle's words.

1. If "Law" here means the Old Testament, that is, the whole Jewish religion, the meaning will be that there is no contradiction between the law and the Gospel, as ch. iv. with its proof from Abraham will show. This is the view taken by some authorities, including Godet. It is thought that the statement is to be closely connected with the preceding and following verses, especially in view of the "then" of ch. iii. 31 and the "then" of ch. iv. 1. According to this interpretation, the Apostle is still showing the essential harmony between the Mosaic law and his doctrine of righteousness by faith, and he adduces Abraham in ch. iv. as an example to prove the inferences that he has drawn in ch. iii. 27-31.

2. If "Law" means the Mosaic institutions of the ceremonial law, then there will be no contradiction between the law and grace, because, as Paul has already shown, and will show again hereafter, Christ is the end of the law for righteousness. Thus, the Apostle's doctrine, as Haldane rightly says, really establishes law by making Christ fulfil its demands, which man could not possibly do, and so the Old Testament law is not made void but really established through the Gospel. As we all have broken that law and are still liable to violate its requirements, so we commit ourselves as sinners to Him Who fulfilled the law and saves from under its curse those who thus entrust themselves to Him. No man can obtain righteousness by law unless he perfectly satisfies its demands, and as it is impossible for sinful man to do this, he turns for righteousness to One who had kept that law perfectly. Thus in Christ as perfect righteousness, law is really established in the only possible way, and the man who seeks righteousness by works will always come short of that perfection which the law demands. This view would give a thoroughly satisfactory meaning to the passage. And if we may assume its truth, there is nothing more humbling or more inspiring than its message. As Hooker put it—

> "Oh that the Spirit of the Lord would give this doctrine entrance into the stony and hard heart which followeth the law of righteousness, but cannot attain to the righteousness of the law; who therefore stumble at

Christ, are bruised, shivered to pieces as a ship that has run itself upon a rock! Oh that God would cast down the eyes of the proud, and humble the souls of the high-minded, that they might at length abhor the garments of their own flesh, that cannot hide their nakedness, and put on the faith of Christ . . . Oh that God would open the ark of mercy wherein this doctrine lieth, and set it wide before the eyes of poor afflicted consciences which fly up and down on the water of their affliction, and can see nothing but only the deluge of their sins, wherein there is no place to rest their feet" (quoted by J. Brown, *Exposition of the Epistle to the Romans,* p. 45).

3. If "Law" here means the moral law, then there is no contradiction between the law and the Gospel, because Christ makes it possible for believers to obey, and thereby to fulfil its requirements. On this view the Apostle just notes and dismisses the objection, which will be dealt with later in chs. vi.-viii. The idea is that as justification reveals a new provision and power of grace, the result will be a fulfilment of the law as would be possible in no other way (ch. viii. 4). Union with Christ not only makes us partakers of the merit of His sacrificial death; it introduces us to a divine fellowship with the living Lord, and this fills the soul with the fruits of righteousness, and thus establishes law. According to this view the argument is that the Gospel does not do away with the requirements of the divine law, for every vital demand of it is as important now as ever, and every breach of it as truly a sin as it was ages ago. Not one of us can violate God's law on the strength of our discipleship of Christ; on the contrary, our trust in Him for salvation carries with it sanctification and power for obedience. This, again, would give a thoroughly satisfactory interpretation of the passage, though with Godet we may perhaps question whether the Apostle would be likely to introduce the sanctifying power of faith at this juncture even for a moment. In the light of the immediate context, before and after, it would seem best to interpret the passage in either of the first two of these three ways. (Yet see Note, p. 160.) Whatever the point of the Apostle's meaning, the general idea is perfectly clear; there is not only no incompatibility between faith and law, but the most perfect agreement and harmony. "Do we then make the law of none effect through faith? God forbid; yea, we establish the law."

Let us mark carefully the key-word of this passage, "Boasting."

1. There is a boasting which is *false.* The Jew boasted in his law, but he never properly obeyed it; he boasted in his God, but in reality he blasphemed Him (ch. ii. 17-24). Works as a means of salvation must be absolutely perfect and not wanting in any respect, a fact which is obviously impossible to sinful man. "Not of works, lest any man should boast" (Eph. ii. 9). Ruskin forcibly says: "I believe that the root of every schism and heresy from which the Christian Church has ever suffered has been the effort of men to earn rather than to receive their salvation."

2. There is a boasting which is *impossible.* It is utterly impossible for a man to boast with regard to faith, for the very essence of faith is the absence of personal pride and confidence in our own powers. The heart goes outside itself to another, and so confesses its need of help. From first to last the soul of the believer is conscious of its own dependence on Christ, and of its own utter unworthiness, and the one adoring expression is ever and increasingly, "Thou art worthy" (Rev. v. 9).

3. There is a boasting which is both *true and possible.* We shall see this in a later chapter, though it is found quite frequently in St. Paul's Epistles. Is it not a striking paradox that there is a boasting for a true Christian which is both legitimate and inspiring? The word "boast" is almost invariably used in unworthy connections, and it is one of the glories of the Gospel that it can take the idea, purge it of its unworthiness, and employ it as one of the most inspiring attitudes of the Christian soul. There are no less than seven aspects of the believer's boasting. He can boast in God (ch. v. 11); he can boast in Christ (ch. xv. 17; 1 Cor. i. 31; Phil. iii. 3); he can boast in the Cross (Gal. vi. 14); he can boast in tribulations (ch. v. 3); he can boast in infirmities (2 Cor. xi. 30); he can boast in the work God has enabled him to do (ch. ii. 7; 2 Cor. xi. 10; 1 Thess. ii. 19); and he can boast in hope of future glory (ch. v. 2).

NOTE.—Those who hold the view stated on p. 158 have much in their favour when they point to the Pauline habit of touching briefly on truths to be elaborated later (see p. 113); and to the fact that these very objections (pp. 153-155) are discussed fully, twice over, in the sections commencing (1) chs. iv. and ix. (2) chs. v. and x.; and (3) chs. vi. and xii.

XVIII

ABRAHAM'S RIGHTEOUSNESS

Rom. iv. 1-8.

1. What shall we say then that Abraham our father, as pertaining to the flesh, hath found?
2. For if Abraham were justified by works, he hath *whereof* to glory; but not before God.
3. For what saith the scripture? Abraham believed God, and it was counted unto him for righteousness.
4. Now to him that worketh is the reward not reckoned of grace, but of debt.
5. But to him that worketh not, but believeth on him that justifieth the ungodly, his faith is counted for righteousness.
6. Even as David also describeth the blessedness of the man, unto whom God imputeth righteousness without works,
7. *Saying*, Blessed *are* they whose iniquities are forgiven, and whose sins are covered.
8. Blessed *is* the man to whom the Lord will not impute sin.

The Apostle now proceeds to adduce in detail the proofs of some of the positions laid down in the important section (ch. iii. 21-31). He had said that righteousness by faith had been witnessed to by the law and the prophets (ch. iii. 21), and also that by means of faith all human boasting was necessarily excluded (ch. iii. 27). Further, he had stated that the Gospel, though apart from law, does not set aside, but really establishes law (ch. iii. 31). He now takes up these points, using Abraham to prove more clearly than ever the necessity and importance of faith in relation to righteousness, and at the same time to give adequate evidence that this teaching on righteousness by faith is in exact agreement with the Old Testament as exemplified in the Father of the Faithful. It was thus not only foreshadowed and predicted, but actually seen as early as Abraham.

The fact of taking Abraham in support of his doctrine is full of significance and importance. The Mosaic law was not by any means the first or fundamental step in the divine act and purpose of redemption. Indeed it was only a temporary addition to a far greater provision. The history of the Chosen People did not begin at Sinai, but in the person of Abraham, with whom God entered into covenant in relation to the whole world. The covenant with Abraham was therefore a covenant of grace, and preceded by centuries the Mosaic covenant of works. It is for this reason that, having considered the righteousness of faith in relation to the law of Moses, the Apostle is compelled to go much further back and discuss the history of God's dealings with Abraham.

The whole of ch. iv. is occupied with this subject. The Apostle argues that righteousness is by faith (vers. 1, 2); not by works (vers. 2,8); nor by circumcision (vers. 9-12); nor by law (vers. 13-17a). Then he indicates how Abraham's faith is an example to us (vers. 17b-25), and he deduces some consequences of his great doctrine of righteousness by faith as laid down in ch. iii. 21-31. The chapter requires very close attention, more particularly as it is so important a part of the Apostle's argument.

I. *The Necessity of Faith* (vers. 1, 2).—The question is now stated, What are we to say about Abraham? That is, how do the statements about righteousness apart from law bear on the case of the patriarch? What was it that he obtained when he entered into covenant relationship with God? What advantage had he through the law, or by his own natural efforts? The question thus asked arises out of ch. ii. 27-31. If boasting is excluded, what about Abraham? Had he any advantage? Was his righteousness by works a position of favor earned or merited?

There are some differences of text in verse 1 which lead to differences of interpretation. Where are we to put the phrase, "According to the flesh"? Does it go with the word "found"? Or with the word "forefather"? Most authorities favor the latter, but the former seems on the whole most in keeping with the context (see Godet, and the American Standard Version). "What did Abraham find, or win, or earn, by his own human, natural efforts as opposed to a divine free gift?" (Luke i. 30). "What did he acquire by religious works?" On this view "flesh" will mean "human nature in the fall as unrenewed and unassisted by divine special grace" (Moule, *Cambridge Bible*). If, however, the phrase "according to the flesh" goes with "forefather," it will simply mean a description of Abraham, and the question will be, "How stands it with our great progenitor in regard to justification?"

The answer implied by the Apostle's question, followed by the "for" of ver. 2, is, "Nothing at all"; for if he had been justified by works he would have had something to boast of, but inasmuch as boasting is excluded from faith (ch. iii. 27) it is impossible to think of Abraham as justified by works. Justification by works would have enabled him to boast, though the boasting would not have availed him in the sight of God. Like the Jews, Abraham had many advantages, especially that of circumcision, but there was one that he did not possess—justification by works. As Godet says, "He had a great deal of which to glory, but it had no effect on his relation to God."

II. *The Object of Faith* (vers. 2, 3).—Abraham's faith is clearly proved by the Scripture (Gen. xv.), which shows that God made Abraham a promise, that he believed God, and that by means of his faith he was reckoned righteous. There is no merit in trusting God, and it was God's mercy and grace that reckoned Abraham righteous through faith. The point has been well illustrated by showing that the value of a bank-note really lies in the bank itself, for, to quote Godet, "Faith consists in holding the divine promise for the reality itself, and then it happens that what the believer has done in regard to the promise of God, God in turn does in regard to his faith." Abraham did the only righteous thing possible; he believed in God, and thus the question of verse 1 is answered. Abraham "found" justification by faith. Let it be said once again that there is absolutely no virtue or merit in faith. Trust is man's answer to God's truth. Faith is the condition, not the ground of salvation. God is the One Whom we trust, and it is His free grace that warrants and elicits our confidence. All through this chapter the emphasis rests on God as the Object of the believer's faith.

III. *The Principle of Faith* (vers. 4, 5).—Now comes the exposition and explanation of Genesis xv. 6 in general terms, showing that God's justification of Abraham was something divinely spontaneous and gratuitous, and cannot be spoken of in terms of work, wages, right, and duty. The man who works has a legal right to his wages, but the man who believes God simply accepts the divine favor and bounty. The reward of a worker implies a debt due, but as Abraham's reward was a gift, it follows that he could not have been a worker. Thus the wrong way of righteousness is definitely barred. "To him that worketh not." The very first step is away from self with all its works, and the hope of being saved by anything we do has to be set aside for ever. Then the right way is clearly shown. "To him that . . . believeth on Him that justifieth the ungodly." How marvelously simple, sufficient, and satisfying is this principle of faith. "Trusting Jesus; that is all." We lean upon Him, resting on His word, and in the rest and acceptance of faith we come to know by experience Him "Who justifieth the ungodly."

We must not fail to observe the striking boldness of the Apostle in using this term, "Justifieth the ungodly," that is, "ungodly when he is justified." Not that it means absolutely depraved, but without piety. It is a strong word, showing the wonderful grace of the Gospel, and is characteristic of St. Paul's exulting confidence in the "God of all grace." Denney has a characteristic and fine comment here:—

> "The whole Pauline Gospel could be summed up in this one word—God Who justifies the ungodly . . . . It is sometimes argued that God can only pronounce just, or treat as just, those who actually are just; but if this were so, what Gospel would there be for sinful men? . . . The paradoxical phrase, Him that justifieth the ungodly, does not suggest that justification is a fiction, whether legal, or of any other sort, but that it is a miracle. It is a thing that only God can achieve . . . . The miracle of the Gospel is that God comes to the ungodly, with a mercy which is righteous altogether, and enables them through faith, in spite of what they are, to enter into a new relationship to Himself, in which goodness becomes possible for them . . . . The whole secret of New Testament Christianity, and of every revival of religion and reformation of the Church, is in that joyous and marvelous paradox, 'God that justifieth the ungodly'" (*Expositor's Greek Testament*, p. 616).

IV. *The Acceptance of Faith* (ver. 5).—"His faith is counted for righteousness." This is an important and difficult statement, for there is an ambiguity in the word "for." We are not for a moment to suppose that it means, as the Authorized Version might suggest, that faith is the equivalent of righteousness. Faith and righteousness are entirely distinct and different, and the former is the means of obtaining the latter. It is best to understand the Apostle's statement "for righteousness" as "with a view to the receiving of righteousness" (Haldane). It must never be forgotten that the Apostle is dealing with the method, not the ground of righteousness. Dr. John Brown says (p. 49 f.), that to reckon a mental act to a person is to reckon that he has exercized it; if it is an action, that he has performed it; if it is a privilege, that he possesses it. To reckon sin to a man is to reckon him a sinner; to reckon faith to a man is to reckon him a believer. "God reckoned Abraham a believer, and as such He justified him." First came the divine revelation, then the response of Abraham's faith, and thereupon God reckoned him a believer, and justified him. We are here concerned, therefore, with the divine method and channel (not the basis) of justification, that it is through faith apart from law. The marvel and glory of divine grace is that God Who is perfect righteousness regards us as righteous in Christ. Christ fulfilled the divine law, and through faith we receive and appropriate Him as our perfect righteousness. He is the ground of our righteousness, and faith is the channel, or method. Godet puts the truth very clearly in these words:—

> "This word *righteousness* here denotes perfect obedience to the will of God, in virtue of which Abraham would necessarily have been declared righteous by God as *being* so, if he had possessed it. As he did not possess it, God put his faith to his account as an equivalent. Why so? On what did this incomparable value which God attached to his faith rest? We need not answer; on the moral power of this faith itself. For faith is a simple receptivity, and it would be strange to fall back on the sphere of meritorious work when explaining the very word which ought to exclude all merit. The infinite worth of faith lies in its object, God and His manifestation. This object is moral perfection itself. To believe is therefore to lay hold of perfection at a stroke. It is not surprising that laying hold of perfection, it should be reckoned by God as righteousness" (*Romans*, vol. i. p. 288).

V. *The Outcome of Faith* (vers. 6-8).—This truth of righteousness by faith is now illustrated from the words of David (Psa. xxxii.), another name which, like that of Abraham, would weigh with the Jews. The same language is found in the Psalms as in Genesis, and goes to confirm the Apostle's argument from Abraham. Man's sin is forgiven, covered, not reckoned, through the abounding mercy and grace of God, and all without any works on man's part, as the Psalm clearly teaches. The imputation of righteousness carries with it of necessity the non-imputation of sin, and so in the quotation from the Psalm the negative side is appropriately brought forward. Thus David is not used as a fresh example, but as an illustration of God's acceptance of Abraham through faith. Here comes into view the "blessedness" of which David speaks; the blessedness of sins forgiven, of unrighteousness covered, and of sins not reckoned. The burden and condemnation of guilt being taken away, and the believer being accepted before God in Christ, blessedness must necessarily be the result in personal experience.

A careful consideration of the words and phrases here quoted from the Psalm will show that righteousness is much more than forgiveness. The believer is not merely a pardoned criminal, but one who has been reinstated in a right position before God. As this state of being right with God covers past, present, and future, we can well understand its "blessedness," and we ought to rejoice in it more and more.

We must notice in this passage how the Apostle dwells on the word "reckon," which occurs eleven times, showing the emphasis placed on it, and the importance of the idea in his mind. It is "a metaphor taken from accounts," and implies something put to a man's credit. Righteousness is "imputed," or "reckoned." God regards, reckons, accounts us righteous because of what Christ has done. He is "the Lord our Righteousness," and His righteousness is put to our account through faith.

This seems to be the place at which to call attention to the relation of St. Paul and St. James in their teaching on faith. At first sight the emphasis by the former on Faith and the latter on Works, both using Abraham as their example, might seem to imply a contradiction, but a more careful study of the use made of Abraham by the two Apostles enables us to see that their teaching is not contradictory but complementary. It should be noted that St. Paul refers to the events recorded in Genesis xv. while St. James deals with those recorded in Genesis xxii., some forty years afterwards. As, therefore, according to St. Paul, Abraham was justified by faith in the first instance, he must have been living a life of faith all those years as a justified man. Then at the end of that time (Gen. xxii.) his faith was proved by his works, and by works his faith of forty years was perfected and brought to its culmination. There is therefore no contradiction between the two Apostles. They are dealing with two different aspects of faith. St. Paul is emphasizing faith as against legalism; St. James is emphasizing works as against formalism. The former uses Genesis xv. to prove the necessity of faith, the latter uses Genesis xxii. to prove the necessity of works. St. Paul teaches that work must spring from faith, St. James shows that faith must be demonstrated by works. One lays stress on faith as against merit, the other on works as against mere orthodoxy. And when we realize that St. Paul is writing about non-Christians with a view to their acceptance, and St. James about Christians with a view to their acceptableness, we see that, so far from any opposition, there is a beautiful harmony between them. It has been well said that St. Paul and St. James are not soldiers of different armies fighting against each other, but soldiers of the same army fighting back to back against enemies coming from opposite directions.

The entire chapter, but especially this section, is occupied with the thought of faith, several aspects of which have been brought before us. But the thought of faith needs special emphasis by reason of its prominence here and elsewhere in Scripture.

1. *The Power of Faith.*—Faith is a great law in the spiritual world, and is at the root of our relation to God. Sin breaks the connection between Him and us. Our Lord came to re-establish the connection, and this chapter is the exposition and illustration of the fact and power of faith. It is emphasized thus strongly because it is the only response that we can make to God and His

grace. Faith can be analyzed as including (1) renunciation of self; (2) reliance on God. These two aspects sum up its meaning. Faith implies the cessation of self-dependence and the commencement of dependence upon another. There is no value or merit in faith, for it derives its efficacy, not from the person trusting, but from the person trusted. It links us to God, and is absolutely useless apart from Him. By trust in Christ we become sharers of the efficacy of His atoning sacrifice, and obviously the power of faith finds its entire source and spring in Him, not in ourselves. Since trust is the essential attitude of the creature to the Creator, and therefore of the redeemed to the Redeemer, it ought to be quite clear and obvious that the power of faith is in Him on Whom we depend, just as the vitality of the branch is in the life of the vine.

2. *The Basis of Faith.*—Faith as a great spiritual and moral principle must have something on which to rest. The Object of faith is none other than God Himself, and the warrant of faith is God's own revelation. Thus, faith in man answers to Grace in God: our trust responds to His Truth; our faith to His Faithfulness. This is the meaning of St. Paul, "Faith cometh by hearing, and hearing by the word of God" (Rom. x. 17). This, too, is the explanation of the emphasis placed on faith in that great chapter, Hebrews xi. "Without faith it is impossible to be well-pleasing unto Him: for he that cometh to God must believe that He is, and that He is a rewarder of them that seek after Him" (Heb. xi. 6, R.V.). It follows that the more we know of God through His Word, the stronger will be our faith; the more deeply we enter into fellowship with Him, the more confidence we shall have in Him; the more accurate and thorough our knowledge and appreciation of His character, the more instinctive, strong, and far-reaching will be our faith. The heart of the believer will thus be continually discovering that God is true, and that therefore the soul can trust Him.

XIX

ABRAHAM'S RIGHTEOUSNESS AND OURS

Rom. iv. 9-17.

9. *Cometh* this blessedness then upon the circumcision *only*, or upon the uncircumcision also? for we say that faith was reckoned to Abraham for righteousness.
10. How was it then reckoned? when he was in circumcision, or in uncircumcision? Not in circumcision, but in uncircumcision.
11. And he received the sign of circumcision, a seal of the righteousness of the faith which *he had yet* being uncircumcised: that he might be the father of all them that believe, though they be not circumcised; that righteousness might be imputed unto them also:
12. And the father of circumcision to them who are not of the circumcision only, but who also walk in the steps of that faith of our father Abraham, which *he had* being *yet* uncircumcised.
13. For the promise, that he should be the heir of the world, *was* not to Abraham, or to his seed, through the law, but through the righteousness of faith.
14. For if they which are of the law *be* heirs, faith is made void, and the promise made of none effect:
15. Because the law worketh wrath: for where no law is, *there is* no transgression.
16. Therefore *it is* of faith, that *it might be* by grace; to the end the promise might be sure to all the seed; not to that only which is of the law, but to that also which is of the faith of Abraham; who is the father of us all,
17. (As it is written, I have made thee a father of many nations.)

With this section the Apostle commences the consideration of the second point in the chapter dealing with the agreement between the Old Testament record and the grace of the Gospel, thus again proving his statement of ch. iii. 21, that the righteousness of God is witnessed by the law and the prophets. Justification by faith has now been proved, and the question to be considered in these verses is whether this method of free justification refers to the Jews only, since Abraham was the father of the Jewish race. The Apostle now sets out to demonstrate the truth that justification by faith is intended for all, both Jews and Gentiles (as in ch. iii. 29, 30), and he does this by showing that Abraham was justified long before he was circumcised. This is the thought of verses 9-12.

I. *Personal Righteousness* (vers. 9-12).

1. The Question (ver. 9). A natural inquiry is whether the blessing pronounced on the man to whom the Lord does not reckon sin (ver. 8) is intended for the Jews only, or for the Gentiles also. Thus far the Apostle has only been speaking about Abraham as the ancestor of the Jews, and it is therefore essential to know whether the blessedness of righteousness through faith is for Gentiles as well, or for Jews alone.

2. The Answer (ver. 10). In a simple though striking way it is pointed out that Abraham was justified by faith (Gen. xv.) at least fourteen years before he was circumcised (Gen. xvii.), and that therefore his righteousness came to him, not as a circumcised Jew, but as an ordinary individual who exercized faith in God.

3. The Proof (ver. 11). What, then, it might be asked, was the advantage of circumcision? Here comes the answer to the question of ch. iii. 1. If the rite did not confer righteousness, what did it accomplish? It did not *confer*, but *confirmed* the righteousness. The ordinance attested the validity and acceptance of Abraham's faith. It was not a means of righteousness, but a seal. It did not "convey," but "attest." It bore witness to an already existing righteousness. As Lightfoot says, it was not a preliminary condition, but a final ratification:—

> "In no dispensation do rites bestow anything; they are the shadow, not the substance; they are a seal. But the seal is worthless apart from the matter or from the document that it attests. The Jew had torn off the seal from the covenant, and then vainly boasted of this meaningless imprint" (Stifler, *The Epistle to the Romans,* p. 74).

This is not to set aside or even to derogate from the importance of divine ordinances. They are seals of promises to be embraced by faith. Such an ordinance as circumcision might well be called a "visible word." Faith lays hold of the promise, and then the ordinance is the seal and assurance of its fulfilment, so that in their place and for their purpose, divine ordinances like circumcision are full of meaning, power and blessing.

4. The Purpose (vers. 11, 12). The divine object in the case of Abraham was to bring blessing to all classes, the Jews and the Gentiles. Abraham was to be "the father of all them that believe," whether they were circumcised or uncircumcised. God's design was the salvation of the world, and not that of the Jews only, and this, through simple faith. We observe how the Apostle entirely destroys the Jewish boasting in circumcision, by showing that Abraham was not circumcised in order to be saved, but was saved in order to be circumcised. In like manner, the Gentiles were not to become Jews in order to be saved, but Jew and Gentile alike were to exercise the same faith for salvation, and would obtain the same spiritual blessings on these terms. It was not for Gentiles to enter by the Jewish gateway, but for the Jews to enter by the same gateway as the Gentiles. This was indeed a striking turning of the tables on Jewish exclusiveness.

II. *Representative Righteousness* (vers. 13-17).—The Apostle has shown that Abraham's righteousness came apart from works, apart from circumcision, and by faith only. He now introduces an additional subject, which is the third point of the chapter (vers. 13-17a). He is still concerned to show that righteousness by faith conforms to the Old Testament (ch. iii. 21). Now he takes up the question of Abraham having received the promise of the inheritance of the world for himself and his posterity. The Apostle had spoken of Abraham as "our father" (vers. 1, 12), and the idea of a world-wide family at once comes into view, and with it the question whether this promise of a universal inheritance was for Jews only, and by means of the law, or for Gentiles also, and by means of faith? Here is the answer.

1. The Meaning of the Promise (ver. 13). Let us notice that the promise mentioned in this verse does not refer to righteousness by faith, which has been discussed and settled. It is the promise of heirship of the world; the promise that Abraham and his seed were to have universal dominion. Not salvation, therefore, but inheritance, is the question, and the very term "world" must necessarily

include Gentiles as well as Jews. The question is no longer one of Abraham's personal faith, but of Abraham in relation to the world. It is a question of universality. Abraham is regarded as the stem of a tree, not merely as a private individual, but as a public man, a representative of the human race. Consequently, it is pointed out that this universal dominion comes not through law, but through faith. The fact that the world includes Gentiles as well as Jews demands a principle of faith, not of works, and the way in which, in verses 11, 12, Abraham is described as "the father of all them that believe" shows that he is here regarded not as an example of faith, but as the founder of a household of faith. The promises of universal dominion and world-wide blessing here in view are mentioned in Genesis xii. 3 and xxii. 17.

2. The Way of the Promise (ver. 14). If it were true that all this blessing came through law, two things would necessarily follow: "faith would be made void, and the promise made absolutely useless." The first of these points has already been taken up in the Apostle's insistence upon the importance of faith, and it is not further dealt with here. The latter point about the promise being made useless is now considered. If the blessing comes by law, there is no room for faith, and the proof is adduced by contrasting law and faith, word and promise. If, therefore, blessing is to proceed from Abraham, the world must be brought under the influence of his spiritual seed.

3. The Principle of the Promise (v. 15). That the promise would be made useless by laws is shown by the fact that law cannot work out, or earn a promise. "The law worketh wrath." This is all that it can do. It leads to divine disapprobation because of transgression. Obedience to law must be perfect, and as no man can provide this, the only result of attempting it would be divine wrath on the worker. Law and transgression are therefore inseparably associated, and it would be absurd to think that law could obtain the inheritance of the world. Thus the Apostle shows the absolute necessity of falling back on the promise.

4. The Proof of the Promise (ver. 16). The conclusion is now drawn that the promise is by grace through faith, in order that

both Jews and Gentiles, as Abraham's spiritual seed, may participate therein. This verse is somewhat obscure because it is so elliptical, and it may perhaps be paraphrased as follows: "Therefore, inasmuch as law cannot produce anything but wrath, the promise of the heirship of the world is by faith, in order that it might be a gift to those who believe, not only to Jews, but also to all, whether Jews or Gentiles, who have the same faith that Abraham had."

5. The Confirmation of the Promise (ver. 17a). The Apostle concludes by showing the agreement between his teaching and Scripture, for the Old Testament itself (Gen. xvii. 5) proves that Abraham was far more than a private individual; he was the head of a spiritual race. "A father of many nations have I made thee."

Two profound spiritual lessons underlie these verses, which deal with the outcome of righteousness through faith.

1. *The Great Prospect.*—The result of righteousness by faith is shown to extend far beyond any individual salvation, and to result in the *heirship* of the world for Abraham and his spiritual seed. As St. Paul says elsewhere, "All things are yours" (1 Cor. iii. 21), and again, "The saints shall judge the world" (1 Cor. vi. 2). God has so conditioned human affairs that the eventual rule and dominion of mankind will be vested in the spiritual seed of Abraham, the Church of Christ, which is His Body. All nations are to come under the influence of Abraham's seed in order to be blessed. Not merely is Abraham to have a number of believers as his spiritual progeny, but very much more is to happen; world-wide dominion is to accrue to Abraham's seed. This far-reaching principle ought to be our greatest inspiration and incentive to world-wide evangelization. Not only are we saved with an everlasting salvation, but our salvation is to issue in the universal dominion of the world. Let us ponder again and again this truly stupendous thought of divine revelation:—

> "'We see not yet all things' fulfilled of this astonishing grant and guarantee. We shall not do so, till vast promised developments of the ways of God have come to sight. But we do see already steps taken towards that issue, steps long, majestic, never to be retraced. We see at this hour in literally every region of the human world the messengers—an always more numerous army—of the Name of 'the Son of David, the

Son of Abraham.' They are working everywhere; and everywhere, notwithstanding innumerable difficulties, they are winning the world for the great Heir of the Promise. Through paths they know not these missionaries have gone out; paths hewn by the historical providence of God, and by His eternal life in the Church, and in the soul . . . . No secular conscious programme has had to do with this. Causes entirely beyond the reach of human combination have been, as a fact, combined; the world has been opened to the Abrahamic message just as the Church has been inspired anew to enter in, and has been awakened to a deeper understanding of her glorious mission. For here, too, is the finger of God; not only in the history of the world, but in the life of the Church and of the Christian. For a long century now, in the most living centres of Christendom, there has been waking and rising a mighty revived consciousness of the glory of the Gospel of the Cross, and of the Spirit; of the grace of Christ, and also of His claim. And at this hour, after many a gloomy forecast of unbelieving and apprehensive thought, there are more men and women ready to go to the ends of the earth with the message of the Son of Abraham, than in all time before" (Moule, *Romans*, Expositor's Bible, pp. 118, 119).

2. *The Sure Promise.*—It is almost too marvelous for us to believe that all this is involved in the divine promise to Abraham (Gen. xii.) as realized in the Lord Jesus Christ. And yet, here it is in plain language for everyone to ponder, to accept, and to rejoice in, and the method of its realization is clearly shown to be by faith. "This is the victory that overcometh the world, even our faith." In proportion as we exercise trust in God we shall find ourselves making progress in the direction of fulfilling and realizing God's purpose of world-wide dominion and blessing in Christ.

XX

ABRAHAM'S FAITH AND OURS

Rom. iv. 17-25.

17. Before him whom he believed, *even* God, who quickeneth the dead, and calleth those things which be not as though they were.
18. Who against hope believed in hope, that he might become the father of many nations, according to that which was spoken, So shall thy seed be.
19. And being not weak in faith, he considered not his own body now dead, when he was about an hundred years old, neither yet the deadness of Sarah's womb:
20. He staggered not at the promise of God through unbelief; but was strong in faith, giving glory to God;
21. And being fully persuaded that, what he had promised he was able also to perform.
22. And therefore it was imputed to him for righteousness.
23. Now it was not written for his sake alone, that it was imputed to him;
24. But for us also, to whom it shall be imputed, if we believe on him that raised up Jesus our Lord from the dead;
25. Who was delivered for our offences, and was raised again for our justification.

In these concluding verses of the chapter we have the Apostle's fourth point, in which Abraham's faith is used as an illustration of faith in us. It is shown that the faith which God requires from us is exactly the same as that which He required from Abraham. Let us ponder carefully some of the characteristics of faith, as here set forth.

I. *Faith in Relation to the Divine Object.*—"Him Whom he believed, even God" (ver. 17). Trust must always be centered upon a person, not upon a thing, and Christian faith always rests upon a Divine Person God Himself. It is the presence of God that elicits, verifies, and guarantees faith. When this simple but all important thought is realized it removes all difficulty from the thought of faith. Someone remarked to a clergyman, "It is so difficult to believe." "To believe *Whom?*" was the reply. Faith is something real, concrete, definite, not theoretical, abstract. The emphasis must always be placed upon the Object of trust rather than upon the act of believing.

II. *Faith in Relation to Divine Power.*—"Who quickeneth the dead, and calleth those things which be not as though they were" (ver. 17). The special point in Abraham's faith is thus seen to be trust in the divine Omnipotence which makes the dead alive, and calls non-existent things as though they were existent. The law of God's higher operations is from death to life, and it was this in particular on which Abraham's faith was concentrated.

III. *Faith in Relation to Natural Probabilities.*—"Who in hope believed against hope, that he might become the father of many nations" (ver. 18). Everything seemed to be against Abraham so far as nature was concerned, and yet he rested absolutely upon God. "On the strength of hope" he believed even against hope.

IV. *Faith in Relation to the Divine Word.*—"According to that which was spoken, so shall thy seed be" (ver. 18). This was the warrant of Abraham's faith, the word of God. All through the Bible the warrant of faith is found in what God says, and this in turn rests upon what God is. "Faith reasons from God and His Word, not from self or circumstances."

V. *Faith in Relation to Special Difficulties* (ver. 19).—There was the difficulty of his own age and also that of Sarah. But these did not concern him in the least. In the A.V. we read, "He considered not his own body now dead"; that is, he took no notice of this fact which might have made many a man hesitate. In the R.V. the negative is omitted, and we read, "He considered his own body now dead"; that is, he deliberately faced the problem, giving it careful attention, and in spite of every appearance persisted in trusting God. In either case, whichever reading we adopt, we see the sobriety and magnificence of his trust during the peculiar circumstances, difficulties, and improbabilities. Against all natural appearances and probabilities he simply rested on God. There was nothing unreal or merely emotional about his trust. He was blind to nothing, but quietly faced the realities of the situation. Stifler well says, "Weak faith looks at difficulties and scarce looks to God. Strong faith looks at God Who has promised, and does not see the difficulties."

VI. *Faith in Relation to Triumphant Expression* (vers. 19-21).—Every phrase of these verses should carefully be noticed. "Being not weak in faith"; "He staggered not"; "Was strong in faith"; "Giving glory to God"; "Fully persuaded"; "He was able to perform." Abraham did not question or discriminate. There was an entire absence of hesitation and indecision. Time had been when his faith swerved, and he was led to question the possibility of God's fulfilment of His promise and so to provide his own method of fulfilment. But God came to His rescue, strengthened his faith, led him to rest once more on the divine word, and Abraham's trust rose again and he was enabled to go forward in hope and joy. His faith was thus reinvigorated, and strong in divine strength he overcame every obstacle and triumphed in his God. Nothing made him quail. He stood, as it were, on the edge of the precipice of possibilities and was unmoved. He rested everything on God's promise, he continued believing until he became "strong in faith, giving glory to God." Faith ever finds its nutriment in the word of God, and can only be strong as it feeds itself thereon. Weak faith is invariably due to a lack of the food of the promises. "God's ability is the foundation of faith's stability."

VII. *Faith in Relation to the Divine Reward.*—"And therefore it was imputed to him for righteousness" (ver. 22). This was how God met His servant's trust. He honored him by reckoning him as righteous from that time forward. God rejoices when our faith goes out to meet Him, resting solely on his word and becoming fully assured that He will do as He has said.

VIII. *Faith in Relation to a Definite Example* (vers. 23-25).—The Apostle now says that the same faith is needed in us, and that the same result of righteousness imputed will accrue to us if we exercise like faith. "It was not written for his sake alone . . . but for our sake also." This personal touch, "our sake," is found here for the first time in the Epistle, though we have had "our forefather Abraham" in ver. 1. Our trust may be centered on God in precisely the same connection as was Abraham's. Thus, the story of Genesis xv. is not merely historical and archæological, but definitely spiritual with reference to us, believers in Christ. "It was not written for his sake alone." Observe this spiritual purpose of the Old Testament. It does not merely say that it did not occur for his sake alone, but that "it was not *written* for his sake alone." The very record of the Old Testament had a definite spiritual purpose for the blessing of all who were to believe in Christ (ch. xv. 4; 1 Cor. x. 11; 1 Pet. i. 10, 11).

Let us look more carefully into the analogy of Abraham's faith and ours. He believed in God "Who quickeneth the dead" (ver. 17), and we believe on Him Who "raised up our Lord from the dead" (ver. 24). He believed in God "Who was able to perform" (ver. 21), we believe in a God Who has performed (ver. 24). And just as the result of Abraham's faith was righteousness in the sight of God, so the outcome of faith in our Lord as having died and risen again is forgiveness and righteousness for us. Our Lord was "handed over" to death "because of our sins," and He was raised from the dead "because of our justification." Godet interprets the words thus:—

> "In the same way, as Jesus died because of our offences, that is our (merited) condemnation, *He was raised because of our* (accomplished) *justification.* Our sin had killed Him; our justification raised Him again. How so? The expiation of our trespasses once accomplished by His death, and the right of God's justice proved in earnest, God could pronounce the collective acquittal of future believers, and He did so . . . . So long as the security is in prison the debt is not paid; the immediate *effect* of payment would be his liberation. Similarly, if Jesus were not raised, we should be more than ignorant whether our debt were paid: we might be certain that it was not. His resurrection is the *proof* of our justification, only because it is the necessary effect of it." (*Romans,* vol. i. p. 312).

There is also a point of very great importance here in the association of faith with our Lord Jesus Christ. In ch. iii. 25 our faith is exercised "in His blood," that is, in His atoning death. But in ch. iv. 24 our faith is exercised in God Who raised Him from the dead, that is, in connection with the resurrection. So faith is concentrated on Him Who once was dead and is now alive for evermore. The resurrection is the proof of our acceptance, and is the antidote against all fear. "Jesus paid it *all*," *and* the resurrection is the receipt, the full discharge of the debt.

The essential unity of the Old and New Testament ideas of faith is thus very significant. Faith and its Object are shown to be the same throughout, and the specific nature of faith is also observable. Anyone could believe God in the abstract, but the specific Christian faith is trust in God as the One Who had raised our Lord from the dead. Faith is no mere abstract thing, but a reality connected with the Object, the ground, and the warrant of our faith. It is this quality in the Object of our trust that constitutes the true and vital nature of Christian faith.

The entire chapter is occupied with the thoughts of justification and righteousness, and it may be useful to bring into one view the various aspects of these truths as they are found here and elsewhere in the New Testament.

1. *Seven Aspects of Justification.*—(*a*) We are justified by God, as the source (ch. viii. 33); (*b*) by grace, as the spring (ch. iii. 24); (*c*) by blood, as the ground (ch. v. 7); (*d*) by the resurrection, as the proof (ch. iv. 25); (*e*) by faith, as the means (ch. v. 1); (*f*) by words, as the evidence (Matt. xii. 37); (*g*) and by works, as the fruit (Jas. ii. 21). It is in the combination of all these elements that the complete truth of justification is found, and the more we ponder them the more we shall see the fulness of blessing associated with it.

2. *Seven Aspects of Righteousness.*—Let us now concentrate attention upon this chapter, and observe the various elements and phases of righteousness brought into view. (*a*) Righteousness is associated no less than eleven times with reckoning (vers. 3, 4, 5, 6, 8, 9, 10, 11, 22, 23, 24). God puts our Lord's righteousness to our account. (*b*) Righteousness is associated nine times with faith (vers. 3, 5, 9, 13, 14, 16, 20, 22, 24). Trust is the channel by means of which God's righteousness in Christ becomes ours. (*c*) Righteousness is said three times to be apart from works (vers. 2, 5, 6). Nothing that man can do can possibly provide an adequate

righteousness. (*d*) Righteousness is said twice to be apart from circumcision (vers. 10, 11). No outward ordinance or ecclesiastical rite can possibly guarantee righteousness; at most it can only prove and seal an already existing righteousness. (*e*) Righteousness is said three times to be apart from law (vers. 13, 14, 16). Law commands, but cannot compel; it requires, but cannot provide righteousness. (*f*) Righteousness is said to be according to grace (ver. 16). This is the divine standard by which God provided Christ and wrought righteousness for man. (*g*) Righteousness is associated with the Person of our Lord Jesus Christ (ver. 25). In Him God has provided and bestows to every believer a perfect righteousness. As we contemplate the marvel and the glory of this divine gift how can we help doing as Abraham did: "giving glory to God"?

"*Once* it was thus; the storm-capped mound,
The thunders echoing loud and deep,
The solemn cordon stretched around,
Bade me, a sinner, distance keep;

For thou, O God, wast unrevealed!
To see Thy glory was to die;
Now, through th' eternal covenant, sealed
In Jesu's blood, I am brought nigh,

And in Thy presence undismayed,
A sinner reconciled by grace,
With unveiled eye, behold displayed
Thy fullest glories in His face."

XXI

THE SECURITY OF THE JUSTIFIED

ROM. v. 1-11.

1. Therefore being justified by faith, we have peace with God through our Lord Jesus Christ:
2. By whom also we have access by faith into this grace wherein we stand, and rejoice in hope of the glory of God.
3. And not only *so,* but we glory in tribulations also: knowing that tribulation worketh patience;
4. And patience, experience; and experience, hope:
5. And hope maketh not ashamed; because the love of God is shed abroad in our hearts by the Holy Ghost which is given unto us.
6. For when we were yet without strength, in due time Christ died for the ungodly.
7. For scarcely for a righteous man will one die: yet peradventure for a good man some would even dare to die.
8. But God commendeth his love toward us, in that, while we were yet sinners, Christ died for us.
9. Much more then, being now justified by his blood, we shall be saved from wrath through him.
10. For if, when we were enemies, we were reconciled to God by the death of his Son, much more, being reconciled, we shall be saved by his life.
11. And not only so, but we also joy in God through our Lord Jesus Christ, by whom we have now received the atonement.

THE harmony and agreement of the law and faith has at length been made abundantly clear. After the enunciation of the great truth of righteousness by faith (ch. iii. 21, 22), and the statement of its historical foundation in Christ (ch. iii. 23-26), it was confirmed by the Old Testament (ch. iii 27-iv. 25), and Abraham's story was adduced to prove that righteousness is through faith, apart from works, apart from circumcision, and by divine grace alone. But now a new question at once arises. Will this new method of salvation really last; will it continue to the end? Is it safe for all the varied and complex needs of human life? Is it a foundation sufficiently strong to stand the wear and tear of human needs? Even if it saves at the commencement will it continue to save in the future? The answer to this is given in the chapter before us. It is inadequate and therefore erroneous to regard this section as dealing merely with the fruits of justification:—

> "The Apostle never thought of explaining in the piece which we are about to study the fruits of justification; he simply finishes treating the subject of justification itself" (Godet, *Romans*, p. 315).

Most readers will also agree with the following words:—

> "Many commentators have entitled this chapter the 'Fruits of Justification!' This fails in both logic and history. Paul's first readers would be amazed to hear him speak here about fruits. Their cry would be, Is this method safe? Doing no works of law, what assurance does this faith in Christ's work give one for the future? Furthermore, fruits are immediate results in experience and do not need the rigid logical proofs exhibited in this chapter. And what 'fruit' is there in the parallel between Adam and Christ?" (Stifler, *Romans*, p. 87).

We are therefore told of the immediate outcome of righteousness by faith in the personal experiences and hopes of the believer, and it is shown that both present experiences and future hopes are all based upon the perfect provision in Christ as the Lord our Righteousness. The results here stated are the saving, gladdening, rather than the sanctifying effects of justification. Sanctification is to be considered later.

One word occurs three times in this section ("rejoice" or "glory," *lit.* boast, vers. 2, 3, 11) and it is the key to the entire chapter, but as we study the passage we find there are altogether four reasons for feeling assured that righteousness will continue unimpaired to the very end.

I. *Present Experiences assure our Hope* (vers. 1, 2).

1. In relation to the past. (*a*) There is justification. "Being justified by faith." "Justified" means pardoned, acquitted, and regarded as righteous in Christ. It is objective; something done for us by God, and not any mere subjective, inward feeling or attitude towards God. We must never limit justification to forgiveness, for it is much more. Nor must we confuse them, for they are very different, even though they are connected. Forgiveness is negative; justification is positive. Forgiveness deals with the sin

that has been committed; justification deals with the new position and relationship of the restored believer. A father can forgive his sinning child, but cannot justify or reinstate the child as though no sin had been committed. Nor can the child justify himself by any obedience in the future, for the act will always remain a fact in the child's history and experience. But God's justification in Christ Jesus covers both past and future, and not only pardons but reinstates us in a right relation and position. (*b*) There is peace. "We have peace with God. Peace in this passage means the cessation of hostility, not mere tranquility of mind. It is not that we have ceased to be hostile to God, but that God has ceased to be in righteous hostility to us as sinners. "God is the enemy of man, the sinner." But when we are justified through faith we have peace. Peace of conscience in the mercy of God; peace of heart in the love of God; peace of mind in the truth of God; peace of soul in the presence of God.

N.B.—The R.V. reads, "Let us have peace," instead of the familiar "We have peace" of the A.V. The difference turns upon one stroke of a Greek letter, and in spite of the great manuscript authority for the reading of the R.V. all the internal probabilities point in the other direction. The Apostle has not commenced his exhortation but is still concerned with his doctrinal statement of justification. Dr. Beet endeavors to meet the difficulty of manuscript authority and contextual probability by suggesting that the Apostle is referring to the abiding state of peace, not to the initial entrance into it, and really means that this permanent condition of peace with God must be preceded by the event of justification. "Let us then, justified by faith, have peace." This interpretation would be in line with the words, "Let us have grace," in Heb. xii. 28, but Bishop Moule's discussion (*Expositor's Bible*, p. 140) seems on the whole far truer to the teaching of the passage, and we may observe that the American Revised Version reverts here to the reading of the A.V.

2. In Relation to the Present. (*a*) There is access; "Access into this grace." The thought includes the possibility of entrance, and also the privilege of introduction, as at a presentation at Court.

There may be a suggestion of the Tabernacle in the words, with the thought of the possibility of drawing near to God. (*b*) There is grace. "This grace wherein we stand." Constant need and continual supply are here suggested. Grace is the home of the soul "wherein we stand."

3. In Relation to the Future. (*a*) There is boasting. "And we rejoice." This is the true spirit of the Christian life; the expression of our overwhelming joy and satisfaction. (*b*) There is glory. "In hope of the glory of God." This is the goal to which we look. In ch. iii. 23, the phrase, "the glory of God," refers to the divine standard for human life. Here it is that in which we rejoice or boast. It is the goal to which we look, and as to which our souls exult in hope.

II. *Afflictions cannot destroy our Hope* (vers. 3-5).—The Apostle not only boasts in hope of future glory (ver. 2), he is able to boast in tribulations also. "And not only so, but also." Five times in his Epistles does St. Paul use this striking phrase (ch. v. 3, 11; viii. 23; ix. 10; 2 Cor. viii. 19). He knows that tribulation works out steadfast endurance, that endurance in its turn works out "approvedness" of experience, that experience works out hope, and hope never puts to shame because God's love is "poured out like a torrent" (Liddon) by the Holy Ghost given to us. This chain of present experience is very striking, and just as ver. 2 culminates in hope, so does ver. 5. The thought all through is the certainty that righteousness by faith must and will last to the end. This is not the attitude of one who submits to the inevitable, but of one who rejoices to know what the process will mean. St. Paul was always confident that his hope in Christ would never be put to shame, and perhaps he had in mind the familiar Greek version of Isa. xxviii. 16, "He that believeth shall not be put to shame" (see 2 Tim. i. 12).

The love of God in these verses is of course the love of God to us. It is His love in our hearts that assures us. God's love to the undeserving is the marvelous conception of the Apostle. There was nothing in us to attract that love. In this passage the Holy Spirit is mentioned for the first time in the Epistle, the subject being only touched upon and left for fuller treatment in ch. viii.

III. *God's Love as shown in the Gift of His Son confirms our Hope* (vers. 6-10).—In this section we have the foundation of the principle by which the Apostle proves that God's love is assured to us, making justification permanent. The stream of ver. 5 is traced to its source in this verse. This love is twofold: (1) as seen in the death of Christ for the ungodly; (2) as seen in the life of Christ for those whom He has saved through His death. The illustration of the righteous man contrasted with the good man is intended to show the difference between one for whom, as upright, we have profound respect, and one who is also beneficent and elicits our love. The argument is brought to a point in vers. 9, 10, with the characteristic phrase, "Much more." If God can save His enemies "much more" can He keep His friends. "My child," said a dying French saint, as she gave a last embrace to her daughter, "I have loved you because of what you are; my heavenly Father to Whom I go has loved me *malgrè moi*" (Moule, *Expositor's Bible,* p. 137). If Love can die for us when "we were in a repulsive state of impotence" much more now that we are reconciled will it cherish and keep us. If the death of Christ was the means of our reconciliation, the life of Christ will be the means of our preservation. "Much more, being reconciled, we shall be kept safe in His love" (Moule). There is thus a triple antithesis; enemies and reconciled; reconciled and saved; death and life.

The term "enemies" and the reference to reconciliation suggest what we have already seen in connection with the "peace" of ver. 1, that it is not merely a question of the change of the sinner's feelings towards God, but primarily and fundamentally a change in the attitude of God to the sinner. We observe also how each Person of the Sacred Trinity is associated in these verses with our complete and permanent salvation.

IV. *God Himself Crowns our Hope* (ver. 11).—This is the deepest secret of all. Here we touch the very foundation. The word rendered "rejoice" is the same as that found in ver. 2 and ver. 3, and means "boast." Not only do we boast in hope of future glory and in present tribulations (ver. 3), but we boast in God Himself, through Jesus Christ by Whom we receive the Atonement, the power and effect of which will be discussed in the remaining verses of the chapter. The word rendered "atonement" in the A.V. should be "reconciliation," and again we see that the Apostle is still concerned with justification. Reconciliation because justified by the blood of Christ is still another proof that the change is not first of all man's feelings towards God, but in the attitude of God to man. As we contemplate this thought of the believer boasting in God we see that nothing short of God will satisfy us, and nothing short of our lives will satisfy God.

It is impossible to mistake the tone of the Apostle in these verses. How he exults in the reality and glory of justification! We can discover still more clearly the secret of his exultation.

1. *Justification is an Immediate Gift.*—It comes through faith the moment a man believes. It is received, not accomplished; obtained not attained.

2. *Justification is a Perfect Gift.*—There are no degrees in justification. "Justified from all things" (Acts xiii. 38, 39). From the moment of conversion to the end of our earthly life justification is absolutely the same. There are stages of grace, but not of justification. The feeblest believer is accepted with God. The realization of his acceptance may differ but not the reality. "A little faith will bring a soul into heaven, but strong faith will bring heaven into the soul." The Word of God is unchanging and unchangeable.

"I change, He changes not;
The Christ can never die.
His love, not mine, the resting-place,
His truth, not mine, the tie."

3. *Justification is a Permanent Gift.*—Once justified, always justified. A man can never be "unjustified," for justification in Christ covers past, present, and future; assuring us of the removal of condemnation and guilt in the past, delivering us from all fear and doubt in the present, and guaranteeing our title to heaven in the future.

4. *Justification is a Divine Gift.*—As we review these verses it is very striking that after ver. 1, all mention of faith is suddenly dropped until ch. ix. 30 (ch. vi. 8 does not really apply). This omission is all the more remarkable because of the prominence of faith up to this time, the verb having appeared at least five times and the substantive twenty-seven. There must be some reason in this, and it is assuredly found in the simple fact that the certainty of a perfect righteousness is grounded in the love of God. We depend, not upon our faith, but upon God's faithfulness.

> "In proportion as we rest the terms upon which we are with God upon real grounds to be found in ourselves, will our relations with Him, our peace, be weak and low and fluctuating. In proportion as we rest it upon what our faith embraces and anticipates of the infinite all that He is to us in Christ and we are in Him in Christ, will our peace even now be full of a glory that may be future in its existence in us but is very present in its existence for us" (Du Bose, *The Gospel according to St. Paul*, p. 132).

Our faith may fail, but His truth will never fail. There seems to be today too great a tendency to rest upon the human aspects of salvation, forgetful of, or at any rate ignoring, the great underlying divine realities which alone make salvation possible. It is probably for this reason that this whole passage is centered in the love of God with its great proof and demonstration in the gift and death of His Son whose atonement brings God near and guarantees an eternal salvation. As a little Irish convert once said, "I often *trimble* on the Rock, but the Rock never *trimbles* under me."

5. *Justification is a gift to be Enjoyed.*—In view of these divine realities we are to "possess our possessions" (Obad. 17), and enter fully into the unspeakable privileges which are ours in Christ. If we were permitted to read the Apostle's words as hortatory instead of declaratory, this would be their meaning. Let us enjoy peace, let us rejoice in hope, let us rejoice in our tribulations, let us rejoice in God. God's act and fact of salvation is to be a fact, factor, and force in our daily life.

> "Near, so very near to God,
> I cannot nearer be;
> For in the Person of His Son,
> I am as near as He."

XXII

THE FOUNDATION OF RIGHTEOUSNESS

ROM. v. 12-21.

12. Wherefore, as by one man sin entered into the world, and death by sin; and so death passed upon all men, for that all have sinned:
13. (For until the law sin was in the world: but sin is not imputed when there is no law.
14. Nevertheless death reigned from Adam to Moses, even over them that had not sinned after the similitude of Adam's transgression, who is the figure of him that was to come.
15. But not as the offence, so, also *is* the free gift. For if through the offence of one many be dead, much more the grace of God, and the gift by grace, *which is* by one man, Jesus Christ, hath abounded unto many.
16. And not as *it was* by one that sinned, *so is* the gift: for the judgment *was* by one to condemnation, but the free gift *is* of many offences unto justification.
17. For if by one man's offence death reigned by one; much more they which receive abundance of grace and of the gift of righteousness shall reign in life by one, Jesus Christ.)
18. Therefore as by the offence of one *judgment came* upon all men to condemnation; even so by the righteousness of one *the free gift came* upon all men unto justification of life.
19. For as by one man's disobedience many were made sinners, so by the obedience of one shall many be made righteous.
20. Moreover the law entered, that the offence might abound. But where sin abounded, grace did much more abound:
21. That as sin hath reigned unto death, even so might grace reign through righteousness unto eternal life by Jesus Christ our Lord.

THE close connection of this section with that which immediately precedes it must be carefully noted. The first word "Wherefore" is literally "on this account," showing that the thought remains unbroken. Justification has been shown to be permanent (vers. 1-11), and the fundamental proof and guarantee of this is God Himself in Whom we boast (ver. 11). This primary reason is now elaborated in the section before us by pointing out that as man's connection with Adam involved him in certain death through sin, so his relation to Christ insures to him life without fail. Thus, these verses give us the logical centre of the Epistle. They are the great central point to which everything that precedes has converged, and out of which everything that follows will flow. The great ideas of Sin, Death, and Judgment are here shown to be involved in the connection of the human race with Adam, but over against this we have the blessed fact of a union with Christ, and in this union righteousness and life. This double headship of mankind in Adam and Christ shows the significance of the work of redemption for the entire race.

Up to the present point the Apostle has been dealing with *sins*, as they are expressed in human life, but now he proceeds to deal with *sin*, the principle from which all expressions proceed. He thus goes to the root of the trouble; original sin, and shows the disease and its remedy. Although he has clearly proved our justification from *sins* there still remains the question of the old nature, and now he is about to show how we obtain deliverance from *sin* as well as from sins. He ranges men under two heads, Adam and Christ. There are two men, two acts, and two results. In this profound teaching we have the spiritual and theological illustration of the great modern principle of solidarity. There is a solidarity of evil and a solidarity of good, but the latter far surpasses the former in the quality of the obedience of Christ as compared with Adam, and in the effects of the work of Christ for justification and life. It will be seen that the purpose of the section is not to teach Original Sin, but assuming it as a fact, to show how divine grace overcomes it in those who are united to Christ. Thus we get the vital truth of the inseparableness of justification and sanctification.

This passage, therefore, is no mere episode or illustration, but that which really gives organic life to the entire Epistle. As ch. v. 11 had completed the formal treatment of justification by faith, so ch. v. 12 is the transition point which leads up to the inseparable consequence of sanctification, to be treated in chs. vi.-viii. The first step being secured, everything is really safe, since God will not leave the work unfinished (ch. v. 5-10). Although sin and death are ours in Adam, righteousness and life are ours in Christ, and these are infinitely more. Consequently we boast in God "on this account," namely, that whatever we have lost in Adam we have more than gained in Christ. That the phrase, "On this account," can be prospective as well as retrospective is evident from ch. iv. 16 and other passages. Thus the object of this concluding paragraph of the chapter is to show how everything necessary for human salvation from justification to glory is secured by Christ's redemption, and the Apostle does this by comparing Adam and Christ, and by contrasting condemnation and justification. As all the evils of the race have sprung from one man, so all the blessings of redemption have come from one Person and one act. There is such a connection between the Person and the race that all can possess what one has wrought. Godet points out that every aspect of ch. iii. 21-26 has hitherto been elaborated except one, that which deals with "unto all them that believe;" and thus the universality of Christ's salvation is here treated in relation to the entire race. This view of the passage, giving the great central feature and focus of the Epistle, is really vital to the true interpretation of Romans, and any view that makes it merely an episode or an illustration must necessarily be inadequate and therefore inaccurate.

Although in some respects difficult and complicated, the section is absolutely essential to the proper understanding of the meaning of the Apostle, for it is the key to the three chapters that follow, and for a true spiritual experience it is essential that we grasp the meaning of the passage. While the general idea of the discussion is on the whole simple, yet the details are difficult and require careful study. They consist of a series of comparisons and contrasts.

I. *Adam and Christ* (vers. 12-14).—Several points of comparison are here instituted between the two Heads of the human race. Through one man, Adam, sin entered, and death by sin, and so the effects of Adam's sin extended beyond himself (ver. 12). Thus the analogy between Adam and Christ is commenced. The meaning of the phrase, "For that all sinned," is a matter of great difference among expositors. Either it means that they sinned when Adam sinned, as proved by vers. 15-19, or else it describes the personal acts of Adam's descendants as the result of a tendency inherited from him. Clearly there is some causal connection between him and them, as the whole passage implies. The reference, however, is not to guilt, which is personal and cannot be transferred, but to an evil nature which he inherited from Adam. The Apostle is commencing his proof of the universality of Christ's work by the fact of the universal prevalence of death through sin.

The reference to death as coming through sin is primarily to physical death, though physical death is the expression and sign of the deeper idea of spiritual death (2 Tim. i. 10). It is impossible to draw any sharp distinction between them in this passage. Even though physical death was in the world before Adam, it was only in connection with sin that the moral meaning and estimate of death became clear.

Then the Apostle points out (vers. 13, 14) that death was in the world from Adam to Moses, but that there was no personal guilt (even though there was an evil nature) apart from personal disobedience. Adam's sin thus exerted an influence where the absence of an expressed law might suggest that death had been abrogated. We have only to think of the application of physical death to infants and the insane to see the truth of this statement.

In all this, Adam was a figure of One Who was to come, Christ, the effect of Whose work, as we shall see, also extends far beyond Himself (ver. 14). So that if it should be said that millions have suffered in the possession of an evil nature through the sin of one, the reply of the Apostle will be that millions are also saved through the righteousness of One. All through the section, the idea is that we possess in Christ infinitely more than we have received in Adam's sin.

II. *Trespass and Gift* (ver. 15).—There is no need to regard vers. 13-17 as a parenthesis. It is much simpler and more natural to regard vers. 15, 16 as giving the details of the analogy mentioned in general terms in vers. 12-14, and it will be in every way clearer and more in harmony with the argument to adopt the interrogative form in these verses and render thus: "But shall not, as the offence, so also be the free gift?" If Adam is a type of Christ will there not be some correspondence between the fall of one and the free gift of the other? Surely they resemble each other in their far-reaching effects, for if by the lapse of the one the many connected with him were involved in death, it is much easier to believe that by the free sacrifice of One Man, Christ Jesus, God's loving favor and His gift of righteousness abounded unto the many connected with Him.

III. *Condemnation and Justification* (ver. 16).—Again we render by means of a question: "And shall not the gift be even as it was by one that sinned?" That is to say, Is there not also a correspondence between God's gift and man's ruin in respect of its being caused by the agency of one man? For indeed the free gift which led to the just acquittal of man was occasioned by many lapses; the judgment which led to condemnation was occasioned by one man's single lapse.

IV. *Death and Life* (ver. 17).—There is undoubted correspondence here, for if by virtue of that one man's single lapse the reign of death was established through the agency of the one man, it is much easier to believe that a reign of a far different kind (that is, more in harmony with God's heart) will be established through the agency of One Man, Christ Jesus.

The above statement of vers. 15-17 seems to be more in keeping with the general bearing of the passage than the ordinary interpretation. Usually it is thought that as in vers. 12-14 the Apostle states the fact of the analogy, so here in vers. 15-17 he proceeds to point out the contrasts, or the aspects in which the analogy does not hold good, but it seems far more natural to read the first clause of ver. 15, and also the first clause of ver. 16 as questions in each case. The "but" does not introduce the contrast, but the details of the analogy. Does it not seem improbable that after introducing the analogy between Adam and Christ the Apostle should develop the contrasts rather than the correspondences? And the thought of a contrast does not give any force whatever to the "also" of ver. 15. Then again, as we shall see, the "so then" of ver. 18 introduces the summing up of the preceding argument, summarizing correspondences rather than contrasts. Of course there are remarkable contrasts between the sin of Adam and the work of Christ, but the very contrasts strengthen the argument for the analogy which is the great point St. Paul wishes to emphasize. The first resemblance between Adam and Christ is that in both Fall and Redemption we have far-reaching effects, for in both "the many" are involved (ver. 15). The second resemblance is that in both the result is brought in through the agency of "one man" (vers. 16, 17).

V. *Trespass and Righteousness* (ver. 18).—Now various points of comparison are gathered up into one conclusion. We have on the one side as the cause one lapse, and the effect extending to all men for condemnation. We have on the other side as the cause one just sentence of acquittal, and the effect extending to all men for a justifying which carries with it life. These differences, however, only strengthen the argument for the correspondences, for grace is stronger than sin. If "the many" were involved in sin and death through the agency of the one man, Adam; "much more" may we believe that "the many" will be involved in righteousness and life through the agency of the One Man, Christ Jesus.

VI. *Disobedience and Obedience* (ver. 19).—One point in the comparison is still incomplete. Adam's sin has not been contrasted with Christ's obedience, but with the cause of that obedience, grace (ver. 15), and with the result of it, a gift (ver. 17, 18). It is now shown that these effects were wrought by means of Christ's obedience, the exact contrast of Adam's disobedience, for as through the disobedience of the one man, Adam, the many connected with him were set down in the class of sin, so through the obedience of the One Man, Christ Jesus, the many connected with Him shall be set down in the class of righteousness.[1]

VII. *Abounding Trespass and Abounding Grace* (ver. 20).—At once a Jewish objection occurs which must be faced and removed. If Adam and Christ are the two sources of Sin and

1 I am greatly indebted, on vers. 14-19, to some MS. notes by my friend, the late Canon Jones, Moore College, Sydney, Australia, who died after these lines were written. A similar view is taken of the interrogative form of vers. 15, 16 by Mr. J. Fort, in *God's Salvation*, and by *The Englishman's Greek Testament*.

Righteousness, where does the Mosaic law come in? What is its purpose? What is its relation to sin and grace? As ver. 13 mentioned "law," why was it given? As ver. 16 mentioned "many trespasses," how came they to be trespasses? If we pass by one step from Adam to Christ, from sin to redemption, surely there is no place left for the law. Here is now the answer. Law came in as a sort of parenthesis, not as the original, or final purpose of God.

It came in alongside of sin, between that and grace; to convince of sin and at the same time as a consequence, that transgressions might be multiplied (see Gal. iii. 19). Yet God, Who is the Author of law, is not responsible for the increase of sin. The law does not compel, but only impels to sin; it does not create, it only calls it forth. The question of law eliciting sin is to be dealt with in ch. vii. Hence, nothing that we have inherited from Adam settles our eternal destiny, but only our use of that nature. Sin lies dormant in the heart until law comes, and then sin is seen in actual transgression. The law by prescribing what is required gives rise to great occasions of offense on the part of sinful man.

VIII. *Reign of Sin and Reign of Grace* (ver. 21).—But although sin abounds through law, grace abounds "more exceedingly" in order that, as sin reigned in death, even so grace might reign through righteousness unto eternal life through Christ. Here again is the parallel. Whatever sin has brought, grace has brought still more. Righteousness will not fail because it is for ever.

As we review this great passage we must take care to enter into the fulness of the Apostle's meaning. Not only does he teach that what we have derived from the first Adam is met by what we have derived from Christ, but the transcendence of the work of Christ is almost infinite in extent.

> "The full meaning of Paul, however, is not grasped until we perceive that the benefits received from Christ, the Second Adam, are in *inverse ratio* to the disaster entailed by the first Adam. It is the *surplusage* of this grace that in Paul's presentation is commonly overlooked" (Mabie, *The Divine Reason of the Cross*, p. 116).

Dr. Mabie also aptly calls attention to the striking rendering, even though somewhat more a paraphrase than a translation, of this section by that classical scholar, Mr. A. S. Way:—

> "This First Man of the Old Life prefigures the destined First Man of the New Life: each gave a gift to humanity—the former the death-fraught transgression, the latter the free gift of Life. But note that transgression and this free gift are in *inverse proportion.* Through that one man's trespass the myriads of humanity died, I grant you; yet the disproportion is as nothing to the *measureless overflowings of the myriads of humanity of the fountain of the grace of God, and of His bounty conveyed by the grace embodied in this one man, Jesus the Messiah* . . . . If, in consequence of that single first transgression, death became king of men's lives, through the one man's demerit, all this will be *far more than compensated* when those who receive the *measureless wealth* of God's grace and God's gift of righteousness shall be kings in the New Life through the merit of the One, Jesus the Messiah" (*The Divine Reason of the Cross,* pp. 117, 118).

This chapter is full of wonderful teaching for the Christian life, and for personal and practical meditation it will be well to review the whole with special reference to the following points:—

1. *Two Aspects of Justification.*—"By faith" ver. 1); "by blood" (ver. 9).

2. *Three Causes of Boasting.*—"In hope of glory" (ver. 2); "in tribulations" (ver. 3); "in God" (ver. 11).

3. *Two Views of Salvation.*—"From wrath" (ver. 9); "in His life" (ver. 10).

4. *Four Aspects of Sin.*—A falling short (vers. 12, 20, 21); a going beyond (ver. 14); a falling aside (vers. 15, 16, 18, 20); a positive act; (ver. 19).

5. *Three Results of Sin.*—Judgment (vers. 16, 18); condemnation (vers. 16, 18); death (vers. 12, 15).

6. *Four effects of Redemption.*—A justifying fact (vers. 16, 18); a justifying result (ver. 17); a justifying process (ver. 18); a life arising out of justification (vers. 18, 21).

7. *Four Descriptions of Grace.*—Grace (ver. 15); gift of grace (ver. 16); free gift (ver. 15, 17); a boon (ver. 16).

8. *Three Expressions of Abundance.*—Grace and gift (ver. 15); abundance of grace and gift of righteousness (ver. 17); grace super-abounded (ver. 20).

9. *Four Reigns.*—Of sin (ver. 21); of death (vers. 14, 17); of grace (ver. 21); of believers (ver. 17).

10. *Five Comparisons.*—"Much more"; this phrase which occurs four times in the Greek (vers. 9, 10, 15, 17), and once in English (ver. 20), is the key to the entire passage. Whatever we have derived from Adam, we derive "much more" from Christ. Whatever the past may have been in relation to sin, "much more" will be the present and the future by reason of Christ's marvelous grace.

XXIII

THE FOUNT OF HOLINESS

ROM. vi. 1-14.

1. What shall we say, then? Shall we continue in sin, that grace may abound?
2. God forbid. How shall we, that are dead in sin, live any longer therein?
3. Know ye not, that so many of us as were baptized into Jesus Christ were baptized into his death?
4. Therefore we are buried with him by baptism into death: that like as Christ was raised up from the dead by the glory of the Father, even so we also should walk in newness of life.
5. For if we have been planted together in the likeness of his death, we shall be also *in the likeness* of *his* resurrection:
6. Knowing this, that our old man is crucified with *him*, that the body of sin might be destroyed, that henceforth we should not serve sin.
7. For he that is dead is freed from sin.
8. Now if we be dead with Christ, we believe that we shall also live with him:
9. Knowing that Christ being raised from the dead dieth no more; death hath no more dominion over him.
10. For in that he died, he died unto sin once: but in that he liveth, he liveth unto God.
11. Likewise reckon ye also yourselves to be dead indeed unto sin, but alive unto God through Jesus Christ our Lord.
12. Let not sin therefore reign in your mortal body, that ye should obey it in the lusts thereof.
13. Neither yield ye your members *as* instruments of unrighteousness unto sin: but yield yourselves unto God, as those that are alive from the dead, and your members *as* instruments of righteousness unto God.
14. For sin shall not have dominion over you: for ye are not under the law, but under grace.

HAVING now arrived at a turning-point in the Epistle, it will be well to view the path hitherto traversed. After the introduction (ch. i. 1-17) we saw that man's unrighteousness through sin demanded the provision of a Divine righteousness (ch. i. 18-iii. 20); that this righteousness from God is provided in Christ through faith (ch. iii. 21-31); that it is warranted by the Old Testament (ch. iv. 1-25); and that it is permanent (ch. v. 1-21). The last point, the permanence of this righteousness, was based on the relation of mankind as a whole to the two Adams, for just as in Adam's sin the whole race had been "constituted sinners," so in the Second Adam, the Lord from heaven, all believers were "constituted righteous." Thus an entirely new order of things was introduced where abounding grace reigns, through righteousness, in our Lord and Savior Jesus Christ.

But at once comes the important question of the life to be lived by the justified man. The past may have been met (ch. v.); but what about the present? This is the problem now to be considered. From ch. iii. 21 to ch. v. 21 the theme has been Justification by Faith in the Crucified Savior; now, from ch. vi. 1 to ch. viii. 39, it is Sanctification by Faith in the Risen Lord. "The matter in question is no longer to efface sin as guilt, but to overcome it as a power or disease." Justification is the strait gate through which we enter the narrow way of holiness, and from this point we are to deal with the way, not with the gate. Hitherto the contrast has been between wrath and justification; now it is to be between sin and holiness. The Apostle's exposition of justification is over, and though it will be referred to again it will only be as a foundation. We shall be concerned with the structure to be built on the basis of justification, and we shall see that justification is not only necessary to sanctification but secures it.

The transition is made by means of an objection (ch. vi. 1). Does not this doctrine of righteousness through faith give encouragement to sin? If grace abounds (ch. v. 21), may not sin abound still more? The Apostle's answer will be given. He will prove the serious and even awful error of such an objection, and will demonstrate that we are not to do evil that good may come (ch. iii. 8), and that his doctrine does indeed establish law (ch. iii. 31). "Unless there is a necessary connection between justification by faith and the new life, Paul fails to prove that faith establishes the law" (Denney).

But before looking at the chapter in detail it is necessary to view the general position. Union with Christ carries with it not one, but two results. First of all there is the efficacy of the Atonement for our guilty past as we share in the merits of Christ's death. On the basis of this the believer is accepted as righteous before God; but forgiveness alone makes no provision for righteousness of character and life, and consequently grace is needed to prevent a recurrence of the past. And so, secondly, there is the efficacy of the Resurrection for our unholy present as we share the power of Christ's life. Up to this point the Apostle has discussed the first, our judicial position; now comes the consideration of the second;our spiritual condition. Even already there have been hints given, as when he spoke of faith establishing law (ch. iii. 31); of our Lord raised for our justifying (ch. iv. 25); and of our being saved by His life (ch. v. 10). But of course the main thought up to the present has been that of reinstatement in position, not renewal of condition.

Before we limit ourselves to ch. vi. it seems essential to take a view of the three chapters (vi.-viii.) which concern this subject of deliverance from the power of sin. And as we shall see, the fundamental thought is that the believer is united to Christ. This new principle makes him dead to sin (ch. vi.); but it also provides a new power which enables him to be free from law (ch. vii.); and still more, it includes a new possibility, for in the gift of the Holy Spirit there is a new position for holiness (ch. viii.).

Now limiting ourselves to ch. vi. we must observe that the key is in verse 5, which of course refers to the present life, not to the future beyond the grave, and we are taught that the believer has been made vitally one with Christ, not as in the A.V., "planted together," but as it should be, "grown together," "combined by birth." The course of thought is given by means of two questions, verse 1 and verse 15; and the entire chapter may thus be summarized:—

(*a*) Verses 1-14: Continuance in sin is impossible to a justified man because of his union with Christ in death and life.

(*b*) Verses 15-23: Even acts of sin are unwarranted because of the believer's position "under grace," and because sin inevitably leads to bondage and death.

As we shall observe in the detailed study, the first question means, "Shall we sin in order to obtain grace?" and the second, "Shall we sin because we are in grace?" The answer of the Apostle is given in this chapter in the form of Declaration and of Exhortation; first a Declaration of what God hath done, and then an Exhortation as to what God expects of us. We have now to consider the first of these sections.

I. *A question* (ver. 1).—The question is asked: "Shall we continue in sin, that grace may abound?" Looking back over the whole section, and especially ch. v. 20., the point is, that if a superabundance of grace is a law of God's working, why may we not continue in sin in order to obtain more grace? If justification be by grace alone without works, why break off sin? Why not continue in it? Then grace will abound in pardoning sin more freely. In the doctrine of redemption by grace through the righteousness of the Second Adam human perversity finds occasion for sinning. It is as though a man should say, "If by the obedience of One I am constituted righteous and grace becomes superabundant, let me remain in sin that grace may continue to abound."

Before considering the Apostle's treatment of this question it is essential to observe that the very fact of such a question being possible shows with unmistakable clearness the true meaning of the Apostle's Doctrine of Justification. It must mean "to regard as righteous," and not "to make righteous"; or else the question now put would be utterly pointless. If Justification means to *make* a person good, then no license to sin could have been inferred from it; but since God by His grace "justifies the ungodly" (ch. iii. 24), the question is important and demands an answer; and the answer does not in the least modify the freeness of the Apostle's teaching on Grace, but shows the profound depth of his teaching on Justification as involved in union with Christ. "If sanctification and renewal form a constituent element and integral factor in the notion of justification, the question "Shall we continue in sin that grace may abound?" has neither reason nor meaning" (Philippi, *Romans*, p. 288). It is particularly important to observe this point, for it proves beyond all question what the Apostle means by Justification.[1]

II. *A Protest* (ver. 2).—Mark how the Apostle commences his treatment of this solemn subject. First of all, he repels the suggestion with scorn. "God forbid." "Let it not be." He shows its utter shamefulness. "We who died to sin, how shall we any longer live therein?" Thus he repels the question as impius before he commences to refute it as wrong. Such is the evil heart, that it has a tendency to turn grace into license, and it is this that calls forth the Apostle's righteous indignation. "True morality is not only not imperilled, but is furthered by the reception of God's righteousness in Christ" (Liddon).

The rendering of the A.V., "We that are dead," needs correction into "We who died," or "We who have died." So also in verses 7, 8, 11; Col. ii. 20; iii. 3; 2 Tim. ii. 11. The change of rendering enables us to understand much more clearly our intimate and essential union with our Lord in His death. We died when He died.

III. *A Reminder* (vers. 3, 4).—Now the Apostle proceeds with his teaching after administering his rebuke. "Or are ye ignorant?" This clearly implies that they ought to have known what was involved in their union with Christ in His death. When Christ died, believers died in Him; and, as dead men cannot sin, so union with Christ Who died involves absolute severance from sin and continuance in it no more. And, if they do not know what death to sin means, he will explain it, by showing to them, what they themselves ought already to have known, namely, the truth which was involved in their acceptance of Jesus Christ. Their union with Him involved union in His death, burial, and resurrection, and at each stage they were so united from the movement of their acceptance of Him as their Savior that everything of spiritual power in His death, burial, and resurrection was theirs also, and at their disposal.

The view of the Cross is thus widened to take in Sanctification as well as Justification, to deal with sinfulness as well as with sins,

[1]The discussion of this great truth in ch. xiv. of Bishop Moule's *Romans* in the "Expositor's Bible" should carefully be studied.

to apply to what we *are* as well as what we *do*; and Sanctification is shown to rest on the same foundation, and to proceed from the same source as Justification, namely, our union with Christ in His death, burial, and resurrection.

We must carefully notice the two aspects of the death of Christ. There is a death *for* sin in which our Lord is unique as our Redeemer. He was made a curse for us, and we have no share in this work. He did it all. As our atonement, He is absolutely alone. But there is also a death *to* sin, which means that sin ceases to have a place in life. It is the latter point which is dwelt upon here and in verse 10. Christ died to sin once for all, to expiate it and to destroy it, thereby robbing it of its penal power for the believer. Thus Sanctification and Justification come from the same source, union with Christ, and are inseparably connected. This point is hinted at in Gal. ii. 20, and 2 Cor. v. 15, but is here made clear as an essential view of the Apostle's Christianity.[1]

IV. *A Consequence* (vers. 5, 6).—Christians should therefore realize what is implied in Christ's death and resurrection. If they have been vitally connected with Him in the one, then necessarily they will also be vitally connected with Him in the other (ver. 5). They know that their unregenerate self ("old man") was crucified with Christ on the Cross in order that the body, in so far as it is the servant or instrument of sin, might be rendered powerless with regard to sin, and prevented from serving it any more (ver. 6).

This is an important verse, and we must clearly distinguish between "our old man," "the body of sin," and "we." The first of these, "our old man," means "our old self"; what we were as unregenerate sons of Adam. It must not be identified with "the flesh,"

[1]Most writers consider that the Apostle has in view the ordinance of Baptism, and that the passage teaches its symbolical meaning. The usual interpretation is that Baptism symbolizes union with Christ in His death, that the sign stands for the thing signified, and that Baptism as a symbol of faith expresses in outward profession our union with Christ. This may be the correct interpretation, and is so stated by the large majority of commentators. But it is at least significant that the ideas of death, burial, and resurrection in the passage are all purely spiritual and are considered quite apart from literal ordinances; so that to be consistent in our interpretation the Baptism also should be spiritual. Besides, whatever the passage means, the burial is not expressed in symbolical language, but as taking place *by*, or *through* Baptism. This, as Bruce aptly points out, if made to apply to the ordinance, introduces very serious difficulties into the Apostle's thought. If, however, the whole passage is interpreted of the believer's spiritual union with Christ's death, burial, and resurrection, everything is consistent and perfectly clear.

or "our sinful nature." The phrase only occurs here, in Eph. iv. 22, and in Col. iii. 9. The "old man" ceased to exist at our regeneration, when it was "put off." We are never exhorted to "put off" the "old man." A careful study of the three passages shows that it is regarded as in the past. An exhortation to "put off the old man" would be tantamount to an exhortation to become regenerate. "The body of sin" does not mean in our modern terminology, "the mass of sin," or that sin has its source in the body. It simply means that the body is the seat, or instrument of sin. The "we" of this verse means our real self as united to Christ. The word rendered "destroyed" should also be carefully observed. It does not mean "annihilated," but "reduced to a state of inaction and impotence." It implies the "inertness" of sin in the believer's life through union with Christ in His death. Thus while it approximates as nearly as possible to the thought of literal destruction, it significantly stops short of it, and shows that sin is not destroyed but only robbed of its power by the counteracting principle of union with Christ. A similar usage of the term is found in Heb. ii. 14, where, quite obviously, it cannot possibly mean the annihilation of the Devil.

V. *A Principle* (ver. 7).—A dead man is discharged from sin and emancipated from it. Death cancels obligations and breaks all ties, so that our connection with sin was broken off at the Cross, and the bondage by which we were formerly held in its fetters was destroyed by our union with Christ. This general maxim about death putting an end to bondage is thus used to confirm the view of the believer's relation to sin. He is released both from the penalty of sin, and also (in union with Christ) from the power of sin. Union with Christ removes penalties and provides an opening for streams of grace to flow into the soul.

VI. *A Conviction* (ver. 8).—"If we died with Christ we believe that we shall also live with Him." Death to sin thus liberates for a new life, and as we were united with Him in His death we are confident that we shall also be united in everything that His resurrection means. If we did not die with Him we have no ground for expecting that we shall live with Him; but if we were united with Him in His death, then we can say with St. Paul, "the life which

I now live in the flesh I live by the faith of the Son of God" (Gal. ii. 20). We must be careful to observe that the "if" in this verse does not imply any doubt, but, on the contrary, assumes a fact.

VII. *A Proof* (vers. 9, 10).—This is the confirmation of the conviction of the preceding verse. We know that Christ having been raised from the dead dies no more. He is no longer in a world disturbed by sin, and no longer lorded over by death, for the death that He died He died unto sin "once for all," but the life that He lives He lives unto God. This statement of our Lord's death as "once for all" seems clearly to indicate the expiatory power of His atonement, that Christ paid all the claims of death on behalf of His people, and that it has now no claim whatever on them.

VIII. *A Call* (ver. 11).—"Even so also reckon ye yourselves to be dead unto sin, but alive unto God in Christ Jesus." In virtue of our Lord's death and resurrection, the Christian is to keep on reckoning himself to have similarly died to all that is sinful, and in the same way to be living unto God. We must be careful not to weaken this profound statement of our death to sin in union with Christ. After the Apostle's wonderful statement of salvation as a gift to believers in Christ (ch. iii. 21-v. 21), we cannot be content with any mere idea, in verse 6, of a subjective death in the heart of the believer. The Apostle widens his view of grace by taking a wider view of the Cross, and shows the fuller meaning of Calvary.

We must also be particularly careful to note that "dead to sin" does not mean the death of sin as a power in the heart. The Apostle does not say that sin is dead to us, but that we in Christ are dead to it, and that we are to keep on reckoning ourselves to be so with the reckoning of simple faith. As Godet points out:—

> "The Christian's breaking with sin is undoubtedly gradual in its realization, but absolute and conclusive in its principle. As, in order to break really with an old friend whose evil influence is felt, half measures are insufficient, and the only efficacious means is a frank explanation, followed by a complete rupture, which remains like a barrier raised beforehand against every new solicitation; so to break with sin there is needed a decisive and radical act, a divine deed taking possession of the soul, and interposing henceforth between the will of the believer and sin (Gal. vi. 14). This divine deed necessarily works through the action of faith in the sacrifice of Christ" (*Commentary on the Romans*, vol. i., p. 404).

Thus the Apostle has shown the new principle of Sanctification and thereby has answered the taunt of his accusers:—

> "He meets them not at all by modifications of his assertions. He has not a work to say about additional and corrective conditions precedent to our peace with God. He makes no impossible hint that Justification means the making of us good, or that Faith is a 'short title' for Christian practice. No; there is no reason for such assertions either in the nature of words, or in the whole cast of the argument through which he has led us. What does he do? He takes this great truth of our acceptance in Christ our Merit, and puts it unreserved, unrelieved, unspoiled, in contact with other truth, of co-ordinate, nay, of superior greatness, for it is the truth to which Justification leads us, as way to end. He places our acceptance through Christ Atoning in organic connection with our life in Christ Risen. . . . The two truths are concentrated as it were into one, by their equal relation to the same Person, the Lord. The previous argument has made us intensely conscious that Justification, while a definite transaction in law, is not a mere transaction; it lives and glows with the truth of connection with a Person. That Person is the Bearer for us of all Merit. But He is also, and equally, the Bearer for us of new Life; in which the sharers of His Merit share, for they are in Him. So that, while the way of Justification can be isolated for study, as it has been in this Epistle, the justified man cannot be isolated from Christ, who is his life. And thus he can never *ultimately* be considered apart from his possession, in Christ, of a new possibility, a new power, a new and glorious call to living holiness" (Moule, *The Epistle to the Romans,* pp. 159, 160).

Sanctification is thus seen to be implied in Justification as the second of two parts of our redemption in Christ. Christ is at once our righteousness and our sanctification (1 Cor. i. 30).

IX. *A Command* (vers. 12-13).—Now the Apostle exhorts them not to allow sin to reign as king in their bodies. This appeal naturally follows from the foregoing teaching. In this "mortal body," that part of us which is destined to die, we who are risen with Christ are for a time open to the temptations of sin and Satan, and we have to resist all efforts to lead us from loyalty to the will of God into subjection to the sinful tendencies of our evil nature. We must not let that mortal part of us be our king. On the contrary, we are to present ourselves to God as those who are alive from the dead, and are to place all our faculties at His disposal for His service. We must prove that we are in reality what we reckon ourselves to be. In this world two claimants are continually seeking us—God, and Satan; and, as the believer has entered into the kingdom of Christ and is united to Him in death and life, he is to devote himself loyally to his Master, and to present every faculty for his Master's use and service in righteousness. It is impossible to avoid noticing the implication of this verse. When the Apostle tells us not to allow sin to reign in our body, he manifestly implies that sin is in it, and that the believer's life cannot therefore imply what is often described as sinlessness.

X. *A Promise* (ver. 14).—A promise fitly concludes this teaching, confirming all that has gone before, especially the appeals of verses 12 and 13. Sin will not, shall not lord it over us, for the simple reason that we are no longer "under law but under grace." This verse is the transition to the next section. In verses 1-11 the Apostle has shown what it means to be united to Christ; in verses 12 and 13 he has shown the consequences and made his appeal to the believer; and now in verse 14 he assures us of the Divine provision for the complete fulfilment of these exhortations. We may take it either as a promise, "Sin shall not"—or else as a Divine assurance, "Sin will not"—have dominion over us.

As we review these verses we shall see that sin is dealt with as a ruling power, as a master, just as in chs. i.-iv. it was treated as an offense, or a disease. The Cross of Christ has not only separated us from the consequences of sin as transgression; it has separated us from the authority of sin as a lord. Christ *for* us means deliverance from penalty; and our union with Christ means deliverance from power.

In these verses we have specially brought before us the human side of Christian holiness, those aspects of holiness which refer to our attitude and duty. Let us give special attention to the following key-words of holiness:—

1. "*Reckon.*"—This is an attitude of faith, not of feeling. It is a calculation based on facts, and may perhaps be described as mathematical rather than emotional. Faith is "to conclude about ourselves what God has declared about us" (Stifler). God reckons us to have died with Christ. We are, therefore, to keep on reckoning ourselves to have died and to have risen with Him. When Christ died, we died; when He rose, we rose. We are to keep on reckon-

ing these facts as absolutely true, and then, as we reckon them, they will become powerful in our lives, for we become what we reckon ourselves to be. When sin makes its appeal we must refuse to recognize it by reckoning that we died to it in Christ, and at once it will go, its power broken. In the same way, when we long to be holy, we simply reckon that we are alive to God in Christ, and, as we reckon this to be true, the power of God's grace will flood our souls. Then we shall see that the Christian life is not a constant battle but a constant victory. Godet uses an illustration which, as he truly says, proves how this saying of the Apostle, apparently so mysterious, "finds an easy explanation in the light of the lively experience of faith.":—

> "The missionary Casilis told us that he was one day questioning a converted Bechuana as to the meaning of a passage analogous to that before us (Col. iii. 3). The latter said to him; Soon I shall be dead, and they will bury me in my field. My flocks will come to pasture above me. But I shall no longer hear them, and I shall not come forth from my tomb to take them and carry them with me to the sepulchre. They will be strange to me, as I to them. Such is the image of my life in the midst of the world since I believed in Christ'" (*Romans*, vol. i., p. 407, note).

2. "*Let not sin reign.*"—This follows as a consequence from the foregoing, and the present tense of the verb is specially noteworthy. It implies a continuous attitude and action of the believer; because of our oneness with Christ in His death and life we are not for an instant to allow any dominion of sin in our being. If it were possible so to render the words, we should say, "Keep on not allowing sin to be king in your mortal body." Herein lies our personal responsibility. Because of what Christ is we are not to allow sin to be our lord.

3. "*Present.*"—This is the other side of truth. Negatively, we are not to allow sin to be our master. Positively, we are to present ourselves to God for His use and service. The tenses of the verb are striking here also. "Do not keep on presenting your members as weapons of unrighteousness to sin, but once for all present yourselves to God as those who are living from the dead, and your

members as weapons of righteousness for God." It is the presentation of ourselves, the deliberate choice based upon our position in Christ Jesus in order that we may be used of God, and serve Him daily in righteousness and true holiness.

The practical, daily, and even momentary use of each of these three key-words will give us the secret of perpetual holiness.

XXIV

CONTINUANCE IN SINNING

ROM. vi. 15-23.

15. What then? shall we sin, because we are not under the law, but under grace? God forbid.
16. Know ye not, that to whom ye yield yourselves servants to obey, his servants ye are to whom ye obey; whether of sin unto death, or of obedience unto righteousness?
17. But God be thanked, that ye were the servants of sin, but ye have obeyed from the heart that form of doctrine which was delivered you.
18. Being then made free from sin, ye became the servants of righteousness.
19. I speak after the manner of men because of the infirmity of your flesh: for as ye have yielded your members servants to uncleanness and to iniquity; even so now yield your members servants to righteousness unto holiness.
20. For when ye were the servants of sin, ye were free from righteousness.
21. What fruit had ye then in those things whereof ye are now ashamed? for the end of those things *is* death.
22. But now being made free from sin, and become servants to God, ye have your fruit unto holiness, and the end everlasting life.
23. For the wages of sin *is* death; but the gift of God *is* eternal life through Jesus Christ our Lord.

THE Apostle is still concerned to show the utter incompatibility of Justification with continuance in sin, and the subject is discussed by means of a fresh question which follows after that in verse 1. He has shown the new principle of union with Christ; now he will show its practical power, especially in the light of his great statement of verse 14, "Ye are . . . under grace."

We have already noticed that verse 14 is transitional, at once summing up the former section and introducing what follows. It is important to see how it governs the entire section onwards to the end of ch. viii.: (*a*) ch. vi. 15-23, what "under law" does *not* mean; (*b*) ch. vii., what "under law" *does* mean; (*c*) ch. viii., what "under grace" means.

I. *The New Problem* (ver. 15).—There is a close relation between the two questions, as we may readily see by putting them in parallel lines.

Verse 1. "Shall we continue in sin *in order that* grace may abound?"

Verse 15. "Are we to practice sin *because* grace does abound?"

Thus the wording of the question is seen to differ. "Shall we continue in sin?" (ver. 1). "Shall we sin?" (ver. 15). And the reason is different; "that grace may abound" (ver. 1); "because we are not under law but under grace" (ver. 15). The first question is "Shall we continue *in* sin?" The second is "Shall we continue *to* sin?" The former deals with the permanent state; the latter with the isolated act. The Apostle has already shown that the justified believer will not be able to continue the life of sin which he formerly led. He has now to show that he will not even commit a single act of sin, if he realizes what it means to be "under grace."

The reason why we are not to sin needs careful attention. "Because we are not under law but under grace." "Under law" means ruled by law as the principle of a covenant of works. Law commands but it cannot control. It orders but it cannot enable. Being "under law" implies at least three things:—(1) a Divine commandment ordering perfect obedience; (2) a Divine promise of reward for perfect obedience; (3) a Divine threatening of punishment for falling short of perfect obedience. This at once proves the utter futility and powerlessness of attempting to live "under law." Now the Apostle will show what it means to be "under grace," and that, as such, it is simply impossible to do actions of sin. "Under grace" implies at least two things:—(1) a revelation of the Divine attitude and will as gracious; (2) a Divine bestowment of inward power to obey. Thus, "under grace" cannot possibly mean license to sin.

II. *The New Protest* (ver. 15).—Again we have the Apostle's indignant "God forbid," as the prelude to a careful statement of the true position. Let us observe his phrase, "Know ye not?" We have already had it in verse 3, and it will come again in ch. vii. 1. But it is particularly noteworthy that, while the first question (ver. 1) is met by the fact of our union with Christ, the present question is met by an appeal to various motives characteristic of those who are united to Christ. He will show that our service betokens the Master served, and that if we sin it is a proof that Christ is not our Master. Godet records that one day Vinet said to him, "There is a subtle poison which insinuates itself into the heart even of the best Christian; it is the temptation to say: Let us sin not *that* grace may abound, but *because* it abounds."

III. *The New Obligations* (vers. 16-18).—Grace reveals and empowers for new obligations. There is a new subjection to righteousness by means of which grace displaces the old subjection to sin. We can choose our Master, but, once we have chosen, we must perforce obey. What a slave shall do is thus absolutely determined by the master to whom he belongs. This new service is our deliberate choice, but once it has been made we are necessarily under the decisive control of the One to whom we belong. The Apostle in reminding them of this great principle, thanks God (ver. 17) that although they had been in former days the bondslaves of sin, they had obeyed from the heart that "mould of doctrine unto which you were handed over." The thought of the believer being placed into a mould and taking shape from it by obedience from the heart is vivid and suggestive. Thus he reminds them of the blessed and holy contrast between their past and their present. This phrase, "Thanks be to God," is characteristic of St. Paul in several connections (ch. vii. 25; 1 Cor. xv. 57; 2 Cor. ii. 14; viii. 16; ix. 15). The result was that, being freed from sin, they became the servants of righteousness (ver. 18), a still more definite statement of the happy change in their life. There is no intermediate moral condition between the one service and the other.

IV. *The New Duties* (vers. 19, 20).—Grace also reveals and equips for new duties. In the past there had been a yielding to uncleanness and sin. Now there is to be a yielding to righteousness with a view to holiness. A transfer of moral energy is thus to take place as we serve our new Master. He uses this illustration of slavery by reason of their lack of spiritual discernment to see all that was really involved in the death of Christ. Bishop Moule thinks that St. Paul as it were apologizes for the superficial repulsiveness of the metaphor, especially as so many of his readers were actually slaves. He uses the illustration of a human bond of man to man, because their yet imperfect state enfeebles their spiritual perception, and demands a harsh paradox to fit it. Of course the weakness here mentioned is not to be confounded with sin. It is not moral, but intellectual and spiritual weakness which makes him thus explain why he uses the illustration.

V. *The New Rewards* (vers. 21-23).—Grace also reveals and guarantees new rewards. First, an appeal is made to their past experience (ver. 21). What were the then existing results of their former service? Surely the only outcome was death. Then in contrast he turns to their present (ver. 22). They have exchanged the service of Satan for the service of God, and they have fruit unto holiness and everlasting life as the culmination. Last of all he states the general law of God's moral universe (ver. 23). "The wages of sin is death, but the gift of God is eternal life." We must never forget that this passage is an appeal to the Christian and not to the sinner, and any use made of it for evangelistic purposes must not set aside the primary application of it to those who are in Christ Jesus. Wages are what is earned, but life is God's free gift. The ruin of sin is earned as a right, but Christ's reward is His own blessed and holy gift to the soul.

Thus the second question is answered. Sinning is absolutely impossible to those who realize and maintain their union with Christ. Union with Him in His death means cessation from the exercise of sin; union with Him in His life means the communication of new life and power.

We have already seen the human side of holiness. The Apostle now bids us look at the Divine side; those aspects of the Divine provision which enable the believer to be holy.

1. *The Promise.*—"Sin shall not have dominion over you." What an assurance this is! It is a promise of infinite meaning, for it speaks of deliverance and freedom for all who are united to

Christ. It is not merely God's desire and purpose. It is His divine decree that we shall conquer in every fight, and never even for a moment be consciously enslaved by the deceit and power of sin. He has provided for us such an abundance of grace that we "may reign in life by Christ Jesus." His purpose for us is a life of perpetual victory and therein of perpetual blessing. How generous are these thoughts and assurances in contrast to our own narrow faithless and hopeless attitude! Shall we not rest our souls afresh on these wonderful words? "Sin *shall* not have dominion," and therefore "Sin *will* not have dominion." We remember that the ten spies said that "the land is good but we are unable to possess it." But we also recall the words of Caleb and Joshua; "We are well able." So, as the soul contemplates even the awful possibilities of sin, it can rest secure in the promise and assurance of Christ, and be "strong in the Lord and in the power of His might."

2. *The Provision.*—"Ye are . . . under grace." It has been well pointed out that in this statement we have a principle of daily living of the very first importance. If I choose deliberately to place myself under the control of grace, by surrendering to Christ and entering into union with Him, grace will necessarily and inevitably work in me and through me. It is as if a man chooses to put himself in front of a large fire, when it is no longer within his choice whether he will feel warm. The law of nature works independently of him from the moment and in so far as he places himself under its sway. So the Christian cannot sin, in so far as he places himself under the control of Divine grace. We submit ourselves to its influence, and then the power commences to operate on our lives, and will produce its spiritual effects. It is at this point that we are enabled to see the transforming and uplifting influence of grace in the soul. "Under grace," our whole inner being becomes affected and directed into other and higher reaches of living. "Did you not say," said a man once to a Christian, "if a man is a Christian he can live as he likes?" "Yes," was the reply, "I did." "Well, then," rejoined the former; "come with me to the theater tonight." "Ah!" said the other, "But I don't *like*." When we "delight ourselves in the Lord," He undoubtedly gives us "the desires of our heart," but they are

no longer our desires but His, for since we have put ourselves "under grace," we delight ourselves in the God of grace. It is open to our choice to go near the fire, or not to do so, but if we go, the law of nature commences to work. So in regard to things mental and spiritual; if we allow our mind to fix itself upon some particular theme, it will have its effect on us apart from any further interference. All that we can do is to select the influence to which we are willing to submit ourselves, and when we subject ourselves thereto it commences to operate independently of us because we are under its sway. Union with Christ is thus a union of life which brings power, and the deliverance is at once from sin and from sinning.

3. *The Position.*—"In Christ Jesus our Lord." Observe the note of triumph with which the chapter ends in these words. Thus the Apostle closes this part of his Doctrine of Sanctification. The same note of triumph is found at the end of ch. v., "through Jesus Christ our Lord." We see it again, at the end of ch. vii., "through Jesus Christ our Lord." And yet once more, at the end of ch. viii., "in Christ Jesus our Lord." This is the true key-note of the Christian life, the triumphant consciousness of union with Christ. From justification and sanctification come courage, confidence, joy, and boasting, as we "triumph in the Name of the Lord our God."

XXV

NOT UNDER LAW

Rom. vii. 1-6.

1. Know ye not, brethren, (for I speak to them that know the law,) how that the law hath dominion over a man as long as he liveth?
2. For the woman which hath an husband is bound by the law to *her* husband so long as he liveth; but if the husband be dead, she is loosed from the law of *her* husand.
3. So then if, while *her* husband liveth, she be married to another man, she shall be called an adulteress: but if her husband be dead, she is free from that law; so that she is no adulteress, though she be married to another man.
4. Wherefore, my brethren, ye also are become dead to the law by the body of Christ; that ye should be married to another, *even* to him who is raised from the dead, that we should bring forth fruit unto God
5. For when we were in the flesh, the motions of sins, which were by the law, did work in our members to bring forth fruit unto death.
6. But now we are delivered from the law, that being dead wherein we were held; that we should serve in newness of spirit, and not *in* the oldness of the letter.

In ch. vi. we have seen set forth union with Christ, whereby the Christian has become dead to sin and made alive to God. In verse 14, "Ye are not under law, but under grace," we have the method of this holy life and the secret of sin having no more dominion over us. Now that the Apostle has made clear what he meant by "Ye are under grace," it remains for him to explain with equal clearness "Ye are not under law." This is the subject of ch. vii.

It was essential that he should deal thus definitely with law, and at last he comes to this subject of its true function, which hitherto has only been hinted at. He has already shown (ch. ii.) that the law did not enable the Jew, or any man (ch. iii.) to attain righteousness by works, but only to arrive at a knowledge of sin (ch.

iii. 20); that law has no part in the revelation of God's righteousness except as a witness (ch. iii. 21); that as a law of works it could not exclude man's boasting (ch. iii. 27); that it was not attached to the inheritance of Abraham's blessings as a condition (ch. iv. 13); that it works wrath (ch. iv. 15); that its effect was multiplication of transgression (ch. v. 14, 20); and that thus under law men were brought into bondage through sin (ch. vi. 14). This negative and disparaging view of law must have been a great stumbling-block both to Jewish and Gentile Christians, and it was essential for Paul to show that it was not binding on them in their relation to God. The necessity was all the greater because he had defended justification by faith from these very Scriptures of the law (ch. iv.). Thus his exposition would necessarily be a genuine encouragement and comfort to believing Jews and Gentiles, and for the same reason it is useful to us today, because of the inherent tendency in human nature to attempt to save itself by law.

Now let us observe carefully what the Apostle has to say. In ch. iii. 20 we have law in relation to justification; in ch. v. 20, law in relation to sin; in ch. vi. 14, law in relation to believers. These three points are now taken up *in the reverse order*, and are carefully elaborated. In ch. vii. 1-6 he shows that the Christian is "not under law" (ch. vi. 14), and how and why he has been delivered. In verses 7-13 he shows that the law is not sinful, even though it makes sin to abound (ch. v. 20). In verses 14-25 he shows that no man can be saved by law because law cannot deliver from the flesh (ch. iii. 20). Thus the whole chapter is concerned with the great truth that law is unable to save from indwelling sin.

The close connection of this chapter with the preceding one must carefully be noticed, and clearly understood. In ch. vi. 21, 22, the Apostle has spoken of fruitfulness and service, and these come to the believer by reason of his union with Christ. But something more is necessary in the way of teaching, for this fruitfulness and service can only come in connection with deliverance from law; and, if the Apostle did not show this, he would leave the Christian man in bondage, not for salvation, but for sanctification and service, struggling in a hard, legal way to please God, instead of finding his source and spring of joyous service in union with Christ. This instruction about the law is therefore necessary, because of the danger to believers being in bondage to law, and not enjoying the liberty of grace. As we shall see, the conflict of this chapter does not represent the normal experience of the Christian soul, and indeed, only in verses 4 and 6 is there any statement whatever of what Christians ought to be and enjoy in Christ.

1. *The Illustration* (vers. 1-3).—The opening words, "Or are ye ignorant?" show how close and essential is the connection with the preceding chapter. What is the precise force of the alternative "Or"? Perhaps it means, after ch. vi. 23, "Or if you are afraid to yield yourselves to your new master, Grace, and think you must still have an external rule like the law, listen to what I now have to say." It should also be noticed that the words, "I speak to men who know the law," necessarily refer to Jews rather than to Gentiles. This can be seen still more clearly by contrast in the phrase, "I speak to you Gentiles" (ch. xi. 13; *cf.* ch. vii. 4, "my brethren"). The Apostle reminds his Jewish brethren of the great principle, that the power of law is terminated by death, and he uses the illustration of a wife who has been freed by the death of her husband to marry another. "As long as he lives" is the key to the Apostle's use of the illustration. The main thought is that death dissolves legal obligation, and that on the death of her husband a wife is legally free to contract another marriage.

II. *The Application* (vers. 4-6).—Let us now follow the Apostle very carefully in order to see the true idea of the passage and his use of the illustration.

1. The "wife" is that inmost self or personality which is the same under all conditions of existence: "I myself."

2. The first husband is "our old man" (ch. vi. 6), our unregenerate self; and as long as he was alive we were under his law.

3. The death of the first husband is the crucifixion of the "old man" with Christ (ch. vi. 6).

4. The wife, set free through her first husband's death and thereby become dead to the law of that husband, is the soul set free by the crucifixion of the old man and thereby made dead to its law.

The first husband being "the old man," verse 6 is to be rendered; "Having died in that (old man) whereby we were held, the "old man" being the bond by which alone the law had dominion over us in our ego. With Godet we may therefore summarize thus the contents of these verses:—

> "As by His death Christ entered upon an existence set free from every legal statute and determined by the life of God alone, so we, when we have died to sin, enter with Him into this same life in which, like a re-married widow, we have no other master than this new Spouse and His Spirit" (*Romans,* vol. ii. p. 8).

This interpretation follows quite closely the view set forth by Gifford. It must be confessed that there are very few commentators who are clear on this point.[1] It is necessary to beware of thinking that the Apostle uses the illustration inaccurately, as though in the illustration the husband dies and the woman lives, while in the spiritual application the wife dies and the husband lives. This is to confuse matters entirely, and is as unnecessary as it is impossible, if only we will allow the Apostle to guide us step by step. We may surely believe that he knew what he was doing in using this simile. Any intelligent explanation of the illustration requires that what the first husband represents should correspond to what the second is, and we know that the second represents the Lord Jesus Christ. It would, therefore, be altogether incongruous to speak of a woman as having for her first husband an impersonal law, and for her second a living person. Besides, verse 2 clearly distinguishes between the law and the first husband, so that the law cannot be the first husband. The first marriage was that between the "mind" and the "flesh"; between the essential "I myself" and our old unregenerate being, and this union has been brought to an end by our unregenerate self being united to Christ in His death, whereby the soul (I myself) is free for union with the risen Lord.

In this passage three aspects of the Christian life are suggested which practically sum up the whole of Christianity.

---

[1]So far as I have been able to discover, the following are the only commentators who take the view mentioned in the text: Olshausen, Gifford, Sanday and Headlam, Headlam (*Expository Times,* vol. vi. p. 356), Garvie, Du Bose, Forbes, and (with modifications) Stifler, and D. Brown.

1. *Union with Christ.*—Three times the Apostle asks the question, "Know ye not?" In ch. vi. 3, "Know ye not" that the old life is impossible by reason of our oneness with Christ? In ch. vi. 16, "Know ye not" that the old service is impossible by reason of our union with Christ? And in ch. vii. 1, "Know ye not" that the old union is impossible because of our new union with Christ? In ch. v. the Apostle mentioned two Heads, Adam and Christ; in ch. vi. two Masters, Sin and Christ; and now in ch. vii. two Husbands, our Old Man and the Risen Christ. Thus under this figure of marriage the Apostle teaches in the fullest form what union with Christ really means. As marriage is the highest form of earthly union, so the spiritual union suggested here transcends every other aspect. Let us ponder this wonderful thought of the believer's union with the Lord Jesus Christ. The penalty of the law has been paid. He has been crucified with Christ, his former connection with the law has gone for ever and a new Bridegroom claims his heart as He betroths him to Himself for ever. The late Marcus Rainsford, Senr., thus applies this truth:—

> "Let faith ring these bells of heaven for our joy. Married to Christ. Himself the measure of our responsibilities; Himself the fulness of our capabilities; Himself the possessor of our hearts' affections; Himself the security of our hopes; Himself the well-spring of our fruitfulness; Himself the law of our hearts, our glory, and our crown. Blessed are they that are called to the marriage supper of the Lamb" (*Lectures on Romans,* vii. p. 28).

2. *Fruitfulness.*—As in ch. vi. 21, 22, so here again, the Apostle shows that our union with Christ enables us to "bring forth fruit unto God." "Fruit" is the expression of life and may be said to indicate character rather than conduct. The "fruit of the Spirit" in its nine-fold description is an expression of the believer's character as indwelt by the Spirit of God. So in this chapter, our union with Christ the Risen Lord necessarily results in fruitfulness to His praise.

3. *Service.*—From union and fruitfulness will come service. "In Christ" we not only "walk in newness of life" (ch. vi. 4), but "serve in newness of spirit" (ch. vii. 6). The contrast between the

service of ch. vi. and the present section is very striking. There it was the service of a slave; here it is the service of a wife to a husband. The service of a slave, or even of a faithful servant, is altogether different from the loving devotion of a wife to a husband, and this is the simile here used. The new obligation involved in the new position enables the soul to serve, apart from all bondage and labor, Him "Whose service is perfect freedom," or, as the terse Latin of the Collect has it, "Whom to serve is to reign." It should be observed that verse 6 gives the theme of ch. viii.; fruitfulness and service to God in newness of spirit. After the discussion in the remainder of this chapter we shall see how wonderfully these things are wrought in us and through us in the power of the Spirit of God.

XXVI

LAW AND SIN

Rom. vii. 7-13.

7. What shall we say then? *Is* the law sin? God forbid. Nay, I had not known sin, but by the law: for I had not known lust, except the law said, Thou shalt not covet.

8. But sin, taking occasion by the commandment, wrought in me all manner of concupiscence. For without the law sin *was* dead.

9. For I was alive without the law once: but when the commandment came, sin revived, and I died.

10. And the commandment, which *was ordained* to life, I found *to be* unto death.

11. For sin, taking occasion by the commandment, deceived me, and by it slew *me*.

12. Wherefore the law *is* holy, and the commandment holy, and just, and good.

13. Was then that which is good made death unto me? God forbid. But sin that it might appear sin, working death in me by that which is good; that sin by the commandment might become exceeding sinful.

At this point the thought of ch. v. 20 is taken up, discussing the question whether the law is sinful because it makes sin abound. The Apostle has already spoken of our being dead to sin, and also dead to law. The objector might at once say that such statements clearly imply that the law belongs to the same evil category of sin, for if the believer is to break from law as decisively as from sin, is there not something wrong or unworthy in law? Thus verses 7-25 really take up the phrase of verse 6, "in oldness of letter." The Apostle commences by indignantly crying out, "God forbid," and then proceeds to show the relation of law to sin. He gives a picture of all men under law in order to show why death to law is a part of the Gospel.

I. *Law Reveals the Fact of Sin* (ver. 7).—Paul looks back on his own experience, either as a child or in his unregenerate state before he became conscious of moral responsibility, and he tells us that he did not know it was wrong to covet until the law said, "Thou shalt not." All through this passage the depth and intensity of feeling expressed shows that the material must be autobiographical.

II. *Law Reveals the Occasion of Sin* (ver. 8).—What he has said does not mean that the law was sin, or brought sin, but that the law when revealed to Paul woke up the sin that was already existing in his heart. Law was not the cause, but the occasion of sin. Observe carefully the phrase, "apart from the law," an expression that occurs three times in the Epistle (here and in ch. iv. 15; vii. 8, 9). Apart from law sin could not make its presence known as sin, for it remained unrecognized. It is knowledge of the requirements of the Divine law that makes sin effective in the conscience of man. Although, apart from law, a man may be conscious of evil acts, yet law is needed to reveal the presence of sin in the nature.

III. *Law Reveals the Power of Sin* (ver. 9).—Before the law came he himself was alive and sin was dormant, practically dead, in his heart. But when the commandment with its "Thou shalt not" came to him, sin rose to life and he himself felt utterly condemned to death. Thus law soon reveals the awful force of evil within us, like a curb to an unruly horse, though it is never the cause, only the occasion of sin. The commandment which God intended for life is thus found by the sinful heart to be unto death.

IV. *Law Reveals the Deceitfulness of Sin* (ver. 11).—Through the commandments sin takes advantage of us and beguiles us. We know it is the demand of the law, and when we endeavor to fulfil it we are soon made to realize the hopelessness of our position.

V. *Law Reveals the Effect of Sin* (vers. 10, 11).—The outcome is death: "unto death" (ver. 10), "slew me" (ver 11). Whenever a commandment is unable to give life it necessarily brings about death, and the condemnation of the sinner must necessarily be death through his inability to fulfil the law.

Vi. *Law Reveals the Sinfulness of Sin* (vers. 12, 13).—Law itself is "holy and righteous and good." "Holy" because it discloses sin; "righteous" because it condemns the sinner to death; "good" because of its intrinsic and spiritual purpose. It was, therefore, impossible to say that that which was good became death to Paul (ver. 13). Law does not solicit sin, it only elicits it, and it was not law, but sin that brought death. This, then, is his answer so far to the question, "Is the law sin?" though he continues the subject in other forms to the end of the chapter. Law is neither sin nor does it work death, for it is no more the author of death than it is of sin. It is sin that slays the man. "The strength of sin is the law" (1 Cor. xv. 56).

All through this section we have the one thought, the relation of law to sin; and the keynote is the repetition of the phrase, "through the law" or "through the commandment" (vers. 7, 8, 11, 13). Let us ponder it once again, especially in view of the solemn fact of human experience that "legality is the great enemy to sanctification" (J. Brown, p. 158).

1. *Law is intended to reveal Sin.*—It brings home to the conscience the fact that a certain thing is wrong. Like a standard, or rule, or plumb-line, it shows at once where and what we are in the sight of God. A stick plunged into a stream will at once show the direction of the current, and, when God's "perfect law" is held up before the sinner, it will reveal to him himself, and "through the commandment" sin becomes exceedingly sinful (ver. 13).

2. *Law is intended to condemn the Sinner.*—Not only does law reveal sin, it shows the sinner his inability to keep that law. God's standard is perfection, and we must "continue in all things that are written in the law," if we are to be saved by law rather than by grace (Gal. iii. 10). But, as this is utterly impossible, the law brings us into condemnation and shows us our true position in the sight of God, and that "no man is justified by the law" (Gal. iii. 11).

3. *Law is intended to constrain and conduct the awakened, condemned sinner to Christ.*—If we carefully study the office of the law, as seen in St. Paul's teaching, we shall easily recognize how this comes about. In ch. iii. 19 the law condemns us as guilty. In Gal. iii. 22 (R.V.) the law imprisons the condemned soul and keeps him safely in ward (Gal. iii. 23). Then in Gal. ii. 19, 20 the

law becomes the executioner of the prisoner, for law cannot possibly show any mercy. And thus it becomes our conductor to Christ (Gal. iii. 24) in order that we might be justified by faith. Happy, therefore, is that man who has come to the end of himself, his own ideas, his own efforts, his own determination to be saved by his own obedience, and has acknowledged his utter sinfulness, his hopeless inability, and has accepted Christ as "the end of the law for righteousness."

XXVII

THE INABILITY OF THE FLESH

Rom. vii. 14-25.

14. For we know that the law is spiritual: but I am carnal, sold under sin.
15. For that which I do I allow not: for what I would, that do I not; but what I hate, that do I.
16. If then I do that which I would not, I consent unto the law that *it is* good.
17. Now then it is no more I that do it, but sin that dwelleth in me.
18. For I know that in me (that is, in my flesh,) dwelleth no good thing: for to will is present with me; but *how* to perform that which is good I find not.
19. For the good that I would I do not: but the evil which I would not, that I do.
20. Now if I do that I would not, it is no more I that do it, but sin that dwelleth in me.
21. I find then a law, that, when I would do good, evil is present with me.
22. For I delight in the law of God after the inward man:
23. But I see another law in my members, warring against the law of my mind, and bringing me into captivity to the law of sin which is in my members.
24. O wretched man that I am! who shall deliver me from the body of this death?
25. I thank God through Jesus Christ our Lord. So then with the mind I myself serve the law of God; but with the flesh the law of sin.

The Apostle here continues his subject and confirms the preceding argument by showing the power of sin in the flesh. It is this that makes the law weak. No one can be saved by law, because law cannot deliver us from the flesh. Law only prescribes, it cannot perform; it proscribes, but does not provide. Just as in ch. iii. 20, he showed that law could not justify, so here he proves the additional truth, that it cannot sanctify. It can neither give acceptance (justification), nor acceptableness (sanctification). The law cannot give holiness, because the flesh is the seat of sin. In verses 7-10 his argument was based upon the distinction, "Not the commandment, but sin by the commandment," but here his argument rests upon the distinction, "Not I, but sin that dwelleth in me."

> "Hitherto he had contrasted himself in respect of his whole being with the divine law; now, however,he begins to describe a discord which exists within himself" (Tholuck, quoted by Denney).

His true self ("the mind") vindicates and approves law even while indwelling sin ("the flesh") resists it.

Now come two familiar questions: (1) Do these verses represent the Apostle's own experiences? To this we reply, Yes, undoubtedly, for it is impossible to read what he says without realizing it as a personal experience. There is such a genuine ring about it that we cannot believe that he is supposing a case, but, on the contrary, is telling an experience. And yet, of course, it is not an experience which is his only, but one that is characteristic of all men in like circumstances. (2) Do these verses refer to the regenerate, or the unregenerate? Great names are found on both sides of the question. (*a*) In favor of the unregenerate, we are pointed to verse 14, "I am carnal, permanently sold under sin" (Greek), which, it is said, could not be true of a Christian, especially after such a statement as ch. vi. 14. (*b*) In favor of the regenerate, we are referred to verse 22, "I delight in the law of God," which, it is said, could not be true of the unconverted, though Isaiah lviii. 2, and the latter part of verse 25 of this chapter, are thought to prove the contrary.

The fact of so much difference of opinion suggests the wisdom of avoiding the question altogether and of seeking another and better solution. The one point of the passage is that it describes a man who is trying to be good and holy by his own efforts and is beaten back every time by the power of indwelling sin. This is the experience of any man who tries the experiment, whether he be regenerate or unregenerate. The experiences here described are certainly not those of the Christian life as it ought to be, and as it may be, the normal Christianity, that is, of ch. vi. 17, 18; vii. 4, 6; viii. 1, 2; 1 Peter i. 8, 9. And yet they may be true of many professed Christians as they now are. One proof beyond all others that the passage cannot refer to the normal Christian life is the teaching about the Christian in relation to law, as is acutely pointed out by Dr. Garvie:—

> "In this passage he assumes that the law is a legitimate authority for the man who approves but does not obey its commands; whereas for the Christian believer, who is not under law, but under grace, for whom Christ is the end of the law, the law is non-existent. If he were referring to the Christian experience in the passage he would be self-contradictory, for he would be admitting the validity of the law, which it is the purpose of his argument to deny (*Romans*, "Century Bible," p. 174).

The passage describes a man who is in real earnest to be holy by his own efforts, by law, and apart from grace. The passage thus teaches the powerlessness of law for salvation and sanctification, and its position immediately after ch. vi., and before ch. viii. seems to show that the verses express the hopeless struggle of the better side of a man with his sinful nature.

Thus the section does not refer either to the regenerate or to the unregenerate, but to one class of one of them. Verse 1, which must never be overlooked in any proper interpretation of the passage, shows that Jews are addressed, and it seems in every way best to regard the description from verses 7-25 as that of a Jew under the Mosaic law, who valued its spirituality but failed to fulfil its requirements. "To the Jew first" is one of the keynotes of the entire Epistle, and all the chapters from iii. to viii. are a chain of reasoning which institute a number of contrasts between law and grace. This is one of the contrasts and depicts the condition of a man aroused by law to see his own sinfulness, and also his own powerlessness to overcome it. It is therefore a picture of a Jew under law, not of a Christian under grace.

> "What it describes is the experience of a conscientious unconverted *Jew,* fully instructed in the Law, and seeking zealously to accomplish a righteousness of his own by 'works of Law.' It is a practical illustration and demonstration of the statement that 'by works of Law shall no flesh be justfied'" (Mauro, *The "Wretched Man" and His Deliverance,* p. 22).

The key to the meaning of the entire section is found in the repetition of "I" thirty times in the chapter, without a single mention of the Holy Spirit. It indicates what "I" am struggling to do, and utterly fail to do in my own strength. The contrast between this and the succeeding chapter is most striking. In ch. viii. there are at least twenty references to the Holy Spirit, and while in ch. vii. Law is mentioned twenty times, in ch. viii. it is found only three or four times.

Now let us look carefully at the verses. Everything here is "under law," and the main point is not that of condemnation, but powerlessness. The conflict is not between the two natures of the believer, but refers to the effect of law on a heart that recognizes its spirituality. When the passage is studied as a whole it will be found to fall into three sections, and each section has three divisions, giving in turn a statement, a proof, and a conclusion. There is a sort of refrain at the end of each paragraph. As Godet aptly remarks, the passage is "like a dirge; the most sorrowful elegy which ever proceeded from a human heart."

I. *The First Confession* (vers. 14-17).

1. The Statement (ver. 14). — "For we know that the law is spiritual: but I am carnal, sold under sin." The "for" with which this verse commences clearly links the passage with that which precedes, and shows that the Apostle is still occupied with the same subject, however much he may elaborate and unfold it. The present tenses which commence at this point do not imply any change of subject, but are necessary because he is now to treat of the character of the law, not of its operation, and the character necessarily remains unchanged. He could not say "the law *was* spiritual," and so the present tenses are not to be regarded as expressive of his own personal experiences in view of the clear connection with what precedes. He is about to trace his experiences to their cause and the tenses used indicate principles. So he says that the law as given by God is essentially spiritual, but man himself is a creature of flesh in permanent bondage to sin. There are two words in Greek for "carnal"; one implying that which is purely material, and the other implying what is ethical. The former suggests man's nature as weak, the latter suggests his character as sinful. It is difficult

to decide which is to be read here though the interpretation is not very materially affected either way.

2. The Proof (vers. 15, 16).—In confirmation of the statement in the preceding verse the Apostle confesses his consciousness of enslavement. Self is unable to hinder what it disapproves. In verse 15, the "I allow not" of the A.V. is incorrect, and should be rendered, "I know not," that is, "I do not recognize the true nature of what I do at the bidding of sin," or else, "I do not approve of it" (Psa. i. 6; Matt. vii. 23). We must carefully note that the Apostle is not expressing the idea of the well-known words, "I see and approve the better, but follow the worse," for the Pagan who used these words confessed that he practised what he knew to be wrong, and that his inconsistency arose from his love of the evil. St. Paul here confesses wrongdoing, but instead of loving he hates the evil.

3. The Conclusion (ver. 17).—"So now it is no more I that do it, but sin which dwelleth in me." That is to say, it was not the true self of the man which was responsible, but the sin which had its abode in him. The Apostle's purpose is not to excuse himself or to explain his failings. He is only showing his wretched thraldom, that he finds a tyrant who compels him to act against his better self.

II. *The Second Confession* (vers. 18-20).

1. The Statement (ver. 18).—"For I know that in me, that is, in my flesh, dwelleth no good thing." Here the Apostle reproduces in substance his statement of verse 14: "I am carnal," though it is put with greater preciseness, including the clear distinction between the "I" and "the flesh." In him, so far as his person was carnal, there dwelt no good thing, though of course there was something more in him besides the flesh.

2. The Proof (vers. 18, 19).—Here is the explanation of the statement in verse 18, and a repetition of what was said in verse 15, with greater definiteness. The will to do good was ever present within reach, but the execution of the good was what he could not find. The contrast between inclination and act is here shown with great force as a contrast between good intention and bad action.

3. The Conclusion (ver. 20).—Once again, as in verse 17, he comes to the conclusion that he is not his own master, that the tyrant now in the place of power is shown to be alien to the true self that wishes to be holy. Not for the purpose of exculpating himself, but simply to describe his profound bondage and misery, does the Apostle speak of "no more I, but sin."

III. *The Third Confession* (vers. 21-25).

1. The Statement (ver. 21). Again he makes his confession, as in verses 14 and 18. We must mark the way in which he introduces each of them. Verse 14, "We know"; verse 18, "I know"; verse 21, "I find." He is ever conscious of a moral contradiction and conflict within, a desire to do good and yet an evil always present.

2. The Proof (vers. 22, 23).—Here again there is a parallel with the proofs of verses 15, 16, and verses 18, 19. On the one hand, in the inward man he delighted in God's law; on the other hand, he saw a different law in his members warring against the law of his mind and bringing him into spiritual bondage. It should be carefully noted that "the inward man" is not the same as "the new man," nor is "the mind" ever used of the renewed nature. It is the immaterial part of man in contrast with the material, or bodily part, and whenever man is regenerated the mind has to be renewed (ch. xii. 2; Eph. iv. 23.)

It will be observed that no less than four laws are mentioned in these two verses; the law of God, which is the moral law whether written or unwritten; the law of sin, which reigns over man since the Fall; the law of the mind, which is the moral sense in man; and the law of the members, which leads to the individual falling under the law of sin (so Godet).

3. The Conclusion (vers. 24, 25).—The outcome of all this contradiction and conflict is a cry of agony: "O wretched man that I am! who shall deliver me from the body of this death?" "A wail of anguish, and a cry for help." This cry is explained by verses 22, 23. The Apostle uses the word "wretched" rather than "guilty," because the point of the conflict was not guilt and condemnation,

but the indwelling power of evil which could not be overcome by man's unaided strength. Denney's comment is that—

> "The words are not those of the Apostle's heart as he writes; they are the words which he knows are wrung from the heart of the man who realizes that he is himself in the state just described. Paul has reproduced this vividly from his own experience, but 'wretched man that I am' is not the cry of the Christian Paul, but of the man whom sin and law have brought to despair" (*Romans*, p. 643).

The Christian Paul has already been made free (ch. vi. 18). "The body of this death" means the body as the seat of the death caused by sin. It would seem to bear the same meaning as "the body of sin" in ch. vi. 6.

But what are we to make of the outburst of thanksgiving, "I thank God through Jesus Christ our Lord"? The true interpretation seems to be that it is a parenthetical expression. As St. Paul momentarily contemplates his own position in Christ, he gives vent to his feelings in the parenthetical ejaculation of thanksgiving, that through the mercy of God the experience just described was no longer his.

On any other interpretation the exclamation of thanksgiving is quite incompatible with the despairing cry of the former verse, and this shows clearly that the two verses represent two distinct stages of experience.

The outcome of it all is now stated (ver. 25). In regard to his "mind" he serves the law of God, while in regard to the "flesh" he serves the law of sin; the flesh cannot be changed or improved. These words which sum up the entire passage, and form the Apostle's settled conclusions under the circumstances, show that the reference cannot possibly be to a regenerate man, for as Garvie clearly shows:—

> "To apply all that precedes this verse to Paul as a Christian, however would be to admit practically that the grace of God is as powerless against sin as the law is (*Romans*, p. 175).

So that what the chapter discusses is not the conflict of the two natures in the believeı, but a very different struggle, namely, "one between the corrupted nature (the flesh) and the mind in a man whose mind has been fully instructed in the Law of God, who fully approves of it, and who endeavours through the flesh to obey it" (Mauro, *The Wretched Man" and His Deliverance*, p. 57).

Thus the Apostle has vindicated two great truths: (1) that in ourselves, apart from grace, there dwells nothing that God can call good; (2) that the law cannot recover us from our evil nature and change our dispositions and powers. So the chapter with its emphasis on "I," descriptive of the life of religious self, culminates in hopeless inability when looked at apart from grace, and contents itself with the division of interest expressed in the closing words. We shall see the contrast in ch. viii. which deals with deliverance in Christ through the Spirit. It is impossible for the Gospel to end with this note of failure and inability, and so he proceeds to speak of the deliverance (ch. viii. 2), which he is now to deal with in detail.

This very solemn passage goes to the heart of some of the deepest realities of the spiritual life, and, while its primary interpretation is to be kept strictly to the class of man intended by the Apostle, there are secondary applications to other classes which call for attention.

1. *Its Message to the Unregenerate.*—There does not seem much doubt in the light of the entire passage from verse 7 that the Apostle has in view an unregenerate Jew, alive to the beauty and spirituality of the law of God, and yet only too conscious of his inability to live a life in accordance therewith. It is a picture of an unrenewed heart "under law," and this was the Apostle's own experience in his pre-Christian days. The law aroused his moral consciousness but could not provide him with moral purpose. "It produced only a deeper sense of discord between duty and desire" (Garvie, *Romans*, p. 182). So is it always, and when the law of God is brought to bear upon an unregenerate and unrenewed heart it is intended to lead to the cry, "O wretched man that I am, who shall deliver me?"

2. *Its Message to the Regenerate.*—The passage is useful by contrast to show what is intended for the regenerate by the grace of God in the matter of sanctification. This, as we shall see, is definitely brought before us in ch. viii., but meanwhile the very contrast helps us to understand what God purposes for the believer. Chris-

tian morality is due not to an external command, but to an internal power. Union with Christ by His Spirit was intended to make a life of holiness possible, in which God's requirements would find their fulfilment (ch. vii. 6; viii. 4). "Faith makes all things possible; love makes all things easy."

3. *Its Message to the Backslider.*—While the primary meaning of ch. vii. is, in our judgment, to be referred to the unregenerate, it must not be forgotten that the wretchedness here depicted may also be true of a Christian who has lost touch with Christ and has come under the power of sin, or self. Like Abraham while in Egypt, like Jacob before he got back to Bethel, it is only too possible for the Christian to have no joy, no power, no real fellowship with God. And it is only as we return by the connected way of repentance, faith, and surrender that we shall regain the liberty and power which are the essential features of the true Christian life.

4. *Its Message to the Untaught Believer.*—To some extent even this section may be applied to the young beginner in the Christian life, though there must be great care exercised not to confuse the conflict depicted in this chapter with the conflict in the life of the Christian. Romans vii. describes a conflict between two opposing powers, the man and the flesh, but the conflict of the Christian is something quite different. Sin has been overthrown in the believer and is always striving to regain its sway. What then is the Christian to do? Is he to be content with a low standard of life and to attribute his failures to the evil nature within? Is he to soothe himself with the Apostle's words, "It is no more I that do it, but sin that dwelleth in me"? And is he to regard Romans vii, as expressive of the normal conflict which will be inevitable to the end of our earthly life? Far from it. To use the Apostle's words, "Not I, but sin that dwelleth in me," as an explanation, not to say, justification, of wrongdoing, is to apply them in a way altogether different from, and opposed to the proper meaning. We are to occupy ourselves with Christ, to allow the Holy Spirit to reign supreme in our hearts, and thus by His divine counteractive power we shall have perpetual victory over the evil nature within. The normal Christian life is in Romans viii., and it is altogether inac-

curate and dangerous to use Romans vii. as in any way descriptive of the believer's conflict.

5. *Its Message to the Immature Believer.*—Once again let it be remarked quite plainly that we must distinguish between interpretation and application, that this chapter is to be interpreted of the unregenerate Jew, not of the regenerate Christian. And yet there is a sense in which the wretchedness here described is applicable to a believer who is struggling to make himself holy by his own efforts. It is a well-known fact of experience that many who have come to Christ for justification try to obtain sanctification by themselves, as though Christianity meant Justification by Faith, and Sanctification by Struggle and Fighting. As we have received Christ Jesus the Lord, that is, by faith, so must we live and walk in Him, that is, by faith, and if the Christian does not abide in Christ he will soon get into the experience of these verses. He will not become *un*regenerate, for that is impossible, but he certainly will become *de*generate. Such is the tendency of the evil nature that if it is allowed to predominate we become powerless against sin. If we take any commandment of Christ's and attempt to obey it in our own powers rather than by appropriating His grace, we are thereby returning from grace to law. While therefore the Christian is not "under law," yet he may easily lapse into a legal spirit.

Conversion does not give any self-sufficiency for righteousness; there is no inherent power given to the new nature. We are as helpless for sanctification as we were for justification. If one is a gift, so is the other. If one came by accepting Christ and coming to the end of self, so did the other. Christ *for* us is our Justification; Christ *in* us is our Sanctification, and both are by Faith. To teach his twofold lesson is the Apostle's purpose in ch. viii., and to learn it is to know vital Christianity.

XXVIII

THE ABILITY OF THE SPIRIT

Rom. viii. 1-4

1. There is therefore now no condemnation to them which are in Christ Jesus, who walk not after the flesh, but after the Spirit.
2. For the law of the Spirit of life in Christ Jesus hath made me free from the law of sin and death.
3. For what the law could not do, in that it was weak through the flesh, God sending his own Son in the likeness of sinful flesh, and for sin, condemned sin in the flesh.
4. That the righteousness of the law might be fulfilled in us, who walk not after the flesh, but after the Spirit.

Before considering in detail this very important and attractive chapter it seems essential to review our position in order to appreciate fully the precise point of its teaching. Godet quotes Spener as having said that, "If Holy Scripture was a ring, and the Epistle to the Romans a precious stone, ch. viii, would be the sparkling point of the jewel." And Dr. David Brown also remarks:—

> "In this surpassing chapter the several streams of the preceding arguments meet and flow in one 'river of the water of life, clear as crystal proceeding out of the throne of God and of the Lamb,' until it seems to lose itself in the ocean of a blissful eternity" (*Romans*, p. 77).

It is undoubtedly the chapter of chapters for the life of the believer, and several streams of thought, which are found in the earlier sections of the Epistle, are here taken up and united in a wonderful and blessed completeness.

The Justification expounded in chs. iv. and v. and the Sanctification of chs. vi. and vii. have union with Christ as their source and foundation. Chs. vi. and vii. have set forth (mainly by contrast) the power of that union to sanctify. Ch. vi. has shown that union with Christ involves the utter incompatibility of union with sin; ch. vii. has shown that union with Christ means the absolute impossibility of union with law. Law in that chapter is to be interpreted as God's requirement for us. This chapter takes up ch. vii. 6, "newness of spirit," and develops its meaning. The Apostle will now show that union with Christ means victory over indwelling sin (as contrasted with ch. vi.), and also that it means the fulfilment of law (as contrasted with ch. vii.). Law in the present chapter is regarded, not merely as God's requirement, but as His *will* for us in union with Christ. Grace is given for obedience. Ch. viii. will thus teach us that the Christian life is something very far different from one long endeavour to be good. It will show that the Gospel of salvation by grace means that grace *gives* before it *requires,* whereas salvation by law would mean that salvation only comes when we have done all that law requires. Ch. viii. will also teach us that not only does knowledge of evil bring no deliverance from sin, but even knowledge of good by itself brings no power to perform it. In contrast with the thirty occurrences of "I" in ch. vii. are the twenty references to the Holy Spirit in ch. viii.

It is also worth while to compare chs. v. and viii., the latter being in several respects the counterpart and complement of the former. The former shows the permanence of righteousness through faith, that it lasts to the end. Ch. viii. shows how it continues in the time between the beginning and the end. Ch. v. deals with the basis and guarantee of righteousness in the fact of redemption; ch. viii. deals with the life of righteousness in the power of the Holy Spirit. Ch. v. treats of the believer's relation to God; ch. viii. deals with his relation to sin, the world, the flesh, and the devil, as well as to God.

It will also help us to remember that the Apostle is still developing his important statement of ch. vi. 14; "Sin shall not have dominion over you: for ye are not under law, but under grace." He has dealt very fully with "ye are not under law," and has shown with great clearness that when a man is "under law" he cannot possibly escape from the dominion of sin. Then again the Apostle has shown what is provided for us "under grace"; namely, a spiritual union with Christ in His death and in His life, whereby we are enabled to walk in "newness of life" (ch. vi. 4), and to serve in "newness of spirit" (ch. vii. 6). Now he will teach us that this new spirit, which is none other than the indwelling Spirit of God, delivers us from the power of sin, and leads us onward step by step, until the final glorification which, as we have seen from ch. v., is already assured to the believer.

The chapter should, first of all, be looked at as a whole. It consists of four main parts: (*a*) Verses 1-11; deliverance from the power of the flesh by the power of the Holy Spirit. (*b*) Verses 12-17; the full realization of our sonship by the same power of the Spirit. (*c*) Verses 17-30; even sufferings do not affect our position because of the power of the same Spirit. (*d*) Verses 31-39; in spite of everything victory will be ours through Jesus Christ our Lord. Thus, as Godet says, the chapter begins with "no condemnation," and ends with "no separation," while in between, as C. A. Fox remarks, there is "no defeat." An American Bible teacher, Mr. W. R. Newell, has helpfully remarked on the entire chapter in the following words:—

> "There is scarcely a passage in the New Testament that is more delightful reading to the spiritual Christian than the eighth of Romans. Even when its verses (and it contains several very difficult verses) are not fully understood, there is, nevertheless, a wondrous charm about the chapter. There is an atmosphere of blessing all through it. Of course there is, for the blessed Holy Spirit breathes throughout it—the indwelling Deliverer, Quickener, Guide Assurer, Helper, Intercessor."

Let us now confine our attention very carefully to vers. 1-4.

I. *The Glorious Fact* (ver. 1).—Observe the four main thoughts as suggested by the following words and phrases: "Therefore"; "Now"; "No condemnation"; "In Christ Jesus." "Therefore" implies under the changed circumstances involving a change of time (see ch. iii. 21). The word looks back to all that has preceded, but perhaps especially to chs. v.-vii. "Now," that is, in the present, just as in ch. v. he referred to the past and the future. "No condemnation." In the Greek the word "No" is very emphatic, implying "no sort of condemnation," whether judicial or experimental. This is the foundation of everything, for it clearly teaches the perfection of our justification. Grace is intended to keep us holy, and to prevent us from lapsing into sin and ever needing justification again. It is only on the basis of "no sort of condemnation" that holiness becomes possible. "In Christ Jesus," that is, those who enter into union with Him by faith and abide there. This is the union already mentioned in ch. vi. 1-11. We are united to Jesus Christ in His death and resurrection, and all the efficacy of His redemptive work is guaranteed to us for holiness of life. We share His merit and His life, and it is this double provision that constitutes our blessed privilege of "No condemnation." (See Additional Note, p. 207.)

Observe that we omit (with the R.V.) the latter part of ver. 1, found in the A.V., because of the weightiest manuscript authority available. The phrase would be quite inaccurate and misleading in ver. 1, though it is appropriate, natural, and necessary at the end of ver. 4.

II. *The Perfect Explanation* (ver. 2).—This teaches us why there is "no condemnation," and how our deliverance is accomplished. Here is the basis of our freedom, in contrast to the seventh chapter, in one single sentence. When we enter into union with Christ Jesus we find a new power, the rule of the Holy Spirit, Who gives life and thereby controls the evil nature. The presence of the Spirit brings life and His power sustains it, and this gives the believer deliverance from the law of sin and death. Thus verse 2 provides the evidence of verse 1, and gives the answer to ch. vii. 23. Indeed, the verse really indicates the theme of the chapter. The principle of the Holy Spirit of life in Christ Jesus delivers us from the principle of sin and death, and this carries with it the guarantee of an immortal life hereafter. The phrase, "The Spirit of life in Christ Jesus," seems to refer to the resurrection power of Christ, ministered to us by the Holy Spirit as the Fount of life to the Christian. We notice here the two contrasted laws; the law of the Spirit of life, and the law of sin and death. The one overcomes the other by the great principle of counteraction; just as at the Red Sea the law of the wind counteracted the law of the tide, and also as the law of the human will often counteracts by its greater power the ordinary law of gravitation. "Sin and death" refer to the source and result of our condemnation, and from both of these Christ by the Holy Spirit delivers us.

III. *The Divine Cause* (ver. 3).—Here we are enabled to see how it comes about that the man in Christ is free from the law of sin. Law had no power to condemn sin in our flesh so as to render sin powerless, but God could, and did, do this in sending Christ. Man was carnal, that is, without the power of obeying; and it was for this reason that the law was weak, because it demanded what human nature could not provide. Hence the only way of deliverance was the provision of a new spirit, and this could only come through God's gift of His Son. We must never forget that law is not a *force,* but only a *method* of the operation of a force. It is because of our depravity that law is insufficient and impotent, and God must therefore do everything for us in regard to salvation.

Observe the wonderful fulness of this verse. Thus, we have the Deity of Christ, "His own Son"; the Incarnation, "In the likeness of sinful flesh," that is, He was like us in all things except sin—Christ's flesh was not sinful, never the seat of sin; and His Atonement, "for sin," which means "as an offering for sin." Our Lord's death was the divine condemnation of sin, and now its rule is broken. The Cross condemned sin in us so as to loose its hold upon us and to remove for ever its claim upon us. This thought of the deliverance by the Cross of Christ from the condemnation of sin is in close harmony with the teaching of ch. vi. 6, and is the complement of the teaching of ch. iii. 21-26. Our Lord's death is at once a propitiation for sins, an expiation of sin, and a redemption from its power and bondage.

IV. *The Practical Purpose* (ver. 4).—We are now told why the man in Christ is made free from the law of sin. It is in order that the righteous requirements of the law may be fulfilled in those who walk (those who live and act) according to the Holy Spirit. Thus, those who are in Christ find a new life and a new power, and the verse "repeats and completes the secret of holiness given in ch. vi. 12, 13, though in more definite language" (Gairdner). Christ thereby secures in us the holiness which the law could not secure, and the Gospel provides and guarantees practical righteousness. Law had failed because of man's inability to work; the Gospel succeeds because of God's ability to give. "The saints 'fulfil' the law's 'claim,' not in the sense of sinless perfection, but in that of a true, living, and working consent to its principles; the consent of full conviction and of a heart whose affections are won to God" (Moule, *Cambridge Bible*). Thus, the exposition of the Apostle's purpose of the law is now finished (ch. iii. 19; v. 20; vii. 13). It demands and yet is impotent and cannot realize its requirements. Hence the introduction of a new law, a new principle, "the Spirit of life in Christ Jesus."

The importance of these verses lies in the fact that they provide a summary of chs. v. to viii., and indicate in brief but sufficient form the secrets of Christian holiness. Verse 1 is a brief summary of ch. v.; that the condemnation of the sinner is utterly removed in Christ. Verse 2 is a summary of ch. vi.; teaching us that the condemnation of sin in the soul is brought to an end by its union with Christ and consequent deliverance. Verse 3 is a summary of ch. vii.; in which the impossibility of the law to produce righteousness is clearly taught, and the power of Christ's death and resurrection to deliver us from its thraldom. Verse 4 is a summary of what is elaborated all through ch. viii.; showing the possibilities of Christian holiness in the power of the Spirit of God.

1. *Our Prerequisite.*—"No condemnation" (ver. 1). The removal of condemnation provides for deliverance from the power of indwelling sin. A condemned sinner, while continuing such, could not possibly become holy. "It is not said there are no falls, no failures, no infirmities, no inconsistencies, no fleshly corruptions. But, thanks be to God, it is said, 'There is now no condemnation' " (Marcus Rainsford, Senr.). "Herein lies the great difference between an unbeliever out of Christ and the believer in Christ. The unbeliever has his judgment day *before* him, but the believer in Christ has his judgment day *behind* him; for him judgment is past and gone: there is no condemnation" (John iii. 18).

2. *Our Position.*—"*In Christ Jesus*" (ver. 2). Both in verses 1 and 2 emphasis is laid on our union with Christ. It is only here,

as obtained and maintained by faith, that we can realize holiness.

3. *Our Power.*—"The Spirit of Life in Christ Jesus" (ver. 2). This title of the Holy Spirit suggests vividly and forcibly the one power for holiness. The life that is in Christ Jesus is made ours by the Holy Spirit who dwells in us.

4. *Our Protection.*—"Hath made me free" (ver. 2). This, above all else, is what the soul needs for holiness. Liberation, emancipation, freedom from the indwelling power and condemnation of sin.

5. *Our Provision* (ver. 3).—Everything necessary for holiness has been provided by God in the gift of His Son, whose Deity, Incarnation, and Atonement are our perfect provision for "all things that pertain to life and godliness."

6. *Our Possibility.*—"That the righteous requirements of the law might be fulfilled in us" (ver. 4). Thus, the very thing that was impossible by means of the law becomes blessedly and gloriously possible in the power of Christ by the Divine Spirit. The fulfilment of the law is realized in definite practice. We "walk," that is, we live, move, act, and make progress, thereby expressing all the realities and activities of the new life in Christ. Walking is one of the three perfect forms of exercise, and the Christian walk implies that all our powers are thereby exercised and used in the glory of God.

7. *Our Principle.*—"According to the Spirit" (ver. 4). This shows that the very Spirit who gives life ((ver. 2), is also the standard according to which the life is lived, and thus, day by day, and moment by moment, the Christian is enabled to live by principle, as taught and led by the Holy Spirit.

From all this it will readily be seen how important these verses are for a proper and complete idea of Christian holiness. Many people seem to think that, while unconverted sinners have no power against sin, believers in Christ Jesus have; that is, that God gives to the new-born soul strength in itself to overcome the force of indwelling sin. According to this idea the teaching of the New Testament is Justification by Faith and Sanctification by Struggle. But this is an utter mistake, and often proves disastrous to the peace and progress of the soul. Many believers are struggling against sin in the idea that God expects them to "fight the good fight" against evil, but they forget that it is "the good fight of *faith*," and their struggling is very largely in their own strength and inevitably results in failure. God does not give even the believer inherent power over sin. This is not His way of deliverance; His method is altogether different, for He Himself becomes the power dwelling in us that overcomes sin. Not, therefore, by our own struggling, but through the mighty energy of the Holy Spirit within us are we enabled to overcome the power of inbred and indwelling sin.

An illustration may help us to understand this. Motor cars are propelled on what is known as the storage principle; so much petrol or electricity for use, and then a further supply. Tram cars are run on what is known as the contact principle; the car is kept in contact with the electric current which thereby is enabled to influence the movement of the car. It is not the former but the latter that God has adopted for holiness. It is not a case of so much grace put into our hearts to be used on the storage system, and then a further supply provided, but on the contrary we are to keep in close spiritual touch with Him Who is the source of all life and power, and then in constant union with Him we find the secret of purity, power, and progress in righteousness and true holiness.

ADDITIONAL NOTE (page 203).

Deissmann (*Bible Studies,* p. 264) shows from the Papyri that ("condemnation") is a civil as well as a criminal term. He renders it "legal burden,' which would be quite suitable to the context of verse 1. In his useful work, *Christ and His Slaves,* the Rev. Harrington C. Lees translates the word by "disability," or, more popularly, "handicap." It will be found that the present exposition of the chapter is in essential harmony with this new and suggestive interpretation.

XXIX

FLESH AND SPIRIT

Rom. viii. 5-11.

5. For they that are after the flesh do mind the things of the flesh; but they that are after the Spirit the things of the Spirit.
6. For to be carnally minded *is* death; but to be spiritually minded *is* life and peace.
7. Because the carnal mind *is* enmity against God: for it is not subject to the law of God, neither indeed can be.
8. So then they that are in the flesh cannot please God.
9. But ye are not in the flesh, but in the Spirit, if so be that the Spirit of God dwell in you. Now if any man have not the Spirit of Christ, he is none of his.
10. And if Christ *be* in you, the body *is* dead because of sin; but the Spirit *is* life because of righteousness.
11. But if the Spirit of him that raised up Jesus from the dead dwell in you, he that raised up Christ from the dead shall also quicken your mortal bodies by his Spirit that dwelleth in you.

The mention of "flesh" and "spirit" in verse 4 leads naturally to a fuller statement of the contrast between them. Sanctification involves an entire change of the believer's life, and it is essential to show why righteousness must be fulfilled in those who walk after the Spirit and not after the flesh. Hence, as in verses 1-4, the Apostle has shown that until and unless a man is justified he cannot possibly be holy, so now, in verses 5-11, he will show that if a man is not holy he cannot possibly have been justified. Sanctification is the evidence of justification, and this is proved by a series of striking contrasts between the flesh and the Spirit, and the two are shown to be mutually exclusive.

I. *The Two Principles* (ver. 5).—Two classes of men are described here; "them that are after the flesh," and "them that are after the Spirit." The "flesh" when used, as here, with a moral meaning, is always to be understood as referring to the old, unrenewed, sinful nature, according to which the unregenerate man lives. It implies the entire unrenewed life lived apart from God; and it should be carefully observed that this does not necessarily mean a gross, vicious life, for the flesh as unrenewed may be educated, refined, and cultured. Indeed, there is even a religion of the flesh that consists in outward ceremonial observances, asceticism, and self-denial, which, however, does not touch the springs of the heart and provide acceptable worship. There are many things described as being "according to the flesh," which are altogether unacceptable to God. It was this to which our Lord referred when he spoke of "that which is born of the flesh is flesh." Herein lies the explanation why righteousness is not, and cannot be, fulfilled in the man who is not in Christ. In marked contrast to this is the reference to those who are "after the Spirit." They have been born from above and in the power of that spiritual life they live "after the Spirit."

II. *The Two Tendencies* (vers. 5, 6).—Another contrast is here drawn; "they that are after the flesh mind the things of the flesh; but they that are after the Spirit the things of the Spirit; for the mind of the flesh is death, but the mind of the Spirit is life and peace." A man necessarily lives according to his nature, and, if he lives "according to the flesh," he will of necessity "mind the things of the flesh." The whole bent, trend, and tendency of his nature will be towards that which actuates him. Natural things suit the natural man and spiritual things suit the spiritual man. As is the life within, so will be the character and conduct, for fruit always comes "according to its kind."

III. *The Two Issues* (vers. 6-8).—The outcome of "minding the flesh" is death, which is to be regarded as separation from God; and this is due to the fact that "the mind of the flesh is enmity against God; for it is not subject to the law of God, neither indeed can it be. So then they that are in the flesh cannot please God." On the other hand, the minding of the Spirit is "life and peace," power and blessedness. Thus, these verses reveal the striking contrast between the man depicted in ch. vii., and "them that are in

Christ Jesus." The two are opposed and incompatible. The carnal mind is not only subject to inability (as in ch. vii.), but is also characterized by hostility (ch. viii. 7). Hence there is a very definite and valid reason why the unrenewed man cannot fulfil the will of God. As long as a man is out of Christ he may be religious after a sort, but it is impossible for him to be pleasing to God.

IV. *The Two Spheres* (vers. 8-11).—The phrases describing the two contrasted lives here suddenly change. Instead of "after the flesh" and "after the Spirit," they are spoken of as "in the flesh," and "in the Spirit." It is no longer a question of standard, or principle, but of sphere in which they live. "In the flesh" means abiding in union with that unrenewed nature which cannot possibly fulfil the law of God, and the Apostle at once reminds his readers that they are not "in the flesh," but "in the Spirit." This is a blessed and beautiful contrast, and may be regarded as a fuller description of the closing words of verse 4. He addresses them as "in the Spirit," and assumes that the Spirit of God is dwelling in them, but he adds a solemn warning that it is only in the possession of the Spirit of Christ that they can regard themselves as belonging to Him.

Then in verses 10, 11 he deals with the deliverance from the law of *death,* as in verses 3-8 he had treated the law of *sin* (see "sin and death," ver. 2). The saints are subject to physical death, and will die by reason of their association with the physical results of Adam's sin, but their spirit[1] is alive in Christ because of the righteousness provided and bestowed in Him, and the indwelling presence of the Holy Spirit now is the guarantee of the future resurrection of the body. Thus the believer will be emancipated from the law of death.

The context seems clear that this quickening of the mortal body does not refer to any accession of physical power in this present

[1]It is a difficult matter to decide where the word "Spirit" in ch. viii, refers to the Holy Spirit and where to the human spirit. A comparison should be made between the A. V. and the R. V. for different interpretations. The A. V. refers almost every verse to the Holy Spirit, while the R. V. distinguishes between the Divine and the human spirit, and interprets particular verses accordingly. The American R. V. is much closer to the A. V. than to the English R. V. and, except in verse 10, interprets every verse of the Holy Spirit. A discussion of this important subject will be found in Dr. Beet's Commentary and the volume in the *Expositor's Bible* by the Bishop of Durham. While it is therefore difficult to decide in every case, it may be said as a general principle that when the human spirit is intended, it is always to be regarded as indwelt, possessed, and ruled by the Spirit of God.

life. That idea, though true in itself, cannot be derived from the present passage, for quite apart from the context which, in the light of verse 2, deals in turn with "sin and death," the word "quicken" means "to make alive," not to give additional strength. It therefore refers to the resurrection. St. Paul carefully distinguishes between our Lord's body being "raised," or "awakened," and our body being "quickened." His death occurred without any dissolution of the body in the three days, so that it was sufficient to "awake" Him; but in our case the body is entirely reconstituted, and this is naturally expressed by the word "quicken." The term "mortal" means here, as it does in other passages, "deadly," or "dying," that is, inevitably involving ultimate dissolution (ch. vi. 12; 2 Cor. iv. 11; *cf.* ch. iv. 16-21); so that in verse 10 St. Paul speaks of the fact of death, and in verse 11 of the nature of the change which will transform our mortal body into that which is incorruptible (1 Cor. xv. 43, 44).

Thus the Apostle closes his first main section of the chapter in which he has brought before his readers the new feature of the Spirit of God with His threefold help to the believer; delivering him from the condemnation of the flesh (vers. 1, 2), from the power of the flesh (vers. 3-8), and from the power of death (vers. 9-11). This at once shows the striking contrast between this section and ch. vii. 14-25. In the latter the conflict was between the law and the natural man who in his mind approved of the Divine will and yet found himself powerless to do it by the indwelling of sin in his body. Here the Spirit takes possession, asserts His authority, delivers from the condemnation of sin, gives life to the believer's spirit, and pledges future redemption for the body at the time of the resurrection.

Again we observe the work of each Person of the Holy Trinity in our sanctification. The three titles of the Holy Spirit used in these verses need special attention.

(*a*) *He is "the Spirit of God"* (ver. 9) in contrast to the flesh, referring to the *past* of the believer's life in its inability to fulfil the law of God.

(*b*) He is "the Spirit of Christ" (ver. 10) in relation to the believer's *present* life, providing the necessary power for holiness.

(*c*) He is "the Spirit of Him that raised up Jesus from the dead" (ver. 11) in relation to the believer's *future* life, guaranteeing his resurrection.

All through this passage the emphasis is placed on the Holy Spirit of God in relation to the believer's life, and it is in proportion as this is realized that sanctification becomes at once possible and easy. The various aspects of the Holy Spirit's work, as stated in this section, should be carefully noted and pondered again and again. It is impossible to exaggerate the importance of honoring the Holy Spirit to the fullest extent in regard to Christian holiness.

1. *The Believer's Power.*—The Spirit of God dwells within the believer's spirit (vers. 9, 11), and in proportion as this indwelling is allowed to possess every part of our being, holiness becomes possible.

2. *The Believer's Purity.*—This is made possible by living "after the Spirit," and "minding the Spirit." The word "mind" should be carefully studied in the various passages where it is found in the Greek (Matt. xvi. 23; Rom. xii. 16; Phil. iii. 19; Col. iii. 2). It always means the entire bent of thought, feeling, motive, and will, and when this is realized and our whole inner being is turned definitely and constantly in the direction of the Holy Spirit, purity becomes our very life.

3. *The Believer's Prospect.*—The indwelling of the Spirit is associated with our resurrection. Whether we read verse 11 as "through His Spirit," or "because of His Spirit," we are reminded that the Holy Spirit's possession of us is the assurance that the body in which He has lived will be raised from the dead and quickened into immortal and everlasting life.

As we therefore contemplate the prominence given to the Holy Spirit in this passage we can readily see the force of the Apostle's solemn word, "If any man have not the Spirit of Christ he is none of His." The Spirit of God is the Spirit of Holiness, that holiness "without which no man can see the Lord."

XXX

OBLIGATIONS

Rom. viii. 12-17.

12. Therefore, brethren, we are debtors, not to the flesh, to live after the flesh.
13. For if ye live after the flesh, ye shall die: but if ye through the Spirit do mortify the deeds of the body, ye shall live.
14. For as many as are led by the Spirit of God, they are the sons of God.
15. For ye have not received the spirit of bondage again to fear; but ye have received the Spirit of adoption, whereby we cry, Abba, Father.
16. The Spirit itself beareth witness with our spirit, that we are the children of God:
17. And if children, then heirs; heirs of God, and joint-heirs with Christ.

Verses 1-11 have shown how by the power of the Spirit we are delivered in Christ from the condemnation of the flesh (vers. 1, 2), from the power of the flesh (vers. 3-8), and from the power of death (vers. 9-11). But privileges involve obligations. God has a purpose in bestowing these blessings (ver. 4). We are to respond obediently to the Holy Spirit Who dwells within us. We are debtors to live "after the Spirit," and this necessarily means a mortification of everything fleshly and sinful. It is only as we fulfil these obligations that we can realize our true life of sonship and look forward with absolute assurance to the coming glory. Thus, after the delineation of the characteristic features of the regenerate life (vers. 1-11) comes the admonition to live accordingly. We observe that the entire section is dominated with the thought of the Holy Spirit of God, in Whom alone the regenerate, renewed, and victorious life becomes possible.

I. *Indebtedness to the Spirit* (ver. 12).—Here follows the practical deduction from the foregoing discussion. Because the Spirit has given life to the soul and will hereafter give life to the body, we are under an obligation to live according to the Spirit and not according to the flesh. As we have derived no advantage from the flesh, we are under no obligation to it. The flesh is in us, but we are not to live according to it.

II. *Life in the Spirit* (ver. 13).—If we do live according to the flesh, spiritual death will be the inevitable result. But if through the power of the Spirit we "keep on making dead" the deeds of the body, spiritual life will be the inevitable result. The issues of the two courses of life are certain. The flesh cannot be destroyed in this life, but the deeds which proceed from it can be mortified, or made dead. It is important for the spiritual life that we should remember that the flesh is still with us and dangerous, and that it is to be dealt with not by extirpation, but by mortification. Stifler thus clearly puts the truth:—

> "The man in Christ is not in the flesh, but it is in him, and the problem of salvation is not how to transmute the flesh into something good, but how to live with this thing every day without being overcome by it. The presence of the Spirit solves the problem" (*The Epistle to the Romans*, p. 148).

It is important to observe this first reference that the Apostle makes to the actual *process* of the new life, for hitherto he has necessarily dealt with the *change* from the old life to the new. Now he tells his readers how precisely and continuously the new life is to be lived (Col. iii. 10). It is a life of momentary victory over the flesh, and the secret of the triumph is the presence of the Holy Spirit in His counteracting power. A little girl once said that St. Paul kept under his body "by keeping his soul on top," and in like manner we keep under the flesh by allowing the Holy Spirit to reign supreme. This mortification by the Spirit is one of the most important factors of the spiritual life. Any attempt to crush down indwelling evil by our own strength will only end in disaster, as ch. vii. has already plainly shown. But by "the expulsive power of a new affection," the presence of the Holy Spirit in the heart, victory becomes not only possible, but easy.

III. *Guidance by the Spirit* (ver. 14).—Now the Apostle will show the meaning of the phrase, "shall live," on the part of those who "by the Spirit mortify the deeds of the body." They become conscious of the Spirit as their Guide as well as their Deliverer, and to be led of the Spirit is thus seen to be the normal Christian life, since "as many as are led by the Spirit of God, these are the sons of God." As we follow the Spirit's leading we realize and prove our Divine sonship. This leading of the Spirit is a significant indication of the personal relation between the Spirit of God and the believer. It is no mere influence or power, but a definite personal action that constitutes our full relationship to the Spirit of God.

IV. *Experience of the Spirit* (ver. 14).—The sonship mentioned in the former verse is here confirmed by an appeal to their personal experience. They had indeed received the Holy Spirit, but this gift was something altogether different from the spirit of bondage which would lead them again into servile fear. It was a "spirit of adoption" in which they were enabled to appeal to God as their Father. This contrast between slavery and sonship is very striking and goes to the heart of the true Christian life. Anything that involves a believer in fear and bondage cannot possibly be the work of the Holy Spirit of God, and must come either from his own heart of unbelief or as a temptation of the Evil One. Our sonship implies perfect spiritual liberty and the absence of all legal features which would bring us once more "under law." It is the work of the Holy Spirit to lead the believer into a position of filial confidence which is the very opposite of all servility and thraldom.

The use here made by the Apostle of the idea of "adoption" is particularly interesting and should be carefully compared with the corresponding thought of our sonship as "regeneration." When it is said that we become God's children by regeneration the reference is to our relationship and union of nature. When we are said to become His children by adoption it refers to our position and privileges. One who has been, as it were, taken out of another family and adopted enters thereby into all the rights and privileges of sonship. So that regeneration concerns our nature and condition, while adoption concerns our position and privileges. The two are complementary aspects of our Divine sonship.

V. *The Witness of the Spirit* (ver. 16). — Once again we are reminded of the purely personal relationship of the Holy Spirit to the believer, for here we are told that "the Spirit Himself beareth witness with our spirit that we are the children of God." Let us carefully observe that this testimony of the Spirit is not *to* our spirit, but *with* it. This means that the Spirit of God bears witness *to God* alongside of our own spirit's witness. We look up to God and call Him Father while at the same time the Holy Spirit Himself bears witness to God to the same effect that we are God's children. In Gal. iv. 6, the cry, "Abba, Father," is actually attributed to the Spirit of God. Thus, there is a double testimony; that of the Holy Spirit and of our own spirit, that we are the children of God, and this twofold witness is no mere emotion or feeling dependent upon ourselves and liable to be changed by any alteration of our spiritual life. It is one of those absolute facts of the Christian position which are independent of our particular emotions or sentiments at any given moment, and, as such, it constitutes one of the most precious realities and assurances of our relation to God.

VI. *Blessings of the Spirit* (ver. 17).—Three words are used to describe the spiritual privileges and blessings that come to us through the possession and power of the Holy Spirit: "Children"; "Heirs"; "Joint-heirs with Christ." In ordinary usage an heir is one who has not yet entered upon his inheritance, one to whom his possessions are still future; but the Bible idea of "heir" and "inheritance" is very much more than this, for it implies actual possession in part here and now with the promise of complete possession and enjoyment in the future. Thus, the Holy Spirit bears witness to God, not merely that we are God's children, but that we are heirs, and (marvel of marvels!) "joint-heirs with Christ."

Thus the Apostle brings to a close the series of proofs that sanctification is an evidence of justification, and that the regenerate and renewed life will be ruled and guided in all things by the Holy Spirit of God.

We have seen that the Holy Spirit is prominent throughout this entire section in relation to the spiritual life of the Christian, and there are three aspects of His relation which seem to be specially prominent.

1. *The Spirit of Sonship.*—The term "children" represents believers as spiritual babes just born and calling upon their Father in heaven. It is the Holy Spirit, as the Giver of Life, Who enables us to do this. He reveals the love of God to us till, with our souls filled with the Divine mercy, we lift up our hearts in thankful adoration, crying, "Father." This is how the Christian life begins.

2. *The Spirit of Fellowship.*—The Apostle is careful to use the term "sons" as well as "children," and we must be equally careful to distinguish between them. The word "son," as distinct from "child," represents the believer as a full-grown son, adopted into God's family as an adult member of the household. Whatever difference there is between the babe and the young man, that in things spiritual is the difference represented between "child" and "son." The chief mark of this full-grown sonship is being "led by the Spirit of God," which clearly implies conscious responsiveness on our part to the teaching and guidance of the Spirit. This characteristic of adult sonship is the true meaning of "the Spirit of Adoption." It is the attitude of whole-hearted trust, joyous obedience, and complete consecration. This is how the Christian life continues.

3. *The Spirit of Heirship.*—The term "heir," clearly suggests something additional to and higher than sonship. Not every son is an heir in things temporal, but it is so in things spiritual. We actually possess in and with Christ everything that God has for us. "All things are yours, and ye are Christ's, and Christ is God's." Many passages in the New Testament indicate the glory of the believer's inheritance in Christ (Eph. i. 20-23). It is for us to accept, to enter upon, and to enjoy this marvelous wealth of privilege. No wonder that the Apostle is so certain, in view of this great prospect, that we shall be saved and kept to the very end. This is how the Christian life will be completed.

XXXI

SUFFERINGS AND GLORY

ROM. viii. 17-25.

17. If so be that we suffer with *him*, that we may be also glorified together.
18. For I reckon that the sufferings of this present time *are* not worthy *to be compared* with the glory which shall be revealed in us.
19. For the earnest expectation of the creature waiteth for the manifestation of the sons of God.
20. For the creature was made subject to vanity, not willingly, but by reason of him who hath subjected *the same* in hope,
21. Because the creature itself also shall be delivered from the bondage of corruption into the glorious liberty of the children of God.
22. For we know that the whole creation groaneth and travaileth in pain together until now.
23. And not only *they*, but ourselves also, which have the first-fruits of the Spirit, even we ourselves groan within ourselves, waiting for the adoption, *to wit*, the redemption of our body.
24. For we are saved by hope: but hope that is seen is not hope: for what a man seeth, why doth he yet hope for?
25. But if we hope for that we see not, *then* do we with patience wait for *it*.

THE prior words, "joint-heirs with Christ," naturally suggested to the Apostle the thought of a coming glory, and led him to contemplate the fact of the final stage of our salvation. But now comes a sudden change to the idea of suffering. Why is this? Perhaps it was because suffering was one of the inevitable results of professing Christianity in that age; as though the Apostle would teach that they could not long be sons of God without having to pay for it in suffering. The goal had not been reached in spite of the wonders of the Holy Spirit's work. So he feels it necessary to show that afflictions are not inconsistent with the reality and permanence of spiritual blessings. The doctrine of sanctification has been considered from every point of view (ch. vi. 1—viii. 17), and as it necessarily commenced from justification, so in this reference to our Divine sonship it returns thither in allusion to our adoption in Christ. Meanwhile, however, the life is one of suffering, and for encouragement to cheerful endurance the Apostle is to show that the glory will be both certain and wonderful. Already, in ch. v. 3, he has shown that tribulations cannot possibly put the believer to shame; and now he elaborates this thought, and teaches that, although our life in Christ is encompassed by suffering and death, the inevitable issue will be everlasting glory.

In some ways the message about suffering as the inevitable experience of sonship is equally true today. A faithful life for God will often involve trial, hardship, suffering, persecution. But the suffering is not for punishment; it is only allowed for chastisement. "Whom the Lord loveth, He chasteneth." The believer in suffering is following his Master's example, and as in the Master's case so will it be with the follower, the suffering will inevitably lead to glory. This is the thought of the section from verses 17-30, for it starts and closes with the word "glorified," and adduces several reasons why the suffering is certain to issue in glory.

I. *Comparisons* (vers. 17, 18).

1. The Association of Suffering with Glory. "If so be that we suffer with Him, that we may be also glorified with Him." Thus, the Apostle shows our fellowship with Christ both in suffering and in glory; the one is as real as the other.

2. The Disproportion of Suffering to Glory. "For I reckon that the sufferings of this present time are not worthy to be compared with the glory." St. Paul had been doing some spiritual arithmetic, and, as it were, had put down in two columns the suffering and the glory (*cf.* ch. iii. 28), with the result that there was no comparison between them (2 Cor. iv. 17, 18). This disproportion will be more fully seen in the following verses.

3. The Certainty of Suffering being followed by Glory. "The glory which shall be revealed to usward." The phrase in the original implies the inevitableness of the glory, that it is absolutely certain to

come, and that it shall be unveiled in all its wondrous beauty towards those who suffer with Christ.

II. *Confirmations* (vers. 19-25).—The Apostle now proceeds to confirm these comparisons of suffering and glory by pointing out certain elements in the life of the world, and in particular of believers in Christ, which support the contention that there is a glory to come.

1. The Appeal of Creation (vers. 19-22). This glory is actually being awaited with eagerness, even by the irrational creation which is longing for the manifestation of the sons of God (ver. 19). Creation is now under the curse of sin, for somehow or other the sin of man has affected the lower orders of creation. Nature is not as it was in its original constitution, but through sin has been "subjected to vanity by reason of God Who subjected it in hope that there would be a deliverance of creation from corruption" into the liberty of the glory of the children of God (vers. 20, 21). The need of this deliverance is seen by the present condition of creation. We Christians know that the entire creation is groaning and travailing in pain until now. Everything points to the fact that the present constitution of the universe is not what it was at first, or what it will be hereafter; and this state of affairs as occasioned by sin is a clear proof of the glory that yet awaits creation.

This is one of the most striking passages in St. Paul's writings. It suggests to us some of the most wonderful lessons connected with the universe. Science, philosophy, and Christianity all unite in testifying to the essential unity of the universe, with man as the crown and culmination, and there seems no reason to doubt that the fact of sin has in some way affected the entire constitution of things created. How this has come about, and what precisely is involved, it is of course impossible to say with definiteness and completeness; but the more we realize the oneness of the universe the more we shall come to the conclusion that everything is somehow involved in human sin. Very much that we see around us goes to show that nature is not now in a normal condition, or in that state in which it was originally created by God. Physical suffering among animals, catastrophes and cataclysms in nature have some moral meaning, we may be sure, and it is by no means certain that they would have been in the world if sin had not entered. Scripture is quite clear as to the certainty of "a good time coming" for the entire universe. Originally creation was "good," but it fell when man fell (Gen. iii. 17-19), and shall be restored when he is restored (Heb. ii. 5-9). Many passages indicate with unerring clearness the wonderful future for nature as well as for man (Psa. xcvi. 11-13; xcviii. 7-9; Isa. xi. 6-9; lxv. 20; Rev. v. 13).

2. The Attitude of Believers (ver. 23).—It is clear from the way in which creation is distinguished from Christians in this passage that the four references in verses 19-22 to "creation" must refer to the visible heavens and earth as distinct from man. But now the Apostle provides a further confirmation of the certainty of coming glory. The very same terms in which the expectations of the irrational creation are described are employed to depict the attitude of the early believers. Not only does creation groan, waiting for the great future, but believers themselves are longing for that full redemption which will come with the resurrection of the body (ver. 23). Indeed, our salvation has always had the element of hope in it. We are "saved in hope" (not saved *by* hope, but *by* faith). The attitude of hope is an integral part of the Christian life, and we are now waiting patiently for that which as yet we do not see, but which one day we shall realize. This waiting amidst adversity is in perfect harmony with the terms of our salvation "in Christ." Although He has given us deliverance by His Spirit from the law of sin and death, He has left us in the tribulation of the world, and with our bodies subject to the law of death (ver. 10). This salvation is something present and complete in regard to deliverance from the guilt and condemnation of sin, but it is still future in regard to perfect deliverance from the power and presence of sin. The very idea of hope shows that there cannot be any present deliverance from tribulation and death.

While the section on Sufferings and Glory is not yet complete, we may pause at this point to dwell upon some of the aspects of the teaching here presented.

1. *The Pressure of Suffering.*—The words used of creation and of Christians, both being said to "groan" as they wait, show how keenly the Apostle felt the presence and effects of sin in the world. Suffering is indeed a great reality and a great mystery. It affects in one way or another the entire universe which God originally created "very good." Nature is in many ways purposeless (ver. 20) and unable to realize its true ideal. There is an arrested development through sin, a consciousness of bondage, and a pressure of pain. So also it is with members of the Christian Church. In spite of all the glories and comforts of grace, no one can doubt the fact and problem of suffering, physical, intellectual, and moral.

2. *The Power of Hope.*—The same passage that describes so vividly our suffering depicts with equal vividness our expectation. The suggestion of creation waiting (ver. 19) is that of someone with outstretched neck looking eagerly and constantly for what is earnestly expected. So with believers the same idea is found (ver. 23), and this expectation constitutes the inspiration and cheer of the Christian heart. The prospect of future glory is absolutely certain, for we have God's Word for it. Hope is an essential element of our salvation and must never be omitted from our contemplation of what the Christian life means. Faith looks backward and upward; hope looks onward. Faith accepts; but hope expects. Faith is concerned with Him Who promises; but hope is occupied with the good things promised. Faith appropriates; but hope anticipates. It is in the power of this hope which the New Testament calls "that blessed hope" that we are to live and labor. Hope is always centered on the coming of the Lord, and included in that, on the resurrection from the dead with complete deliverance from sin, likeness to Christ, and the full revelation of our sonship to God in Him (1 Cor. xv. 51-57; Phil. iii. 20, 21; 1 Thess. iv. 15-17; 1 John iii. 1, 2).

XXXII

GUARANTEES OF GLORY

ROM. viii. 26-30.

26. Likewise the Spirit also helpeth our infirmities: for we know not what we should pray for as we ought: but the Spirit itself maketh intercession for us with groanings which cannot be uttered.
27. And he that searcheth the hearts knoweth what *is* the mind of the Spirit, because he maketh intercession for the saints according to *the will of* God.
28. And we know that all things work together for good to them that love God, to them who are the called according to *his* purpose.
29. For whom he did foreknow, he also did predestinate *to be* conformed to the image of his Son, that he might be the firstborn among many brethren.
30. Moreover whom he did predestinate, them he also called: and whom he called, them he also justified: and whom he justified, them he also glorified.

THE Apostle is still occupied with the thought of coming and certain glory, and he is engaged in adducing reasons for feeling assured that the glory is as inevitable as the suffering. Already he has given us two confirmations in the appeal of creation and the attitude of believers. There are two more of these proofs which complete the discussion.

I. *The Action of the Holy Spirit* (vers. 26, 27.—The present help of the Holy Spirit is shown to be another guarantee of the glory that will follow the suffering. As the sons and heirs of God, we possess as yet only "the firstfruits of the Spirit" ((ver. 23), but the very thought, from the Old Testament, of firstfruits implies a complete harvest later on (Jas. i. 18). The complete deliverance of our spirit, soul, and body (1 Thess. v. 23) from the "law of sin and death" is a matter of hope for which we are waiting patiently; and now amidst present sufferings the indwelling Spirit does far more than inspire us with hope, He actually helps us in our present distress. Just as hope assists us (ver. 25), so "in like manner the Spirit helps our weaknesses," for we have no power unaided to realize our hopes. The word employed for the help of the Spirit is very striking. It is only found here, and in one other passage (Luke x. 40), and implies "assistance against all opposition." The Holy Spirit makes common cause with us against every foe, by taking hold of us and providing adequate aid. In particular He helps us in our weakness about prayer, all the helplessness and weariness which tend to come to the believer amidst suffering and perplexity. "We know not how to pray as we ought," but the Holy Spirit intercedes for us with unuttered and unutterable groanings. We feel as if we could not pray, but the Holy Spirit prays for us; and we know that this intercession will be effectual because God, the searcher of hearts, knows the meaning of the Spirit's intercession and interprets the inarticulate utterances as they are offered on our behalf.

How great a help all this assurance is to the believer amidst his weariness, perplexity, weakness, and pain is only too well known to personal experience. God Who is greater than our hearts understands us perfectly, and while our lips may be unable to utter anything, the Holy Spirit is all the while making intercession within, just as in a later verse we shall see that the Lord Himself is making intercession above.

> "But the darkness that is so dark to us is no darkness with God. . . . The process of our redemption is not all our own, and it goes on by methods not all or always understood by ourselves. We are often nearest when we think ourselves farthest off, and farthest off when we think ourselves nearest. God reads order where we see only confusion; our groanings that cannot be uttered are the intercessions of the Holy Ghost to Him for us, and however unintelligible to us, it is all clear to Him whose, after all, are all the wisdom and the power of our salvation" (Du Bose, *The Gospel according to St Paul*, p. 279).

It is significant that once again we have the word "groan," so that there are the three groanings: of creation (ver. 22), of believers (ver. 23); of the Spirit (ver. 26).

II. *The Assurance of God's Providence and Purpose* (vers. 28-30).—Here the Apostle reaches the highest point of his wonderful statement that glory is the inevitable outcome of suffering.

1. The Providence of God is working on our behalf (ver. 28).—While "we do not know" what to pray for as we ought (ver. 26) "We do know" (ver. 28) by personal experience, and by God's dealing with others, that all things in the universe are continually working together for good to those that love God. Let us ponder the fulness of this verse and its encouragement.

(*a*) The Fact of a constant working; "Work." Life is made up of many forces, and though at times they seem to be quite stationary they are constantly at work.

(*b*) The Comprehensiveness of the Working; "All things work." Some people are fond of distinguishing between general and particular providences, and seeing God's hand in the great events and not in the smaller details of life; but the true Christian soul refuses to think of anything as outside the direct or else the permissive will of his Heavenly Father.

(*c*) The Harmony of the Working; All things work together." Is it possible for the cold north wind to harmonize with the warm southern breezes? Can sunshine and tears be harmonized? They can; and instance after instance might be given to prove the truth of this contention.

(*d*) The Beneficence of the Working; "All things work together for good." This is the tendency, however mysterious and difficult may be the process. A staircase may wind, but each step is higher than the preceding one, and it is "still upward." The diamond setter cuts and polishes the jewel very long and thoroughly before its facets of brilliancy are visible.

(*e*) The Limitation of the Working; "To them that love God." This restriction must be carefully observed, for godlessness and sin work wrath, and it is only in connection with the believer that these wonderful words are true. Of the man of the world who deliberately continues without Christ it may be fearlessly said that everything is against him: God's character, God's law, God's holiness, God's judgment. But, granted the condition of "them that love God," everything will work harmoniously for good as the result of God's marvellous providence.

2. The Purpose of God is working on our behalf (vers. 28-30). —Now the Apostle turns the subject round and looks at it from its Divine standpoint. The providence of God has its human outlook, while the purpose of God looks within and relates to God Himself. From the human side, the reference is "to them that love God"; but these are now looked at from the Divine side and described as "them that are called according to His purpose." This Divine purpose is thus emphasized, and we are assured that no circumstances of life can possibly harm those who are included in it; for the fact that they love God implies and presupposes His dealings with them in several definite stages or links in the chain of His relationship, all of which shall be realized in due time.

(*a*) They were foreknown. God fixed His regard on them, noted them with favor, and this favorable regard is the commencement of the whole process of redemption.

(*b*) They were predestinated. God's will follows His knowledge and He foreordained them to be conformed to the image of His Son. They were to find in the glorified Son of God their pattern, their power, and their goal.

(*c*) They were called. This, in the Apostle's meaning, is always to be understood as what is known as "effectual calling," not merely invited by God, but also as having accepted the invitation.

(*d*) They were justified. This was the next stage and followed naturally and necessarily from the invitation and its acceptance.

(*e*) They were glorified. Thus the work was completed and crowned and salvation fully realized. So the Apostle's thought after commencing with the promise of glory (ver. 17) goes back again to the assurance of this completion of the Divine work. The past tenses in these verses have often been noted by writers, and especially the past tense of the last word "glorified." Denney finely says, "The tense in the last word is amazing. It is the most daring anticipation of faith that even the New Testament contains."

And so from beginning to end God's people are certain of the glory as they now boast in hope of it (ch. v. 2). It should be carefully noted that the Apostle does not attempt even to introduce, still less to reconcile, the divine and human aspects of this great passage. It is for this reason that everything is looked at from the Divine point of view, and that there is no reference to sanctification between justification and glorification. Even the phrase "conformed to the image of His Son" seems to point almost wholly, if not quite, to the future culmination rather than to the present process of being conformed. It was essential in view of the context that the Apostle should emphasize the Divine side since he is concerned to show that no vicissitudes can possibly rob believers of their eternal glory. Of course we must not forget that in other passages the human side and the various human conditions of this complete work are equally clearly brought to our notice. But safety will be found at this stage in keeping strictly to the Apostle's statements without attempting to reconcile every aspect of truth. Those who are most deeply impressed with the marvel, power, and absoluteness of Divine grace will never fail to realize their own responsibility, their own duty, and the conditions by means of which God works out His purpose concerning them.

Everything in the believer's life will depend upon how he understands and accepts the fact of suffering, if he is to enjoy to the full the Divine grace here and the glory hereafter.

1. *The Believer in the Shadow.*—Jacob once said, "All these things are against me." What a wrong view of life this was can easily be seen from the story. It was due to a very partial knowledge of the facts. He spoke in ignorance. Joseph was not dead, Simeon was not dead, Benjamin was to be kept quite safely. He spoke, too, with a defective memory. How marvelously God had led, kept, and blessed him during the past years! Surely God might still be trusted to be faithful to His promise? An illogical mind was also his. He limited the God of Israel, ignoring God's character, forgetful of His power, and oblivious of everything God had said to him in promise and assurance. Above all, he spoke out of an untrustful heart. With feelings unhinged it seemed as though he could not confide in his God and so dishonored the One Who had so richly blessed him, by crying out "All these things are against

me." If ever we are in a similar case we shall never be otherwise than in a spiritual shadow-land. Surely we may trust our Heavenly Father! Two Christians were once speaking of their experiences, and one said, "It is terribly hard to trust God and realize His hand in the dark passages of life." "Well, brother," said the other, "if you cannot trust a man out of your sight, he is not worth much; and, if you cannot trust God in the dark, it shows that you do not trust Him at all." Psalm xci. does not say, "under His wings thou shalt see," but "under His wings thou shalt trust."

2. *The Believer in the Sunshine.*—This is the right view of life, and is in marked contrast to that of Jacob; for the true heart exults in saying, "All things work together for good." Many years ago an eminent French engineer was detained in the Mediterranean by a tedious quarantine. It was hard for one of his active temperament to endure such confinement; but as he waited on the deck of the vessel he read, and the book, to which he gave extra attention, prompted him to the conception of the Suez Canal, the execution of which has made him so famous and has been of such great service to the world. Did M. de Lesseps afterwards regret those dragging days of quarantine? And if the child of God could realize more fully the constant presence and guidance of a loving Father he would more readily perceive that all things are really working together for his good. Let us ever live in this love of God. The more we trust the more we shall love, and the more we love the more fully we shall trust. Life is dark, but love can see. Life is difficult, but love can understand. Life is sad, but love can rejoice while waiting for that day when we shall no longer see through a glass darkly but when we shall know even as we are known.

XXXIII

EXULTANT ASSURANCE

ROM. viii. 31-39.

31. What shall we then say to these things? If God *be* for us, who *can be* against us?

32. He that spared not his own Son, but delivered him up for us all, how shall he not with him also freely give us all things?

33. Who shall lay any thing to the charge of God's elect? *It is* God that justifieth.

34. Who *is* he that condemn*eth*? *It is* Christ that died, yea rather, that is risen again, who is even at the right hand of God, who also maketh intercession for us.

35. Who shall separate us from the love of Christ? *shall* tribulation, or distress, or persecution, or famine, or nakedness, or peril, or sword?

36. As it is written, For thy sake we are killed all the day long; we are accounted as sheep for the slaughter.

37. Nay, in all these things we are more than conquerors through him that loved us.

38. For I am persuaded, that neither death, nor life, nor angels, nor principalities, nor powers, nor things present, nor things to come,

39. Nor height, nor depth, nor any other creature, shall be able to separate us from the love of God, which is in Christ Jesus our Lord.

Now comes the Apostle's paean of triumph, as he closes this magnificent view of the life of the people of God. After emphasizing God's side of the Christian redemption he describes the resulting feeling of absolute confidence, and shows how that confidence rises into positive assurance. As Gairdner says:—

> "The impassioned but subdued tones of verses 18-30, which succeeded the calm logic of verses 1-17, now pass into a sort of lyric outburst, which quickens and swells to its magnificent climax' (*Helps to the Study of the Epistle to the Romans*, p. 77).

Fearlessly the Apostle asks, "What then are we to say to these things" (ver. 31)? "These things" are not only the aspects of truth presented in the verses immediately preceding, but include the whole discussion of righteousness, its character and results, from ch. iii. 21-viii. 30. Having asked the question, implying that there is nothing to fear either here or hereafter, he answers it by "saying" three "things." He glories in the blessedness and security of believers by dwelling on three fundamental reasons for his triumphant confidence.

I. *Their Relation to God* (vers. 31b-33).

1. God is their Advocate (ver. 31).—"If (or since) God be for us." Everything that he has had to say about the Divine redemption implies that God has interposed on behalf of His people.

2. He is their Protector (ver. 31).—"Who can be against us?" Since God is ours nothing else in the world matters at all.

3. He is their Provider (ver. 32).—Once again, but in a fuller and more elaborate form, we have the argument of ch. v. 6-10. God, Who gave the very best He had in the Person of His Son, will not fail after all to give in Christ everything that pertains to life and godliness. Like Abraham of old (Gen. xxii. 16), God did not spare His own dear and well-beloved Son; and, having handed Him over as a sacrifice on our behalf, He is not likely to be lacking in those provisions for the spiritual life which can only come from Him.

4. He is their Justifier (ver. 33).—Is there anyone who will dare to lay a charge against the elect of God? No one, since God Himself is their justifier. As Marcus Rainsford, Senr., in his fine book on this chapter, so well says, "There is no ground for condemnation since Christ has suffered the penalty; there is no law to condemn us since we are not under law but under grace; there is no tribunal for judgment since ours is now a Throne of Grace, not a judgment; and, above all, there is no Judge to sentence us since God Himself, the only Judge, is our Justifier."

II. *Their Relation to Christ* (ver. 34).—Now comes another question. Is there anyone to condemn us? No one at all, since believers have a fourfold protection in Christ. (*a*) The protection of His death as the propitiation for our sins. (*b*) The protection of His resurrection as the proof of our justification. (*c*) The protection of His ascension since He is at the right hand of God as our Advocate (1 John. ii. 1, 2). (*d*) The protection of His intercession which in the power of His endless life saves us to the uttermost (Heb. vii. 24, 25). Surrounded by this perfect provision there can be no possible condemnation. The ascension is mentioned only here in this Epistle. Usually the stress is on the resurrection. It is in Ephesians that we have the converse and complementary thought which emphasizes in particular the ascension of Christ and ours in Him. Thus, as the Apostle faces this question and throws out his challenge against any who might condemn, he shows at once that Christ is "our righteousness, sanctification, and redemption" (1 Cor. i. 30).

III. *Their Relation to Circumstances* (vers. 35-39).—One more question is asked in this great challenge of the Apostle. "Who shall separate us from the love of Christ?" Is it conceivable that anyone shall separate believers from the love of their Master? Are there any circumstances, however pressing and painful, that can do this? (vers. 35, 36). On the contrary, in the midst of these very untoward circumstances believers are "super-conquerors" through Him that loved them (ver. 37). Not merely do they have victory, but something far more, an overwhelming defeat of all enemies. Circumstances are those things that "stand round us," but they cannot hinder our access to Christ, or prevent His coming to our rescue. A modern French version vividly renders the phrase, "more than conquerors' by *vainqueurs et au-délà,* "conquerors, and more than that." This love of Christ is so certain, so constant, and so changeless that it elecits the perfect persuasion (ver. 38) that nothing in space or time will be able to separate believers from the love of their God in Christ. Every conceivable enemy is contemplated in this wonderful enumeration—the most extreme changes of condition (death and life), the most potent orders of being in the universe (angels and principalities), the possibilities of time present and future (things present and things to come), everything that is involved in space (height and depth), and last of all, anything and everything to be found in creation; and, as he faces them all, resolutely and definitely, he comes to the absolute conviction that not one of them can separate believers from the God Who loves them. Let us observe all through the passage that the emphasis is laid upon God's love to us as a reason for this triumphant confidence and perfect certainty. It is recorded that Spurgeon once saw on a weathercock the words, "God is love," and on remarking to his companion that he did not think that it was appropriate on so changeable a thing, he was met with the answer that he had misinterpreted it, that it really meant, "God is love, whichever way the wind blows."

Some authorities favor a different punctuation of the questions in verses 33-35, a few great names consider that the passage would be still more vivid if everything in these verses were put in the interrogative form. "Who shall lay anything to the charge of God's elect? Shall God that justifieth? Who is he that condemneth? Shall Christ that died? Who shall separate us from the love of Christ? Shall tribulation?"

But it seems to the present writer that, following Godet, "there is still much to be said for the punctuation of the A.V.," more particularly as there is a striking coincidence between the three results of sin recorded in Genesis iii. with the three questions of verses 33-35.

1. Adam and Eve were conscious of *guilt* before God. To the believer there is no guilt (ver. 33), because of God's justification.

2. Adam and Eve were sentenced to *condemnation* by God. To the believer there is no condemnation (ver. 34), because of Christ's redemption.

3. Adam and Eve were sentenced to *separation* from God. To the believer there is no separation (ver. 35), because of God's love.

We must not fail to observe the rapturous and triumphant ending "in Christ Jesus our Lord," and to observe the same close to chs. v., vi., vii. At each stage of the Apostle's discussion of his great theme he bursts forth into the praise of his Lord; "Christ is all."

As we review these eight chapters and pay special attention to the last of them, we naturally ask again the Apostle's question, "What then shall we say to these things?"

1. *These Things.*—What are they? They are all concerned with God's righteousness (ch. i. 17; iii. 21); righteousness provided, accepted, guaranteed: righteousness complete, continuous, permanent: righteousness universal, full, victorious. And as we concentrate attention on this particular eighth chapter, what are "these things" to which the Apostle bids us look. There is a sevenfold emphasis running through these verses: (1) No condemnation; (2) no guilt; (3) no weakness; (4) no defeat; (5) no despair; (6) no want; (7) no separation.

2. *What then shall we say?*—Herein lies the personal application of it all. What shall *we* say? Let each believer ask himself these questions: Is this *my* experience? Is this the Christianity of *my* life? If not, why not? It may be, it ought to be. Shall we not add, It *shall* be? Then our life will "say to these things," "Unto Him that loved us and washed us from our sins in His own blood, and made us kings and priests unto God and His Father, to Him be the glory and dominion for ever and ever."

XXXIV

REVIEW OF CHAPTERS I.-VIII.

THIS is a convenient opportunity to look back over the entire section hitherto considered in order that we may have clearly before us the teaching as a whole. A constant danger in connection with this Epistle is that of being occupied with verses and small sections and thus of failing to see and grasp the general line of thought. It would be well to read these chapters through at one time and thus to refresh the mind with the main ideas.

The one great theme is that of the Gospel as the revelation of the righteousness of God (ch. i. 17), that is, the revelation of God's personal character as righteous, together with the revelation of His gift of righteousness in Christ to guilty man. All through these chapters this theme is brought before us specifically in opposition to the righteousness of the law. Righteousness by *God's gift* is contrasted with righteousness by *man's work.* The chapters are occupied with the answer to Job's question, "How should man be just with God?" (ix. 2). Or, to put it otherwise, "Where shall righteousness be found?" In ch. i. 17, we have the quotation from Hab. ii. 4, which rendered quite literally is, "The righteous by faith shall live." Taking these six words and dividing them into three pairs they give us an outline of chs. i.-viii. "The righteous"—"by faith"—"shall live."

I. *"The Righteous"* (chs. i. 18-iii. 20).—Here we are shown the need of a Divine righteousness.

1. The wrath of God is revealed against all unrighteousness (ch. i. 18-32). This is first considered with special reference to the Gentiles who, by reason of the corruption of their nature, had brought upon themselves the judicial displeasure of God, and were therefore "worthy of death."

2. The Jew was equally under condemnation, notwithstanding his special privileges (ch. ii. 1—iii. 8). He had failed to use his great opportunities, and had become censorious of others, thereby proving his own unrighteousness, which could not escape the righteous judgment of God.

3. This condition of universal unrighteousness, together with man's inability to work out righteousness, is proved from Scripture as well as by the facts of life, with the result that "every mouth is stopped, and the whole world is guilty before God" (ch. iii. 9-20).

II. *"By Faith"* (ch. iii. 20-v. 21).—Here we are shown the method of the reception of righteousness.

1. Human unrighteousness with its consequent inability is met by the Divine provision of righteousness in the Gospel. This is specially wrought by the Atoning Sacrifice of Christ, and is to be received through faith, which excludes all human boasting, and establishes on a firm foundation the law of God in relation to man (ch. iii. 21-31).

2. This Divine righteousness received through faith is proved from the Old Testament by the case of Abraham, and confirmed by that of David. Faith in our case is shown to be exactly of the same nature as that of Abraham in relation to God (ch. iv. 1-25).

3. This Divine righteousness through faith introduces the believer to a state of blessedness even amid afflictions (ch. v. 1-11), for the simple reason that it deals effectively with the principle of sin which is derived through our race connection with Adam (ch. v. 12-21). Though sin abounds, grace in Christ super-abounds.

III. *"Shall Live"* (chs. vi.-viii.).—Here we are shown the life of righteousness, with its secrets of power, victory and permanence.

1. This life of righteousness provides victory over sin (ch. vi. 1-14) and transfers the soul from bondage to liberty (ch. vi. 15-23). *Grace* and *sin* are here contrasted, and it is seen that grace does not lead to sin (ch. vi. 1, 15).

2. This life of righteousness cannot be lived by means of law (ch. vii.). *Law* and *grace* are here contrasted, and the former is seen to be utterly powerless for holiness.

3. This life of righteousness is lived in the power of the Holy Spirit (ch. viii.). *Flesh* and *spirit* are here contrasted, and the Spirit of God is seen to be the Divine power for holiness triumphing over the flesh (ch. viii. 1-17), triumphing in the midst of affliction (ch. viii. 17-30), and triumphing over every actual and conceivable opposition (ch. viii. 31-39).

Thus chs. i.-v. show how we are *accounted* righteous by grace through faith (Justification), and chs. vi.-viii. show how we are *made* righteous through faith (Sanctification), and how, too, we are *kept* righteous (Glorification). Salvation emanating from God's righteousness is based upon justification, built up in sanctification, and crowned in glorification. And it is received at each point by *faith.* From God's side, Salvation is Righteousness by Grace *for* Faith. From man's side, it is Righteousness by Grace *through* Faith.

The one practical point of all this is, whether these great doctrinal themes have become part of our personal experience. Doctrine separated from life is dry, abstract, unprofitable, and even dangerous; but doctrine received into, experienced by, and manifested through life is the secret of clearness of perception, and vigor of activity. St. Paul ever kept doctrine and life closely associated, for they were inextricably bound up in his experience and service. The life of truth and the life of obedience are both necessary, and it is the characteristic feature of these chapters that doctrine is set forth as the root and foundation of life, and life is set forth as the fruit and expression of doctrine. This is true Christianity, and for a genuine, balanced, Christian life there are few passages more essential, more valuable, and more powerful than these eight chapters.

XXXV

PURPOSE AND OUTLINE OF CHAPTERS IX.-XI.

THE change from chapter viii, is abrupt and striking, and yet there is a close and necessary connection between the sections. Though there is no formal link of association there is a very definite psychological relation. This is the second great division of the Epistle, and it deals with the relation of the Jew to the Gospel of Righteousness treated of in chs. i.-viii. Chs. ix.-xi. have not received from writers anything like the attention that the earlier ones have had, and perhaps as a consequence of this neglect some commentators hold that the chapters represent an episode, or parenthesis, or appendix which may be to some extent overlooked in the study of the Epistle. But this is an entirely incorrect view, for the chapters are an integral part of the Epistle and are essential to its true interpretation. Any view which regards them as a mere corollary or appendix can be safely set aside, for in some respects they are the very heart of the Epistle when judged from the personal and historical standpoint of St. Paul. The teaching of these chapters (the relation of the Jew to the Gospel) has really been in evidence from the start. In ch. i. 2, the Gospel is said to be "according to the Scriptures"; in ch. i. 16, it is spoken of as "To the Jew first"; in ch. iii. 1, the question is asked, "What advantage hath the Jew"; in ch. i. 18-iii. 20, Jew as well as Gentile is proved to be unrighteous; in ch. iv., the Old Testament is used to prove justification by faith; in ch. v., all men are included in racial connection with Adam; and the inability of law to justify (ch. iii.) and to sanctify (ch. vii.) is applied to all men, whether Jew or Gentile.

And yet there were two great arguments continually used against Paul's Gospel. If, said the Jewish objector, the Gospel of Righteousness by faith is true, how are we to account for two things: (1) the exceptional position and privileges of the Jews, as compared with the Gentiles, which faith seems entirely to remove (Gal. iii. 28)? How are we to account for and explain the wonderful promises of the Old Testament assuring a seed to Abraham which was to issue in blessing to all the world? If there is "no difference" (ch. iii. 22) what advantage had the Jew? (2) The rejection of the Gospel by the Jewish nation. We might have supposed that all would gladly accept Christ. With all the remarkable opportunities they had, how was it possible for the Jews to reject Him? Surely, then, a Jew might argue, If Jesus Christ is what Paul teaches, either God has broken His special promises to Israel, or if He has not, then this Gospel of Paul is not of God. The Apostle answers the two questions in these chapters; the latter in chs. ix. and x., and the former in ch. xi.

This question of the relation of the Jew to the Gospel was one of the great problems of St. Paul's ministry, and to men of Jewish blood it was particularly acute. At the time that Romans was written it had very special point and meaning for the Apostle himself. His evangelistic work in the East was almost finished, and he was free to pay his visit to Rome, which would be the crowning point of his Apostleship to the Gentiles. The time had come to survey the entire field. Surrounded by Jewish opponents he considers the contention that his Gospel of grace which puts Jewish salvation entirely on a level with Gentile might be regarded as entirely blotting out the Jew and removing him from his position of special privilege in the purpose of God. He therefore addresses himself to the task of showing the true state of the case. As the years went on after the Death and Resurrection of our Lord, and the Jewish national rejection of Him as Messiah became more and more evident, the solemn and awful meaning of Christ's own words about the nation's disobedience became more obvious and profound. It was becoming clearer and clearer that their house had been left to them desolate and that the Kingdom of God had been transferred elsewhere (Matt. xxi. 43). And as these facts pressed upon thoughtful minds we cannot wonder that the great Apostle desires to deal with the entire subject as he does in these chapters.

The problem was primarily historical, and the historical facts must be ever kept in view. The simple but adequate explanation of Jewish rejection is seen in John i. 11. "He came unto His own, and His own received Him not." And the whole of the Fourth Gospel is occupied with the theme of Jewish opposition to Christ. But although all that receive Him become one in Him (John i. 12), there are certain facts of history which must not be overlooked.

While grace makes Jew and Gentile one, there is still a place for the Jew, which will be seen in God's own time. Although most Christians now are Gentiles, yet the day of the Jew is not over. He is not to be regarded merely as a member of the Church. He will have a place yet. It is impossible to spiritualize all the Old Testament and apply it to Christianity. There is a marked contrast between Hebrews and Romans. In Hebrews the Jew is considered spiritually. Here he is considered nationally, and in relation to the whole world, while preserving his individuality. St. Paul's view is that for the present Judaism is as it were on a by-path, while the Gentiles are going forward to salvation and blessing along the highway. Nevertheless God's purpose had not failed, and the day was coming when He would return to Israel to take them up again into His purpose and make them a channel of blessing to the world (ch. xi.).

The general course of thought should be grasped before entering upon the details. The Apostle's teaching proceeds along three main lines:—

(I) Ch. ix. 6-29; God's absolute freedom as against any claim of man.
(II) Ch. ix. 30-x. 21; Jewish sinfulness in rejecting Christ.
(III) Ch. xi. 1-36; Present events are to be overruled for the the future glory of both Gentile and Jew.

Thus, as Godet points out, the one problem all through is how God can reject those whom He has elected, and this question is met in the three ways just stated: (1) God preserves His entire liberty (ch. ix.). (2) God shows that Israel's sin is the true explanation (ch. x.. (3) God vindicates His action by foretelling future consequences (ch. xi.)

Now let us consider a fuller outline of the thought in order to see its bearing as a whole:—

1. The Apostle's intense sorrow because of Israel's rejection of Jesus Christ (ch. ix. 1-5).

2. This rejection, however, is not at all inconsistent with God's Word or with His character for veracity. There is nothing in God's action to Israel which lays Him open to the charge of unfaithfulness to His promises to Abraham and his seed. The rejection is not against the promises, but in complete harmony with God's method with Israel from the beginning, the method of Divine, sovereign election (ch. ix. 6-13).

3. Nor is the casting away of unbelieving Israel inconsistent with God's perfect and absolute justice (ch. ix. 14-29).

(*a*) The righteousness of this Divine method with Israel is shown to be according to Scripture, Moses and Pharaoh being cited as examples (vers. 14-18).

(*b*) This method is then shown to be righteous, because God, as God, has sovereign right over His creatures, and any questioning of Divine procedure is really rebellion (vers. 19-24).

(*c*) This method of God is seen from the prophets to be that of Divine sovereignty, calling the Gentiles and rejecting Israel (vers. 25-29).

4. The present condition of Israel is really due to their sin of unbelief and their unwillingness to submit to God's righteousness. It was solely of Divine grace that the Gentiles were accepted, while Israel's rejection was caused by refusal of grace and reliance on their own works (ch. ix. 30-x. 4).

5. God's righteousness is perfectly free as a gift through faith (ch. x. 5-11).

6. It is also universal in its scope, being intended for all mankind (ch. x. 12-18).

7. Israel failed to realize that all this, as well as their own disobedience, was actually predicted in their own Scripture (ch. x. 19-21).

8. But the present rejection of the Jews is not total and complete (ch. xi. 1-10).

9. Nor is it final and irremediable, for they are to be turned and become a blessing to the whole world (ch. xi. 11-36).

It is a considerable help to the proper understanding of these chapters to view them in strict relation to the preceding section of the Epistle, for, as we have seen, the Jew is in evidence from the outset, and these chapters have a close and necessary connection with what has gone before. Thus we may first of all look at the three objections raised by the Jew in ch. iii. 1-8, and observe how these are answered fully in ch. ix. 1-33.

(*a*) Ch. iii. 1, 2. "What advantage hath the Jew?" His privileges remain intact (ch. ix. 4, 5).

(*b*) Ch. iii. 3, 4. Is God unfaithful? He is not unfaithful (ch. ix. 6-13).

(*c*) Ch. iii. 5-8. Is God unrighteous? He is not unrighteous (ch. ix. 14-33).

Again, we may compare the great section (ch. i. 18-iii. 20) with the chapters before us and find in them the twofold relation of Jew and Gentile to Divine righteousness.

(*a*) In ch. i. 18-iii.20 this relation is considered from the standpoint of law, and both Jew and Gentile are shown to need Divine Righteousness.

(*b*) In ch. ix.-xi. this relation is considered from the standpoint of grace and faith, and both Jew and Gentile are shown to need them.

Yet again, we may look at these three chapters as illustrating the truth of ch. iii. 29, 30, that God is the God of the Gentiles also. In ch. i. 18-iii. 20 both Jews and Gentiles are shown to have sinned and to need God's righteousness, while in ch. ix-xi. righteousness is offered to both but received by one only through faith. Let it be once again strongly emphasized that these three chapters have an intimate connection with all that precedes. As we study the

Apostle's great argument in ch. i.-viii. we can readily understand his determination to set the great facts of the national history of his people in their true relation to the question of Divine righteousness, for he knew only too well that many of his fellow-countrymen were building false hopes upon a perverted interpretation of those facts.

Reviewing the entire argument and endeavoring to summarize it, we observe that the Apostle, first of all, examines with great care the relationship into which God entered with the nation of Israel (ch. ix. 6-29), and the Divine conduct is vindicated in excluding the main body of Jews from the blessing of the Gospel. The Apostle demonstrates the fact that the relationship of God to Israel was one that left Him perfectly free to take the course He had actually pursued without laying Himself open to the charge of unfaithfulness or unrighteousness. From the very beginning the blessings were never intended for them as a nation. God was sovereign in the bestowal of His blessings from the outset. His covenant throughout was essentially one of grace to be appropriated through faith, so that if men believed, whether Jews or Gentiles, they would receive, and if they would not believe, they would not receive. Moreover, the Apostle not only proves that the nature of the covenant left room for their national rejection, but he also shows that the covenant was not cancelled by that rejection, and that, hereafter, in God's own time and way, it would reassert its marvelous influence and bring about unspeakable blessing to the Jewish nation and to the world.

Thus Israel's rejection provides the most solemn warning that history affords as to the awful results of spiritual pride and self-sufficiency. They refused to accept and maintain their unique spiritual advantages and a humble and grateful dependence upon the Giver, and they were thereupon set aside and broken off as a branch. And they will remain in that condition as long as they are in unbelief; but when they are willing to become poor in spirit and submit themselves to the righteousness of God, He will graft them in again and make them possessors of that wealth of blessing which He has all along had in store for them.

As we look carefully at these chapters we can readily see that they open "a wide door to intelligence in the ways of God" (J. N. Darby). The Apostle meant this letter to be a systematic and circular one, dealing with some of the most difficult and important problems of his day. "The extraordinary daring of the end of ch. xi. is not unrelated to the extraordinary passion of the beginning of ch. ix. The whole discussion is a magnificent illustration of the aphorism that great thoughts come from the heart" (Denney).

These chapters are a fine corrective to merely individualistic views of God's salvation. It is essential to keep ever in mind: (1) God's purpose for the individual; (2) God's purpose for the Church; (3) God's purpose for the world. The last of these is by no means the least; indeed, it is the climax and culmination of the rest. These three chapters, especially ch. xi., deals with the third of these points, and it will be well for us to dwell upon it and have it constantly before our mind. Among other things it will be the finest possible encouragement and inspiration against pessimism. We are so apt to grow weary, depressed, and disheartened with the fight against sin and the slow progress of good and right and truth. These chapters should hearten us by reminding us that this old sin-stricken world is still to have its golden age when "All the ransomed Church of God" (God's heavenly company) shall "be saved to sin no more," and reign with Christ over the earth. And also when Israel (God's earthly company) shall be "saved in the Lord with an everlasting salvation" and become a blessing to the whole world. In the light of these glorious hopes how *can* we be depressed and discouraged? What manner of persons ought we to be not only in all holy conversation and godliness, but in all buoyancy of hope and courage, and in all strenuousness of life and service?

XXXVI

ST. PAUL AND ISRAEL

Rom. ix. 1-5.

1. I say the truth in Christ, I lie not, my conscience also bearing me witness in the Holy Ghost,
2. That I have great heaviness and continual sorrow in my heart.
3. For I could wish that myself were accursed from Christ for my brethren, my kinsmen according to the flesh:
4. Who are Israelites; to whom *pertaineth* the adoption, and the glory, and the covenants, and the giving of the law, and the service *of God,* and the promises;
5. Whose *are* the fathers, and of whom as concerning the flesh Christ *came,* who is over all, God blessed for ever. Amen.

This personal introduction to his great theme is characteristic of the Apostle. His heart was rent in twain by the trouble of his nation's rejection of his Savior. The outburst of confidence and thanksgiving, with which ch. viii. closes is in sharp contrast to his unceasing sorrow as he realizes that the glories of God's grace in Christ are not being enjoyed by his fellow-countrymen. In ch. i. 16 he had spoken of the Gospel as intended for "the Jew first," and yet the Jews as a nation were not sharing in the glorious opportunity. These verses, as we ponder their meaning, reveal the great heart of the great Apostle.

I. *Sincerity of Feeling* (ver. 1).—His constant controversies and conflicts with Jews and Judaisers might suggest doubts of his assertions of sorrow, and so he solemnly affirms his sincerity. He knew that he was regarded as a traitor (Acts xxi. 33; xxii. 22; xxv. 24), and so he makes these very strong protestations. He affirms his sincerity both positively and negatively. He speaks "in Christ," that is, in union with Him, a position in which it was quite impossible to lie, since Christ is the Searcher of hearts (Eph. iv. 15; Col.

iii. 9). His conscience bears witness with him (ch. ii. 15; viii. 16) in the presence and power of the Holy Spirit, and on this account he is able to speak with all possible clearness and force as he stands in the presence of the God of truth. This threefold reference to Conscience, Christ, and the Holy Spirit, as indicative of his sincerity, is very striking. Although he has had to pour contempt on Jewish pride and self-sufficiency it was not because of any lack of love to his brethren.

II. *Intensity of Feeling* (vers. 2, 3a).—Here we find a twofold statement of his sorrow which is thereby intensified by repetition. His grief is not only "great" but "unceasing." It is at once mental and physical. "Paul cannot find words strong enough to convey his feeling" (Denney).

The proof of this intensity is seen in the usual interpretation of the Apostle's words, that he is prepared to go the length of being severed from Christ, were that possible, if only thereby he could ensure the salvation of Israel. His love was ready to forego his best, if by so doing he could save some. On this view the words are parallel to those of Moses (Exod. xxxii. 32, 33), and they are the fervent outburst of an unselfish devoted love. Paul could wish this if the wish could be realized for the good of his people. This intense desire has been well described as "a spark from the fire of Christ's substitutionary love."

III. *Reasons for Feeling* (ver. 3).—But the question arises whether the Apostle really meant this, however familiar and akin to the wish of Moses it may be. Would St. Paul be likely to wish a thing that was impossible? When we carefully look at the Greek text we feel inclined to doubt this familiar interpretation, for there is no "could" in the Greek, which is quite literally, "I used to wish," or, "I was wishing." Suppose we render the phrase, "I myself used to wish (or pray)," thus contrasting himself with the Jews. On this view, the words are to be regarded as a special explanation of his sorrow for Israel, based upon his own former unconverted state of hostility to Jesus as the Messiah. Let us read the words in this light. "I have great heaviness and continual sorrow in my heart (for I myself used to pray to be accursed from the Messiah) for my brethren, my kinsmen according to the flesh." When read thus, the words form a parenthesis, and give special point to his sorrow. At any rate, this view is worth mentioning, even though very few commentators favor it. But whether true or not, the passage, as a whole, shows the marvelous revolution that Christ made in Saul of Tarsus. From the position of an intensely bigoted devotee of Judaism, he had been transformed into a servant of Christ, whose intensest desire was for the salvation of his brethren.

IV. *Basis of Feeling* (vers. 4, 5).—He has already pointed out some grounds for his strong desire, such as the greatness of the misery of being accursed from the Messiah, and the closeness of his own relationship as an Israelite. But now he will elaborate and emphasize the chief reason for his feeling, in the greatness of the privileges that the Jews are losing by their rejection of Jesus Christ. This is the culminating point, for the losses sustained by Israel in refusing to accept Jesus as the Messiah rise above everything else in the Apostle's mind. There are eight marks of the Divine favor to Israel mentioned here, and they especially sum up the whole of the history of the nation from Egypt to the coming of Christ. Each separately and all combined constitute the crowning reason for the Apostle's grief.

1. "The Adoption"; that is, of the nation as God's family (Exod. iv. 22. See also the Greek version).

2. "The Glory"; that is, the Shekinah, or special token of God's presence (Exod. xvi. 10).

3. "The Covenants"; that is, the various covenants made with the people, and the successive renewals from the time of Abraham onwards.

4. "The giving of the Law"; that is, the legislation through Moses, as recorded in the books of the Pentateuch from Exodus to Deuteronomy.

5. "The Service of God"; that is, the Temple ceremonial in all its branches and aspects of spiritual meaning.

6. "The Promises"; that is, those found all through the Old Testament from Genesis to Malachi.

7. "The Fathers"; that is, the ancestors of the Jewish race of St. Paul's day.

8. "The Christ"; that is, the Messiah as the Jew. Observe the two sides of the Messianic revelation here stated, the human and the Divine (*cf.* ch. i. 3, 4). This last point is the climax of all the rest, for the Rejected One is He Who is over all, God blessed for ever.

In spite of Dr. Denney, we venture to hold that the interpretation that makes a full stop at the word "Christ," and interprets the rest as a Doxology to God, is exegetically impossible and quite opposed to the spirit of the context. Even Denney himself admits that the doxology is somewhat hard to comprehend in such a statement: "It seems at the first glance without a motive, and no psychological explanation of it yet offered is very satisfying." No other interpretation than the familiar one provides the proper climax to all these statements concerning Israel.[1]

The points mentioned not only show the preeminence of Israel's privileges, but also heighten their sin in rejecting Christ. At the same time they indicate the real difficulty of the situation in the Apostle's day. It is as though he had said that all these glories belong to Israel and yet they were rejecting Jesus Christ as the Messiah.

Two pictures of the Apostle, or rather two aspects of one picture, stand out very clearly in these verses.

1. *Paul the Patriot.* The intensity of his love for his fellow-countrymen is peculiarly interesting and significant. His acceptance of Jesus Christ had made no difference to his Jewish heart, except to increase his loving desire for the highest interests of his nation. Patriotism is not destroyed but intensified by Christianity. Paul did not cease to be a Jew when he became a Christian, and he shows his love for his brethren in the best possible way by desiring and working for their salvation. This should ever be the main object of Christian patriotism—the evangelization of those who are one with us in ties of blood and nationality. How profoundly this thought of Christian patriotism should stir the hearts of citizens of the British Empire as they contemplate the various nationalities in

1 Dr. Fairbairn has a note on this page in his *The Place of Christ in Modern Theology* (p. 308) which seems quite convincing.

our Dependencies who are citizens with us and subjects of the same Monarch! A Christian man cannot possibly show his patriotism in a better way than by doing his utmost to evangelize India, British Africa, and every other part of our Empire where Christ is not yet known.

2. *Paul the Soul-winner.* But this patriotism is only expressive of the intenser desire of the Apostle as a winner of souls. He had this great burden upon him. He not only loved man, but men; definite, concrete, individual men. He loved with a yearning and burning love of compassion. He himself was in Christ and longed for them also to be there. He knew what men miss when they reject Jesus Christ, and he is sure that all other privileges, however great, can never compensate for this loss. "Paul was sad for them, just as many today . . . are sad because some whom they love are away from Christ. . . . It is in moments when our joy in Christ is brightest and when we feel ourselves to be completely victorious . . . that this sadness comes to us with greatest bitterness" (Beet, *Romans*, p. 253).

And so Paul loves, and longs, and prays, and strives, and writes, and works for Israel's salvation. Have we these marks of a soul-winner? What a rebuke they are to our dulness, dryness, and deadness. A clergyman once asked a friend to find him a Curate, and said that he wanted a man "whose heart was aglow with the love of souls." Such was the Apostle, and such ought we to be. If we are not, shall we not seek to "abound in this grace also?"

XXXVII

ISRAEL'S REJECTION AND GOD'S FAITHFULNESS

Rom. ix. 6-13.

6. Not as though the word of God hath taken none effect. For they *are* not all Israel, which are of Israel:
7. Neither, because they are the seed of Abraham, *are they* all children: but, In Isaac shall thy seed be called.
8. That is, They which are the children of the flesh, these *are* not the children of God: but the children of the promise are counted for the seed.
9. For this *is* the word of promise, At this time will I come, and Sarah shall have a son.
10. And not only *this;* but when Rebecca also had conceived by one, *even* by our father Isaac;
11. (For *the children* being not yet born, neither having done any good or evil, that the purpose of God according to election might stand, not of works, but of him that calleth;)
12. It was said unto her, The elder shall serve the younger.
13. As it is written, Jacob have I loved, but Esau have I hated.

The Apostle now addresses himself to the task of justifying God's ways in relation to Israel, and his first point (see analysis, p. 116) is that God's rejection of Israel is not at all inconsistent with His Divine veracity and purpose, and must not be interpreted to mean the failure of His Word. The Apostle has expressed his grief at the sad condition of Israel, but he has not yet stated plainly that this condition is due to unbelief. Later on he will deal with this plainly (ch. ix. 30-xi. 36). Meanwhile he puts forth his argument in vindication of God.

The subject is introduced very abruptly, and before considering the details of the argument it is essential to gain a view of the general line of thought. Every statement is a link in a chain of very close reasoning, and we must constantly keep in view the place and purpose of the Apostle's argument. The main theme is that though the Jews have failed, God's Word has not failed. The promises made to Israel were not based upon physical descent and national life, but were associated from the first with spiritual blessing. The real, that is, the spiritual Israel, is therefore within the limits of the natural and national Israel. This distinction between the national and spiritual Israel is seen in the Old Testament, and it proves that God's sovereignty had not failed, so that without in any way trenching on Jewish promises God could admit the Gentiles to a share in that Gospel which was the theme of the Old Testament promises.

I. *The Word of God had not Failed* (ver. 6).—"But the case is not such as that the Word of God has utterly failed." This abrupt opening seems to suggest that the Apostle's thought should be interpreted to mean that it is not such a matter as failure of God's Word which has caused his grief, but something very different. In spite of his grief he does not mean that. The rejection of Israel does not imply any unfaithfulness in God, or any failure of His purpose. The emphatic phrase in this statement is "the Word of God," and the Apostle is about to defend it in the face of the fact that Israel is not saved. He will show that the unbelief of some of the Israelites does not make void God's promise, that the rejection of Israel does not for an instant imply any failure of Messianic assurances. The Jews had come to think that God's pledge on their behalf was absolute and irrevocable, and with this idea in their mind it is no wonder that they were resentful of Paul and his Gospel.

II. *The First Proof* (vers. 6-9).—The promise to Israel was not made to the whole nation, but to a limited portion of it. Even Abraham's natural seed were not all in the covenant, and therefore God's blessings did not proceed along the line of mere natural descent. This is shown by the choice of Isaac instead of Ishmael. Isaac was born according to God's purpose, power, and time, and not according to ordinary nature. He is therefore called "a child of promise." This means a child who would never have existed except for the promise; a child, moreover, to whom God's promise would come in power. Hence, there was a distinction from the very first, and it was not Abraham's position, but God's promise that determined the true seed. Since, therefore, God limited His original promise to one son of Abraham, this limitation necessarily excludes the purely natural descendants as well. If God drew the distinction at the outset, it could not be wrong to draw it subsequently all through the ages. Thus the Apostle distinguishes between the seed as a whole and the promised seed, in order to emphasize Divine election as the fundamental principle (vers. 7-9).

III. *The Second Proof* (vers. 10-12).—A further and still more striking and decisive proof of this principle of election is seen in the choice of Jacob rather than of Esau; and the illustration is much more conclusive than the case of Isaac, not only because Esau and Jacob were both legitimate children, while Ishmael was not, but still more, because the promise about Jacob being superior to Esau was given by God before their birth, and could not therefore be based upon the personal character or action of either of them. There was nothing in the parentage or in the life of Esau to cause rejection. The source of the choice of Jacob was the will of God alone, and the Divine freedom is shown to be His prerogative. It should be carefully noted that St. Paul is referring to the seed of Abraham typically and spiritually (*Cf.* Gal. iv. 29). The true Israelites are not within the seed of Isaac or Jacob according to the flesh, nor was Ishmael excluded simply because he was born of Hagar. It was therefore the Divine promise, and not fleshly descent, that gave the title even to external Messianic privileges quite apart from spiritual blessings which we know are not fleshly, but spiritual.

Special attention should be given to the phrase, "that the purpose of God according to election might stand" (ver. 11). This means that the selection might remain unchangeable even until the present time.

IV. *The Word of God is Confirmed* (ver. 13).—The Apostle's argument is confirmed from the prophecy of Malachi, which was uttered centuries after the original choice, and after centuries of opposition between Edom and Israel. The reference is, of course, to Jacob and Esau in their national capacity, and not to any "hate" of Esau while yet unborn. It is shown that ages of history had but confirmed the original choice. The phrase, "Esau I hated," should be compared with Luke xiv. 26 for its meaning of "loving less" (*cf.* Matt. vi. 24). There is no question of personal feeling, but a deliberate decision in favor of one rather than of the other. God's choice was not dependent on personal merit or individual privilege. It is therefore no question of personal salvation by absolute decree, but only of Esau and Jacob as individuals whose relation to God's purpose was settled before they were born.

Thus the Apostle shows that God's promises are not destroyed by Israel's failure as a nation, because from the very first there had always been distinctions which were explicable only by the sovereignty of God. And yet, though sovereign, the Divine choice is never arbitrary, *i.e.*, non-rational, or non-moral. As Denney well says, "The fact that many had not received the Gospel no more proves that the promise has failed than the fact that God chose Isaac only and not Ishmael."

Let us gather up the main points of the argument thus far. The Apostle has met the Jewish contention that salvation was by physical descent and legal works by showing (1) that a true interpretation of God's promise to Abraham and God's attitude to the children of Isaac, proves conclusively that no man can claim to be a child of God merely because he has descended physically from Abraham; (2) that from the very outset the special blessings bestowed on Abraham and Jacob were not due to human works, but sprang wholly and solely from the Divine free will and grace. Under these circumstances, it was utterly impossible for the Jew to object to a Gospel which proclaimed salvation for all men by grace through faith, and any thought on the part of Israel that this universal offer involved unfaithfulness in God was altogether a baseless charge.

Leaving for the present the Godward side of the truth here taught until the Apostle's entire treatment comes before us, let us note two special lessons that stand out clearly from these verses.

1. *A Solemn Possibility.* We may belong to the visible Church without belonging to the invisible. All Jews were Israelites according to the flesh, but were not thereby members of the spiritual Israel. In like manner it is possible to belong to a Christian community

and not to be a Christian. As Denney says, "It is not what we get from our fathers and mothers that ensures our place in the family of God." We must never forget our Lord's words, "That which is born of the flesh is flesh." It was an awful error of the Jews to suppose that they were inheritors of God's promises simply because they were natural children of Abraham (Matt. iii. 9; John viii. 33, 37, 39, 53). The failure of natural descent to secure spiritual position shows the fundamental unity of the Old and New Testaments in regard to salvation. Even in the old covenants the necessity of the new birth is clearly taught. There is scarcely anything that needs clearer and more constant emphasis today than the distinction between outward privilege and inward life. The Baptismal register or the Communicants' roll is never to be regarded as equivalent to the "Lamb's Book of Life." The distinction between the Church as visible and the Church as invisible, the Church as expressed in outward worship and the Church as united inwardly to Christ by the Holy Spirit, is a vital fundamental, and eternal distinction.

2. *An Absolute Necessity*. It follows, therefore, that the possession of a Divine life is an essential requirement for membership in the invisible Church. Before the people of Israel could become the people of God they needed genuine faith in Him, and the acceptance of His Word of promise as the means of spiritual life. Neither physical descent nor personal merit counted for anything in this respect. So must it ever be. "He that hath not the Son of God, hath not life" (1 John v. 12). "If any man have not the Spirit of Christ, he is none of His" (Rom. viii. 9). "They which be of faith are blessed with faithful Abraham" (Gal. iii. 7). "Ye are all the children of God by faith in Christ Jesus" (Gal. iii. 26). "If ye be Christ's, then are ye Abraham's seed" (Gal. iii. 29). This necessity of a Divine, spiritual life, to be received through faith, must be pressed home upon heart and conscience at all costs, for all people, in all circumstances, and at all times.

XXXVIII

ISRAEL'S REJECTION AND GOD'S JUSTICE

Rom. ix. 14-18.

14. What shall we say then? *Is there* unrighteousness with God? God forbid.

15. For he saith to Moses, I will have mercy on whom I will have mercy, and I will have compassion on whom I will have compassion.

16. So then *it is* not of him that willeth, nor of him that runneth, but of God that sheweth mercy.

17. For the scripture saith unto Pharaoh, Even for this same purpose have I raised thee up, that I might shew my power in thee, and that my name might be declared throughout all the earth.

18. Therefore hath he mercy on whom he will *have mercy*, and whom he will he hardeneth.

The Apostle had shown that God's Word had not failed even though Israel had failed. The blessing comes, not through man's physical descent, or by reason of his personal merit, but by the grace of God, grace that is due solely to the will of God. He has now refuted the charge that the condemnation of Israel meant God's failure in faithfulness, and he has commenced to show that their history, when properly interpreted, really led up to the great doctrine of righteousness by faith.

But this at once starts another objection: What about God's character as righteous? It is this question of God as a just God that occupies attention all through the following section. Now St. Paul will take another step and prove that Israel's rejection did not lay God open to the charge of unrighteousness. In making salvation a matter of Grace, and in rejecting the Jews who sought it by works, and in receiving the Gentiles who welcomed it by faith, God is not unjust.

The passage is long and difficult and must be considered in the fullest possible detail. It extends to the end of verse 29, and can hardly be understood aright, unless it is taken as a whole.

I. *Mercy according to the Divine Will* (vers. 14-16).—But the objector now raises another problem. "What shall we say, then?" By this phrase the Apostle usually introduces the view of an objector (ch. iii. 5; iv. 1; vi. 1; vii. 7; viii. 31; ix. 30). Is not the restriction of the promises to one line (Isaac and Jacob, not Ishmael and Esau), and to Christian Jews (not the majority of the nation), unjust on God's part? If He chose Jacob for no good in him, and rejected Esau for no evil in him, is He not unrighteous and unfair (ver. 14)?

The Apostle, as elsewhere, repels the idea with scorn (ver. 14). "God forbid." "Perish the thought." This phrase is very characteristic of the Epistle, and all its occurrences should be noted.

Instead of seeking to explain and justify God's action to human reason, Paul quotes from Scripture (ver. 15), as though to say, "That ought to close the matter." "God says Himself that He shows mercy with . . . freedom . . . and this principle of action which God announces as His own cannot be unjust." God's choice is thus not inconsistent with His justice, for He has a sovereign right to dispense mercy, as He said to Moses. The passage is from Exod. xxxiii. 19, and the context should be studied. Israel had sinned by idolatry, and Moses had asked for mercy. Then God spoke, enunciating the principle of unmerited favor as that by which He Himself works. Moses received mercy, not because of anything in himself, but because God willed to give it. The principle was one of Divine grace. God acted with perfect freedom in exercising compassion.

Hence God's mercy (ver. 16) is not merely a response to human resolve ("him that willeth"), or to human effort ("him that runneth"). His own Divine will is the one and only source of His mercy. All men are sinners, and as God pardoned Israel when they were rebels, why may He not pardon the Gentiles also? This verse, therefore, confirms verses 12, 13, and the idea is developed in ch. ix. 30-x. 3.

Thus in these verses (14-16) the Apostle proves from God's word to Moses, that, within the limits of the chosen nation, He deliberately retained His own absolute liberty in the exercise of His mercy. To say that a Jew had a right to God's favor, was to assume that he was in a position where he could win that favor by his own works. It was to ignore and set aside the plainest revelations of God's mind and will. So that when God refused to save the Jew who rejected the Gospel, He was acting in the most perfect harmony with His declaration to Moses.

II. *Judgment according to the Divine Will* (ver. 17).—But now the Apostle goes further, and cites the opposite case of one who did not receive mercy. God has also a perfect right to execute judgment, as is seen in the case of Pharaoh. The reference to Moses (ver. 15) illustrates Divine mercy in the choice of Jacob. The reference to Pharaoh (ver. 17) illustrates the Divine judgment in the rejection of Esau. Pharaoh is used to prove God's sovereignty and freedom in His dealings with men, and this shows that Scripture represents God as acting with freedom in regard to severity as well as to mercy (Exod. ix. 16). No Jew would complain of this argument, because it was so manifestly in his own Scripture. He might object to Paul, but not to the Word of God. According, therefore, to his own Scripture, which he would naturally accept, the Jew is taught that to show mercy and also to harden are Divine prerogatives manifesting God's absolute sovereignty. He has never given up this liberty of action, and in His attitude to unbelieving Jews he was only carrying out these righteous principles of His government. It is therefore impossible to say that He is unrighteous. This would be an argument exactly suited to the Jewish objector. God was only acting upon the same principle as He acted upon in regard to Pharaoh when He hardened unbelieving Israel.

But although the Apostle's words are adequate to meet the purely Jewish objection, the problem is acute for us today who read this reference to Pharaoh. It does not mean that Pharaoh was hardened for the mere sake of hardening, for we are told ten times in Exodus of Pharaoh hardening himself. He is used here as an illustration of Divine power as manifested and revealed in the outcome of the monarch's self-will and hardening of his own heart. "I raised thee up," does not mean that he was created for the purpose of being hardened, but as Denney renders it, "Brought thee on the stage of history." It simply states that God brought about everything that belonged to Pharaoh's history, even though Pharaoh himself was perfectly free in his action. God would let all men know His Name and attract general attention to Himself and His people. God's direct object in raising up Pharaoh was thus to use him. The manifestation of the Divine power in the miracles of Egypt had a natural tendency to soften rather than to harden, and consequently Pharaoh's heart was hardened by means of Divine displays of power that were fitted and intended to have a precisely opposite effect. The reason why Pharaoh was chosen as an example of judicial hardening is quite beyond our knowledge, and is a matter of the Divine will alone; but we know from the history that it was Pharaoh's disobedience alone that led to his being hardened. Neither Pharaoh nor anyone else is ever created in order to be hardened, though secret disobedience on the part of a sinner may lead to his being made a public example, as was Pharaoh, of God's judicial displeasure against sin. The Apostle all along is dealing with human pride, and for this reason he does not in any way soften his statements.

III. *The Divine Principle* (ver. 18).—Here we see the solemn and comprehensive conclusion based on the whole section from verse 14. God has mercy on the one hand and hardens on the other, even though man is free.

Let us observe how the Apostle thus far has dealt with the subject from God's side alone. The human aspect will come later (ch. ix. 30-xi. 21). The reconciliation of God's sovereignty and man's responsibility is beyond our power. The Bible states and emphasizes both, and then leaves them. We shall be wise if we do the same.

1. *God is Righteous in Judgment.* Everything that He does is absolutely just and is based upon reasons, whether we know them or not. We do not know why Jacob was chosen and not Esau; we only know God's will in the matter as expressed in the choice. But we are perfectly certain that the choice was due to reasons of

His own. We must pay special attention to the three references in Ephesians i. to the will of God. In verse 5 we read of "the *good pleasure* of His will." This is the supreme point. God wills to do a thing, because it is His pleasure. In verse 9 we notice "the *mystery* of His will." This is found in the passage before us about Isaac and Jacob, and we observe it again and again in the providences of life. God's will is indeed mysterious. In verse 11 we have "the *council* of His own will." This teaches us that His will is never arbitrary, but is based on reason. He takes counsel with Himself. Let us, therefore, rest upon this fundamental fact, that, in spite of all mystery, God is righteous, or He would not be God.

2. *God is Righteous in Mercy.* Here is the perfect balance of the Divine character. There is no respect of persons with Him. He has no favorites. While His grace is abundant, it is never bestowed apart from strict justice. Even in the story of Moses we can see this profound truth. In spite of all his magnificent service for God, the great Lawgiver was not permitted to enter Canaan because of his sin. We must never allow ourselves to presume on Divine mercy, or to forget the profound and searching truth; "There is forgiveness with Thee, that Thou mayest be feared."

XXXIX

ISRAEL'S REJECTION AND GOD'S POWER

Rom. ix. 19-29.

19. Thou wilt say then unto me, Why doth he yet find fault? For who hath resisted his will?

20. Nay but, O man, who art thou that repliest against God? Shall the thing formed say to him that formed *it*, Why hast thou made me thus?

21. Hath not the potter power over the clay, of the same lump to make one vessel unto honor, and another unto dishonor?

22. *What* if God, willing to shew *his* wrath, and to make his power known, endured with much longsuffering the vessels of wrath fitted to destruction:

23. And that he might make known the riches of his glory on the vessels of mercy, which he had afore prepared unto glory,

24. Even us, whom he hath called, not of the Jews only, but also of the Gentiles?

25. As he saith also in Osee, I will call them my people, which were not my people; and her beloved, which was not beloved.

26. And it shall come to pass, *that* in the place where it was said unto them, Ye *are* not my people; there shall they be called the children of the living God.

27. Esaias also crieth concerning Israel, Though the number of the children of Israel be as the sand of the sea, a remnant shall be saved:

28. For he will finish the work, and cut *it* short in righteousness: because a short work will the Lord make upon the earth.

29. And as Esaias said before, Except the Lord of Sabaoth had left us a seed, we had been as Sodoma, and been made like unto Gomorrha.

Now comes another objection, and one still stronger. Human nature will insist on working out these great problems. If, says the objector, God is sovereign, supreme, and also righteous, why then does He find fault with sinners who cannot resist such a power as His will? This objection, as we shall see, goes to the very heart of the problem, and demands our most careful consideration.

I. *The Divine Right* (vers. 19-21).—This objection is really the same as that of verse 14, only put in an intensified form. In that verse the question was raised whether God was just. In this (ver. 19), the question is raised whether He is not unjust. If, says the objector, Pharaoh did what was God's will, why, then, was he punished? Cannot the hardened man say, "I am what Thou madest me, and therefore Thou shouldest not find fault?" Thus moral distinctions would be at an end if God's power were shown to be incompatible with human responsibility.

"No," replies the Apostle (ver. 20), "that is not the question. The real question is one of a reverent attitude to God." St. Paul could have introduced here the question which comes later, namely, man's freedom and consequent responsibility, but he withholds it in order to show how blameworthy is the attitude to God implied in the question. Dr. Shedd calls it "an irreverent equalizing of man with God." The objector should rather ask whether the thing created should say to its Creator, "Why hast Thou formed me thus?" Whatever God does is necessarily just, since God is God; and for man to judge God is foolish and wicked. The Apostle thus answers by pointing to God's sovereignty. God does not give His reasons, and it is blasphemous to judge Him by weak, puny, limited self. It is noteworthy how St. Paul meets this objection, not by reasoning, but by rebuke, not by exposing the fallacy, but by denouncing the spirit of the question. He repels rather than refutes; he silences the opponent by saying that he has no right to put this objection.

It is absurd and monstrous for man to question God's dealings. "Hath not the potter a right over the clay?" (ver. 21). This illustration, together with the word "formed" rather than "created" in verse 20, deserves attention, as showing the Apostle is not referring to original creation, but to spiritual destination. God is regarded as taking men as He finds them, just as the potter does not create the clay but uses it. With great force the Apostle presses the alternatives. Either we must be silent before God's absolute authority, or else we must say that the potter has no power over the clay. Thus again the Apostle illustrates God's sovereignty by this metaphor. He does not touch the question as to why men are sinners, but accepting the fact that they are, he shows that God has a perfect right to deal with them as such. He shows that the exercise of

Divine power is ruled, first of all, by the principle that God has a right and a responsibility to make that use of the creature which He judges best in view of all the facts.

II. *The Actual Exercise* (vers. 22-24).—Paul's argument, while still insisting on God's freedom, now begins to enter into the realm of human experience. Thus we have in this section the second answer to the objection of verse 19. After asserting God's absolute right (vers. 19-21), the Apostle proceeds to justify His actual dealing as characterized by long-suffering. This fact shows how unbecoming is the attitude implied in verses 19-21. It is as though he had said: "You may argue against God's freedom, but if you find His actual treatment of man marked by patience and long-suffering, what can you say but that His relations with man are not fully explained by the idea of the potter and the clay?" So that even in His judgment God deals mercifully and with benevolent purposes for man, whether Jew or Gentile.

The contrast here between "vessels of wrath" and "vessels of mercy" should be closely examined. The "vessels of wrath" are described generally as "fitted to destruction," that is, fitted by themselves, through their own sin. On the other hand, the "vessels of mercy" are described very significantly as those which "He had afore prepared," that is, God through His grace and mercy prepared them. Men fit themselves for hell; but it is God that fits men for heaven. The same contrast is found in Matt. xxv. 34 and 41. The kingdom is prepared for "YOU"; the everlasting fire is prepared (not for you, but) for the "DEVIL and HIS ANGELS." God is not responsible for sin, only for grace.

In verse 24 we are perhaps to assume the answer to the "What if?" of verse 22. The Apostle seems to ask, Will man be entitled to find fault with God? He answers, Surely not. As Godet says (*Romans*, vol. ii. p. 175), "Do not all the Divine perfections occur harmoniously in realizing God's plan, and has not the freedom of man its place in the course of history in perfect harmony with God's sovereign freedom in His acts of grace as well as in his judgments?"

We see that the Apostle has proved three points. (1) God's power and right to do all things; (2) His wonderful endurance with the wicked; (3) His demonstration of glory on behalf of the vessels of mercy.

It is to be observed that at the close of verse 24 the calling of the Gentiles is introduced for the first time. Hitherto the argument has only been concerned with two distinct portions of the Jews.

III. *The Scriptural Anticipation* (vers. 25-29).—Here St. Paul proceeds to show that even in the Old Testament the calling of the Gentiles and the preservation of a Jewish remnant were foretold, and this fact ought to have been observed by the Jews. Verses 25, 26 refer to the Gentiles, quoting from Hosea ii. 23, and i. 10; verses 27-29 refer to the Jewish remnant, quoting Isa. x. 22, 23, and i. 9. Thus the Old Testament shows that long ago God had declared His intention of acting on these very principles. The Scriptures announced that many among the Gentiles would be called "sons of God," and it was therefore very far from true to say that a man would be saved simply because he happened to be an Israelite. Hosea's words about Israel's recovery are here applied to the Gentiles by St. Paul, and Isaiah is seen to teach the great law of history that progress comes through a faithful few, not through an entire nation. If a remnant had not been elected, there would have been none left, so that if God saves the remnant, it must be by grace alone. Thus the Apostle calls up the witness of prophecy to the facts of his own day in regard both to Gentiles and Jews, to the vessels of mercy and to the vessels of wrath, and this double dispensation of Gentile reception and Jewish rejection is shown to be nothing but a fulfilment of God's Word announced ages before. This fact of prediction is another proof that the rejection of Israel and the choice of the Gentiles do not imply any unfaithfulness or unrighteousness, but rather the fulfilment of God's ancient promises. If God's rejection of the ten tribes for idolatry was no breach of His covenant, neither was the exclusion of the Jews in Paul's day any violation of the Divine promise to Abraham and his seed.

This double reference to Scripture (Hosea and Isaiah) requires very special study. Of the Gentiles God speaks plainly in Hosea, telling the Jews that those who had not been His people were to be called "sons of the living God." Of the Jewish remnant Isaiah speaks equally plainly, and the very fact of God's election of a remnant was a proof of His kindness, not His severity, for if an elect seed had not been preserved by Divine power, the whole nation would have rushed to a doom similar to that of Sodom and Gomorrah (ver. 29). It was only of God's saving mercy that a remnant of Israel was kept from being overwhelmed in a similar judgment of Divine righteousness. In the face of this fact, surely no one but a wilful opponent would object to God's sovereign election.

To sum up: in this great division of the Epistle (chs. ix.-xi.) Paul is concerned with the solemn fact that the mass of the Jewish nation was refusing God's righteousness in Christ, and was in a hardened state; and in the portion we have just been considering (ch. ix. 6-29), he proves that the condition of the children of Abraham argues neither unfaithfulness, nor unrighteousness, nor an arbitrary exercise of power on God's part. Further, that in refusing to accept as His sons those Jews who persisted in seeking righteousness by their own works, while receiving from the Gentiles all who were willing to come through faith in Christ, God was only acting in accordance with declarations made centuries ago in their own Jewish Scriptures. Hence the doctrine of righteousness through faith could not be overturned, or even challenged by anything in Scripture, or in history, or in the condition of the Jewish nation.

1. *God is Sovereign.*—All through this section, as we have seen, the Apostle is looking at his subject from God's standpoint. He is rebuking human presumption and showing that God has prerogatives which must be upheld. The other side, the human, will be considered in the next section, and for the time being this is almost wholly shut out (except in vers. 22, 23). St. Paul here declares a profound conception of God. God is God. What He says is true, and what He does is right, because He is God. He alone has an absolute right; man has none. But while the Apostle points out that God's exercise of sovereign choice is independent of man's

physical descent or personal merit, He nowhere hints that the choice works independently of human character or choice. While mercy and judgment belong to God alone, He has clearly revealed the conditions under which He exercises His awful sovereignty. The Scriptures are full of statements as to the kind of people upon whom God wills to have mercy (Isa. lv. 7). Nor has He left us in ignorance as to those whom He wills to harden. The case of Pharaoh itself is perfectly clear, for in spite of overwhelming manifestations of God's power, Pharaoh stubbornly and defiantly refused to let Israel go (Exod. ix. 17). It was then that God stepped in and prevented him from doing as selfish policy, what he was unwilling to do as righteousness. So also with Israel; they claimed to base their privileges on birth, and the Apostle therefore says that the Divine choice was entirely independent of this, and that Gentiles who were not born Israelites might prove truer to God after all. As we shall see in the next sections, Israel was disobedient and defiant (ch. x. 21; xi. 20), and on this account they were hardened.

This sovereign exercise of Divine power to harden is, however mysterious, one of the vital and fundamental realities of God's righteous government. The hardening of the heart is the process by which the almighty power of God deals with a creature who rejects His will. The influence of the creature is thus limited, and without any disregard of genuine human freedom, the man is used for purposes altogether outside his own thought and wish. In all this emphasis on the Divine sovereignty, the Apostle is not teaching anything that is arbitrary, or characterized by favoritism and partiality. While therefore we remember the subsequent sections, in which he shows that Israel's rejection was due to their own sin, let us never forget this profound conception of God as sovereign in all things. The more we ponder it the more fully we shall enter into its deep, true meaning, and the more thoroughly we shall accept and trust Him of Whom it is declared.

2. *Man is Responsible.*—The hints given in verses 22, 23, which will be amplified in the remaining sections, show that man is not lost because he has been hardened, but that he has become hardened because he is lost through sin. God is not responsible for sin, and

no one will be able to say with regard to his sin when he stands before God, "I could not help it." The figure of the potter and the clay must not be overpowered, since man has a will which the clay has not. The figure does not cover the entire relationship of God to man. Besides, to keep the metaphor, it must never be forgotten that the potter is not responsible for the *composition* of the clay, but only for its form and fashion. As we observed on verse 20, Paul is not discussing God's original creation, but man's ultimate destination. Even with regard to Pharaoh the expression is "raised up," and we must not read it as though it meant "created." Paul is treating of God's right to harden an already unbelieving and disobedient people. As is the potter with the clay, God is not responsible for the composition of the sinner's heart as it now is, and if God so deals with him as to make his wilfulness promote His glory, He is not compelling him to sin, but only treating him according to his nature.

There comes a point in the case of the obedient and of the disobedient, where the question is as to what God is to do with man. In the case of the "vessels of mercy" He treats them according to His own grace, and prepares them for the glory which He has in store for them. But He also appoints a use and destiny for the disobedient. When Israel refused God's righteousness and wilfully rejected Him, it was for Him, not them, to decide their destiny. The New Testament idea of judgment is not something arbitrarily inflicted on man from without, but is the inevitable result of man's own work as he takes up and maintains an attitude of opposition to God. Future judgment will be nothing more than the clear revelation of an already existing and inevitable state of mind which man has fashioned for himself through sin. The issues of the solemn power of choice rest with God and not with man. God takes up into His Divine purposes the decisions of the obedient and the disobedient, and uses His grace in the one case, and His power in the other, to lead on to results, whether of honor or dishonor. As it has been well pointed out, it is open to a man to choose whether he will or will not take poison, but if he takes it the result cannot be fixed by his own will; the power of God in the laws of nature settles the issue. The clay of human life can be *moulded* by surrender; it can also be *marred* by disobedience; and above all it can be *made* by obedience.

Those two truths, God's Sovereignty and Man's Responsibility, are to be believed firmly, held tenaciously, proclaimed fully, and our life is to be lived in the light thereof.

XL

IRAEL'S REJECTION AND GOD'S RIGHTEOUSNESS

ROM. ix.. 30-33.

30. What shall we say then? That the Gentiles, which followed not after righteousness, have attained to righteousness, even the righteousness which is of faith.
31. But Israel, which followed after the law of righteousness, hath not attained to the law of righteousness.
32. Wherefore? Because *they sought it* not by faith, but as it were by the works of the law. For they stumbled at that stumblingstone;
33. As it is written, Behold, I lay in Sion a stumblingstone and rock of offence: and whosoever believeth on him shall not be ashamed.

THE Apostle here takes a fresh step in his argument. The question is turned round and treated from the human point of view. He passes from the consideration of God's sovereignty to that of man's responsibility. He shows that Israel had no right to salvation, that their history proves God to have proceeded on quite another principle. If, then, Israel's failure is not due to failure on God's part, how is it to be accounted for? This is answered in the present section. As a matter of historical fact, the failure of Israel was due not to any compulsion on the part of God, but to their own attitude of wilful disobedience to God and His Gospel. It is not that the Word of God has failed, but that the prophecies of ch. ix. 24-29 have become history in the Jewish rejection of the Gospel. And what is more, many of the Gentiles had secured what the Jews had failed to obtain.

I. *The Plain Question* (vers. 30, 31).—What then is to be said? Simply this: not that God has been faithless, or unrighteous, but that the Gentiles who did not seek righteousness have found it, while Israel who sought it has not attained to it. Observe the striking paradox in these verses. The Gentiles did *not* pursue righteousness and yet overtook it. The Jews pursued after righteousness and never arrived at it. This is another illustration of the principle laid down in ch. ix. 16: "It is not of him that willeth, nor of him that runneth." When it is said (ver. 31) that "Israel followed after a law of righteousness," we are perhaps to understand the term "law" as principle, or external standard (as in ch. iii. 27). Denney thinks it means a goal which enjoins righteousness. Careful note should be made of the strong and persistent emphasis laid on righteousness all through this passage.

II. *The Definite Answer* (ver. 32).—Why did this twofold result take place? The explanation is that Israel did not seek righteousness by faith, but by works, while the Gentiles received righteousness not by works, but by faith. This is the simple but sufficient solution of the problem which pressed so heavily upon the Jews in the Apostle's time. "Not by faith, but by works" (ch. i. 17); iii. 21, 22).

III. *The Simple Explanation* (ver. 32b).—The Apostle goes on to show that this avoidance of faith, and insistence on works, is due to the guilt of Israel in stumbling at the doctrine of righteousness by faith in the Messiah, an attitude which carried with it the rejection of the Messiah Himself. "They stumbled at the stone of stumbling."

IV. *The Scriptural Confirmation* (ver. 33).—Paradoxical as it may appear, this twofold attitude of stumbling and rejecting on the part of the Jews is confirmed by what Scripture foretold about them (Isa. xxviii. 16; viii. 14; *cf.* 1 Pet. ii. 6, 7). And yet if they had only realized the truth, they would have found that by faith in the Messiah would have come all available blessing; for while it is true, on the one hand, that He is a stone of stumbling to those who seek Him the wrong way, yet, on the other hand, it is equally true that "He that believeth on Him shall not be put to shame." Observe how this passage is repeated in ch. x. 11.

All through this section and that which follows, it is impossible not to notice the persistent emphasis placed on righteousness by faith as the fundamental idea of the Apostle, thus repeating what he had generally taught in ch. iii. 21 ff.

Observe the twofold attitude to Christ suggested in these verses. Some stumble over Him; others build on Him.

1. *Christ as a Stumbling-block.*—This is a striking statement; at first sight astonishing and incredible, and yet only too true to life. Christ has become a stumbling-block and a cause of offense to some men. "Blessed is he whosoever is not caused to stumble in Me."

Why is it that men stumble in Christ? One explanation is pride; another is prejudice; yet another is sin. Some men stumble at the way Christ came in lowliness to Bethlehem; others stumble at the work He did on Calvary; many today find Him "a stumblingstone and a rock of offense" in much the same way as did the Jews. God offers the gift of a Divine Savior as the one and only refuge of the sinful soul; but there is an absence of that consciousness of sin, that poverty of spirit, that realization of utter helplessness which constitute the true attitude of deep need. Multitudes in their pride will not consent to learn the profound necessity of Divine mercy and grace for salvation, and thus the Gospel of Christ becomes a stumbling-block to them. Yet our Lord's word about true blessedness is this; "Blessed are the poor in spirit, for theirs is the kingdom of heaven." So long as a man insists on going his own way, and believes that by his own unaided efforts he can secure righteousness, the glad tidings of the free gift of salvation by faith in Jesus Christ will offend, and even enrage him.

And yet it is a thousand pities that men should miss Divine blessing through their own pride and prejudice. There is always a danger lest preconceptions should become misconceptions, and it is not only unsafe but exceedingly perilous to take offense at Jesus Christ. A better way would be to inquire humbly and earnestly into the causes of those things which give us offense, for we may easily find in them the very elements which they do not appear to us to possess. Thus in the Apostle's time the Jews required a sign, and were offended at such a powerless Messiah as they considered Jesus to be. And yet the Christian finds in Him that very element of power: "Christ the power of God" (1 Cor. i. 24).

On the other hand, the Greek, with his love of philosophy and wisdom, despised Christ for what was considered a lack of wisdom, since a crucified Savior was the very opposite of philosophy. And yet the Christian finds in the Lord Jesus that very element of wisdom: "Christ the wisdom of God" (1 Cor. i. 24). It is never wise or safe to allow preconceptions to rule us unless we first test them on the hard rock of simple fact.

2. *Christ as a Stepping-stone.*—"Blessed is he, whosoever shall not be offended in Me." "He that believeth on Me shall not be put to shame." A willingness to be taught by Christ, and to accept what He is and gives, always brings blessedness. He asks for trust even though He does not explain, and the result of our trust in Him is that we are not put to shame. Faith gives insight and foresight. Faith gives fearlessness and fortitude. Faith uplifts and transforms life. Faith brings salvation and satisfaction. Faith inspires life and elicits hope. Faith gives value to all problems and mysteries in life. Faith gives victory over all the conflicts of life.

XLI

THE CAUSES OF ISRAEL'S FAILURE

Rom. x. 1-4.

1. Brethren, my heart's desire and prayer to God for Israel is, that they might be saved.
2. For I bear them record that they have a zeal of God, but not according to knowledge.
3. For they being ignorant of God's righteousness, and going about to establish their own righteousness, have not submitted themselves unto the righteousness of God.
4. For Christ *is* the end of the law for righteousness to every one that believeth.

This chapter develops the solution of the problem which was stated in ch. ix. 30-33. Israel's rejection is seen to be due not to the withholding of grace, which as a matter of fact was freely offered by God, but to their own sinful inability to use and accept God's way of life. Notwithstanding their zeal they were blinded by self-righteousness, and they failed to see several essential and important things.

I. *The Feeling Described* (ver. 1).—Another expression of the Apostle's earnest regard for Israel. In unveiling their ignorance and sin, he again expresses his own emotions. As Denney says, "The Apostle cannot enlarge on this melancholy situation without expressing once more the deep grief which it causes him." He desires to prove by his own feelings that he is not their enemy, and that he still hopes for their salvation, and believes in its possibility. It is noteworthy that each chapter commences with a warm personal testimony to his pity for Israel (ch. ix. 1; x. 1; xi. 1).

II. *The Reason Assigned* (ver. 2).—The explanation of his intense desire and earnest prayer for their salvation is that they are so zealous for God, though their zeal was absolutely void of all real knowledge. He appreciates their good qualities, but at the same time points out that they are not regulated by adequate knowledge. The words, "Not according to knowledge," may be regarded as the key to the whole chapter. Sincerity is not enough; we must be in the right way. The Jews had persisted all through the centuries, and yet had not submitted themselves to God. As someone has aptly pointed out, a locomotive engine has enormous power of usefulness as long as it is running on the track, but once it is off the rails it becomes a power for destruction.

III. *The Error Indicated* (ver. 3).—This zeal, which was not actuated by knowledge, was in turn due to a lack of spiritual discernment. They were ignorant of God's righteousness," that is, the righteousness demanded and provided by God, and all the while they were seeking to establish their own private righteousness (see Greek). As a consequence they were altogther unwilling to submit themselves to the righteousness of God (Phil. iii. 9). Like the man in the parable, they were without the wedding garment, even though it had been provided for every guest (Matt. xxiii 11-13). Thus Israel's condition was marked by the three elements of (*a*) ignorance, (*b*) effort, (*c*) failure.

IV. *The Truth Stated* (ver. 4).—All this deliberate and wilful attitude on the part of the Jews was entirely inexcusable, since Jesus Christ, their Messiah, was the end of the law for righteousness (ch. viii. 3, 4). He is the object to which the law points, the goal, the termination (Eph. ii. 15). The law could not bring righteousness, but Christ did and does. With Christ before us, legal righteousness is necessarily at an end, and in not submitting to Christ, the Jews were refusing to submit to God Who gave them the law (Luke xvi. 16).

It is of the greatest possible importance to keep in mind this statement of the Apostle as to the cause of Israel's rejection. It was not that they were indifferent to righteousness, but that they wilfully sought it by their own efforts, rather than in God's way by faith. As we observe this reference to Israel's obstinate refusal to seek righteousness by faith, we can readily understand the appropriateness of these chapters concerning Israel in an Epistle specially devoted, as we have seen, to the consideration of God's righteousness received by faith, and we can also fully understand why St. Paul dwells at such length, in this chapter, on the contrast between the righteousness of self-effort and the righteousness of faith.

In this simple passage, expressive of the true state of the case in regard to Israel, several points emerge which are of particular application to Christian life and work today.

1. *The Intense Desire and Earnest Prayer* of a true Man of God for the salvation of others. He was solicitous and prayerful on behalf of Israel with a view to their salvation. The sincerity of the Apostle's life should characterize that of all workers for God. It is the very heart of Christian discipleship. In particular this desire on behalf of *Israel* should be noticed. Paul loved the Jew, and, although we have not the same kinship of blood, there should be a love in our hearts for God's people Israel, and the desire for their salvation.

2. *The Element of Zeal without Knowledge* indicates a useless expenditure of vital force. What a splendid outcome would have arisen from Jewish effort, if only it had been rightly directed to good influence in the service of God! The combination of religious zeal and ignorance of Bible truth is unutterably sad and very regrettable, more particularly as zeal should always be tempered with knowledge.

3. *The Astonishing and Deplorable Lack of Discernment* in those who were presumably familiar with their own Scriptures. Is it not marvelous that people can read the Bible and all the time fail to see its essential teaching and its personal application to themselves? There is scarcely anything more surprising and saddening than the presence of intellectual knowledge of God's Word with an utter failure to appreciate its spiritual meaning and force.

4. *The False Idea of Righteousness* which is expressed by the attempt to gain Righteousness by Works. This is one of the fundamental characteristics of human nature. The Pharisee with his phylacteries; the Chinaman burning his bits of paper in his ancestor worship; the Hindu plunging into the Ganges; the Roman Catholic counting his beads; the moral Protestant satisfied with intellectual

knowledge, Scripture reading, and regular attendance at Church—all express this inherent tendency of human nature to go about to establish its own righteousness. When a man comes to realize that life demands righteousness he can proceed along one of three ways: (1) He may endeavor to restore himself; or (2) to rest upon the mercy of God; or (3) endeavor to blend the two methods and divide the work between God and himself. But he very soon comes to see that the second course is the only possible one. He cannot remove the guilt of his own past, for God only can do this. Nor can man guarantee by his own efforts the absolute perfection of righteousness in regard to character and conduct. Hence it is wholly impossible for him to be saved, unless he is willing to be saved in God's way.

5. *The Secret of all Failure in Life* in relation to God is unwillingness to submit to His Word and Will. This is always the explanation of a life that does not realize its true purpose. When the will of man opposes the will of God, spiritual disaster must be the result.

6. *The Secret of all Blessing and Power of Life* is in the willing submission of the heart to God and the acceptance of His Word by simple trust. Dr. John Brown thus puts the case:—

> "The Divine method of Justification requires nothing but to be submitted to. There is no great work to be done. Its two radical principles are that man is restored to the Divine favor not by his own doings and sufferings, but by the doings and sufferings of Another; and that in these doings and sufferings of the Justifying Savior he is interested, not by working but by believing . . . But while it requires nothing but submission, it does require submission, unqualified submission of the understanding and heart" (*Romans*, p. 364).

It is the element of surrender and teachableness that gives life its real power, for when the heart of man is willing to be dependent upon God, it ceases to be self-dependent and rebellious.

XLII

RIGHTEOUSNESS BY WORKS AND BY FAITH

Rom. x. 5-11.

5. For Moses describeth the righteousness which is of the law, That the man which doeth those things shall live by them.
6. But the righteousness which is of faith speaketh on this wise, Say not in thine heart, Who shall ascend into heaven? (that is, to bring Christ down *from above*:)
7. Or, Who shall descend into the deep? (that is, to bring up Christ again from the dead.)
8. But what saith it? The word is nigh thee, *even* in thy mouth, and in thy heart: that is, the word of faith, which we preach;
9. That if thou shalt confess with thy mouth the Lord Jesus, and shalt believe in thine heart that God hath raised him from the dead, thou shalt be saved.
10. For with the heart man believeth unto righteousness; and with the mouth confession is made unto salvation.
11. For the scripture saith, Whosoever believeth on him shall not be ashamed.

The statement that Christ is the "end," or goal of the law for righteousness to everyone that believeth (ver. 4), is now taken up and proved from the Old Testament, by a contrast between righteousness by works and righteousness by faith. Israel ought not to have been ignorant of righteousness by faith, for their own Scriptures bore witness to this method of obtaining it. The law (ver. 5) says, "Do and live by this means," but the Old Testament also bears witness (vers. 6-8) to a righteousness by faith, in direct contrast to righteousness by works.

1. *Righteousness by Law Described* (ver. 5).—Righteousness must be by faith, for Moses wrote about it and described the righteousness by law as one of doing. Moses' testimony is beyond all question, and so if righteousness comes by doing, it would be

man's own righteousness and not God's. There is all the difference between *obtaining* and *attaining*. If man had really kept God's law he would have had life; but no one has done, or can do this (ch. iii. 9-20). The use of law is not to save, but to discover sin. The emphatic word in this phrase is "doing."

II. *Righteousness by Faith Described* (vers. 6-8).—In contrast to the foregoing, God's righteousness is clearly brought forward, and is actually based on an Old Testament passage (Deut. xxx.). It is particularly interesting that in these verses there is no reference to Moses, as in verse 5, although the quotation comes from a book of Moses, Deuteronomy. The Apostle has shown that the zeal of the Jews is not God's righteousness, but the very opposite and contradiction of it. Righteousness by the law is righteousness by man's own works, while righteousness in Christ is righteousness by faith. Now he goes on to show that righteousness in Christ by faith is the only genuine righteousness, and that there is no other.

Note carefully the use made of Deut. xxx. 11-14, with the Apostle's explanations interposed. It is sometimes said that St. Paul here applies to the Gospel what Moses applied to the law, and that therefore the Apostle freely reproduces and accommodates the passage to his own use. But this is not the case, for such an accommodation would be against his object, which is to reason with the Jews out of their own Scriptures. A close study of the original chapter will show that the passage comes from Moses' last public exhortation, and contemplates the condition of Israel when they should have broken the law and be suffering its consequences. It points forward to the New Covenant after the Mosaic, or legal dispensation, when the fulfilment of the law would have become impossible, since Israel had been driven out of their land for having broken it. Deut. xxx. refers to the ultimate gathering of all Israel, when God should accept them if they would turn to Him with all their hearts (ver. 10). Then would come the blessing mentioned in these verses (vers. 11-14). The chapter is therefore an anticipatory intimation of the higher dispensation for which the Old Testament was the preparation. Thus the passage in Deuteronomy supplies the Apostle with a proof of the great principle of righteousness by faith.

Observe, too, that Deut. xxx. speaks of both kinds of righteousness, mentioning not only "commandments" (plural), but "commandment" (singular). It thus speaks both of keeping the commandments, and also of turning to the Lord with all the heart. It was the Gospel that gave the Apostle the clue to the latter idea, and so he quotes the passage as exactly describing Gospel-righteousness, not law-righteousness. Israel in Deut. xxx. was no longer the people of God, and God was addressing them, not on the ground of law, but on the basis of faith. This being the case, says the Apostle, it is Christ Who is its object, and in Him Israel was intended to gain what they had lost by disobedience to law. Thus the Old Testament bears witness at once to righteousness by law and righteousness by faith, and this exactly corresponds with St. Paul's earlier statement that righteousness by faith was witnessed to by the law and the prophets (ch. iii. 21, 22). And as the Apostle had already found the righteousness by faith in Abraham who believed God, so here he finds the essence of the same position in one who turns to God with all the heart and soul (Deut. xxx. 6-10). As Beet says, "This appeal to Moses is a remarkable example of skillful and correct exegesis" (*Romans*, p. 285).[1]

The Apostle therefore quotes such terms as exclude "doing" on the part of man. Righteousness springs out of the finished work of Christ (vers. 3, 4), and there can be no "finished" work while man is endeavoring to be saved by law, for this would be virtually to undo what Christ has done. That which would be impossible to man, God has already done in Christ. All the "doing" required by the law, has been accomplished by Jesus Christ, and everything that is required now from men is to believe what Christ has done. Christ has neither to be brought down from heaven, nor to be raised again from the dead; everything has been accomplished, and all that is left is to accept in trustful thankfulness. Faith has not to acquire or win a Savior, but to accept One Who has already accomplished the work of redemption. God's righteousness is not distant and difficult, but near and easy. It only requires the act of believing, and its proof in confession. It is easy of comprehension by the

[1]The two writers who shed most light on this passage are Gifford and Forbes.

heart, and ready for utterance by the mouth. Alford's words on this are specially worthy of notice:—

> "The anxious follower after righteousness is not disappointed by an impracticable code, nor mocked by an unintelligible revelation; the word is *near him,* therefore *accessible; plain and simple,* and therefore *apprehensible;* and, we may fairly add, deals with *definite historical fact,* and therefore *certain;* so that his salvation is not contingent on an amount of performance which is *beyond him,* and therefore *inaccessible; irrational,* and therefore inapprehensible; *undefined,* and therefore *involved in uncertainty.*"

And the familiar words of Cowper are much to the point:—

> "O! how unlike the complex works of man,
> Heaven's easy, artless, unencumber'd plan!
> No meretricious graces to beguile,
> No clustering ornaments to clog the pile:
> From ostentation as from weakness free,
> It stands like the cerulean arch we see,
> Majestic in its own simplicity.
> Inscrib'd above the portal, from afar
> Conspicuous as the brightness of a star,
> Legible only by the light they give,
> Stand the soul-quick'ning words—'Believe and live.'"
> (Cowper, *Truth.* II. 21-31).

III. *Righteousness by Faith Realized* (vers. 9, 10).—The "word of faith" is here shown to include the consent of the heart and the mouth, with reference to Jesus as Lord (see R.V.), and as proved by the resurrection (ver. 9). The terms "heart" and "mouth" are set in contrast with law.

Then follows the explanation of what is meant by believing in Christ. The term "heart" in Scripture always means the centre of the moral being, and invariably includes the three elements of intellect, feeling, and will. We never find in the Bible that contrast between "head" and "heart," between "intellect" and "emotion," which is so characteristic of our usage today. Trust always includes the assent of the mind and the consent of the will; the credence of the intellect and the confidence of the heart. Saving faith dominates the entire being, mind, feelings, and will, and as a consequence, this faith will express itself in confession.

Observe also the distinction here made between "righteousness" which comes from believing, and "salvation" which comes from confession. This does not seem to be any mere Hebrew parallelism, but rather two sides of the same thing. If we render "salvation" by "safety," we have perhaps the best equivalent. We receive righteousness through believing, and we realize that righteousness as "safety" by continual confession of Christ as *Lord.* This allusion to the *Lord,* has a clear reference to the place occupied by the will. Our "safety" is at once present and future, and we thus see that, while believing in Christ brings man into a right relation to God, confession of faith maintains him in that right relation, and keeps him continually safe until the final salvation, "ready to be revealed in the last time" (1 Pet. i. 5). Righteousness thus issues in "safety." This twofold emphasis on heart and mouth is important; the mouth without the heart might be hypocrisy, while the heart without the mouth might be cowardice. It should never be forgotten that the Bible word "salvation" includes past, present, and future, the precise element and point of application in each passage being left to be decided by the context.

IV. *Righteousness by Faith Assured* (ver. 11).—Righteousness is now shown to be based on Scripture. The office of faith is illustrated by a quotation from Isaiah, repeating ch. ix. 33. Thus the prophet supports and vindicates the Law giver in the matter of believing wih a view to righteousness. "Under law" a man creates by his action the facts by which he lives, but under the Gospel Christ creates the facts, and it is for faith to accept and appropriate them. If, therefore, Christ does create all the facts necessary for our reinstatement in righteousness, and then offers these facts to men for acceptance by faith, He must of necessity be the end of the law, for the law said to a man, not "Believe and live," but "Do and live." The difference between the two methods is aptly expressed by the words "do" and "done."

The elements of the Gospel as here stated are all worthy of special notice. The Apostle seems to rejoice in reiterating the great realities which were his theme in the earlier chapters.

1. *The Substance of the Gospel* (ver. 10).—In two words, "righteousness," and "salvation," we have the very heart of the redemptive work of Christ. Righteousness means, as we have seen, "rightness" with God, and covers past, present, and future. In relation to the past we are "righteous" by justification. In relation to the present we are "righteous" by sanctification. In relation to the future we shall be "righteous" by glorification. Salvation is the same great fact viewed from another standpoint. Salvation means deliverance, and therefore safety, and this also concerns our past, present, and future. In relation to the past, it is salvation from the penalty of sin. In relation to the present, it is salvation from the power of sin. In relation to the future, it is salvation from the presence of sin. Well may the Apostle call this "the glorious Gospel."

2. *The Foundation of the Gospel* (vers. 6, 7).—This is seen in the finished work of Christ. His resurrection and ascension are shown to be the ground of certainty. Everything that God does is perfect and permanent, and He has left nothing unfinished that was necessary for man's salvation. The covenant is "ordered in all things and sure." The resurrection and ascension are facts of history which have perpetual and perennial spiritual force. "On Christ the solid Rock I stand."

3. *The Accessibility of the Gospel* (ver. 8).—The Apostle is particularly anxious to show that everything has been made available and easy for our acceptance of Christ. "The word is nigh thee." We have not to cover great distances to bring it. We have no insuperable difficulty to overcome in order to obtain it. He Who provided Christ, has provided the possibility of our simple, immediate, and easy acceptance of Him in the proclamation of His everlasting Gospel.

4. *The Channel of the Gospel* (ver. 8).—The way in which the Apostle calls attention to faith is for the purpose of showing us how all these blessings come into our hearts and lives. Not by works of righteousness which we do, but by His mercy, through faith, God saves us, and faith is the hand that receives and the mouth that tastes the goodness of His grace.

"No hope can on the law be built,
Of justifying grace;
The law, that shows the sinner's guilt,
Condemns him to his face.

Jesus, how glorious is Thy grace,
When in Thy Name we trust,
Our faith receives a righteousness,
That makes a sinner just."

5. *The Maintenance of the Gospel* (vers. 9, 10).—When once the heart has received, the life must retain the Gospel of redeeming love. The retention is by "confession." This is the great law of the spiritual world. "There is that scattereth and yet increaseth." The more we confess and profess our faith, the more it will obtain a hold upon our own lives. It was never intended for mere private enjoyment, or even personal use; it was expected of us that we should spread it far and wide by confessing what Christ is to our souls.

6. *The Scope of the Gospel* (ver. 11).—The word "whosoever," as based on Isaiah must in the Apostle's meaning refer to Gospel days, and this thought of universality, which is to be elaborated in the next section, is one of the glories of the Pauline Gospel, as it is one of the glories of today. "To the Jew first, and also to the Greek." This was why the Apostle was not ashamed of the Gospel, since it was God's power to the salvation of "every one that believeth."

7. *The Certainty of the Gospel* (ver. 11).—St. Paul is particularly anxious that those to whom he is writing should not have any fear, and it is for this reason that twice over he quotes from Isaiah the word that "every one that believeth shall not be ashamed." There is no reason why we should, and every reason why we should not, be ashamed of a Gospel which provides such abundant satisfaction for time and eternity.

XLIII

RIGHTEOUSNESS BY FAITH FOR ALL

ROM. x. 12-21.

12. For there is no difference between the Jew and the Greek: for the same Lord over all is rich unto all that call upon him.
13. For whosoever shall call upon the name of the Lord shall be saved.
14. How then shall they call on him in whom they have not believed? and how shall they believe in him of whom they have not heard? and how shall they hear without a preacher?
15. And how shall they preach, except they be sent? as it is written, How beautiful are the feet of them that preach the gospel of peace, and bring glad tidings of good things!
16. But they have not all obeyed the gospel. For Esaias saith, Lord, who hath believed our report?
17. So then faith *cometh* by hearing, and hearing by the word of God.
18. But I say, Have they not heard? Yes verily, their sound went into all the earth, and their words unto the ends of the world.
19. But I say, Did not Israel know? First Moses saith, I will provoke you to jealousy by *them that are* no people, *and* by a foolish nation I will anger you.
20. But Esaias is very bold, and saith, I was found of them that sought me not; I was made manifest unto them that asked not after me.
21. But to Israel he saith, All day long I have stretched forth my hands unto a disobedient and gainsaying people.

THE Apostle here glides into the additional thought of the universality of the Gospel of righteousness, which has already been implied in the "whosoever" of verse 11. He now proves once again that this free Gospel is for all; and the recurrence of the principal topics of the Epistle (ch. i. 16, 17) seems essential in order that he may vindicate the equal offer of the Gospel made to everybody. In view of all that he has said about the acceptableness and facility of the Gospel, it is clear that it must be preached everywhere; and if this universal preaching was predicted in the Old Testament, and has been carried out, a fresh proof is offered of the universal destination of the Gospel, and the guilt of Israel in neglecting the opportunity of accepting it. The promise from Joel involves and necessitates a universal proclamation, and although this had been done when the Apostle wrote this Epistle, Israel nevertheless had not believed.

I. *The Universality of the Gospel Declared* (vers. 12, 13).—Two proofs are adduced in support of the contention that the free gift of God's Righteousness is for Jew and Gentile alike.

1. The first proof lies in the Character of God. "The same Lord is Lord of all, and is rich unto all that call upon Him." He is "over all" without any distinction, and is "the same" to all, ready to pour out the wealth of His grace to any one and every one who seeks Him. No one has ever approached Him and found Him lacking that graciousness of attitude which expresses itself in forgiving mercy and love. "Thou, Lord, art good, and ready to forgive, and plenteous in mercy unto all that call upon Thee" (Psa. lxxxvi. 5). The phrase "no difference" is particularly noteworthy, because it has occurred in ch.iii. 22, though in a significantly different connection. As in ch. iii., there is "no difference" in human sinfulness; so here, there is "no difference" in the wealth of God's grace. The Greek phrase is also equally striking. The same Lord over all is "continually wealthy to all those who are continually invoking His aid." Observe, too, in verses 11-13 the strong and striking emphasis on "all" and "whosoever."

2. The second proof is the Promise of God. "Whosoever shall be saved" (ver. 13). Already (ver. 12) there has been a reference to calling upon God, and here it is repeated in the form of a promise. If only His Name, which means His revealed Character, is invoked by the needy sinner, salvation will be the inevitable and glorious result. So that there is a double assurance of salvation, namely, what God is, and what He promises to do.

II. *The Universality of the Gospel Proved* (vers. 14, 15).—But opportunities for fulfilling the prophetic word "call" were needed. If the Jewish Scriptures spoke of every one, then the calling involved an offer to "all." How were they to call on Him in Whom they had not believed? Then the Apostle works backward by stages, dwelling on the (1) calling, (2) believing, (3) hearing, (4) preaching, (5) sending. Point by point he shows conclusively, by arguments based upon the plain words of their own Scriptures, that a universal proclamation of the Gospel was absolutely necessary, if the prophet's words were to be fulfilled.

III. *The Universality of the Gospel Disregarded* (vers. 16, 17).—Opportunities were therefore afforded, and were deliberately refused. The fact remains that Israel had not obeyed the Gospel, and this is confirmed from the well-known word of the prophet Isaiah, "Lord, who hath believed our report?" (ch. liii. 1). Mark the form of expression in the Apostle's statement, that "they did not all hearken." This is similar to his statement in ch. iii. 3, "What if some were without faith?" This is his way of speaking with mildness and large-heartedness of the national and almost universal rejection of the Gospel by Israel.

IV. *The Universality of the Gospel Scorned* (vers. 18-21).—There are no excuses for Israel's neglect and rejection. It was not merely an instance of not hearing and not believing, but of something far worse; it meant definite neglect and deliberate refusal, rejection, and contempt. Two pleas are advanced on Israel's behalf and are carefully examined in turn.

1. Did Israel really hear (ver. 18)? Yes, undoubtedly they did, for the words of Psalm xix. 4 can be applied to the universal proclamation of the Gospel. It was not lack of hearing, but lack of obedience.

2. But did Israel know (vers. 19-21)? Yes, assuredly they did, for they were warned beforehand, first by Moses (Deut. xxxii. 21), and then later on by Isaiah (ch. lxv. 1, 2). This unbelief and disobedience had characterized the Jews all through their history, and culminated at length in their rejection of Jesus as the Messiah.

Reviewing this section from ch. ix. 30, we now see the real reasons of God's rejection of Israel. Although warned beforehand by their own Scriptures, and although the glad tidings had been clearly and fully proclaimed, they deliberately refused God's gift of righteousness in Christ. Blinded by pride, they endeavored to maintain their exclusive position by making permanent their law. They repelled with scorn the idea of a free salvation (ch. x. 5-11), and a universal salvation (ch. x. 12-17). They were thus absolutely without excuse, and God was only righteous in setting them on one side and offering salvation to the Gentiles. This is how the chapter closes, and by itself we might think there was no further hope for Israel; but, as we shall see, the next chapter proceeds to reveal God's method of mercy even with His wilful people.

The practical messages of this section are solemn and important.

1. *The Marvelous Mercy of God to All* (ver. 12).—There is no distinction between Jew and Greek, between cultured and ignorant, between bond and free. The same Lord in heaven is ready to pour out His abundant provision of grace to all mankind. This is the glory of the Gospel. "All souls are Mine." And we can never reach a place or time on earth where anyone is outside the mercy of "the God of the spirits of all flesh."

2. *The Exquisitely Simple Terms of Acceptance* (ver. 13).—For the purpose of salvation, all that is required is to "call upon the Name of the Lord." This means the prayer of faith. The publican lifted up his heart as he prayed, "God be merciful to me the sinner." And the "same Lord" is ready to hear the prayer of every repentant, believing soul who is willing to lift up the heart for forgiveness and grace.

3. *The Call to the Universal Preaching of the Gospe*l (vers. 14, 15).—Here are four questions commencing with "How," which every Christian ought to face. All who profess to be among the people of God ought either to go themselves, or to help others to go, or to let their near and dear ones go. God has so conditioned the knowledge of His Gospel for all the world, that unless Christians say, "Here am I, send me," or "Here am I, use me," the world cannot possibly hear of Him Who loved them and gave Himself for them. The beauty and glory of missions are seen in the prophetic word, "How beautiful are the feet of them that bring glad tidings of good things." The Gospel is "beautiful," because of its revelation of its bestowal of God's grace, and because of all the spiritual influences God's love, because of its manifestation of God's truth, because of that flow from the living Christ.

4. *The Rejection of the Gospel* is no warrant for not sending it all over the world (ver. 16). Even though it is not heeded, we must still proclaim it far and wide. The responsibility for proclaiming it rests with us; the responsibility for receiving or rejecting it lies with those who hear it.

5. *The Simple Secret of Faith* (ver. 17).—This is a point of primary importance in the Christian life and experience. Faith comes from a message heard. This message comes by the Word of God. Hence, the more we know of God through His Word, the more faith we shall possess. Faith does not come by asking, but by getting to know God. We need not pray for faith, but if we come to know God, faith will spring up as the certain result. "They that know their God shall be strong." We trust people by knowing them. The longer we spend with our Bible in getting acquainted with God, the stronger, more practical, and more blessed will our faith be.

6. *The Certainty that some will accept the Gospel,* even if others reject it (vers. 19, 20).—God's Word cannot possibly return to Him entirely void, and the faithful proclamation of the Gospel will never be without some definite results. If one rejects, another will accept. This is the inspiration and encouragement of all true service.

7. *The Divine Longing for Man's Salvation* (ver. 21).—Let us observe carefully the metaphor here used. God is depicted as stretching forth His hands for an entire day. If we try the experiment of holding out our arms for a few minutes only, we shall find how tiring it is, and yet God waits and waits "all the day long" in His "incessant pleading and love" (Denney). He is "not willing that any should perish, but that all should come to repentance." And the more thoroughly we can enter into this Divine longing, and yield ourselves to God for the grace of long-suffering patient service on behalf of others, the more Christlike will be our character and the more blessed will be our life.

XLIV

THE REMNANT OF ISRAEL

ROM. xi. 1-10.

1. I say then, Hath God cast away his people? God forbid. For I also am an Israelite, of the seed of Abraham, *of* the tribe of Benjamin.
2. God hath not cast away his people which he foreknew. Wot ye not what the scripture saith of Elias? how he maketh intercession to God against Israel, saying,
3. Lord, they have killed thy prophets, and digged down thine altars; and I am left alone, and they seek my life.
4. But what saith the answer of God unto him? I have reserved to myself seven thousand men, who have not bowed the knee to *the image of* Baal.
5. Even so then at this present time also there is a remnant according to the election of grace.
6. And if by grace, then *is it* no more of works: otherwise grace is no more grace. But if *it be* of works, then is it no more grace: otherwise work is no more work.
7. What then? Israel hath not obtained that which he seeketh for; but the election hath obtained it, and the rest were blinded.
8. (According as it is written, God hath given them the spirit of slumber, eyes that they should not see, and ears that they should not hear;) unto this day.
9. And David saith, Let their table be made a snare, and a trap, and a stumblingblock, and a recompence unto them:
10. Let their eyes be darkened, that they may not see, and bow down their back alway.

THE Apostle has proceeded a considerable way in his discussion of the problems raised by the rejection of unbelieving Israel. He first showed that God never entered into any obligations towards the nation which in any way fettered His liberty to reject those who would not accept His terms of salvation by faith (ch. ix. 5-29). Then he went on to show quite plainly the essential reason of Israel's opposition to righteousness by faith, and to prove that this very opposition had necessarily brought about the situation of which the prophets had spoken centuries before (ch. ix. 30-x. 21.

From the last verses of ch. x. we might almost think that the Divine long-suffering towards Israel was utterly exhausted, and that the threats of judgment were about to be fulfilled; but the Apostle's thought takes another turn, and we are introduced to the glorious hope which God set before Israel. St. Paul raises the inquiry whether the present situation is final and ultimate; whether it must always be that the majority of the nation will remain outside the kingdom, while the Gentiles are rejoicing within it. He replies in the most emphatic way that this cannot possibly be, that the present situation is not only temporary, but also really contains within itself God's means for securing a glorious future for Israel. The blessedness of the Gentiles as they experience God's righteousness by faith, will at length provoke unbelieving Israel to emulation, and they in turn will regain by faith their lost fellowship with God. Not only so; this restoration of Israel will be associated with marvelous blessings to the whole world.

Twice already St. Paul has said that Israel's unbelief had not cancelled God's promises (ch. iii. 3; ix. 6). This thought is now closely associated with the certainty of the salvation of those whom God has forknown (*cf.* ch. viii. 28-39). God "has not cast away His people whom He forknew." Although the true Israelites are not the mass of the nation (ch. ix. 6), but a godly remnant representing those who are "Israelites indeed," yet the fact of this remnant, existing amidst national degeneracy and apostasy, shows that God is still mindful of His people as a people.

Let us once again have clearly in mind the two great outstanding facts and problems which occupied general attention in the Apostle's time: (1) that the Christian Church, mainly composed of Gentiles, had set aside Israel in the position of God's believing ones; (2) that nevertheless the promises of God to Israel, as recorded in the Old Testament, still remained unfulfilled and unrealized, and, as they were a matter of national position and blessing, could not be realized and fulfilled at all by the Gentile Church. The first of these two questions the Apostle has dealt with in chs. ix. and x., showing that Israel had been set aside because of their sin. With the second of these great facts we are concerned in this chapter. Israel as a people and nation is to be restored, and is yet to realize the promises made in the Old Testament. Israel's failure is neither complete (vers. 1-10), nor permanent (vers. 11-32).

I. *A Solemn Question Answered* (ver. 1).—"What I mean is, Has God cast away His people?" The very thought is impossible. In view of their rejection of God's righteousness in the Gospel, did God, Who necessarily foresaw this, determine to bring to an end His special relationship with the nation? And is such a determination on the part of God the explanation of the present sad position of Israel? The Apostle answers with characteristic emphasis, "God forbid." "Perish the thought." But, as we shall see, he goes very much further than a mere rejection of the thought, however emphatic.

II. *The Answer Illustrated* (ver. 1).—The Apostle brings forward his own case, and calls himself "an Israelite of the seed of Abraham, of the tribe of Benjamin." Some writers think that he adduces his own conversion as one proof that God has not rejected Israel altogether; that, since he himself was an Israelite of the most approved and unquestioned type, his own conversion would never have taken place if God had ceased to deal graciously with the nation. There is very much to be said for this reference to himself as the first proof of his negative answer to the question. Other writers think it hardly likely that he would adduce himself as a proof, and they therefore suggest that this reference is merely an illustration. In either case the allusion is a manifest proof of the impossibility of God's rejection of Israel. We must not fail to observe this third reference of the Apostle to himself (ch. ix. 1; x. 1). It is the third mention of his own profound sympathy with his people.

III. *The Answer Reiterated* (ver. 2).—"God hath not cast away His people whom He foreknew." The whole course of Israel's history was thus foreseen and foreknown, and at no point did God ever contemplate ceasing to be their faithful covenant-keeping God. They are "His" and He "foreknew" them, a twofold proof that He has not cast them off. The word "foreknew" is to be interpreted as in ch. viii. 29, as meaning something a little more than foresight, and a little less than fore-ordination. It means to "note with pleasure." This is another way of saying what we find described in Heb. vi. 17 as "the immutability of His counsel."

This reference to God's foreknowledge of Israel as a nation shows the uniqueness of that people, for they were the only nation fore-known in this way by Him. Individuals, as such, may be foreknown, but not so a nation, except Israel.

IV. *The Answer Proved* (vers. 2-4).—The Apostle has already instanced his own case, and also brought forward Divine fore-knowledge, in support of his contention that God has not cast away His people. Now he proceeds to adduce historical analogy, in the fact that the very same state of affairs occurred in the time of Elijah. Appearances are not the reality, and there is still a godly remnant, though unknown to, or disregarded by the entire nation. And as the unfaithfulness of the majority in Elijah's time did not carry with it the Divine rejection of the nation, neither did it in the time of St. Paul. When Elijah on Mount Horeb brought an accusa-tion against his countrymen of such unfaithfulness to God that he himself alone was left, the Divine response quickly showed him that there was a kernel of loyalty. In exactly the same way, in the Apostle's day, the mass of the people were unfaithful, but there was a remnant of loyal Israelites who had thankfully accepted the Divine righteousness by faith. Like the quiet pious group that welcomed the birth of Jesus at Bethlehem, there were many in this remnant who "waited for the salvation of Israel." The wording of God's answer to Elijah is particularly significant. "I have re-served for Myself." And yet this was no arbitrary decree, because the character of this reservation is at once described as those "who have not bowed the knee to Baal."

V. *The Answer Confirmed* (vers. 5, 6).—Now the Apostle's thought is definitely applied to the present. This remnant is related to God on a basis of grace, not of works. The election is by means of grace, not partly by grace and partly by works (ch. ix. 6-13). Grace and works are mutually exclusive (ver. 6), and it is by means of the remnant, according to the election of grace, that God makes provision for future restoration. Law elects those who obey its requirements, Grace elects those who are willing to receive everything through faith, not as a matter of right, but as undeserved and unmerited favor at the hand of God.

VI. *The Answer Explained* (vers. 7-10).—How, then, does the case stand? On the human side, the nation of Israel has sought, but has not obtained righteousness (ch. ix. 31, 32). On the Divine side, the godly remnant has obtained righteousness, the rest being hardened (not as A.V., "blinded"). Then from three passages of the Old Testament (Isa. xxix. 10; Deut. xxix. 4; Psa. lxix. 22, 23), this judicial hardening is proved and explained to be due to Israel's sin. Thus the Divine action in the present entirely agrees with similar action in the past. The chosen nation lacked spiritual discernment (ver. 8), and they had become burdened with ceremonialism and servility (vers. 9, 10), until at length they had wholly departed from the Divine idea and ideal. The majority had persisted in seeking righteousness by works (ver. 10), and the result had been failure and hardening. But what the many had not secured by their own efforts, the few, who were willing to receive, had obtained by grace through faith.

These quotations show that the hardening of the unbelieving Israel is in entire agreement with what Israel had known all along from their own Scriptures. God has never allowed rebellious men to pursue their own way without limits and restraints. This profound, even though mysterious, doctrine of the Divine hardening of the heart, is a positive proof that God limits man's defiance ot His will, and will never allow him to proceed beyond a certain point. It is a sad representation of the religious state of the people, and though it is of course true that the hardening comes from man's unbelief, yet here the Apostle ascribes it directly to the will of God. But this, as we know from experience, is nothing arbitrary, but the solemn and inevitable outcome of God's law of righteousness. If we place our hand in the fire, we may say, if we will, that the fire did it, or that we ourselves did it, or that God did it, the last-named expression being equivalent to saying that it was by the law of nature that comes from God. So in the moral world, when we rebel we set in motion the laws of God's universe which act upon our soul and tend to blind and harden us. The great truth of the Divine blinding and hardening is proof that God limits man's wilfulness and says, "Thus far shalt thou go, and no farther."

The entire passage calls for very definite meditation and personal application.

1. *The Apostle Paul as a Monument of the Divine Mercy* (ver. 1).—This is a word of cheer. What God did for and with Saul of Tarsus and Paul the Apostle, He is willing, ready, and able to do for every one. We need never despair of the hardest case. "He is able to save to the uttermost."

2. *The Jewish Nation as a Monument of the Divine Faithfulness* (ver. 2).—This is a word of comfort. As we contemplate the devious paths of Israel's unfaithfulness, we might readily think that there was no hope and no possibility of recovery, but even in the "hardening," mercy is blended with judgment, for God would not cast away His people. God is ever true to His Word.

3. *The Godly Remnant as a Monument of the Divine Grace* (vers. 4-6).—This is a word of counsel. In the most corrupt churches God has some true followers. Let us take care not to forget this. Let us cultivate charity. All people have not our opportunities. Elijah did not dream of the possibility of a loyal remnant, and the majority of the Jews in St. Paul's day never imagined that there were a faithful few in whom the promises were being fulfilled. So is it today. In many a place of which we know nothing, God has His true followers. God is never without witnesses.

4. *The Rebellious Majority as a Monument of Divine Justice* (vers. 7-10).—This is a word of caution. Their fate should be a warning to us. Neglect of God and His truth is a terrible sin. It is only too possible to become "Gospel-hardened," and familiarity with Divine truth is perhaps one of the most serious and hopeless of positions. Our responsibility is heightened in proportion to our knowledge, and God must deal with neglect and contempt. God cannot regard sin with indifference.

XLV

INSTRUCTIONS ABOUT ISRAEL

Rom. xi. 11-16.

11. I say then, Have they stumbled that they should fall? God forbid: but *rather* through their fall salvation *is come* unto the Gentiles, for to provoke them to jealousy.

12. Now if the fall of them *be* the riches of the world, and the diminishing of them the riches of the Gentiles; how much more their fulness?

13. For I speak to you Gentiles, inasmuch as I am the apostle of the Gentiles, I magnify mine office:

14. If by any means I may provoke to emulation *them which are* my flesh, and might save some of them.

15. For if the casting away of them *be* the reconciling of the world, what *shall* the receiving *of them be*, but life from the dead?

16. For if the first-fruit *be* holy, the lump *is* also *holy*: and if the root *be* holy, so *are* the branches.

Here the Apostle turns to consider the great mass of the people of Israel. He has already shown that the cause of their fall was their own sin and wilfulness, but this sad condition is not the last thing to be said. The fall is not final, and we are now to consider the purpose of God and the glorious result of everything. The temporary hardening of Israel will be seen to be a powerful factor in preparing the way for their restoration. Out of the two great factors of His favor to the Gentiles, and His judgment on Israel, He Himself will eventually bring about a glorious result.

I. *Israel's Fall is not Permanent* (ver. 11a).—"What I mean is, Have they stumbled in order to fall?" Was this the only purpose? Are they irrecoverably lost? Can this fall be the climax of their marvelous history? "Perish the thought." Such an idea was utterly inconceivable. Thus the Apostle opens the subject by rejecting with scorn the idea that Israel's ruin was final and permanent.

II. *Israel's Sin has been Over-ruled* (ver. 11b).—So far from the fall being final, God over-ruled it in such a way as to bring about the accomplishment of His purposes. There was a wonderfully far-reaching aim in their rejection. As the Jews would not receive the Gospel, its preachers naturally turned to the Gentiles, and this resulted in Gentile salvation. If the Jews had only been believing, they would have become missionaries to the world. This fact of Gentile salvation was in turn intended to stir the Jews to emulation (not "jealousy"), and if possible to lead them to wish for and accept the same Savior. Thus two results have accrued from the fall of the Jewish nation; salvation has come to the world, and an opportunity has been given to the Jews to be saved.

III. *Israel's Return will bring Abundant Blessing* (vers. 12-15).—Not only are the truths of the preceding verse to be kept in mind, but the Apostle has something even more important to say. If by the fall of the Jews, the world has received the Gospel, how much more will the world be blessed through the return of the Jews to Christ. Observe the striking contrast between "fall" and "riches"; between "diminution" and "riches," and note that the word "fulness" means the future occupation by Israel of the present vacancy caused by their unbelief. Denney renders the word "diminution" by "defeat," or "loss," and suggests that the word "fulness" means "making up to a full number," "that which fills an empty space" (Denney, *Romans*, p. 678; Armitage Robinson, *Expositor*, April, 1898). If, then, the sin of Israel led to the salvation of the Gentiles, much more will their restoration be the means of blessing to the entire world. Their reception back again is to be of infinitely greater value to the world than their fall (ver. 12).

Then in a sort of parenthesis (vers. 13, 14), St. Paul addresses the Gentiles direct, explaining to them by way of justification, the teaching which he, as the Apostle of the Gentiles, has been giving in regard to the future of Israel. He has shown such zeal on behalf of Israel that an explanation seems due to the Gentile Christians at Rome. They might well be asking what he means by this prolonged reference to Israel, seeing that he is so pre-eminently the Apostle of the Gentiles. He replies by showing that all this discussion about his fellow-countrymen affects very closely the Gentile Christians, and that he is really glorifying his office of Apostle to the Gentiles in so writing, especially as universal blessing to the Gentiles is so closely connected with the return of the Jews to God. Thus it is actually in the interests of the Gentiles that he is doing all this.

Once again (ver. 15) he states his greatest reason for trying to save the Jews. This is a repetition of verse 12, and its climax. If the rejection of the Jews was the reconciliation of the Gentiles in Christ, the reception back again of the Jews shall be life from the dead to the world. Let us carefully observe that "life from the dead" refers, not to the Jew themselves, but to the whole world through them. To save a Jew at any time is a great thing, for it involves "unimaginable blessing." And in the future, the salvation of the Jews will mean a spiritual revival to the world. Thus there always has been, and always will be, some sort of blessing in connection with the Jews, directly or indirectly. Their rejection brought blessing to the Gentiles, and their restoration will bring blessing to the world.

IV. *Israel's Future is Guaranteed by its Past* (ver. 16).—Here the Apostle adduces a further argument for the restoration of the Jews, as in accordance with the original consecration of the race to God. There are two metaphors: the "first-fruits" and "the lump," and the "root" and the "branches." The idea of the first-fruits as the pledge of the rest comes from Numbers xv. 19. The first-fruits were the portion set aside from the meal offering, which imparted its consecration to the whole mass of which it was the representative. In this verse the "first-fruits" are the patriarchs, from whom the people (the "lump") had descended. The word "holy" means consecrated, and the thought is that the patriarchs, as consecrated to God, were the representatives and pledge of the consecration of the whole nation. The spiritual glories of the patriarchs are thus regarded as the earnest of the future which awaits the race. The same truth is taught under the second figure of the root and the branches; the root is Abraham, and the branches his natural descendants.

The Apostle is still concerned with Israel's sin and the way in which God met and dealt with it. The problem of sin in relation to God is still with us, and is as acute as ever.

1. *God's Promise and Human Sin.*—We know how all through the Old Testament God promised a Messiah and spiritual blessings in Him, and yet from time to time through the centuries, reaching to, and culminating in the time of Jesus Christ, the Jews manifested their unbelief in the promise, their pride of position and privilege, their boasting in mere natural connection with Abraham, and their deliberate unwillingness to receive the Gospel of righteousness by faith. God's promise of salvation is still being met on many hands by the same attitude of proud unbelief and wilful rejection.

2. *God's Providence and Human Sin.*—We see how God dealt with the evil of His people Israel. He used it first of all to bring about the salvation of the Gentiles, and then used that in turn to stir up the Jews to a consciousness of their need of the same Divine Righteousness.

3. *God's Purpose and Human Sin.*—How marvelously God overruled the deepest iniquity for the purpose of blessing the whole world! It is a familiar saying that there is "a soul of goodness in things evil." But this is absolutely incorrect, and morally dangerous. There is no goodness in things evil, and God never can bring good *out of* evil, because there is no good in it to bring out. What God does is to bring good to pass *instead of* evil.

4. *God's Power and Human Sin.*—We are sometimes inclined to think that sin will be victorious, but if we wait long enough we shall see that the Divine power is not really thwarted. God deals with the situation in such a way that His will is accomplished by reason of His omnipotent grace. Whatever, then, we may think about sin, let us never forget that it is limited, and that in spite of all appearances to the contrary, "The Lord God omnipotent reigneth."

XLVI

WARNINGS FOR GENTILES

Rom. xi. 17-24.

17. And if some of the branches be broken off, and thou, being a wild olive tree, wert graffed in among them, and with them partakest of the root and fatness of the olive tree;
18. Boast not against the branches. But if thou boast, thou bearest not the root, but the root thee.
19. Thou wilt say then, The branches were broken off, that I might be grafted in.
20. Well; because of unbelief they were broken off, and thou standest by faith. Be not highminded, but fear:
21. For if God spared not the natural branches, *take heed* lest he also spare not thee.
22. Behold therefore the goodness and severity of God: on them which fell, severity; but toward thee, goodness, if thou continue in *his* goodness: otherwise thou also shalt be cut off.
23. And they also, if they abide not still in unbelief, shall be graffed in: for God is able to graff them in again.
24. For if thou wert cut out of the olive tree which is wild by nature, and wert graffed contrary to nature into a good olive tree: how much more shall these, which be the natural *branches,* be graffed into their own olive tree?

From instruction (vers. 11-16) the Apostle makes a sudden change to warning addressed direct to Gentiles, and these verses form a long parenthesis inculcating humility, and, at the same time, confirming the hope about Israel already expressed. It was essential to point out that the Jews were the channel of blessing to the Gentiles, and not the Gentiles to the Jews. On this account the Gentiles should have a feeling of profound regard for Israel, even though the present condition of the nation was so sad (vers. 17, 18). A remembrance of their own former state should also lead them to truehearted fear, for if the rejection had come upon such a highly privileged people as the Jews, it would be far easier to bring upon the Gentiles a similar Divine discipline (vers. 19-21). The future of the Jews is once again shown to be more than a possibility (vers. 22-24). Let us now give heed to the Apostle's solemn warnings.

I. *Against Boastfulness* (vers. 17, 18).—If some of the Jewish branches were broken off, and the Gentiles were grafted in, it is no occasion for Gentile boasting, for in any case the root of the Gentile life was Abraham, as the covenant father (ch. iv. 11, 12; Gal. iii. 16). Gentiles are therefore not to boast, as though they were the root and the Jews the branches. There is a similar danger today in Gentiles despising the Jews, and forgetting the source and channel of their own spiritual blessings.

It should be carefully observed that the olive tree in this section is not the Church, but the Jewish nation as a whole. To introduce the Church at this point is to cause nothing but confusion. The Apostle was making a practical appeal to the Gentiles to be humble and self-distrustful. The illustration of grafting found here calls for some attention.

> "It has been objected to the figure used here by the Apostle, that a gardener never engrafts a wild branch on a stem already brought under cultivation; but, on the contrary, a stem is taken which still possesses all the vigor of the wild state to insert in it the graft of the cultivated tree. There are two ways of answering this objection. It may be said that, according to the reports of some travelers, the course taken in the East is sometimes that supposed by the figure of the Apostle. A wild young branch is engrafted in an old exhausted olive, and serves to revive it. But there is another more natural answer, viz., that the Apostle uses the figure freely and without concern, to modify it in view of the application. What proves this is the fact that in verse 23 he represents the branches broken off as requiring to be engrafted anew. Now this is an impracticable process, taken in the strict sense" (Godet, *Romans*, vol. ii. p. 247).

As Denney has pointed out, the Apostle knew that he was referring to that which was spiritual, not natural (ver. 24), and the force of the reproof turns on this fact.

II. *Against Pride* (vers. 19-21).—Another ground of boasting is possible to the Gentiles. Although St. Paul has already said that the rejection of the Jews meant the enrichment of the Gentiles (ver. 11), it would be intolerable to say that the advantage of the

Gentiles was the only cause of God's rejection of Israel. Such selfishness as is expressed by the emphatic "I" is impossible. Jewish rejection was due solely to unbelief, and Gentile continuance is due solely to faith and not to merit. Gentiles are therefore to avoid pride, and to cultivate reverential fear, for God will not spare even them if they manifest a similar spirit to the Jews.

III. *Against Presumption* (vers. 22-24).—God is at once gracious and severe; gracious to those who abide in His goodness, severe to those who reject His grace and boast proudly in self-sufficiency. If the Jews should not continue in unbelief they will be grafted in again, since God is able to do this, for since the Gentlies were grafted in contrary to nature, much more can the Jews be grafted in because of their original relation to God. The restoration of the Jews is therefore more probable in itself than the reception of the Gentiles had been. God's favor is still upon them as the people of His promises, and their restoration would only be a recurrence to an old order of things.

This contrast between Jew and Gentile is particularly important. While it is true that the appeal to God's power ("God is able") shows the great difficulty of bringing Israel back, yet on the other hand there were reasons for believing that the process would not be so difficult as the conversion of the Gentiles had been. Keeping up the idea of the grafting the Apostle teaches that the converted heathen (1) were cut out of a wild tree of heathenism; and (2) were grafted contrary to nature on to a people who possessed Divine revelation. Neither of these things would be necessary with the Jew. In his case there would be no separation from an irreligious society, and his conversion would only place him back among the people of God. As we have seen (ver. 17), we must be careful in our interpretation of this figure of the olive tree and its branches. The figure is not to be pressed.

As we ponder these solemn and searching words addressed to the Gentiles, we can readily see their direct application to ourselves as Gentile followers of Jesus Christ.

1. *Three things about the Believer.*—The Apostle lays stress upon three aspects of Church life as the secret of preservation from the

evils about which he warns: (*a*) the necessity of faith (ver. 20), "thou standest by thy faith." Faith always implies the cessation of dependence on self and the assertion of dependence on another. It was by the absence of this faith that the Jews were "broken off," and it will only be by faith that we are enabled to maintain our true position in the sight of God. "By faith" is the key to everything in the believer's life. We are "saved by faith" (Eph. ii. 8); "sanctified by faith" (Acts xxvi. 18); "purified by faith" (Acts xv. 9); we "live by faith" (Gal. ii. 20); "stand by faith" (Rom. xi. 20); "walk by faith" (2 Cor. v. 7). It is the only, as it is the adequate response to God's revelation of Himself in Christ. (*b*) The necessity of fear (ver. 20). "Be not high-minded, but fear." There are two kinds of fear, that of the slave and that of the son. The one implies fright, the other awe and reverence. This latter is one of the great essentials of a true Christian life, for it expresses that holy sensitiveness to sin, and that quick perception of God's will which constitute true sonship. "There is forgiveness with Thee, that Thou mayest be feared." (*c*) The necessity of faithfulness (ver. 23). "If they continue not in their unbelief." God's absolute requirement for Christian living is loyal obedience to His will. The life that commences with faith is to be continued in faithfulness, and in this will be found power, joy, and blessing. "God is faithful," and He expects us to be faithful too. "Be thou faithful unto death."

2. *Three things about God.*—The same passage that teaches us these solemn truths about ourselves reveals to us the character of God for our guidance and protection. (*a*) The goodness of God (ver. 22). This means His loving kindness as expressed in beneficence, and every believer knows how true this is in his own personal experience. All things in his life bear witness that "God is good." (*b*) The severity of God (ver. 22). This means the penal severity of His justice. God is righteous, and cannot be indifferent to human sin, especially the wrong-doing of His professed people. His character demands that He should manifest His righteousness; otherwise He would not be God. Let us never presume for an instant to think that the free grace of God in our justification in any way modifies the Divine character of absolute holiness. (*c*)

The ability of God (ver. 23). "God is able." This is our supreme encouragement. The power of God is exercised on behalf of all those who are willing to put themselves unreservedly in His hands. What is said here of the Jews, that God is able to graft them in again, is equally true of his attitude to all believers, that He is "able to do exceeding abundantly above all that we ask or think" Eph. iii. 20).

XLVII

ISRAEL'S FUTURE SALVATION

ROM. xi. 25-32.

25. For I would not, brethren, that ye should be ignorant of this mystery, lest ye should be wise in your own conceits; that blindness in part is happened to Israel, until the fulness of the Gentiles be come in.
26. And so all Israel shall be saved: as it is written, There shall come out of Sion the Deliverer, and shall turn away ungodliness from Jacob:
27. For this *is* my covenant unto them, when I shall take away their sins.
28. As concerning the gospel, *they are* enemies for your sakes: but as touching the election, *they are* beloved for the fathers' sakes.
29. For the gifts and calling of God *are* without repentance.
30. For as ye in times past have not believed God, yet have now obtained mercy through their unbelief:
31. Even so have these also now not believed, that through your mercy they also may obtain mercy.
32. For God hath concluded them all in unbelief, that he might have mercy upon all.

THE Apostle brings his great theme to a conclusion by dwelling on the bright future in store for Israel notwithstanding the present failure of their majority. This is one of the most distinctly predictive of all the utterances of St. Paul. From argument he proceeds to revelation. He has discussed probabilities and adduced reasons; now he will bring forward God's Word. The future conversion of Israel has been proved to be both possible and probable, and here it is shown to have been the subject of direct Divine revelation, thus confirming the hope of verse 24.

I. *A Great Revelation* (vers. 25, 26).

1. The Subject had a Supreme Importance.—"I do not wish you to be ignorant." This is the Apostle's characteristic phrase for drawing attention to some special and important truth (*cf.* ch. i. 13). It should be noted with great care wherever it appears in his writings.

2. The Subject had a Special Character.—"This mystery." The word "mystery" in the New Testament always refers to something that was once hidden, but is now revealed, a secret told. It applies to something which could not be discovered by natural faculty, something which, if not revealed, would never have been known, a piece of revelation. Dr. Sanday points out that whereas among the heathen, the word was always used of a mystery concealed, with St. Paul it is a mystery revealed (*Romans*, p. 334). This meaning of the term must be carefully distinguished from our modern idea of a mystery as something difficult of comprehension, or "mysterious." The New Testament word is variously applied: (1) To the Gospel (Mark iv. 11; Matt. xiii. 11); (2) to the union of Jews and Gentiles in one body (Eph. iii. 3); (3) to the union of Christ and the Church (Eph. v.); (4) to the change at the resurrection of the body (1 Cor. xv.); (5) to the revelation of evil (2 Thess. ii.); (6) to the future conversion of Israel, as here.

3. The Subject has a Practical Intention.—"Lest ye be wise in your own conceits." The Apostle was particularly anxious that his Gentile readers should have clearly in view the Divine truth on this far-reaching topic, for this alone would prevent them from self-sufficiency, vanity, and pride. God's revelation is intended to produce humility and to abolish all false conceit.

4. The Subject had an Immediate Aim.—"That a hardening in part hath befallen Israel, until the fulness of the Gentiles be come in." The mystery now revealed is that "partial" hardness has happened to Israel. "In part," means that there were many exceptions, as in the case of Jewish believers. The phrase, "until the fulness of the Gentiles shall have come in," is very difficult. Some think it means, "until the void made in Israel by the fall is filled up from the Gentiles" (*cf.* the parables in Luke xiv. 16-24, and Matt. xxii. 1-14). But it is perhaps better to refer it to the time when God shall close this Gentile dispensation, and when Israel's national salvation shall take place. Liddon refers it to the time when "the full number of the heathen have been converted" (*cf.* Luke xxi. 24).

5. The Subject had an Ultimate Object. "And so all Israel shall be saved." The words "And so" indicate the casual connection

between the foregoing and what is now said. It will happen when the partial hardness shall have been removed. "All Israel" does not necessarily mean every individual Israelite, but the whole nation, a future national conversion, as distinct from the present conversion of individuals.

II. *A Great Vindication* (vers. 26-32).

1. This Subject is in harmony with Divine Prophecy (vers. 26-27).—The future restoration of Israel is proved from Scripture (Isa. lix. 20, 21; xxvii. 9).

2. This Subject is in harmony with the Divine Plan (ver. 28).—The national restoration is not inconsistent with present facts, which are part of God's plan for extending mercy to all. Israel has a double aspect. In regard to the Gospel they are "enemies" for the sake of the Gentiles, but in regard to the election they are "beloved" for the sake of their fathers. This phrase, "enemies for your sake," is very remarkable. Godet thinks that it may mean that if Israel had universally accepted the Gospel it might have become Judaized, and so hindered; or else it may mean that by the enmity shown to the Gospel, the Gentiles had been given their opportunity.

3. This Subject is in harmony with the Divine Principle (ver. 29).—The confirmation of this prediction of Israel's future is found in the fact of God's unchangeable attitude to them. His gifts to, and calling of, Israel are without any change of mind on His part. This is the proof that they are still the objects of His Divine love, for that love has not been annulled by disobedience. This is another way of putting the truth of ch. ix. 4, 5, and is also a restatement of everything which has been said by the Apostle from ch. xi. 11. God is incapable of revoking His Word.

4. This Subject is in harmony with the Divine Providence (vers. 30, 31).—The general truth of verse 29 is confirmed by an explanation of the way in which it will one day be realized. The history of God's providential dealings with Jews and Gentiles is summed up in a series of comparisons and contrasts. Mark the striking repetitions, and also the anthithesis of disobedience and mercy.

5. This Subject is in harmony with the Divine Purpose (ver. 32).—The crowning proof of the restoration of Israel is found in its entire agreement with God's purpose. Jew and Gentile are, as it were, in two great divisions, and God has arranged to lock them both up in a prison-house of disobedience, in order that He may have mercy on all alike. This is a bold and remarkable declaration of how God uses and even forces sin into the service of His mercy. We have a similar idea in ch. v. 20 (R.V.). "The law came in besides, that the trespass might abound." An earthly parent may occasion disobedience in a child, when to a wrong tendency he opposes a command which makes the child transform the tendency into an act of disobedience. The providence of God puts men in such circumstances that the perverted human will shows itself in disobedience. And yet we must never forget that the latent sin had really revealed and expressed itself, long before God's judgment began to act. The Divine severity is thus wonderfully vindicated in the purpose of grace which it serves.

The word "all" in this verse refers to Jew and Gentile viewed in the mass, and not individually. It is necessary to keep in mind the fact that "all" in some passages means "all without exception," and in others "all without distinction." It has the latter meaning here.

Let us observe the glorious thought of this verse; that at the close of the present dispensation there will be a wonderful fresh dispensation of grace, in which salvation shall be offered to all the nations living on the earth, and that, somehow or other, this magnificent opportunity will be the discipline through which Jew and Gentile will have passed in the present period of time.

Frederick the Great is recorded to have asked his Chaplain to give him in a sentence the strongest evidence for Christianity. The Chaplain replied, "The Jew, Sir." We see the truth of this as we contemplate the revelations of the Apostle in this entire chapter.

1. *The fall of the Jews* was overruled for mercy to the Gentiles.

2. *The salvation of the Gentiles* was intended to stir the Jews to the acceptance of Christ.

3. *The salvation of the Jews* is to issue in still greater blessin
to the human race.

4. *The glorious future* that is yet to dawn on the world by th
mercy of God.

The more we ponder these profound truths the more deeply w
shall enter into the very heart of the Apostle's thought, and, sti
more, into the very heart of the Divine purposes of love and grac
for the entire world.

XLVIII

THE APOSTOLIC DOXOLOGY

Rom. xi. 33-36.

33. O the depth of the riches both of the wisdom and knowledge of God! how unsearchable *are* his judgments, and his ways past finding out!
34. For who hath known the mind of the Lord? or who hath been his counsellor?
35. Or who hath first given to him, and it shall be recompensed unto him again?
36. For of him, and through him, and to him, *are* all things: to whom *be* glory for ever. Amen.

The wonderful truth of verse 32 compels the Apostle to burst forth in adoring wonder at the marvel of God's mercy and grace. And yet it is probable that the doxology is due to the whole discussion. The remarkable way in which the Divine will is to be accomplished, and evil overruled and made subservient to God's purposes, constrains him to this note of praise. The Divine intention is to be realized in spite of, and even by means of human disobedience.

I. *The Divine Attributes Contemplated* (ver. 33).—There are three elements of adoring wonder at the Divine attributes contemplated here, and they are in view throughout the whole section (ch. ix.-xi.). It is perhaps best to read the R. V. rather than the A.V., and to regard the Apostle as referring not only to two, but to three aspects of the Divine character; riches, wisdom and knowledge. The word "depth" refers to inexhaustible fulness rather than unfathomable mystery, though some writers think that the latter is to be included. It would, however, seem hardly likely that St. Paul meant to emphasize the darkness and depth of God's counsels, which would really forbid rather than elicit contemplation.

1. The Depth of Divine Wealth. This refers to the exhaustless grace of God, the superabundant wealth of His resources. The Apostle seems particularly partial to the metaphor of "wealth" or "riches" to express the fulness and abundance of Divine grace (Rom. ii. 4; x. 12; Eph. i. 7; ii. 4, 7; iii. 8; Phil. iv. 19; Tit. iii. 6).

2. The Depth of Divine Wisdom. This refers to God's providence in arranging in the best possible way His practical wisdom and providence in the affairs of men.

3. The Depth of Divine Knowledge. This concerns His omniscience, His perfect knowledge of everything, past, present, and future.

II. *The Divine Attributes Described* (vers. 33-36).—Now the three elements thus contemplated are expanded, but are taken in the reverse order.

1. The Depth of Knowledge in God's unsearchable Judgments (ver. 33). His secret decisions are beyond the power of human explanation.

2. The Depth of Wisdom in God's "untrackable" Ways (vers. 33, 34). He has no confidant, and His procedure cannot be "tracked" by any human discovery.

3. The Depth of Wealth in God's independence of all gifts (vers. 35, 36). The initiative has always been God's, not man's, and He is the Source ("of Him"), the Means ("through Him"), and the End ("unto Him"). There can be no possibility of His indebtedness to man.

Thus the doxology is a beautiful expression of adoring awe, as the soul contemplates the marvels of God's working in providence and grace. This attitude of praise is particularly characteristic of the Apostle, and at each important stage of the Epistle his soul is uplifted in adoration to the God of all grace (see close of chs. v., vi., vii., viii.).

It has been well said that "we have learned Paul's meaning only when we can join in this ascription of praise" (Riddle).

1. *The Character of God.*—The soul of the Apostle is possessed with the thought of the greatness, goodness, and glory of God. His far-reaching purposes have filled his mind as he contemplates the

glorious future when "all Israel shall be saved" (ver. 26). His unchanging faithfulness has cheered his heart as he had dwelt on the irrevocableness of God's gifts to, and calling of, Israel (ver. 29). His abundant mercy has fired his heart as he has pondered the wonder of Divine grace in relation to all mankind (ver. 32). And thus we have what has been well called the Divine philosophy of history. Starting with a dualism in the call of Abraham and the preservation of Israel as a separate nation, the Divine purpose is to develop into a glorious universalism in which there will be a fusion of Jew and Gentile in the great unity of the human race. We are accustomed to think that history sheds much light on the Bible, but it is evident from these chapters that the Bible sheds still more light on history. The revelation of God's character should possess and inspire the soul of every believer.

2. *The Contemplation of God.*—The attitude of the Apostle is one of adoration, and he cannot say more, because there is nothing more to say, than "To Whom be the glory for ever." Again and again this reference to the glory of God comes before us in this Epistle, and in other writings of the Apostle. It is the Divine requirement for man's life from which sin has fallen short (ch. iii. 23). It constitutes the Divine prospect for man's future life as the believer rejoices "in hope of the glory of God" (ch. v. 2). And it is the Divine standard for the Christian's present life as he does "all to the glory of God" (1 Cor. x. 31). Very appropriately, therefore, does the Apostle ascribe the "glory" to God. "The supreme Sun of the spiritual universe, the ultimate reason of everything in the world, and the work of grace, is the glory of God. Whole systems of truth move in subordinate relations to this; this is subordinate to nothing" (Moule, *Union with Christ*, p. 10).

XLIX

A RETROSPECT

We have now come to the close of the second main division of this Epistle. All through, from ch. i. 18 to ch. xi. 36, we have seen how the Apostle, with keen thought and in striking language, brings before his readers the revelation of God's wrath against ungodliness (ch. i. 18-iii. 20); the revelation of God's righteousness in Christ (ch. iii. 21-viii. 39); and the revelation of His all-embracing mercy to Jew and Gentile (chs. ix.-xi.). As it has often been pointed out, there was nothing local in the circumstances of the Church at Rome to call forth this magnificent statement of truth. It was doubtless due to the inspiration of the Holy Spirit and intended for all ages of the Church. "It is a far-reaching glance over the Divine plan of the history of the world" (Godet).

But these later chapters (ix.-xi.) are so important, and so difficult as well, that it seems essential to endeavor to gather up some of their main truths, and to view the section as a whole now that we have pondered the details of the verses.

I. *The Divine Dispensations.*—The word "dispensation" is often used in connection with God's revelation to man. Thus we speak of the Jewish dispensation and the Christian dispensation, meaning thereby the particular times of God's dealings respectively with Jews and Christians. But there are at least seven periods of time described by this word, and they indicate in turn the fact and method of God's dealings with mankind, or with some portion of it, in regard to sin and to the purpose of His own mercy and grace. We have (1) the Eden dispensation (Gen. i. ii.); (2) the antediluvian dispensation (Gen. iii. 23); (3) the dispensation of Noah (Gen. viii. 20); (4) the Abrahamic dispensation (Gen. xii. 1); (5) the Mosaic dispensation (Exod. xix. 8); (6) the Christian dispensation (John i. 17); (7) the future dispensation (Eph. i. 10). Now it is vident that these dispensations must be carefully distinguished rom one another, if we are to understand fully the various aspects f the Divine revelation, and it is the attempt to distinguish in this vay that underlies the familiar phrase, "dispensational truth." It s possible, and perhaps probable, that when St. Paul counsels 'imothy about "rightly dividing the word of truth" (2 Tim. ii. 15), e had in mind some such distinction as is now under consideration. As St. Augustine said, "Distinguish the dispensations, and the criptures will agree." We must endeavor to interpret each passage r section of Scripture according to the dispensation for which it s intended, and we must also be particularly careful to draw a lear distinction between the primary interpretation and the econdary spiritual application of any passage. This effort at istinction is particularly true of the differences between Romans .-viii. and ch. ix.-xi. The former quite evidently refers mainly to he Christian dispensation, and the latter to the Jewish in relation o the Christian. Already, in ch. i.-viii. St. Paul had dealt briefly vith the three periods, or dispensations, of Adam, Moses, and Christ (ch. v.), and now in chs. ix.-xi. he is especially concerned vith the relation of Moses and Christ. The dispensations of Sin, aw, and Grace, are thus in turn considered and discussed.

All this makes it the more important to have clearly before our yes the true position and teaching of chs. ix.-xi.

II. *A General View of Chs. ix-xi.*—The main line of thought is, s we have seen, national rather than individual. St. Paul's object s to prove the essential harmony (even amid the difference) of e dispensations. In this section he shows that the Gospel is not pposed to, but is in perfect consistency with the earlier revelations f God. To make this quite clear it will be worth while looking once gain at these chapters in their entirety. They form a perfect whole hen considered alone, even though they have their rightful place s an integral part of the Epistle. In order that we may appreciate e completeness of this section we will endeavor to put it in a rm that will enable the eye to see and the mind to grasp its roportion and perfection.[1]

1The following outline is a modification of the view found in *The Church of the pistles*, by Dr. Bullinger (p. 78).

A. Ch. ix. 1-5. Paul's sorrow regarding Israel's failure.

B. Ch. ix. 6-13. God's purpose had respect only to a portion.

C. Ch. ix. 14-29. God's purpose regarded only a remnant.

D. (*a*) Ch. ix. 30-33. Israel's failure in spite of the Prophets.
(*b*) Ch. x. 1-13. Israel's failure in spite of the Law.
(*c*) Ch. x. 14-21. Israel's failure in spite of the Gospel.

E. Ch. xi. 1-10. God's purpose regarding the remnant accomplished.

F. Ch. xi. 11-32. God's purpose will ultimately embrace the whole.

G. Ch. xi. 33-36. St. Paul's joy regarding God's purpose.

It will be seen that this conspectus agrees closely with the detailed analysis already given. But it should be also observed that A answers to G; B to F; C to E; while D (in three sections) is the center and heart of the section. And as Denney says, the Apostle's interpretation proceeds along three lines: (1) In ch. ix. 6-29 he asserts God's freedom and sovereignty as against any claims or right of man; (2) in ch. ix. 30-x. 21 he turns to the human side and shows that the rejection of the Jews is due to their rejection of the Gospel, for if God had been arbitrary He would have been unjust, and yet He is not unjust since the Jews fell through their own sin; (3) in ch. xi. he shows how the unbelief of the Jews and the salvation of the Gentiles are to issue in the great future, in which God's promises to Israel are fulfilled. Thus chs. ix-xi. meet the objections of those who said that the Gospel could not possibly be true because it was inconsistent with God's covenant with Israel. On the contrary, the Apostle shows that they are in the most absolute harmony, and both covenants are shown to come from the same source, God Himself.

III. *The Dispensational Teaching of these Chapters.*

1. The covenant with Abraham is here referred to his natural seed and is regarded as of permanent validity. It is inaccurate to speak of the Jews as God's "ancient" people. They are His "permanent" people, because of the perpetuity of the Divine covenant with Abraham. We must beware of spiritualizing the Old Testament and making references to Israel and Jacob refer to the Church.

Much of the Old Testament remains unfulfilled to this day. As Dr. David Brown says:—

> "Those who think that in all the Evangelical prophecies of the Old Testament, the terms 'Jacob,' 'Israel,' etc., are to be understood solely of the Christian Church, would appear to read the Old Testament differently from the Apostle who, from the use of those very terms in Old Testament prophecy draws arguments to prove that God has mercy in store for the natural Israel" (*Romans,* p. 119).

The preservation of the Jews today is a proof of this perpetual covenant of God with Israel.

2. A clear distinction is made throughout between Jew and Gentile. Although in the present Christian dispensation, individual Jews and individual Gentiles combine to form one Church, the Body of Christ, yet in the great future to which the Apostle looks, national distinctions will remain, and the Jew, the Gentile, and the Church of God will be kept separate until that day when "God shall be all in all."[1]

3. There is no possibility of questioning the Apostle's prediction of a future national restoration for Israel. His words cannot be interpreted in any other way. Whether we are to understand, "There shall come out of Zion, the Deliverer" (ch. xi. 26), as referring to the first or the second coming; the fact remains that Israel as a whole is to be saved. But with this fact St. Paul is content, and no details are given. As to whether the Jews will go back to Palestine, or what will happen there, he says nothing, but what he does say is perfectly clear.

4. It is absolutely necessary to distinguish between Christ's first and second coming. In chs. i.-viii. He is described as having come for redemption, but in chs. ix.-xi. the salvation of Israel is still in the future. When this distinction between the first and second comings is seen, we can realize the futility of many objections to Christianity. Dr. Broughton gives a typical illustration of the confusion in many minds on this subject, and also of the way in which the confusion may be removed:—

> "One day on a train I got to talking with a Jewish Rabbi, a very intelligent man. He said, 'Do you know, the objection I have to your

1See Stifler, *Romans,* ch. xi., and Scofield, *Rightly Dividing the Word of Truth* (p. 3).

teaching is that it is not sincere. As I read the Scriptures, I read that Jesus Christ is to rule in the affairs of the earth. Don't you? Well, you know that he did not. He never got anywhere near His Father's throne, nor to ruling this earth. Then, how do you claim Jesus to be the Messiah? I tell you when the Messiah comes He is to sit on His father David's throne and rule this earth, and then you are going to be ashamed that you did not wait until He came. I said, 'You have got the cart before the horse. You do not rightly divide the Scriptures. Jesus Christ is coming again, my friend, and He is prophesied in your Scriptures to come again. When He does come again He is not coming in a manger. That is the reason you despised Him. You say that I am not sincere. I say that you are not sincere, because the Scriptures tell you that He is to be born in a manger, and to be born of a Virgin. You expected Him to come with a blast of trumpets as a King.' Well, he had never seen that. I said further, 'When He comes again He is coming as you are expecting Him to come, as a King, and He is going to sit on His Father's throne, and then you are going to say that "the Messiah has really come at last." He is going to say to you, "I am the Jesus of the manger. I am the Jesus of prophecy. I am the One crucified, and I am come back and am going to sit on My Father's throne and rule this nation according to the program of heaven." Then you are going to say, "Oh, I wish I had accepted Him before this, but since I did not I will accept Him now." Then the Jews are going to be restored, and then the great world-wide Evangelistic sweep will begin,'" (*Salvation and the Old Theology,* p. 172).

1. *Missions to the Jews* ought to occupy a prominent place in every Christian heart and life. "To the Jew first" is a great principle. Nothing can be sadder than the way in which Jewish Missions have been neglected even by godly men. It is hardly credible that these are the words of Martin Luther:—"The Jewish heart is so stock-stone, devil, iron hard, that it can in no way be moved. They are as young devils, damned to hell. To convert those devil brats (as some fondly ween out of the Epistle to the Romans)is impossible" (Quoted by John Brown, *Romans,* p. 410).

And yet there is proof positive on every side, that, in proportion to the work of Jewish Missions, the results are even greater than among the Gentiles. It is sometimes asked why we need to give the Gospel to the Jews, if they are not to be converted as a nation until the Lord's return. But "all the world" surely includes Jews, and although the present is mainly, it is not exclusively, a Gentile dispensation. The Jews need Christ as much as do others, and we owe the Gospel to the Jew because it is through him we have received our Lord and the Bible.

There is no fear of lessening blessing among the Gentiles by prosecuting Missions to the Jews. The facts of the case are all against it. Besides, we are told distinctly that the reception of the Jews into the kingdom of God, is to be life from the dead to the whole world (ch. xi. 15).

2. *The Message to Gentile Christians* is only too clear. "Be not high-minded, but fear." It is not from any special privilege, and certainly for no personal merit, that the Gentile nations of the world have heard and received the Gospel, and it will be neither by privilege nor merit that they will retain that Gospel, but only by faithfulness to its great realities. Further, if Gentile Christians are not faithful, God may do to them what He has been compelled to do to the Jews (Rom. xi. 22).

3. *The Practical Purpose of Election* is a subject for careful consideration. There are many difficulties and consequent differences of opinion on this point, and we do not here touch the problems of the general subject.[1] The primary thought of the Apostle in these chapters is not individual salvation, but the philosophy of history, though of course the fundamental mystery still remains as to the relation between the Divine and the human wills. Yet chs. ix.-xi. clearly teach that while there is a Divine law of election which has a principle of selection, and behind which we may not penetrate to know the reason (ch. ix. 6-21), yet the outcome and purpose of this selection is seen in the service which God intends the elected man or nation to render. Whatever we may think or say about eternal salvation, no one can question the teaching of these chapters that Israel's election had for its object the service of his fellow-men. St. Paul is concerned not so much with individuals, as with nations and masses of people. He speaks of God's choice of Israel, not to eternal life as such, but to the privilege and duty of receiving His grace in order to work for and with Him for the establishment of His kingdom. When Israel refused to rise to this

1For these questions reference may be made to several works on *Romans;* Sanday and Headlam (p. 347), Garvie (*Century Bible,* p. 221), Woule (*Cambridge Bible,* p. 167). Forbes (p. 347), Beet (p. 279), Chalmers (vol. iii., p. 362).

high calling, the Gentiles were summoned into the kingdom. Israel was chosen to be a blessing; the Gentiles were saved to be a blessing; the Church is chosen to be a blessing. "Saved to serve." God's chosen men are His "choice" men, and all through Scripture His choice men do not lie on "flowery beds of ease" but endure hard, strenuous sacrificing on behalf of others. We must never forget this.

4. *The Great Future* to which we are bidden to look. Nothing can be clearer than the glorious outlook set before us by the Apostle. Amid all the shadows, disappointments, discouragements, and sin of today, we must lift up our hearts and our eyes and contemplate that future which God purposes for His people.

5. *The Confidence and Authoritativeness of the Apostle.*—In spite of his sorrow, he was filled with strong hope and perfect assurance:—

"It is not my intention to defend the inspiration of this great Apostle; that has a thousand times been done with such consummate ability, as to leave no necessity for any feeble efforts of mine: but I wish to notice the consequences that follow, as it appears to me, inevitably, from the manner in which the Epistle is written. Either Paul had incessant, infallible guidance of the Holy Spirit of God, or he was a vain pretender (fanatic, or enthusiast, as you please), who assumed, without right, the demeanor of a prophet; and whose dogmas every man is at liberty to reject, or receive, at his pleasure. There is no middle path between these conclusions admissable (Walford, *Curae Romanae,* p. 216).

In ch. xi. 25 the Apostle leaves argument for revelation, and as Dr. Denney says:—"How much a revelation of this kind will weigh with the modern reader depends on the extent to which on general grounds he can recognize in Paul an inspired interpreter of Christianity."

Certainly the words must be either true or false, for history does not offer the faintest glimmer of light on the subject. To quote once again the writer already referred to on this page:—

"The only state of mind that fits men to read this book of God, so as to derive from it the inestimable instruction and improvement which it was designed to convey, is that by which the writer of it was manifestly actuated when he penned the last verses of this chapter: 'O, the depth of the riches, and wisdom, and knowledge of God! How unsearchable His purposes, and inscrutable His ways! For who hath known the mind of the Lord? or who hath been His counsellor? or who hath first given to Him, that He should be recompensed? For from Him, and by Him, and for Him are all things! To Him be glory for ever, Amen" (Walford, *Curae Romanae*, p. 217).

L

THE PRACTICAL APPEAL

ROM. xii.-xvi.

AFTER doctrine comes duty; after revelation, responsibility; after principles, practice. We now turn to the third main division of the Epistle. The Apostle has said, "The just shall *live*" (ch. i. 17). But this has been dealt with in ch. vi.-viii. only in regard to the life of character; it is essential to show its meaning in the life of conduct. We must observe the three pivots of the Epistle suggested by the word "Therefore." In ch. v. 1 we have the "Therefore" of Justification; in ch. viii. 1, the "Therefore" of Sanctification; in ch. xii. 1, the "Therefore" of Consecration. This is the order: Salvation, Sanctification, Service. Only thus can the Christian life be realized and truly lived.

Before passing on, it seems essential to review the course of thought. The Apostle has shown how through faith in Christ sinful man is reinstated in righteousness (ch. i.-viii.). The Gospel is "the power of God unto salvation" because in it the Divine righteousness is revealed (ch. i. 16, 17). After man has received that reinstatement in righteousness which we call Justification (ch. iii. 21-v. 21), St. Paul proceeds to describe those relations of the believer which make possible a definite Christian experience (ch. vi.-viii.). These relations are two, to *sin* and to *law;* and in each of them there is the element of death and the element of life. In the first place, the believer is "dead unto sin and alive unto God" (ch. vi. 11); in the next place, he is "dead to the law in order to be married to Him Who is raised from the dead" (ch. vii. 4). This two-fold relationship, involving a break with sin and law, introduces the soul to that ample fellowship with the living Christ which enables him to realize what is meant by the righteousness of God in personal experience. And thus united to Christ in death and life the righteousness of the law is fulfilled in the believer, and he walks "not after the flesh, but after the Spirit" (ch. viii. 4).

The Apostle has also taught us that this gift of Divine righteousness for guilty man has been deliberately refused by the Jews, the very people who should have been the first to receive it. By their wilful persistence in seeking righteousness in their own way, and in their refusal to accept God's gift of righteousness in Christ, they have become God's enemies, though ultimately they too will abjure their own righteousness and accept the righteousness of God in Christ (ch. ix.-xi.).

Now we are to see the moral and practical consequences of these doctrines in order that we may reproduce in our life "the fruits of righteousness" (Phil. i. 11). The Apostle's mind has been convinced, and his heart stirred by the revelation of God's righteousness. It now remains to emphasize the practical, joyous expression of this in daily living. When the soul has entered into the true Christian relation of union with Christ, as taught in the earlier chapters, his life will run along the lines laid down in the section which is now to be considered.

Before entering upon the details it will be well to take a brief view of the general lines of practical application set forth.

I. Foundation Principles of Christian Consecration (ch. xii. 1, 2).

II. Christian Consecration in Ordinary Life (ch. xii. 3-21).

1. Humility in Service (vers. 3-8).
2. Love to the Brethren (vers. 9-13).
3. Love to all (vers. 14-21).

III. Christian Consecration in Relation to the State (ch. xiii. 1-14).

1. Obedience (vers. 1-7).
2. Love (vers. 8-10).
3. Motive to obedience and love (vers. 11-14).

IV. Christian Consecration in Relation to Special Duty (ch. xiv. 1-xv. 13).

1. The weak brother (ch. xiv. 1-12).
2. Principles for the strong (ch. xiv. 13-23).

3. The example of Christ (ch. xv. 1-13).

We have in this a picture of an all-round Christian life, and the material is as systematically arranged as that in the entire doctrinal part which precedes. As Godet points out, the idea which governs the arrangement of this section is that the Apostle deals successively with the two spheres of the believer's activity; the religious (ch. xii.), and the civil (ch. xiii.). "These are the two domains in which he is to manifest the life of holiness which has been put within him. He acts in the world as a member of the Church and as a member of the State." Godet proceeds to remark that this double walk has one point of departure and one of aim. The point of departure is the consecration of the body as the basis of activity, and the point of aim is the Lord's coming again; and so we have, "a point of departure; two spheres to be simultaneously traveled; a point of arrival. Such in the view of the Apostle is the system of the believer's practical life."

Three main thoughts are to be pondered at this point.

1. *The Fundamental and Essential Connection between Doctrine and Exhortation.* There is no contradiction or even incongruity between the preceding teaching about holiness by faith and the practical consequences here emphasized. If it should be thought that Justification inevitably produces Holiness as an absolute necessity, just as the tree bears fruit of itself without any appeal, it is essential to remind ourselves that "moral life is subject to quite different laws from physical life" (Godet). The fact of free-will makes human life unique and necessitates the appropriation and application of grace moment by moment in order to realize the Divine purpose. Added to this, there is ever before us the fact and power of indwelling sin, and this is an additional call to the use of that Divine grace which is provided for us in Christ, and is only available for us through faith. This is why we are enabled to speak of the righteous man living "by faith." It is by faith he receives Christ for justification; it is by faith he receives Christ for sanctification; and it is equally by faith that he receives Christ by momentary appropriation for that consecration of life in all its

parts which the Apostle here delineates. Godet's view of the truth on this point needs careful attention:—

> "The believer is *dead unto sin,* no doubt; he has broken with that perfidious friend; but sin is not dead in him, and it strives continually to restore the broken relation. By calling the believer to the conflict against it, as well as to the positive practice of Christian duty, the Apostle is not relapsing into Jewish legalism. He assumes the inward consecration of the believer as an already consummated fact, implicitly contained in his faith, that he proceeds to call him to realize his Christian obligation" (*Romans,* vol. ii., p. 277f.)

2. *Holiness as the Proof of Grace.* Let it therefore be constantly before our mind that holiness of life is the supreme, indeed, the only proof that Divine grace is our personal possession. All our professions, our desires, our ideals, our hopes, our intentions, will count for nothing unless we manifest holiness in thought, word, and deed in all the circles of daily life and activity.

3. *Holiness as the Expression of Life.* Holiness is very much more than a proof of our possession of grace:—

> "It is the expression of life; it is the form and action in which life is intended to come out. In our orchards the golden apples are evidences of the tree's species, and of its life. But a wooden label could tell us the species, and leaves can tell the life. The fruit is more than label or leaf; it is the thing for which the tree is there" (Moule, *Romans,* "Expositor's Bible," p. 325).

It is of the utmost importance that we bear in mind this constant characteristic of Holy Scripture, the close association of humblest duties with the profound revelation of spiritual blessing. As the sun descends millions of miles to open the petals of the tiniest flower, so the highest Christian doctrine is intended to affect the lowliest Christian duties. The interests of morality are sometimes thought to be served best by a foundation of works, but this is not true; indeed, the truth is just the opposite. The most powerful incentive and the greatest safeguard of morality come from Divine grace. Richard Cecil, one of the greatest Evangelical teachers that ever lived, used to say that if he had to choose between preaching precepts and preaching privileges he would preach privileges, because the latter would inevitably lead to the former, while the former alone could not possibly provide the necessary grace for duty

(Moule, *Romans*, "Expositor's Bible," p. 323). The connection between doctrine and exhortation is thus put with all his characteristic quaintness by the great Bishop Joseph Hall:—

> "Those that are all in exhortation, no whit in doctrine, are like to them that snuff the lamp, but pour not in oil. Again, those that are all in doctrine, nothing in exhortation, drown the wick in oil, but light it not; making it fit for use if it had fire put to it; but as it is, neither capable of good nor profitable for the present. Doctrine without exhortation makes men all brain, no heart; exhortation without doctrine makes the heart full, but leaves the brain empty. Both together make a man, one makes a wise man, the other a good; one serves that we may know our duty, the other that we may perform it. Men cannot practice unless they know, and they know in vain if they practice not" (Quoted by C. Neil, *Romans*, p. 380).

We must therefore keep constantly in memory the secret of Christian living. It starts with the acceptance of Christ for justification; it continues in the constant appropriation of Christ for sanctification, together with that break with sin and law which forms part of our fellowship with Christ. It is impossible for us to live the true life without maintaining this break. We are "dead unto sin" and "dead unto law." But when we surrender all known sin and break with it in our will, abandoning all efforts of self, we find in Christ the ample source of power for obedience. It is this fellowship with Christ which makes the real Christian life possible. When the branch is truly united to the vine it begins to live its genuine life. We must enter into fellowship with Christ, and then abide in Him by using the resources made available for us in order that we may reproduce in life the character and conduct of our Master. This is true sanctification, the attitude of abiding in that relation of fellowship with Christ, in which alone it is possible to go forward step by step, having our fruit unto holiness.

LI

PRINCIPLES OF CONSECRATION

Rom. xii. 1, 2.

1. I beseech you therefore, brethren, by the mercies of God, that ye present your bodies a living sacrifice, holy, acceptable unto God, *which is* your reasonable service.

2. And be not conformed to this world: but be ye transformed by the renewing of your mind, that ye may prove what *is* that good, and acceptable, and perfect, will of God.

As every building rests on its foundation, so the Christian life of practical consecration must be based upon principles such as the Apostle here inculcates.

The tone of the writer is particularly noticeable as he introduces these searching requirements. "I beseech." This is his favorite word (Eph. iv. 1; 1 Thess. iv. 1). "Moses commands; the Apostle exhorts" (Bengel). It is noteworthy that not once in the writings of St. Paul do we find him "commanding" his converts. He himself constantly exemplified his own words: "Not that we have dominion over your faith, but are helpers of your joy" (2 Cor. i. 24). This is the true spirit for all Christian teachers; the beseeching, pleading, exhorting attitude.

I. *The Ground of Consecration* (ver. 1).—The pivot word "therefore" must be carefully studied (*cf.* Eph. iv. 1). It connects this section with all that has gone before and emphasizes the essential unity of doctrine and life. As we have already seen, Christian morality is inextricably related to the Christian revelation. Our relationship to God dominates and determines our attitude to Him, and the new position which is ours in Christ requires and provides for new duties corresponding to it.

"The mercies of God." These "mercies" are the theme of the former eleven chapters, and the Apostle emphasizes "mercies," not "power" or "authority." Mercies, too, because salvation is due to them and not to any human merit. The grace that saves has already been established as the foundation principle of salvation, and this is necessarily the ground of all Christian consecration and morality. It is because we are already recipients of the mercies of God that we must and can live the true life. We work *from*, not *for* salvation. Morality needs a dynamic. Conduct requires a power behind it. This is found in "the mercies of God," in that Gospel which is "the power of God unto salvation" (ch. i. 16). The soul that is united to Christ by faith is ready to learn and to do its duty, for the simple but sufficient reason that it knows it can appropriate without reserve the marvelous resources of Divine grace. It is for this reason that the Apostle emphasizes the mercies of God, and exhorts us to place ourselves unreservedly in God's hands for grace to live the true life.

II. *The Character of Consecration* (ver. 1).

1. It is voluntary. "Present." This is a term associated with gifts for the Temple (Lev. i. 3; xvi. 7). It occurs in Rom. vi. 13, where it is translated "yield," and thus this chapter closely connects itself with the former section (see also Luke ii. 22; Col. i. 28).

2. It is complete. "Your bodies." A comprehensive phrase, meaning *themselves*—spirit, soul, and body. The body is the instrument of the inner life, and if this is really consecrated it carries the soul and spirit with it. This thought of the body is found frequently in St. Paul's teaching. It is fundamental to his complete presentation of the Gospel of Redemption. Christ is the Savior of the whole man, and redemption necessarily includes spirit, soul, and body. No religion values the body like Christianity. Through the Incarnation we have been delivered from that ancient dualism that considered the body purely materialistic and unworthy of regard. It is through the body that the entire life reveals itself. It is the body that receives impressions, possesses tendencies, and expresses powers; not merely our emotions and energies are to be consecrated to God, every part of our life is to be His. Since we

are united inwardly by faith to Christ and our will is already God's, it necessarily only remains to present our body to Him for the purpose of carrying out that will.

3. It is sacrificial "A living sacrifice, holy, acceptable unto God." The Jewish sacrifices consisted of two main classes: (*a*) those associated with reconciliation (sin and peace offerings), and (*b*) those associated with consecration which was based on reconciliation (burnt and meal offerings). It is the latter class with which we are now concerned, just as the former came before us in connection with propitiation in ch. iii. 25. We observe that in Lev. i. the burnt offering comes first as the necessary result of the Jewish believer being on redemption ground by virtue of the great passover sacrifice. In the same way, the Christian is redeemed in order that he may be consecrated. "Christ expiated that the Christian might be dedicated." The Old Testament sacrifices were offerings of dead animals, but the Christian's sacrifice is "living." Yet even so the sacrifice of the Old Covenant represented the life of the offerer, and so now, the Christian's sacrifice is living, because of our new life in Christ (ch. vi. 13). As such, it is "holy" and "well pleasing" to God, for in it our Lord sees "of the travail of His soul and is satisfied" (Isa. liii. 11). When the life of the believer is thus devoted to God the fulness of the Divine purpose is realized, and it can be said of us in our sphere and degree, "This is My beloved son, in whom I am well pleased."

4. It is practical. "Your . . . service." This is the end and outcome of consecration, definite work for God. Not merely for personal salvation, but that "we being delivered out of the hand of our enemies might serve Him without fear, in holiness and righteousness before Him, all the days of our life" (Luke i. 74, 75).

5. It is rational. "Your reasonable service." Consecration is intelligent as contrasted with the unintelligent offering of the animal in the Jewish sacrifices. The word rendered "rational" is literally "logical," and the phrase may almost be rendered, "your logical service," that is, the service which is the "logical" outcome of our position as believers in Christ. The word refers to an act of the mind, or reason, and Godet well points out that the true meaning

is "the service which rationally corresponds to the moral premises contained in the faith which you profess." Such a service is appropriate to a being like the believer whose essential nature is rational and spiritual.

III. *The Demand of Consecration* (ver. 2).

1. Negative. "Be not conformed to this world." The word "world" is literally "age," and is always opposed to "the age to come." It is invariably described as evil (Gal. i. 4), with Satan as its ruling power (2 Cor. iv. 4). Any definition of "world" or "age" is admittedly difficult, but it really means everything in the existing order of things which is outside the kingdom of God. It therefore applies to condition rather than to position, to atmosphere rather than to sphere. The spirit of this present age is absolute selfishness as contrasted with Divine love. Its object is the gratification of self rather than the doing of the will of God, and its authority springs from Satan because it has rejected the one true Ruler of the universe (John xiv. 30; Eph. ii. 2). The believer must therefore avoid taking his shape from the world around. Its life is so entirely different to that which comes from God that it is impossible for the true follower of Christ to be conformed to it. Unless we are particularly careful we shall find ourselves influenced by and fashioned like the world and given up to its spirit and life. All this gives special point to the appeal of the Apostle not to be conformed to the age in which we live, but to be separated in heart and spirit from it. This is the spiritual "nonconformity" required from all Christians.

2. Positive. "But be ye transformed by the renewing of your mind." The only way to prevent the outward shape of our life from being fashioned like that of the world is to take care that the inward spirit of our being is transformed by the renewing of our mind. The Holy Spirit is to be allowed continually to work in the realm of our intellectual and moral knowledge and thought. The "mind" in Scripture is much more than mere intellect, for it has a moral aspect as well (chs. i. 28; vii. 23, 25; xi. 34). It blends the intellectual and the moral, and may be described as "the faculty by which the soul perceives and discerns the good and the true." As the result of sin this faculty has been injured and disturbed; self

has darkened the mind, and led it to regard everything from a purely personal and selfish point of view. It is the Holy Spirit alone Who can renew in us this faculty of mental and moral perception. By reason of sin it is under the power of the flesh, but when delivered from this sway and controlled by the Holy Spirit the faculty recovers its power of discernment and is enabled to realize what is right and true. It is very important to ponder this idea of moral transformation by means of what we *think*. "As a man thinketh in his heart, so is he."

(To those who understand Greek the words and tenses of these two phrases will prove of great interest. See Sanday and Headlam on this subject; Lightfoot on Phil. ii. 7 ; and Gifford, *Incarnation*, pp. 22 ff., 88 ff.)

IV. *The Effect of Consecration* (ver. 2).—"That ye may prove what is that good, and acceptable, and perfect, will of God."

1. The will of God *known*, is the first result of the consecration effected by presenting ourselves to God and by avoiding conformity to the world and becoming transformed within. To "prove" means to prove and approve, to test and attest. It refers to spiritual discernment, which is the inevitable result of inward transformation. "The result of this purification is to make the intellect, which is the seat of moral judgment, true and exact in judging on spiritual and moral questions" (Sanday and Headlam, p. 354). It is only the regenerate who can discern between what is and what is not pleasing to God. The New Testament makes much of spiritual discernment. St. Paul prays that the eyes of our heart may be opened (Eph. i. 18), and in his later Epistles places great emphasis on "knowledge," that is, spiritual discernment. Indeed, a favorite word of his means "full knowledge," implying maturity of preception which is a mark of the ripening believer. St. Peter's second Epistle reveals the same characteristic, for in the short space of three chapters the thought of knowledge, or of "full knowledge" appears several times. Again, in the first Epistle of St. John the key-note of the entire writing is "That ye may know," and when the Apostle of Love comes to describe the three stages of the Christian life; the children, the young men, and the fathers, has nothing more to say about the

fathers than the twofold statement that "they know Him that is from the beginning." There is thus no surer mark of a growing, progressive, ripening Christian life than this faculty of spiritual discernment.

2. The will of God *done,* necessarily follows from the knowledge of it, and this is the practical object, outcome, and effect of consecration, for God's will is everything in the believer's life. By the power of the Spirit of Christ he is to make his life in the body the manifestation of God's will as opposed to the realization of the mind and spirit of the world. And thus:—

> "To the false model, presented in every age by the mundane kind of life, there is opposed a perfect kind of type, that of the will of God which is discerned by the renewed mind of the believer, and which he strives to realize, by means of his God-consecrated body, at every moment and in all the relations of his life" (Godet, *Romans,* vol. ii., p. 284).

3. The will of God *enjoyed,* as well as known and done, is suggested by the words "good," "acceptable," and "perfect." By daily consecration we "prove," and thereby "approve" God's will in these three ways, and thus we reach the climax and culmination of Christian consecration, the acceptance and enjoyment of God's will in daily life. Our experience is to be ever progressive, rising from the positive to the comparative and superlative. We are to seek the very best that God can give, and the normal attitude of the spiritual life is that it is at once full and yet always craving for more. Our new experience deepens our capacity for greater blessing, and as we yield ourselves continually to the grace of God, we find His will essentially good, and our obedience well-pleasing to Him, and ethically realizing the end for which we are intended. And so the renewed mind obtains a discernment for daily living which leads it to a gladsome service in correspondence with the will of God. That will is free from evil, acceptable to those around us, and in every way complete for human life.

While the entire passage calls for patient, detailed, and prolonged meditation, there are some main thoughts which summarize the Apostle's teaching.

1. *The Basis of Holy Living—Revelation.*—It is of course true that in Matthew Arnold's phrase "conduct is three-fourths of life," but it is equally true that the other fourth is the spring, the source, and the guarantee of the rest, because it concerns the motive and the power. At the cost of repetition this thought must be pressed home because it is so often forgotten. If a man stands before one of the great masterpieces of Turner, and is told to reproduce it on a canvas provided for him, he will soon realize his utter helplessness to accomplish the task. The ideal is too high; the genius of the great painter is infinitely above him. But if by some possibility Turner could become incarnated in the man, could see through his eyes, think through his brain, and work through his hand, it would be possible to reproduce the picture because it would be no longer by him, but by Turner dwelling in him. In the same way in morals, the prior question is always as to the power to do what is required. The example of Christ, the will of God, the ideal life; these things are far above our powers, and it is only when Christ dwells in us by the Holy Spirit that they become practical possibilities. This is why the Apostle dwells on "the mercies of God"; these facts about Jesus Christ, which when received into the soul and made vital by the Holy Spirit, guarantee that "power of God" which enables the believer to realize God's ideal for him.

2. *The Method of Holy Living—Consecration.*—This, in a word, is the response of the soul to the mercies of God. As we contemplate what Christ has done, what He is, and what the Holy Spirit gives, our hearts rise up in thankful trust and deep adoration as we yield ourselves to God. Consecration is often found in connection with the priesthood of the Old Testament, and the Hebrew word for "consecrate" is quite literally "fill the hand." "Who then is willing to consecrate his service this day unto the Lord" (1 Chron. xxix. 5)? That is to say, who is willing to come to God with his hands full, ready for service, with every faculty to be presented to, and used by God?

"I will not work my soul to save,
For that my Lord has done;
But I will work like any slave
For love of His dear Son.'

3. *The Outcome of Holy Living—Transformation.*—Not growth, but transformation, which is very much more, and more important. Growth suggests progress, but transformation indicates change. Our Lord "grew," but He never needed to be transformed, because there was nothing in His character that required to be altered. At every stage of His "growth" He was perfect, without any element to mar that perfection, but with the Christian it is different, for when he has come into fellowship with Christ he requires not only growth, but transformation. This transformation, as we have seen, is effected by inward renewal. The mind of Christ takes the place of the mind of self, and just as the new character becomes adjusted to the new conditions, those who are united to Christ and are filled with His Spirit will both grow and become transformed. They will often view themselves, as in the sight of God, with many marks of sinfulness and imperfection, and they will always feel the necessity of basing their acceptance with God on the gift of His righteousness in Christ, but with the acceptance will come an ever-increasing acceptableness, and this will be the ambition of the soul (2 Cor. v. 9, Greek) as it momentarily yields itself to God to be possessed and transformed by His wondrous grace.

LII

HUMILITY

Rom. xii. 3-8.

3. For I say, through the grace given unto me, to every man that is among you, not to think *of himself* more highly than he ought to think; but to think soberly, according as God hath dealt to every man the measure of faith.
4. For as we have many members in one body, and all members have not the same office;
5. So we, *being* many, are one body in Christ, and every one members one of another.
6. Having then gifts differing according to the grace that is given to us, whether prophecy *let us prophesy* according to the proportion of faith;
7. Or ministry, *let us wait* on *our* ministering: or he that teacheth, on teaching;
8. Or he that exhorteth, on exhortation: he that giveth, *let him do it* with simplicity; he that ruleth, with diligence; he that sheweth mercy, with cheerfulness.

The principle of Consecration is now to be applied to various aspects and departments of daily life, starting from its exercise in the Church ((ch. xii. 3-13), and extending to the believer's relations to all men (ch. xii. 14-xiii. 14). St. Paul opens with his characteristic phrase, "For I say" (ver. 3), that is, "I will illustrate my meaning." His first message consists of an appeal for Christian humility.

I. *The Call of Humility* (ver. 3).—After a right relation to God comes a right relation to our fellow-believers; from the spiritual emerges the social. Humility is the direct effect of consecration, because pride is, and ever has been, the great enemy of true righteousness. Even the Apostle in making this appeal expresses his own true Christian lowliness, for he speaks "through the grace that was given." He could therefore rightly teach and press this upon them without pride. He makes his appeal to every Christian without exception. "To every man that is among you." Each one is urged to think soberly of himself, and not to think more highly than he ought to think. This play upon the word "think" is specially noteworthy. The first need of the enlightened mind is the consciousness of our proper attitude to our fellow-Christians and the right use of spiritual gifts. There is an inherent tendency from the highest spiritual life to the lowliest to exalt self, and every form of spiritual pride is disastrous to life and godliness. Each Christian man is only a part of the great whole, and unless his opinion of himself agrees with God's opinion of him his life will inevitably result in failure. Action is to be strictly limited by the Divine gift; "according as God hath dealt to each man a measure of faith." Some writers (like Godet) would limit the phrase, "Every man that is among you," to those who are engaged in some form of ministry, urging that it would be superfluous to use such words if the Apostle merely intended to indicate the members of the Church. But the whole context would seem to imply something wider than purely ministerial gifts, great and varied as they were in the primitive Church. It is a solemn and searching thought that upon everyone some gift has been bestowed (Eph. iv. 7). It must be used. On the other hand, it is equally important to remember that no one Christian possesses all the gifts. Accordingly, we are to minister our gift just as we have received it, neither more nor less, "as good stewards of the manifold grace of God" (1 Pet. iv. 10).

II. *The Reason for Humility* (vers. 4, 5).—The fact that there is a variety of gifts in the Christian Church constitutes one main reason why each Christian man should be humble. No one can possess and exercise all the gifts, and it is obviously impossible for every Christian to take the lead and occupy the most important places. As the vine has many branches, and the body many members, so the Christian Church is made up of a large number of individual members, each with his own gift, intended to be exercised in its proper place and way. Our duty, therefore, is to note our province and to stay there, to recognize our limitations and work accordingly. Usefulness is never increased by going beyond our proper sphere. The Church is an organism rather than an organization, and this figure of the body with its several members is a definite reminder of the place and limits of each individual Christian. St. Paul amplifies the figure in 1 Cor. xii. 12-27. Three great thoughts are thus emphasized, or at least suggested in these words: Unity, Diversity, and Harmony. And it is only when all three are realized and blended that the Church of Christ can live its true life and do its proper work. We may vary the old phrase and say that in the Church of Christ there is "a place for everyone and everyone in his place," and the more thoroughly we face this two-fold truth the more effectively will the work of the Church be done. The trouble is that there is far too little of this recognition of different gifts and different spheres in the one body of Christ.

> "What good work is there which is not in more or less continual danger of suffering, or even being abandoned, because fellow-Christians, zealous fellow-Christians, will plainly, and it must be wilfully, yield to the ambition to be first: will not be content to be second or third: will not do the unobtrusive work: will think 'How can I shine?' rather than 'How can I serve'?" (Gore, *Romans,* vol. ii., p. 112).

III. *The Expression of Humility* (vers. 6-8).—Humility will therefore show itself in a variety of ways according to the gifts that we possess and the work we have to do. While there are different functions there will be one Spirit actuating everything. Seven ministerial gifts are mentioned here. The first four are official: prophecy, teaching, ministry, exhortation. The last three are general: giving, ruling, showing mercy. Prophecy is put first as the most important. It was the inspired declaration of the will of God. It did not necessarily consist of prediction, but of proclamation, the announcement of the Gospel in the power of the Holy Spirit (1 Cor. xiv. 1-5; Eph. ii. 20; iii. 5). This prophetic work is to be done "according to the proportion of faith." The phrase is perhaps best interpreted of the prophet's own faith in relation to God. He is to prophesy within the limits of his own trustful insight, according to the measure given to him by God. Most writers take this view, though others (Godet in part, Philippi, and Liddon) prefer to understand it as prophecy according to the proportion of "the faith," that is, the substance of the Gospel. Godet suggests that while the original meaning is personal faith, it also implies that the prophet should exercise it in connection with the whole Church, and this, according to Philippi, comes in substance to "the faith," the collective normal faith of the community. If this is the true interpretation, the prophet is to proclaim each side of the truth in turn. But it may be questioned whether this view of faith, as "that which we believe," is quite so early as the Epistle to the Romans. It seems far better to understand by the phrase that the prophet is to proclaim the message God has given him to deliver, neither more nor less.

It is important for a man to express *all,* and yet not more than his faith warrants. Each has something to say for God. Let him see that no false humility prevents him from expressing it fully.

In the case of ministry, or teaching, or exhortation, the Christian is to give himself to his own special work. He is to exist in, and to be absorbed by his own service. He is to know his province and abide therein.

The three general gifts are equally important. "He that giveth" is to do it with liberality, communicating freely of his own possessions for the good of the community. "He that ruleth" is to proceed with earnestness and singlemindedness, remembering the need of impartiality. "He that shows mercy" is to do it with cheerfulness. The word is literally identical with our English term, "hilarity," and

> "denotes the joyful eagerness, the amiable grace, the affability going the length of gaiety, which make the visitor, whether man or woman, a sunbeam penetrating into the sick-chamber and to the heart of the afflicted" (Godet, *Romans,* vol. ii., p. 293).

This point of cheerfulness, brightness, joyousness in Christian work is specially important. It is not so very many years ago that an advertisement appeared in a religious paper for a clergyman who was to be "pious but cheerful"; and on another occasion a little girl said of a certain clergyman, "He must be an excellent man, he looks so sad." Christianity is the opposite of sadness, and it is a duty to show by our manner and words that "the joy of the Lord is our strength."

As we contemplate afresh these various gifts we realize that their differences are intended to be expressed on every occasion, because our exercise of them is with a view to the Body of Christ and not to our own individual desires and preferences. A clear recognition of what we possess and a whole-hearted determination to exercise our gift to the utmost will form the best possible means of glorifying God and blessing those around us.

IV. *The Secret of Humility* (vers. 3, 6).—The Apostle does not fail to remind us how all this humility is possible. "According as God hath dealt to each man a measure of faith" (ver. 3). "Gifts differing according to the grace that is given to us" (ver. 6). The recognition that all we are and possess comes from God is the constant safeguard against pride. We are members one of another, and, as such, we are to be humble. This can only be realized by finding out God's will for us, and this in turn will only be practicable by keeping close to God. The fact that all our powers are gifts, not attainments, Divine graces, not human accomplishments, will ever tend to keep us humble and true to God.

1. *Humility the Primary Need.* It is significant that humility comes immediately after the emphasis on consecration. Pride takes various forms. It prevents the sinner from accepting God's gift. It led the Jews to refuse and reject Jesus Christ of Nazareth as "the Lord our Righteousness." But of all forms of pride spiritual pride is the most specious and deadly. The soul may be very easily tempted to think that because the life is wholly devoted to God it may disregard all else in the contemplation of this wonderful privilege and honor. It is against the possibility of this spirit that the Apostle teaches us that consecration will express itself in humility. A right relationship to our fellow-believers who are presumably equally consecrated to God with ourselves is to be instantly recognized and fully realized. Indeed, our life of humility among our brethren is only second to the surrender of our life to God. A consecrated believer is to seek at once from his Divine Lord a true, modest estimate of himself. Humility has been defined as "unconscious self-forgetfulness." It is certainly "the most beautiful flower in the Christian garden," and the more the Apostolic direction

is followed the more completely will our Christianity be recommended. There is perhaps no form of Christlikeness so beautiful and so influential as "being clothed with humility."

2. *Humility the Perfect Possibility.* And for this God has made abundant provision in Christ. There is no excuse for pride, nor any justification for that false humility which tends to think that it has no gift, or "talent." To everyone something has been given in the great provision of righteousness, and this may be expressed and manifested to the praise and glory of God, and to the blessing of those around us. For humility, as for everything else, the word is true: "My grace is sufficient for thee."

LIII

BROTHER-LOVE

ROM. xii. 9-13.

9. *Let* love be without dissimulation. Abhor that which is evil; cleave to that which is good.
10. *Be* kindly affectioned one to another with brotherly love; in honor preferring one another;
11. Not slothful in business; fervent in spirit; serving the Lord;
12. Rejoicing in hope; patient in tribulation; continuing instant in prayer;
13. Distributing to the necessity of saints; given to hospitality.

FROM the thought of humility the idea of love naturally follows, for humility will necessarily express itself in affection for those around. Indeed, in the closing words of the preceding verse the thought of love is already present, and now it is to be abundantly illustrated. This connection between humility and love seems worthy of special note. Godet says, "First self-limiting, self-possessing: this is what he has just been recommending; then self-giving: this is what he proceeds to expound." In the present section the sphere for the exercise of love is the Church of God, and this brings before us the specific Christian idea of "brother-love" or *philadelphia.* It is a little unfortunate that our English versions render this "brotherly love," which means "brother-like love," or love similar to that of brethren. But the true idea is very much more, and means "brother-love," that is, love because we are brethren. The prominence given to this grace in the New Testament is quite striking (1 Thess. iv. 9; Heb. xiii. 1; Pet. i. 22; iii. 8; 2 Pet. i. 7). It is the carrying out of our Lord's words, "A new commandment give I unto you" (John xiii. 34, 35), and a careful consideration of His actual words shows clearly that the "newness" lies in the object of love, for three times in two verses we find the words "one another." Love to fellow-Christians was an entirely new fact based on an entirely new tie.

The principle of love is first of all laid down in the opening words, "Let love be without dissimulation," and then the fact and sincerity of love are brought before us in a variety of ways. Let us dwell a little on the fundamental principle. Love is to be sincere; without dissimulation," and we may add, without simulation. There must be no hiding of what we are, or pretending to what we are not. Feigned love is the most horrible thing in life, and a pretence to brother-love is wholly harmful to self, to our brother, and to the world. This emphasis on the sincerity of love is very characteristic of St. Paul, for elsewhere he speaks of "love unfeigned" (2 Cor. vi. 6), just as previously he had spoken of giving with "single mindedness." The same call to genuineness is associated with faith (2 Tim. i. 5), and love (2 Cor. viii. 8), just as in like manner St. John urges as to a love which is not in word or in tongue, "but in deed and in truth" (1 John iii. 18). When this absolute transparency of love is once realized we are prepared to look at the twelve aspects which are in turn brought before us.

I. *The Sensitiveness of Love* (ver. 9).—"Abhor that which is evil." The Christian soul is to hate and shrink from what is wrong. The power of love to hate that which is not good is one of the prime marks of a true life. Unless there is this scorn of and opposition to evil our love is lacking an essential feature.

II. *The Purity of Love* (ver. 9).—"Cleave to that which is good." The use of the word "cleave" in the Old and New Testaments offers much opportunity for thoughtful, practical meditation. It of course implies the closest possible adherence. Indeed, one writer suggests that the Apostle's injunction is literally, "Be glued to that which is good." The Old Testament is full of the thought of "cleaving to the Lord" (Josh. xxiii. 8; 2 Kings xviii. 6). Our love will necessarily show itself in this determination to hold fast by that which is good.

III. *The Reality of Love* (ver. 10).—"Be kindly affectioned one to another with brother-love." Here specially and definitely we have the reminder of the new family tie in Christ, and the call to show it in thoroughness and reality of affection. This brother-love is one of the proofs of real discipleship.

"We know that we have passed from death unto life because we love the brethren" (1 John iii. 14). And while we are to do good unto all men we are specially to exercise our goodness towards "the household of faith" (Gal. vi. 10). No wonder that in the early Church the heathen were so deeply impressed with the new spirit as to say, "Behold how these Christians love one another."

IV. *The Humility of Love* (ver. 10).—"In honor preferring one another." The Church has been described as "the noblest school of courtesy," and the Apostle's words mean that every Christian man is to "lead the way" in giving honor to his fellow-believers. He is to regard others by preference to himself and thereby show the true spirit of humble love. It is a beautiful paradox that each one is to do this to all others (Phil. ii. 3, 17; 1 Thess. v. 13). If only this spirit of preference for others, and determination to sink our own position and reputation had been more in evidence in the Christian Church, what differences it would have made in individual and corporate life.

V. *The Faithfulness of Love* (ver. 11).—"Not slothful in zeal." The familiar word "business" is not to be understood in its modern sense, but in the quite literal idea of "busy-ness" or earnestness. In point of earnestness the Christian man is not to be slothful; "in zeal not flagging" (Sanday and Headlam). Or as Luther remarks, "Be not lazy as to what you ought to do." It is equivalent to the Old Testament word, "Whatsoever thy hand findeth to do, do it with thy might" (Eccles. ix. 10).

VI. *The Earnestness of Love* (ver. 11).—"Fervent in spirit." This is the inward attitude, as the former phrase expresses the outward. In our spirit we are to be "boiling." Our Lord rebuked the Church of Ephesus for having left its first love (Rev. ii. 4), and a still more solemn word was uttered to the Church of Laodicea, wishing that it were either cold or hot (Rev. iii. 15). Among our Lord's prophecies of the future was one to the effect that the love of many would "wax cold" (Matt. xxiv. 12). All the more reason, therefore, for the Christian life to be full of fervency.

VII. *The Genuineness of Love* (ver. 11).—"Serving the Lord." Some few manuscript authorities favor the word "season," or "time," instead of "Lord," in which case we should understand the injunction to mean, "Use the present opportunity to the best of your ability." But it seems in every way preferable to adhere to the familiar reading, and to understand it to mean that in all our service the one supreme principle must be our relation to Jesus Christ. Whatever we do to others it will always have Him and His Glory for its supreme object.

VIII. *The Buoyancy of Love* (ver. 12).—"Rejoicing in hope." This was a very pertinent injunction in the presence of suffering and tribulation, for there was doubtless a tendency from time to time to fear the overwhelming pressure of outside forces. Against all this the Apostle urges the Christians to joy and hope. "In the matter of hope, rejoicing." In the midst of all their tribulations there was the one hope of future glory in which they were to "rejoice with joy unspeakable and full of glory." If only they walked by faith and not by sight, they would by patient continuance in well-doing be enabled to exult in hope of the glory of God (ch. v. 2).

IX. *The Endurance of Love* (ver. 12).—"Patient in tribulation." This is the other side of the experience. The same hope which causes joy is intended to guarantee patience. The joy comes at the contemplation of the future prospects; the patience is to be exercised under the pressure of present sufferings. Like their Master, the Roman Christians were to live with their minds occupied with the future, as they suffered day by day in the present. "Who for the joy that was set before Him endured the Cross" (Heb. xii. 2).

X. *The Devotion of Love* (ver. 12).—"Continuing instant in prayer." The connection of prayer with hope and tribulation is particularly interesting, because it is through prayer that we are enabled to rise above our present circumstances and fix our hope more steadfastly on the coming glory. The familiar phrase "Continuing instant," represents a picturesque word in the original. We might render the whole phrase, "In the matter of prayer, staunch." It suggests the idea of firm adherence and constant waiting, and the various connections of the term illustrate the true attitude of the soul. Thus it is used of the little boat that was to "wait on our Lord continually" (Mark iii. 9). It is connected with the prayer-life of the primitive Church (Acts i. 14; ii. 46). It is associated with the ministry of the Word of God (Acts ii. 42; vi. 4). And it is employed by St. Paul in at least two other passages in connection with prayer (Eph. vi. 18; Col. iv. 2).

The three thoughts of hope, suffering, and prayer, are thus helpfully associated in Hofmann's paraphrase of the verse:—

> "In so far as we have cause to hope, let us be joyful; in so far as we have cause of pain, let us hold out; in so far as the door of prayer is open to us, let us continue to use it" (Quoted by Godet, *Romans*, vol. ii., p. 297).

XI. *The Unselfishness of Love* (ver. 13).—"Distributing to the necessity of saints." The word "saint" as descriptive of all Christians calls for renewed attention. Its simple meaning is "belonging to God," and it refers invariably to our position, not our condition, to our standing in Christ, not our actual state. It is most unfortunate that the word has been so frequently associated with an exceptional holiness, when it means nothing of the kind, but only the actual fact that from the moment of conversion every Christian soul is consecrated and devoted to God, and belongs to Him (Rom. xvi. 1, 2; 1 Cor. i. 2; vi. 2). The needs of God's people must have been great at the time these words were written, and we know how keen St. Paul was in encouraging the Gentiles to help their poorer brethren in Jerusalem. In the same way he appeals to all the Christians in Rome to communicate to their fellow-believers whatever might be necessary, and this duty was one which the earliest Christians evidently performed with remarkable generosity (Acts iv. 34, 35; xi. 27-30; Rom. xv. 25-27; 2 Cor. viii. 1-4; ix. 1-4).

XII. *The Large-heartedness of Love* (ver. 12).—"Given to hospitality." Christian hospitality was another characteristic prominent in New Testament life (1 Tim. iii. 2; Tit. i. 8; Heb. xiii. 2; 1 Pet. iv. 9), and the thought underlying the Apostle's exhortation is that they were not to wait to be asked, but on the contrary, to be ready to welcome their fellow-Christians, keeping "open house." This hospitality was a point of very great importance in the primitive

Church when "it had begun to appreciate with full consciousness the importance of inter-communication" (Ramsay, *The Church and the Roman Empire*, p. 288. See also p. 368).

All these aspects of love should be closely studied in the text of Scripture and under the guidance of a good Commentary in order that the words and phrases may be understood, and their full meaning and practical power elicited. We see that the Epistle is at once individualistic and corporate. The Christian who is related to Christ soon finds that he is associated with others in common life, common grace, common needs, common duties, common hopes.

1. *The Connection of Humility and Love.* After thus dwelling on each separate section of this very practical appeal of the Apostle it may be well to revert once more to the close and essential connection between humility and love, as seen in this and the preceding sections. These two aspects of Christian living show how essential it is to realize that the first elements, in true righteousness are to be expressed in a lowly, loving fellowship with our brethren as we endeavor to fulfil to the utmost our duties as members of Christ, and members one of another. Faith is to work by love, and love will naturally express itself first of all towards those who belong with us to the family of God. The more we can reproduce this spirit of humility and brotherly affection the more thoroughly we shall glorify God and recommend our Christianity to others.

2. *The Secret of Humility and Love.* Never may we tire of emphasizing Divine Grace as the source and guarantee of consecrated life. It is by the "gentleness of Christ" (2 Cor. x. 1) we become humble in the power of the fruit of the Spirit "gentleness" (Gal. v. 22). And it is by the love of Christ shed forth in the soul (ch. v. 5) that love to others becomes possible.

LIV

LOVE

Rom. xii. 14-21.

14. Bless them which persecute you: bless, and curse not.
15. Rejoice with them that do rejoice, and weep with them that weep.
16. *Be* of the same mind one toward another. Mind not high things, but condescend to men of low estate. Be not wise in your own conceits.
17. Recompense to no man evil for evil. Provide things honest in the sight of all men.
18. If it be possible, as much as lieth in you, live peaceably with all men.
19. Dearly beloved, avenge not yourselves, but *rather* give place unto wrath: for it is written, Vengeance *is* mine; I will repay, saith the Lord.
20. Therefore if thine enemy hunger, feed him; if he thirst, give him drink; for in so doing thou shalt heap coals of fire on his head.
21. Be not overcome of evil, but overcome evil with good.

The same spirit of love is still before us, though in this section the exercise of it is directed to "them that are without." The Christian has social relationships and duties to others besides his fellow-Christians, and just as verses 9-13 are concerned with love which is exercised mainly in an atmosphere, so here in verses 14-21 it is to be shown mainly to those who are hostile to Christianity. As Dr. John Brown remarks:—

> "Having thus stated how the Roman Christians ought to behave to their fellow-sufferers, the Apostle proceeds to show how they should conduct themselves to the authors of their sufferings" (*Exposition of the Epistle to the Romans*, p. 467).

In verses 17-19 the passive attitude of forbearance is the main thought, while in verses 20, 21, the active form of beneficence is urged. Love is the principal thought, giving unity to the whole section, and every word and phrase calls for careful consideration.

I. *Love blessing our Persecutors* (ver. 14).—"Bless them which persecute you: bless, and curse not." It is suggestive that the word in verse 13, translated "given to," is literally "pursuing," and is identical with the "persecutors" of this verse. Thus we are to "pursue" hospitality, and we are also to bless those who "pursue" us. It is a very different "pursuit," and a truly severe test of the Christian life is here afforded. The words are an echo of the Sermon on the Mount. "Blessed are they which are persecuted for righteousness' sake. Blessed are ye, when men shall revile you, and persecute you" (Matt. v. 10, 11). If we acknowledge God in all our ways we shall seek for grace to say with David, "Let him curse" (2 Sam. xvi. 10).

II. *Love interesting itself in Others* (ver. 15).—"Rejoice with them that do rejoice, and weep with them that weep." It is comparatively easy to "weep with them that weep," but much more difficult to "rejoice with them that rejoice." We find it a simple matter to condole, but not so simple to congratulate. The reason is that the latter calls for much more unselfishness and the entire absence of any envy or jealousy at another's success. But self-forgetfulness will enable us to do both, and thereby to manifest the true spirit of Christ in deep interest for others.

III. *Love finding Points of Agreement* (ver. 16).—"Be of the same mind one toward another." We are to have the same concern for the welfare of others as for our own. This spirit of disinterested thought of others is one of the finest elements of the Christian character. It is so easy to accentuate differences and to overlook elements that tend to unite. But if we have the same solicitude for the well-being of others as we have for our own, it will enable us to be of "the same mind one toward another." As the Apostle says elsewhere, we are in lowliness of mind to esteem others better than ourselves (Phil. ii. 3).

IV. *Love spurning unworthy Ambitions* (ver. 16).—"Mind not high things." Another call to humility. It is impossible not to recall the Apostle John's solemn word about Diotrephes, "Who loveth to have the pre-eminence" (3 John 9). We can see what trouble was thereby caused in the Church. The contrast to this is found in the only other place where the same word occurs, "That in all things He might have the pre-eminence" (Col. i. 18). When Christ is first in our life it is impossible to "mind high things."

V. *Love consorting with the Lowly* (ver. 16).—"Condescend to men of low estate." The word "condescend" is a little unfortunate because of its modern idea of unworthy patronage. Here the meaning is something very different, and is literally "Let yourselves be carried away with." It is also found in Gal. ii. 13. In its good sense it suggests the necessity and wisdom of accomodating ourselves to people and things very different from ourselves and our own tastes. The R.V. renders the phrase, "things," not "men," and, as far as the Greek is concerned, it may refer to either. Tyndale renders the verse, "Make yourselves equal to them of the lower sorte"; and another version has, "Let yourselves be drawn away with lowly things." We must avoid anything in the way of cliques or coteries exclusively bent on their own special interests, and instead we must give ourselves to everybody and everything alike, showing preference, if preference be necessary, to men and things outside our own sphere. We can readily see how searching a test this is of true spirituality.

VI. *Love avoiding Self-Esteem* (ver. 16).—"Be not wise in your own conceits." There is nothing more despicable than conceit, especially as it is almost invariably associated, not with real gifts, but with their absence. It is the empty and shallow man who is vain. The corn when it is green is upright, but when it is ripe it bends low.

VII. *Love refusing to take Revenge* (ver. 17).—"Recompense to no man evil for evil." There is an intimate connection between the self-forgetfulness of the preceding verses and the love which is here shown to be exercised in pardoning evil done to us. It is well known that pride is easily wounded, and as easily is ready to take vengeance, and yet there is nothing more Christlike than the grace of forbearance, and nothing more calculated to recommend the Gospel to others. As Sir Matthew Hale once said, "Though it is manly to punish, it is God-like to forgive."

VIII. *Love endeavoring to Attract* (ver. 17).—"Provide things honorable in the sight of all men." The word "honorable" is literally "beautiful," and when read thus it shows very plainly the need of attractiveness in the Christian life. "Provide things beautiful." We read of the beauty of holiness," and if we take our Lord's words literally we may read, "I am the Beautiful Shepherd" (John x. 11). When St. Paul urges upon his converts the importance and necessity of good works, sometimes he uses a word which means that which is intrinsically good. But at other times, especially in the Pastoral Epistles, he uses a word which means that which is also outwardly attractive. "Let our's learn to maintain beautiful works" (Tit. iii. 14). The thought of "providing" is also to be noticed. We are to use forethought to disarm enmity by means of that which is morally and spiritually attractive:—

> "It is a happy thing when worldly men are constrained to say of a Christian what Tertullian makes a heathen say of a Christian in his time, 'He is an excellent man, that Caius Servius, only he is a Christian'" (John Brown, *Exposition of the Epistle to the Romans*, p. 474).

There is no contradiction between this injunction and that of "contending earnestly for the faith" (Jude 3). As Haldane points out, we must never sacrifice truth to peace, and we must be willing, if necessary, to be unpopular if thereby alone we can be faithful to the trust committed to us. While, therefore, we fulfil the pastoral injunction and maintain with earnestness the true faith of Christ, we must be particularly careful lest in our championship of the truth the "old Adam" creeps in and really spoils our testimony. It is only too possible to be faithful in a hard, not to say censorious spirit, and while we may think we are only loyal and true to our trust, our testimony is being colored by the hard, bitter spirit with which we express it.

IX. *Love keeping the Peace* (ver. 18).—"If it be possible, as much as lieth in you, live peaceably with all men." Every part of this injunction needs attention. "If it be possible" seems to refer our own attitude, because as to this, we have the power of exercising control. Thus, according to the old saying, "It takes two to make a quarrel"; and this endeavor to keep the peace will mean hard work, to those around us. "As much as lieth in you," naturally refers to but it will be worth while. This is another echo of our Lord's words,

"Blessed are the peacemakers: for they shall be called the children of God" (Matt. v. 9).

X. *Love entrusting its Cause to God* (ver. 19).—"Avenge not yourselves, but give place unto wrath." Twice St. Paul uses the phrase, "Give place," here and in Eph. iv. 27. In the present passage we are to make room for wrath, to stand on one side as it comes rushing towards us, allowing it to go past leaving us untouched and unharmed. But in the other case we are not to "give place to the devil." On the contrary we are to withstand him, and when we see him coming, to take up our position boldly, knowing that if we resist he will flee. One writer thinks that the passage here means, "Give room for God's wrath to work." But this thought does not seem to be introduced until the quotation from the Old Testament, "Vengeance is Mine; I will repay, saith the Lord." If we take care of our character God will take care of our interests. He is absolutely just, and we can fully trust Him to plead our cause and guard our position.

XI. *Love returning Good for Evil* (ver. 20).—"If thine enemy hunger, feed him." This is the very opposite of the policy of the world, and when it is exercised it will have the effect of heaping "coals of fire" on the head of our enemy. This must mean "coals of red-hot love," involving the fire of shame (Prov. xxv. 21 and 22). Of course it cannot possibly refer to punishment, but to the best possible kind of revenge, the fire that melts the ore in the furnace.

XII. *Love winning the True Victory* (ver. 21).—"Be not overcome of evil, but overcome evil with good." Here as the crowning point we have the expulsive power of goodness. This is the true secret of Christianity, and nothing like this is to be found anywhere among the nations and teachers before the time of Christ. The thought of overcoming evil with good only became possible through the redemptive love of God in Christ (see Dr. John Brown, *Romans*, p. 482).

It is noteworthy that in this passage there are three distinct references to the book of Proverbs, indicating the Apostle's knowledge and use of the Old Testament. A Christian merchant was in the habit of giving a copy of Proverbs to every boy who came into his establishment. He considered it the best book of practical ethics available for human life.

As we review this and the former sections we should note that verses 9-21 are no mere cluster of spiritual rules or regulations. One theme, that of love, runs throughout, and it is another version of the great chapter on love in 1 Corinthians xiii. It covers the entire range of our religious and social life.

1. *Being and Doing.* The emphasis is on Being rather than on Doing, and on Doing as the result and expression of Being. While the active and passive sides are balanced, yet the chief emphasis is on what we are rather than on what we do. This is always characteristic of New Testament morality (see Moule, *Romans*, "Expositor's Bible," p. 346).

The writers are much more concerned with our character than with our conduct, because they feel sure that if the former is right the latter will be right also. Some years ago a missionary was leaving China for a furlough at home, and before sailing Mr. Hudson Taylor said to him, "When you get into the Homeland and speak at meetings, never mind about China." The missionary was surprised, but quickly understood the meaning when Mr. Taylor added, "Never mind about China, but when you get before your audiences may this be your constant prayer, that you may be able by the Spirit of God to bring all those who hear you face to face with Jesus Christ, and Jesus Christ will take care of China." In like manner we may say, without any hesitation, that if we take care of our character our conduct will take care of itself. As is the source, so will be the stream.

2. *The Supreme Power for Being and Doing.* These blessed and glorious practical details of the life of righteousness are such as the law cannot accomplish, but the Spirit of Christ can work them in the believer. Self-effort is unfruitful, but the law of the Spirit of Life in Christ Jesus is the source of love, and the possession of life is proved by the practice of love.

3. *The Outcome of Being and Doing.* A careful consideration and a detailed personal application of all these aspects of love reveals to us what true Christianity means in relation to those around us. What a difference it would make if our home life, our Church life, and all our relations to others were actuated by this spirit. Our professions of full consecration will go for nothing unless this spirit of Christlikeness actuates us in all our dealings with our fellow-men.

LV

CHRISTIAN CITIZENSHIP

Rom. xiii. 1-7.

1. Let every soul be subject unto the higher powers. For there is no power but of God: the powers that be are ordained of God.
2. Whosoever therefore resisteth the power, resisteth the ordinance of God: and they that resist shall receive to themselves damnation.
3. For rulers are not a terror to good works, but to the devil. Wilt thou then not be afraid of the power? do that which is good, and thou shalt have praise of the same:
4. For he is the minister of God to thee for good. But if thou do that which is evil, be afraid; for he beareth not the sword in vain: for he is the minister of God, a revenger to *execute* wrath upon him that doeth evil.
5. Wherefore *ye* must needs be subject, not only for wrath, but also for conscience sake.
6. For this cause pay ye tribute also: for they are God s ministers, attending continually upon this very thing.
7. Render therefore to all their dues: tribute to whom tribute *is due*; custom to whom custom; fear to whom fear; honor to whom honor.

In chapter xii. the Apostle dealt with the obligations of love which are directly spiritual and fraternal. But the believer has other relationships besides these, and it is to some of them that attention is now to be drawn. Just as chapter xii. treats of spiritual duties to our fellow-Christians and to others, so chapter xiii. deals with our natural relationships, especially in regard to civic and civil duties. The Christian is a citizen as well as a Church member, and, as such, his duties must be carefully performed. This is another application of the great law of righteousness under which the soul is to live. There is a natural transition from the thought of peace in the closing verses of the preceding chapter to our duty to the State, as here inculcated.

The reference to the relation of the Christian to the State is very rare in St. Paul's Epistles (1 Tim. ii. 2). It seems pretty clear, therefore, that there must have been some local circumstances to account for the present emphasis. The Jews at Rome were notorious for their turbulence. Their ideas of their position and theocracy made submission to government by Gentiles intolerable, and they had lately rebelled and suffered expulsion (Acts xviii. 2). Since Christians were regarded by many as a Jewish sect, a suspicion of revolutionary tendencies was easily turned against them. All this may have weighed with the Apostle in bringing this matter forward. There may have been danger also lest the Christians should be misled by false ideas of the kingdom of Christ and its relation to the kingdoms of the world, and as in Rome Christianity was naturally brought face to face with the Imperial power, it was essential that the true relations of Christians to the State should be clearly definied. But whether local circumstances account for this reference or not, it is the permanent principle, and no mere local need, that is mainly emphasized.

The chapter may be analyzed as follows:

(*a*) Vers. 1-7: The Christian's duty to the State.

(*b*) Vers. 8-10: The Christian's duty to the citizens of the State.

(*c*) Vers. 11-14: The Christian enforcement of these civil duties.

It is the first of these which must now occupy our attention.

I. *The Duty of Civil Obedience* (ver. 1).—"Let every soul be in subjection to the higher powers." Not a single Christian is exempt from obedience to the State. Submission is the great law (1 Pet. ii. 13-17). The description of the State as "the higher powers" is particularly noteworthy, both in the light of the Apostle's day, and also of our own.

II. *The Reason for Civil Obedience* (ver. 1).—"For there is no power but of God: the powers that be are ordained of God." Civil authority thus derives its source and sanction from God Himself. Society needs government, and this proves that God intended man to live under authority. But He has not laid down any definite form, so that the principle of governmental authority can take any form, so long as it has authority. Bad conduct tends to weaken, good conduct to strengthen authority.

III. *The Denial of Civil Obedience* (ver. 2).—Resistance to the power of the State is condemned as equivalent to resistance to God Himself. It is of course true that we are not to do at the bidding of the State that which is morally wrong, but short of this, submission, not resistance, is the Christian law.

The question has been asked whether St. Paul's teaching forbids Christians taking part in a rebellion. It is obvious that Christians can agitate for better government, but must they, according to this passage, never oppose the government that exists? In reply, it should be observed that two things are omitted here: (1) the Christian's duty if the State should persecute Christianity; (2) the Christian's duty of the State should fail to do its duty. We must therefore be careful not to read into the Apostle's word what is not found here. At the same time, every one admits that rebellion is only to be regarded as the very last resource. The Christian will be slow to head a rebellion, but where circumstances absolutely compel, there does not seem anything in this passage to prohibit it.

IV. *The Vindication of Civil Obedience* (vers. 3, 4).—Additional reasons for submission are here adduced. Civil government has a providential purpose, for rulers are really servants of God. They cause no fear or trouble to those who do their duty, but only to the evil-doers. The Apostle himself often used the Roman authority for personal protection (Acts xviii. 12-17; xix. 35-41; xxii. 25). This is a remarkable testimony to the essentially Divine character of civil authority. Twice the civil ruler is called "the minister of God," and the word is all the more striking when it is remembered that it is used in connection with the Temple services.

V. *The Spirit of Civil Obedience* (ver. 5).—A further step is here taken, and the Apostle inculcates his teaching, not merely on the ground of expediency, but for moral reasons as well. Principle as well as prudence is involved. Not only are we to be afraid of the consequences of disobedience to the State, but we are to obey "for conscience sake." This reference to conscience suggests both the spirit and the limit of obedience. As the State governs in God's name, it must not do anything contrary to God's law. Hence this teaching, as Godet points out, leaves the Christian free to witness against the State if it should prove necessary (See Moule, *Romans*, "Expositor's Bible," p. 353).

VI. *The Illustration of Civil Obedience* (ver. 6).—An example is now given from the payment of taxes. "Ye pay," states a fact and acknowledges the truth of verse 5. This is one of the simplest and yet clearest instances of our duty to the government under which we live.

VII. *The Call to Civil Obedience* (ver. 7).—The teaching is now summed up by a practical appeal. "Render to all their dues." Four aspects of civil authority are mentioned: (1) Personal, or property taxes, "Tribute to whom tribute is due"; (2) Export, or import, "Custom to whom custom"; (3) Fear, or veneration of the chief authority, "Fear to whom fear"; (4) Honor, or respect to his subordinates, "Honor to whom honor." Nothing could be finer than this emphasis on duty and courtesy, and, again, we cannot help recalling our Lord's own words about the true ministry of service as expressive of the noblest, highest life (Matt. xx. 25-28).

These are refreshing lessons for Christians in relation to the country in which they live. Let us mark carefully the principles here emphasized.

1. *How beautifully applicable is this Teaching to every form of Government.* Whatever country may be ours and whatever the form of authority these great principles apply. The institution of the State is according to the will and plan of God. But while the Divine right of civil authority is plainly asserted, no particular aspect, or method of it is necessarily expressive of the Divine will.

2. *How clearly the Apostle insists on the Christian's fulfilment of his Duties to the State.* They are as truly an obligation as the most spiritual of our Church functions. Paying taxes is just as Christian as praying at a meeting. It is the duty of faith to see God in these relationships, and we must take care that the duties to the State are made part of our Christian conduct. And yet, as we have observed, in making conscience the ground of obedience the Apostle shows the true limit of civil submission (Acts v. 39, 40, 42).

3. *How entirely independent of the moral character of the civil government is this fulfilment of our Duty to the State.* The Jewish priesthood in our Lord's time was very corrupt, but He approved of the widow paying her Temple tax (Luke xxi. 2, 3). So also, our

Lord Himself in His relations to the Roman government fully exemplified the teaching here given (Matt. xxii. 21; xxvi. 52; xxvii. 26, 27). In relation to the State, questions as to its precise moral character do not touch our duty, so long as the demand does not entrench on the domain of the conscience. Thus the Apostle has a far higher idea of the State than anything merely utilitarian. In spite of the fact that Christians were compelled to witness day by day the corruption which reigned in State affairs, the Apostle insists that the State is an essentially Divine and moral institution. We must therefore carefully distinguish between use and abuse, between the actual condition of the State at any given time and the idea of the State when viewed from the standpoint of God's will.

4. *How entirely satisfactory it would be to the Progress and Welfare of Christianity if such loyalty and submission were invariably practiced.* If our duties as citizens were fully realized, it would constitute a splendid witness for God. In the State as well as in the Church we are called upon to "prove what is that good, and acceptable, and perfect will of God."

LVI

DEBTS—PAID AND UNPAID

ROM. xiii. 8-10.

8. Owe no man any thing, but to love one another: for he that loveth another hath fulfilled the law.
9. For this, Thou shalt not commit adultery, Thou shalt not kill, Thou shalt not steal, Thou shalt not bear false witness, Thou shalt not covet; and if *there be* any other commandment, it is briefly comprehended in this saying, namely, Thou shalt love thy neighbor as thyself.
10. Love worketh no ill to his neighbor: therefore love *is* the fulfilling of the law.

THE Christian has relationships to the citizens of the State as well as to the State itself. The duty of the believer to his fellow-citizens is here definitely inculcated.

I. *Debt that can fully be Paid* (ver. 8).—"Owe no man anything." The phrase, "no man," is evidently not the Christian brother, for that aspect of duty is considered in ch. xii., and is not here repeated. The term covers the entire field of our duties to our fellow-men. The "neighbor" is not a brother in Christ, but one who is bound to us by the ties of common humanity. The relation of the Christian to God is spiritual, not legal, but to the world it is legal rather than spiritual, the spiritual being expressed in the legal.

The negative duty emphasized is the avoidance of debt. "Owe no man anything." The Christian is not to incur anything which he is unable to pay, and knows that he is unable when it is incurred. He ought to be able to render back what is rightfully claimed from him. If he should have to borrow anything and the repayment is required, he ought to be able to meet his liability. How simple, and yet how searching is this requirement. Men judge Christians by their promptness in fulfilling obligations and in paying their bills, and it is a fine, natural, and legitimate test. A spirituality that is not ethical carries its own condemnation and is certain to elicit the disgust and opposition of all practical, honest people. A man who owed a Christian brother some money was once heard to pray in a meeting, "Lord, give us faith, give us devil-driving faith." The brother to whom the money was owing said to himself quietly, "Amen, Lord, and give us debt-paying faith." We have known of instances where teaching has been inculcated of a very spiritual nature by those who were notorious for not paying their tradesmen. As a result the fair name of Christianity was clouded and dragged in the mire. On the lowest ground it is a great satisfaction to feel that we have no pecuniary liability which we are unable to meet, for then we are free to give, not as a matter of duty, but as one of privilege and joy.

And yet perhaps we are intended to go far wider afield and to consider our debts in the fullest possible sense. There are many other ways of fulfilling our obligations besides that of monetary repayment, and the more fully we realize our debt to others the richer will be our Christian life. When St. Paul said, "I am debtor" (ch. i. 14), he was conscious of a debt of obligation as binding as any monetary responsibility could be. Christ had done so much for him that it was a simple duty to endeavor to repay something of his obligation. So also, when he said, "We are debtors, not to the flesh, to live after the flesh" (ch. viii. 12), he was conscious of the same spiritual pressure of obligation from another point of view, and felt it incumbent upon him to repay the debt by living to the Spirit and mortifying the deeds of the body.

II. *Debt that cannot be Paid* (vers. 8-10).—"Owe no man anything, but to love one another . . . love is the fulfilling of the law." The avoidance of debt is by no means the whole of our duty. Abstinence from wrong-doing is only part of the Christian attitude. Our life is to be rooted positively in love, and this constitutes a debt which we are always to pay and yet can never discharge in full. Our duty to the State, as we have seen, is virtually fulfilled by the avoidance of injury, but our duty to God goes much further and involves the active expression of love. We have already observed this love, as it affects our fellow-Christians (ch. xii. 10), and those who are hostile to us (ch. xii. 20). Here, however, it is inculcated in the widest possible way. We must ever continue the positive duty of love; not merely "thou shalt not hurt," but "thou shalt help." Love is the foundation of justice, and the Second Table of the law is mentioned because the context refers to our neighbor, and therefore to justice to him. But justice is negative, not doing wrong; while love is the means of fulfilling justice. Every commandment of the Second Table is summed up in the positive word, "Thou shalt love thy neighbor as thyself." Our love to self is obviously positive and definite, and our love to our neighbor must be similar in character. Here again we find the echo of our Lord's own words (Matt. xii. 39, 40), and especially of His parable of the Good Samaritan. This constitutes the heart of Christianity. We are to love because God is love, and because He first loved us. This is the Divine way of working.

Godet helpfully indicates the essential connection between the various parts of the long passage from ch. xii. 3-xiii. 10.

(*a*) In ch. xii. 3-18, our life is to be limited by humility.

(*b*) In ch. xii. 19-21, our life is to give itself in love.

(*c*) In ch. xiii. 1-7, our life is to be limited by submission.

(*d*) In ch. xiii. 8-10, our life is to give itself in love.

1. *Life by Rule and by Principle.* Living by rule and by principle finds in this passage a very striking illustration. There is all the difference in the world between these. We teach children to live by rule, a regulation for this and a regulation for that; so is it also with races and communities in their moral childhood. But Christianity is a religion of principle rather than of rule. A rule is a law for certain given circumstances and it mainly acts from without. A principle is a law for all circumstances, and is invariably applied from within. The rule is necessarily limited by the circumstances. The principle has no limit because it applies to all conditions.

2. *Illustrations of life by Rule and by Principle.* Let us observe the application of the distinction in some familiar ways. (*a*) In the matter of forgiveness, St. Peter asked his Master whether he should

forgive "until seven times" (Matt. xviii. 21). That was the suggestion of a rule; very simple, and so far, very easy, but after the seventh time there would be a difficulty if the offender came with his eighth appeal. So the Master laid down a principle, "Until seventy times seven." It is the spirit of forgiveness and no mere rule that will suffice. "Even as God in Christ forgave you" (Eph. iv. 32). (*b*) The question of neighborliness. The Jew asked our Lord, "Who is my neighbor?" This was to make himself the pivot around which others were to turn. He looks round and asks, "Who"; but our Lord's reply reversed the order, and as Bishop Lightfoot points out, the true question is, "Who my neighbor *is*" that is, "What is he like?" We must find out all we can about him. There must be no picking and choosing, but a full recognition of all as our neighbor. (*c*) The problem of giving. How much ought I to give? Is it to be one-tenth, or what? The New Testament lays down no rule, but emphasizes the principle of giving, "as God hath prospered," and this, together with the corresponding principles, "as we have opportunity," and "as he hath purposed in his heart," shows what Christian giving really means.

Additional illustrations can be given of this distinction between rule and principle, as we think of such questions as the time required for religion, the way and times for realizing the worship of God, the true methods of guidance, and the question of certain forms of amusement. Not one of these can be settled by rule. They must be decided by principle. It is exactly the same with the passage now before us. There is one principle which includes everything: the great, essential, fundamental principle of Love. Everything we say and do is to emanate from love, and nothing is to be excluded from its all-embracing power.

3. *The power for life by Principle.* Does someone say that this is difficult? It is; because Christianity is for men, not for children. It emphasizes character instead of mere conduct under given circumstances and character is only possible by means of principle. But if difficult, it is not impracticable, because of God's gift of the

Holy Spirit. He is the Spirit of Love, and if only He controls our life according to the Apostle's teaching in chapter viii. it will not be impossible to fulfil our obligations to the uttermost. "The love of the Spirit" is ours for this very purpose, and the love of God is shed abroad in our hearts by that Spirit (ch. v. 5), in order that filled with love we may love as Christ loved, and live as He lived.

LVII

THE GREAT INCENTIVE

ROM. xiii. 11-14.

11. And that, knowing the time, that now *it is* high time to awake out of sleep: for now *is* our salvation nearer than when we believed.
12. The night is far spent, the day is at hand: let us therefore cast off the works of darkness, and let us put on the armor of light.
13. Let us walk honestly, as in the day; not in rioting and drunkenness, not in chambering and wantonness, not in strife and envying.
14. But put ye on the Lord Jesus Christ, and make not provision for the flesh, to *fulfil* the lusts *thereof*.

HERE comes the Christian enforcement of these duties. Some writers think that the verses are to be limited strictly to the preceding section, dealing with our duties to our fellow-citizens. Others suggest that they sum up the whole of the duties dealt with in chapters xii. and xiii., applying them in the light of the Second Coming. There is perhaps no real contrariety between these two views. The one thought is that everything is to be done in the light of the coming of our Lord.

I. *The Solemn Appeal* (ver. 11).—"And that, knowing the time, that now it is high time to awake out of sleep." We may read this abbreviated phrase as follows: "And this (you are to do), knowing (as you do) the season (*cf.* 1 Cor. vii. 29; Eph. v. 16; 1 Thess. v. 1)." Their life was to be lived in the light of the great event of our Lord's coming (Heb. x. 25). This spiritual insight into the true reason and meaning of the time in which they lived is a point of great importance in Scripture. Our Lord rebuked His enemies for not knowing the signs of the times (Matt. xvi. 3), and one of the characteristic needs of Israel was that of men who had "understanding of the times" (1 Chron. xii. 32). Christians are called upon to observe carefully and scrutinize closely the spiritual aspects of the time in which they live, in order as far as possible to note the signs of God's presence and working.

This knowledge of the time was especially incumbent on them, because it was already the occasion for alertness ("high time to awake out of sleep"). "Sleep" suggests the thought of forgetfulness of God, while being awake implies spiritual readiness and shows responsibility. The words are addressed to Christians, and therefore apply, not to spiritual death, but to languor in the Christian life. "They all slumbered and slept" (Matt. xxv. 5).

II. *The Clear Explanation* (ver. 11).—"For now is our salvation nearer than when we believed." We have already observed that salvation in the New Testament is threefold: past, present, and future; and in this passage the third aspect alone is intended. The complete salvation which is to be ours in Christ (1 Pet. i. 5, 6) is nearer now than when we first commenced our Christian life. Observe the expression of salvation being nearer to us rather than of our being nearer to it. We see the meaning of this teaching in the next verse.

III. *The Glorious Expectation* (ver. 12).—"The night is far spent, the day is at hand." The night of Christ's absence is nearly over and the day—dawn of His appearance is at hand. Our perfect salvation is to be brought when He appears, and in this lies the call to alertness and expectation. The contrast of night and day as expressive of the present life and the coming of our Lord is a favorite one with St. Paul (Eph. v. 7-16; 1 Thess. v. 1-11). Christ's coming will indeed be "the day" in all its effulgence of brightness and glory.

IV. *The Practical Exhortation* (vers. 12, 13).—In a threefold way the Apostle exhorts to holiness of life. "Let us cast off"; "Let us put on"; "Let us walk." Everything characteristic of darkness is to be laid aside, and all that is appropriate to the day is to be put on. We are to walk "becomingly." The true life is to be one of "seemly behavior" in the light of the great event. Sins of the flesh and sins of the mind will alike be set aside. We notice the six sins here mentioned. There are three classes of two each: (*a*) intemperance (public sins); (*b*) impurity (private sins); (*c*) discord (personal and social sins). The climax of all these in "strife and jealousy" is specially significant. It is remarkable that licentiousness and envy should be put on the same level. God's classification of sins differs greatly from man's.

V. *The Complete Provision* (ver. 14).—The true secret of Christian living is stated, first positively and then negatively.

1. Positively; the Christian is to put on Christ as a garment. He is the soul's true clothing.

2. Negatively; no forethought is to be taken for the sinful nature. No preoccupation of mind with anything except with Christ. This is the Christian's twofold method of victory. He is not to fight in his own strength, but commit himself to Him Who has won the victory. The flesh is referred to as the seat of sin, as in earlier chapters, and no provision of any sort is to be made for it. We are to say "No" to the flesh on every occasion and occupy ourselves solely with the Lord Jesus Christ in the personal appropriation of faith.

This passage will always be memorable in connection with the conversion of St. Augustine of Hippo. While he was in a garden one day he heard a voice, as from a neighboring house, repeating frequently, "Take up and read." As he did so, he opened to this passage: "Not in rioting and drunkenness . . . But put ye on the Lord Jesus Christ." Then he adds, "I did not choose to read more, nor had I the occasion. Immediately at the end of this sentence, as if a light of certainty had been poured into my heart, all the shadows of doubt were scattered." Archbishop Trench, referring to this conversion, remarks, "God's Word, if only we will suffer it to work in us, may be as potent now as ever it was of old, showing itself His power unto salvation by the same infallible proofs" (quoted by Neil, *Romans*, p. 434).

There are two favorite expressions of the Apostle in this passage which call for special attention: the use of the word "clothe," or "put on," and the reference to "armor."

1. *The Soul's Attire.* This figure of "putting on" is frequently found in St. Paul. (*a*) We are to put on Christ (ch. xiii. 14). By an act of simple but all-embracing faith we are to accept and appropriate Him as our complete salvation for past, present, and

future. Everything that He is and has done is intended for our use, and when we "put on" Christ we take Him from the beginning to the end of our Christian life for all that we need (*cf.* Gal. iii. 27). (*b*) We have "put on the new man" (Eph. iv. 24). This is no exhortation (see Greek), but the statement of a fact. When we accepted Jesus Christ as our own personal Savior we there and then put off our "unregenerate self," everything we were in Adam, and at the same time we put on our regenerate self, the "new man" (Col. iii. 10), everything we are in Christ, and it is an essential part of the Christian life to realize this regeneration and live in its power. (*c*) We are to "put on" Christlikeness (Col. iii. 12). The Christ Who died is the Christ Who lives, and the grace within us is to be expressed in holiness of character and conduct. (*d*) We are to "put on" the power of the Holy Spirit with which it is promised we shall be clothed (Luke xxiv. 49). All available grace is ours in the power of the Spirit. (*e*) We are to "put on" the Christian armor (ch. xiii. 12; Eph. vi. 11-14; 1 Thess. v. 8). Clothed in this provision no foe can possibly touch us. (*f*) We are to look forward to the time when we shall be "clothed with immortality" (1 Cor. xv. 53, 54; 2 Cor. v. 3). Thus from first to last God has made marvelous provision for what Godet calls "the toilet of the soul."

2. *The Soul's Armor.* This is another characteristic metaphor of St. Paul and is a further assurance of God's complete provision for our needs. The idea is found in three different connections which suggest in turn the three foes of the Christian against which he needs protection. (*a*) There is "the armor of righteousness" (2 Cor. vi. 7). This seems to be the protection against the world. On the one hand, the world would tempt the believer to *despair* by asking what is the use of religion. At this point comes in "the armor of righteousness," because whatever the past may have been "the Lord our Righteousness" covers it all. On the other hand, the world may easily tempt the believer to *despise* and disregard uprightness by urging him to be content with a low standard and not to be so particular. Against this God provides "the armor of righteousness" for the present, since the Lord Jesus Christ is not only

God's righteousness for our justification but also for our sanctification. No wonder, therefore, that the Apostle speaks of the armor of righteousness "on the right hand and on the left." From whatever quarter the enemy may come the provision is adequate. (*b*) There is "the armor of light" (ch. xiii. 12). This seems to be the protection against the flesh. All lower animals have a struggle for life, and so God gives many defenses. Among these is that of color. Insects which live in plants are mostly green. Grouse which live in the heather are mostly brown. Arctic animals which live in the North are mostly white. But the simplest protection is clear light; light protects by dazzling and baffling the foes. The little creatures in the sea which flash their light are thereby kept safe in the brightness. It is exactly the same in things spiritual. There is the light of *sincerity* which protects us against the deceits of the flesh; the light of *purity* which protects us against the defilements; the light of *love* which protects us against the delights; the light of *joy* which protects us against the despair. And when we put on this armor we find it altogether unnecessary to make any provision for the flesh, or to be preoccupied with it in any way whatsoever. (*c*) There is "armor of God" (Eph. vi. 11). This seems to be the protection against the devil. His *works* (1 Tim. iii. 6, 7) are overcome by the greater work of God, for "greater is He that is in you than he that is in the world"; and his *wiles* (Eph. vi. 11) are overcome by the wisdom of God, so that when Christ is made unto us wisdom we are able to say of the devil, "we are not ignorant of his devices." And thus our three enemies are more than met by this threefold armor provided in Christ. Let us therefore appropriate Him and put Him between ourselves and our foes. Let there be but contact of the soul with Christ, committal of the soul to Christ, and control of the soul by Christ, and there will be safety to self, victory over foes, and glory to God.

LVIII

STRONG AND WEAK BRETHREN

Rom. xiv. 1-12.

1. Him that is weak in the faith receive ye, *but* not to doubtful disputations.
2. For one believeth that he may eat all things: another, who is weak, eateth herbs.
3. Let not him that eateth despise him that eateth not; and let not him which eateth not judge him that eateth: for God hath received him.
4. Who art thou that judgest another man's servant? to his own master he standeth or falleth. Yea, he shall be holden up; for God is able to make him stand.
5. One man esteemeth one day above another: another esteemeth every day *alike*. Let every man be fully persuaded in his own mind.
6. He that regardeth the day, regardeth *it* unto the Lord; and he that regardeth not the day, to the Lord he doth not regard *it*. He that eateth, eateth to the Lord, for he giveth God thanks; and he that eateth not, to the Lord he eateth not, and giveth God thanks.
7. For none of us liveth to himself, and no man dieth to himself.
8. For whether we live, we live upon the Lord; and whether we die, we die unto the Lord: whether we live, therefore, or die, we are the Lord's.
9. For to this end Christ both died, and rose, and revived, that he might be Lord both of the dead and living.
10. But why dost thou judge thy brother? or why dost thou set at nought thy brother? for we shall all stand before the judgment seat of Christ.
11. For it is written, *As* I live, saith the Lord, every knee shall bow to me, and every tongue shall confess to God.
12. So then every one of us shall give account of himself to God.

The Christian love of chaps. xii. and xiii. is now to be applied to a special case (*cf.* ch. xii. 3, 10 with ch. xiv. 19). The R.V. rightly inserts the word "but" at the beginning which has curiously been left out of the A.V. This enables us to consider and, if possible, discover the true connection between the present and the preceding sections. Bishop Moule thinks that it may be found in the thought of the alert Christian of ch. xiii. 11-13, finding some weak brother, and being tempted to protest against or despise him as a trouble and a hindrance. Then the present chapter would suggest the opportunity for the strong brother to show Christian considerateness, while the weak one also is not to think the strong brother self-indulgent or careless because he happens to use his liberty in Christ. Another suggestion of the connection between the sections is in the association of subordination as a citizen with toleration as a Christian, each being adduced as an example of the Christian consecration inculcated in chap. 1, 2. Christianity thus holds a perfect balance between the highest devotion and the lowest duty.

Hitherto the Apostle has been speaking to his readers as believers in Christ who are in the enjoyment of full liberty, and are divinely equipped for all righteousness. He has taken for granted the normal and free vigor of the true life of faith, but experience has shown him that this fulness of liberty was not properly understood, appropriated, and enjoyed by all believers. Side by side with those who were experiencing liberty in Christ were others who were weak in faith and troubled by scruples about things which were in themselves without moral significance.

Circumstances had thus arisen which troubled the Christians and were causing dissension, and so it becomes necessary for St. Paul to inculcate the spirit of Christian love by means of mutual forbearance in things indifferent. It was very difficult for a Jewish Christian to rid himself at once of all ideas of differences between days and between foods. Indeed, conscience about diet and observances seems almost inherent in human nature. A Gentile Christian, on the other hand, having entirely given up his old religious system as idolatrous would not usually be troubled by such scruples, but the Jewish converts often could not quite make up their minds to abandon the private observance of rules such as those to which they had been formerly accustomed. They therefore judged other Christians harshly for not observing rules, while they themselves in turn were despised for their scrupulosity.

The question does not seem to have been so serious in Rome as in other Churches (1 Cor. viii. 8), nor was it connected with the great controversy on Justification, as in Galatia (*cf.* Gal. ii. 12-21). It was simply a matter of local difference of conscience between Christians; mainly, as it would seem, though not exclusively, between Gentile and Jewish believers. It has been suggested that the trouble was due to the idea of the superiority of vegetarianism over flesh diet (Gen. i. 29; ix. 3), and if so, no Christian principle was involved. It was a matter for mutual consideration on both sides. Godet thinks these differences probably broke out at Love Feasts, and gave occasion to sad expressions of disharmony between believers at these solemn and, as they should have been happy times.

The subject covers ch. xiv. 1-xv. 13, and is treated thus:

(*a*) Ch. xiv. 1-12: Some general principles and rebukes to both sides.

(*b*) Ch. xiv. 13-23: Exhortations mainly to the strong.

(*c*) Ch. xv. 1-13: The subject considered and widened in the light of our Lord's example.

I. *The Call to the Strong* (ver. 1).—The man who is weak in his Christian confidence as to the extent of his liberty in matters of eating and drinking is to be welcomed cordially to Christian fellowship. "Him that is weak in faith receive ye." The last clause of the verse is differently interpreted. In the A.V. and English R.V. we read, "But not to doubtful disputations." In the American R.V. it is, "Yet not for decision of scruples." Weymouth renders it, "But not for the purpose of deciding mere matters of opinion." Rutherford in his able version translates the entire verse thus: "Although in his faith a man shows weakness, I bid you welcome him to your society without desiring to contest his opinions." Strong Christians are not to sit in judgment on the scruples of their weak brethren, but to show a spirit of toleration and sympathy. Difficulties are not to be discussed, doubts are not to be discriminated, still less is judgment to be passed. The brother is to be welcomed cordially into fellowship and loved rather than argued out of his difficulties. Sanday thinks that the meaning is, "Not to pass judgment on his thoughts," while Gifford says, "Not to discuss his doubts." Garvie writes, "They are not to be made to feel that the community tolerates them but condemns their scruples." Godet suggests that the fundamental idea is against getting into any debate which would only end in vain reasonings.

The weakness of faith here mentioned refers, not to any essential or inherent defect of character, but simply to the lack of true spiritual breadth and moral perception. Faith in Christ saves us from sin, but it does not at once and always enable us to see the application of this salvation to the small matters of daily life. "Grace sanctifies the heart much more easily than the head." It has been aptly said that God washes hearts in this life, but He washes brains in the life to come.

II. *The First Difference and its Adjustment* (vers. 2-4).—One kind of question referred to in the preceding verse had to do with eating. One man had confidence that there was no essential difference between foods; another, lacking this perception, hesitated, and so limited himself to herbs as the only safe way of avoiding moral pollution (ver. 2). This was the problem, and we shall see how it was to be faced by both parties. The strong is not to despise the weak; the weak is not to be censorious against the strong. Since God has received the strong brother, why should not the weak one welcome him to fellowship? If God has received him into fellowship it is clearly a case which is not to be despised, especially as God's reception means that he is to be dealt with at a Divine and not a human tribunal of judgment (ver. 3). Then follows a severe rebuke to the weak for judging the strong. He is the servant of another, and hence there must and can be no intrusion into the household affairs of another party (ver. 4). "To his own master he stands or falls," and although the Apostle has made use of the word "fall," he goes on to say that the strong brother will not fall because God's mighty power will keep him upright. It would seem best to make this assurance (that God is able to make the strong brother stand) refer to his moral and spiritual position in the present life, though there are interpreters who think the reference is either to Church status as the good standing of Church membership, or the Jewish status of acceptance in the last day (See Neil, *Romans*, p. 440).

III. *The Second Difference and its Adjustment* (ver. 5).—Another question was the observance of days. Perhaps the reference was to the permanent binding character of Jewish feasts, though Sanday and Headlam think that it is impossible to distinguish between Jewish rites which are condemned and Christian rites which are enjoyed. On this subject the great rule for all parties was full persuasion of mind or moral conscience. "Let every man be fully persuaded in his own mind." Let there be such a fulness of conviction that no room will be left for the least hesitation.

IV. *The Right Standpoint* (ver. 6).—The true attitude as to days and foods is found in the words "to the Lord." Everything was to be done or left undone in the light of this great thought. This is the reason why both lines may be followed, by the strong and the weak respectively. He who has any feeling on the matter gives it careful thought and practices it in relation to his Master, just as in the same way he who refrains does so in the same spirit of loyalty to his Master, since he too has fellowship with God concerning it.

A word seems necessary here about the Christian observance of Sunday. It is sometimes thought that the regular observance of one day in seven is altogether incompatible with Christian spirituality and liberty as here inculcated by the Apostle. But, as Godet points out, the context does not warrant us in coming to this conclusion. There is no doubt that even the observance of Sunday can be undertaken in a spirit of anxious scrupulosity which is utterly opposed to Christian liberty, and if a believer observes the day in this spirit he will inevitably come under the bondage here deprecated. But when we fully realize the true spirit of the observance of that day as based upon our physical nature, promulgated from creation, and constituting one of the essential features of true religion, we observe it as "under law to Christ," without the faintest possibility of any spiritual bondage detrimental to the Christian soul (see Sanday and Headlam, *Romans*, p. 387).

Another question of supreme moment seems to be settled by this teaching of the Apostle. The young believer is often puzzled by certain practical questions of daily life. May I do this? May I go there? May I read that? The answer is clear in the light of this principle: "Yes, if I can enjoy it to the Lord, and while giving Him thanks for it; No, if I cannot receive it as a gift from His hand and bless Him for it" (Godet, *Romans,* p. 334).

V. *The Fundamental Reason* (vers. 7-9).—The great principle in all these matters is "Not I, but Christ." We are all related to one another in Him, and the questions now discussed are only special examples of what is true of the entire Christian life (vers. 7, 8). Our relation to Christ is based on His death and resurrection, and this means His Lordship. Indeed, the Lordship of Christ over the lives of His people was the very purpose for which He died and rose again (ver. 9).

VI. *The General Reproof* (vers. 10-12).—The two parties are again rebuked. Why should the weak judge censoriously the liberal-minded? Why should the strong brother despise the scrupulous? We are to stand before God's judgment, not the judgment of one another. Our relation to Christ is incompatible with any similar relation to man. Earthly Christians are not our lords, neither are we theirs, and although Christians are to judge angels (1 Cor. vi. 3), that time is not yet come. This teaching about judgment is confirmed from Scripture (Isa. xlv. 23), and the practical conclusion is that each one of us is to give an account to God (ver. 12). "The preceding context (ver. 10) signified: Judge not thy brother, for God will judge him; this verse signifies: Judge thyself, for God will judge thee" (Godet, *Romans,* p. 338). Hence the true attitude is holy fear. The strong will fear to grieve the weak, and the weak to judge the strong, and in both cases it will be because of their relation to Christ.

This reference to judgment needs careful distinction in the light of other passages of the New Testament. In John v. 24 we read of judgment on sins as past in the case of the believer, but in the present passage, and in 2 Cor. v. 10, the reference is to Christ's tribunal for the faithfulness of His own disciples who will there receive as Christians the reward of grace according to their works.

The great principle laid down throughout this section is the Lordship of Christ. "That He might be Lord." This is true, not only of the subjects here mentioned, but also of the whole of the believer's life.

1. *For Pardon.* We have to acknowledge Christ as our Lord. Sin is rebellion, and it is only as we surrender to Him as our Lord that we receive pardon from Him as our Savior.

2. *For Peace.* We have to accept Him as our Lord. He is the Lord of Peace (2 Thes. iii. 16). It is first, government, and then, peace (Isa. ix. 7).

3. *For Holiness.* We have to admit Him to reign on the throne of the heart, and it is only when He is glorified in our hearts as King that the Holy Spirit enters and abides (John vii. 39).

4. *For Victory.* We have to appropriate Him as Conqueror of Satan, sin, circumstances, and self.

5. *For Fellowship.* We have to allow Him to be the Lord of our Christian assemblies. It often happens that earnest souls are thrown into contact with uncongenial fellow-Christians, and it is difficult for the strong uncompromising believer not to be hindered and hampered. The one secret of power and blessing is the recognition of the Lordship of Christ. He is our Lord, He is their Lord, and the most profitable Church for the development of Christian character is often the Church which is characterized by trying surroundings.

It is the Lordship of Christ which will enable us to tolerate differences so long as they do not involve disobedience to the Word of God, or denial of some fundamental principle of the Gospel. In the latter case, as we can see from St. Paul himself, we must not give place, even for an hour (Gal. ii.). But this apart, the realization of the Lordship of Christ will enable us to become large-hearted Christians, emphasizing unity in things essential and liberty in things non-essential. Loyalty to Christ will inevitably bring about freedom from anxiety as to any choice made by self, or any misunderstanding between fellow-Christians. Fellowship must not be broken for trifles, since we have no right to insist on such slight conditions of communion; indeed, the fear of breaking the bonds of fellowship between those who are under the Lordship of Christ ought to act as one of the strongest deterrents. When the strong brother realizes how dear the weak one is to our Father in Heaven, how can he despise him? And if the weak brother only recalls the common attitude of accountability to their one Lord and Master, how quickly he will shrink from all censorious judgment. Thus loyalty to the Lord will ever keep us from occupying the Master's judgment seat.

And so for everything the secret is found in the Lordship of Christ. "He is thy Lord" (Psa. xlv. 11). "Speak, Lord, for Thy servant heareth" (1 Sam. iii. 9). "My Lord and my God" (John xx. 28).

LIX

HIGH DOCTRINES FOR HUMBLE DUTIES

Rom. xiv. 13-23.

13. Let us not therefore judge one another any more: but judge this rather, that no man put a stumblingblock or an occasion to fall in *his* brother's way.

14. I know, and am persuaded by the Lord Jesus, that *there is* nothing unclean of itself: but to him that esteemeth any thing to be unclean, to him *it is* unclean.

15. But if thy brother be grieved with *thy* meat, now walkest thou not charitably. Destroy not him with thy meat, for whom Christ died.

16. Let not then your good be evil spoken of:

17. For the kingdom of God is not meat and drink; but righteousness, and peace, and joy in the Holy Ghost.

18. For he that in these things serveth Christ *is* acceptable to God, and approved of men.

19. Let us therefore follow after the things which make for peace, and things wherewith one may edify another.

20. For meat destroy not the work of God. All things indeed *are* pure; but *it is* evil for that man who eateth with offence.

21. *It is* good neither to eat flesh, nor to drink wine, nor *any thing* whereby thy brother stumbleth, or is offended, or is made weak.

22. Hast thou faith? have *it* to thyself before God. Happy *is* he that condemneth not himself in that thing which he alloweth.

23. And he that doubteth is damned if he eat, because *he eateth* not of faith: for whatsoever *is* not of faith is sin.

The Apostle has been laying down the general principles with reference to our responsibility to the law in connection with difficult circumstances. Now he will speak of the right and true use of Christian liberty. He has shown that all such matters as foods and days are in themselves indifferent; but he proceeds at the same time to emphasize the great principles associated with Christian love. He addresses mainly to the strong, untrammelled, vigorous Christian, though indirectly, and in passing, the weak, hesitating, scrupulous brother is not overlooked. The main thoughts of the section seem to be as follows: (*a*) vers. 13-19: Do not grieve the weak brother; (*b*) vers. 19-23: Do not destroy God's work in Him. Let us give careful attention to the high principles here inculcated for the observance of lowly practices.

I. *An Earnest Exhortation* (ver. 13).—Because of the judgment of God before which we shall all have to stand (ver. 12), "let us not therefore judge one another any more." Judgment is God's work, not ours. If we must judge at all, let us decide on this, that we will not be the cause of stumbling to any Christian brother. We may fully give the powers of our mind to this form of judgment, but to no other. It is a primary duty to avoid anything which will cause a shock, and, still more, a fall.

II. *A Strong Assertion* (ver. 14).—In the clearest, most definite, and even most solemn way, as expressed by the opening words, "I know, and am persuaded in the Lord Jesus," St. Paul states that distinctions of foods are groundless, and yet that every Christian has not realized this truth. Indeed, this exception is the argument of the present section in which he appeals to the strong. It is just because all Christians cannot take this high ground that the Apostle has to speak as he does (1 Cor. x. 26; 1 Tim. iv. 3-5; Tit. i. 15). It is a fine testimony to St. Paul's clearness of sight, and at the same time to his Christian love, that he is able to write in this way.

III. *A Loving Entreaty* (vers. 15, 16).—The strong Christian who has come to the conclusion that nothing is unclean of itself must be careful to respect the scruples of the one who has not yet learned the lesson, for fear he should hurt the spiritual health of his brother. Our brother's weakness is the measure of our duty. For a trifling bit of food we must not grieve a brother in Christ and perhaps lead him astray (1 Cor. viii. 7-13; x. 23-33). As Dr. David Brown helpfully says, "The wilful violation of conscience contains within itself a seed of destruction."

Liberty is given, but it must not degenerate into license. Wrangling and differences between Christian men will cause the enemy to blaspheme. We must therefore give special care lest our good be evil spoken of. This "good" may be that Christian liberty which the strong enjoy, or it may refer to the Christian cause, which is thereby reproached through our lack of true consideration. Both ideas may be included, for we all know how definite and practical a bearing individual conduct has on the general interests of Christianity. Our stronger faith and wider liberty must be held in check and not given full play, lest we hurt and trouble others both in the Church and outside.

IV. *A True Attitude* (vers. 17, 18).—That all this action is necessary is shown by the fact that the essence of Christianity is no matter of food and drink. The Kingdom of God is occupied with far greater matters than the mere questions of eating and drinking. Christianity is internal, not external, and its main principles are righteousness, and peace, and joy in the Holy Ghost. The "righteousness" of love which is moral uprightness; the "peace" of fellowship which is union and communion among Christians; the "joy" in the Holy Spirit which involves genuine exaltation in the Christian community—those are the essential realities of the Gospel, and when this is clearly understood it becomes utterly impossible to dwell on any smaller matters. This is the true attitude of the genuine man of God, and the life thus lived with constant regard to helpfulness to our fellow-Christians will have the twofold effect of being acceptable to God and approved of men (ver. 18). Such a life will stand the supreme test of Divine examination, and will be seen to be well-pleasing to the Father, and to possess the approbation of those around.

V. *An Urgent Necessity* (vers. 19, 20).—All this points clearly to the duty of both strong and weak to pursue the things that make for peace and mutual edification. They must not merely live so as to avoid irritation, but, much more, they must so live as not to do any harm to the work of God's grace already experienced in a brother's heart. "Peace" and "edification" are thus the two aspects, negative and positive, of every genuine life. For a mere piece of food no one must destroy the work of God's grace in a human soul (ver. 20). Mark the striking contrast between "meat" and "God." In verse 13 the appeal is made with reference to personal pain and trouble, but here the Apostle goes much further and urges it in the light of God's work. The strong must not give any occasion to another to stumble. The issues of life are profoundly solemn, and it is essential to live the true life in Christ moment by moment. While everything is pure in itself it becomes base to the man whose conscience is stumbled by eating it ((ver. 20).

VI. *A Simple Privilege* (ver. 21).—Now comes a thought which covers and summarizes the whole subject. It is a "beautiful" thing not to eat, or drink, or do anything which causes a brother to stumble (1 Cor. vii. 1). Nothing could well be finer than this statement of what ought to be regarded as the high joy and true satisfaction of a Christian brother who is willing to avoid even the most harmless things as he regards them for the sake of a weak brother. If God puts such a privilege before us we ought to rejoice in the possibility of doing such a "beautiful" thing.

VII. *A Closing Reminder* (vers. 22, 23).—In two successive verses the Apostle makes a virtual appeal, first to the strong, and then to the weak brother. To the strong this is what he has to say (ver. 22): If you have faith that these things are pure matters of indifference, keep that faith to yourself; do not parade it in public and shock your weak brother. At the same time be quite sure that in this attitude of liberty you are not condemning yourself and going beyond your own conscience. Happy is he who has no misgivings in that of which he approves; happy is the man whose practice does not go beyond his convictions. This is a motive for restraint; the strong brother is to be content with the absence of scruples, and is to avoid the use of liberty for the sake of another who cannot see as far as he can. This appeal to the strong to cherish and enjoy his faith alone with God is a reminder that he can well afford to be generous to his weak brother. The quiet, yet searching word with which the verse closes is particularly significant. That man is happy who feels no scruples or points of conscience in what he has determined to do.

Now he turns to the weak brother, and this is his message to him (ver. 23): Here is your danger; if you have any doubt or hesitation about a matter of food, you are thereby self-condemned. If you cannot exercise faith about it, you must by all means leave it alone. Whenever you are in doubt, give Christ the benefit of the doubt, and if you cannot do a thing as Christ's follower, do not do it at all.

The Apostle's words, "Whatsoever is not of faith is sin," are apt to be misunderstood and misused. We must be careful to apply them to the point at issue. Stifler's words are very pertinent:—

> "It must be carefully noted that Paul is not speaking here of absence of saving faith, but of defect in it. Hence this is not a general but a Christian principle. Paul is prescribing for what is before him in the Church and not for mankind" (*The Epistle to the Romans,* p. 248).

This question of the relation of the strong to the weak brother is one of great, pressing, and constant importance in the Christian life. The weak and the strong are still with us, and if we would maintain that Christian fellowship which is of the very essence of true life we must constantly learn how the weak is to regard the strong, and, even more, how the strong is to regard the weak. There is a great possibility of hurting our fellow-Christians by actions lawful in themselves, and by insisting on rights which God has undoubtedly given to us. We are therefore bound to consider others and the effect of our actions on them. The position is rendered all the more difficult from time to time by the fact that the same action may do harm to some and good to others. St. Paul had directly in mind the unwisdom and danger of doing something that another thinks is wrong, and thereby of tempting him to do it, and thus making him doubt as well the other man's right intention. There is also, however, the possibility of approaching someone who is engaged on that about which he has no scruple and which is for him wholly innocent, and perhaps making him think that it is wrong and thereby bringing him into condemnation. In the latter case the man is stumbled, because he is still tempted to go on doing what he did before, though the question has now been raised in his mind as to its lawfulness. Thus there are two corresponding duties: first, that of a reasonable concern for the conscience of other men by avoiding the doing of what they would regard as wrong, even though we ourselves do not regard it so; second, the duty of doing our utmost to cultivate a discerning and discriminating conscience in the other person, and thereby training him to think for himself and to distinguish between things that differ. We have then to balance results and consider on which side, on the whole, the scale of our influence will fall. We shall be helped by a careful consideration of the principles insisted upon by the Apostle all through this chapter.

1. *The Christian Life must be lived in the Light of the Lordship of Christ* (ver. 8). We have already dwelt on this, and only recall it here for the purpose of associating it with the other principles found in the chapter. "Lord, what wilt Thou?" is the test of all problems.

2. *The Christian Life should be lived in the Light of the Judgment* (vers. 10, 12). It is a great help to true life in the present when it is viewed in its proper perspective. We must continually ask ourselves how such an attitude, or such an action will look in the light of eternity.

3. *The Christian Life should be lived in the Light of Love* (ver. 15). If only we take care to walk "charitably," or "according to love" we shall soon find that our brother's interest will take a foremost place in our thought, and the fact that we love him will do as much as anything to prevent us from violating his conscience.

4. *The Christian Life should be lived in the Light of Calvary* (ver. 15). This is the supreme motive. The weak brother is one for whom Christ shed His blood and in whom the work of God's grace in Christ has already been commenced (ver. 20). If, therefore, we keep ever in view the marvel of God's mercy in the gift of His dear Son, it will do more than anything else to preserve our souls in the same attitude of loving regard, unselfish consideration, and willing self-sacrifice.

As we contemplate these profound principles and the fact that they are brought to bear upon the simplest and most ordinary practices of daily life, we have a fresh illumination of the greatness and glory of the Apostle to the Gentiles.

LX

THE IMITATION OF CHRIST

ROM. xv. 1-7.

1. We then that are strong ought to bear the infirmities of the weak, and not to please ourselves.
2. Let every one of us please *his* neighbor for *his* good to edification.
3. For even Christ pleased not himself; but, as it is written, The reproaches of them that reproached thee fell on me.
4. For whatever things were written aforetime were written for our learning, that we through patience and comfort of the scriptures might have hope.
5. Now the God of patience and consolation grant you to be like-minded one toward another according to Christ Jesus:
6. That ye may with one mind *and* one mouth glorify God, even the Father of our Lord Jesus Christ.
7. Wherefore receive ye one another, as Christ also received us to the glory of God.

THIS section is closely connected with the foregoing subject and, indeed, forms its conclusion. It is concerned with pressing home the true relation between the strong and the weak Christian. From the special discussion, however, of the former chapter, St. Paul passes to the general considerations underlying all such questions, and he appeals to his readers to honor them heartily in their life. We shall also see as we proceed to verses 8-13 that the Apostle has in view something still more important than even these relations between the weak and the strong. He is concerned for the promotion of that joyous and trustful harmony with which the entire Church should be waiting the full consummation of all its marvelous hopes in Christ.

I. *Obligation* (ver. 1).—"We, the strong ones, ought to keep on bearing the weaknesses of the powerless ones, and not to be wanting continually to please ourselves." We observe the emphatic way in which the Apostle associates himself with them. Christians are to bear, not merely to forbear; there must be patient submission and the endeavor to support the weakness of our brother by loving forethought and tenderness. This regard for the weak is particularly characteristic of the strong Apostle of the Gentiles (Gal. vi. 1, 2).

The keynote of the verse is in the word "ought," implying the consciousness of a profound obligation. Even the etymology of "we ought" is suggestive. It always means, "we owe it." There are many weaknesses arising from prejudices, faults, and errors, and they inevitably and invariably come from weakness of faith. For the carrying of burdens love is the great power. A little girl was once carrying a baby, and someone asked, "Is he not heavy?" "No," was the reply, "he is my brother."

II. *Edification* (ver. 2).—The aim of each and every individual Christian should be to please his neighbor for good, with a view to building him up in the Christian faith and life. This is the supreme law of brotherhood, and the Apostle practiced what he preached (1 Cor. ix. 19-22; x. 32, 33).

III. *Imitation* (ver. 3).—For Christ also pleased not Himself." The Master did the very same thing as the Apostle here urges his fellow-Christians to do. This is the first reference to the example of Christ in the Epistle. The lack of prominence is doubtless due to the fact that the Epistle as a whole is mainly concerned with the Person and Work of our Lord. All references to the example of Christ should be carefully collected and studied. They will be found closely associated with that redeeming grace of God by which alone any true "imitation of Christ" becomes possible (John xiii. 34; xv. 2; 2 Cor. v. 13-16; Phil. ii. 4-8; 1 Pet. ii. 21-25; 1 John iv. 10, 11).

IV. *Confirmation* (ver. 3).—"As it is written, the reproach of them that reproached thee fell on me." The Scripture foretold the action of the Messiah in this very respect (Psa. lxix. 9). It is striking to observe that there are more references to Psa. lxix. in the New Testament in relation to Christ than to any other, and this would seem to show that in many respects the Psalm is intended to express Messianic experiences.

V. *Inspiration* (ver. 4).—The reason for quoting the Old Testament is now seen to be in the purpose of that book as a whole. It was written to uphold believers in their life of patient hope. They were to learn, and from learning to derive endurance and comfort, which in turn would lead to hope.

VI. *Supplication* (vers. 5, 6).—From the Scriptures the Apostle turns to God Himself as the Source of endurance and comfort. Wherever the Greek word here rendered "patience" is found we are to understand active endurance, not passive resignation. It suggests the presence, not the absence of difficulty, and the attitude of determined, deliberate steadfastness under pressure.

> "The use of the word *endurance,* which always implies difficulty, to describe our treatment of weaker brethren, and the example of Christ under raillery of the enemies of God, reminds us how difficult it sometimes is to act towards weaker brethren in a spirit of love. Our Christian character is seldom so severely tried as when we are put to inconvenience by the spiritual childishness of members of the Church" (Beet, *St Paul's Epistle to the Romans,* p. 344).

This grace comes from God through the Scriptures, and will in turn bring us and our fellow-Christians into unity, Christ being the standard: "according to Christ Jesus." Oneness with God will lead to oneness among brethren. When God is first the result will be unity. Not identity of union but harmony of feeling. It is to be observed that of the two unities emphasized by the Apostle in Ephesians iv., one is present and the other is future: "the unity of the Spirit" (ver. 3) we are to keep with all possible endeavor; but "the unity of faith and knowledge" (ver. 13) will not come yet, but will be reached some day (*cf.* Phil. iii. 15-17; iv. 2, 3). And the ultimate object which is in the mind of the Apostle as he prays is that unitedly and in harmony they may all glorify God in Christ (ver. 6). This was the supreme purpose of the Apostle, the union of the entire Church. For this he has been praying, and striving, and teaching many years.

VII. *Application* (ver. 7).—Now comes the closing exhortation and appeal to both parties. Each is to acknowledge and treat the other as Christians. They are to welcome one another (see the same word in commencing the subject, ch. xiv. 1), as Christ had welcomed them all without exception, to the glory of God. Both are to do their utmost to bring about this result. If Christ has received a brother, I must receive him too. And yet Christ's reception of us does not destroy differences even while it prevents disunion. Amid harmony there is variety, and there is no reason why with many differences among Christians essential unity may not exist.

As we contemplate the various principles and ideals set before us by the Apostle in this entire section (ch. xiv. 1-xv. 7) the thought naturally arises, "How can these things be?" It is in some ways the supreme question of a believer's life, the possibility of realizing ideals and fulfilling the obvious Divine purpose. We frequently hear of Emerson's counsel, "Hitch your wagon to a star," but the problem is how to connect our wagon with the star in the sky. It is this point that the Apostle very specially brings before us in the present passage. After insisting upon great, powerful, and essential principles he reveals a threefold secret to enable us to fulfil them.

1. *The Pattern of Christ's Example.* Twice in this brief passage is this truth taught. In His earthly life our Lord did not please Himself (ver. 3), and we are to "follow His steps." In His heavenly life we are to be of one mind, "according to Christ Jesus" (ver. 5). In like manner, St. John's First Epistle lays great stress on Christ as our pattern. No less than six times he uses the phrase, "even as He." We are to "walk in the light, as He is in the light" (ch. i. 7). We are to "walk, even as He walked" (ch. ii. 6). We are to "purify ourselves, even as He is pure" (ch. iii. 3). And we are to "love, as He gave us commandment" (ch. iii. 23). But it is the special and unique feature of the New Testament treatment of the example of Christ that it is never far away from the thought of Christ as the Source of grace and power. He is not only, or even chiefly, our Example; He is our Redeemer, and as Savior He provides the grace that enables us to imitate Him. When St. Peter speaks of Christ "leaving us an example, that ye should follow His steps" (1 Pet. ii. 21), he quickly refers to our Lord as the Sin-Bearer, as the Life, and as the Shepherd and Bishop of our souls (vers. 24, 25). Thus the example of Christ, so far from causing us despondency

and despair by reason of our inability to realize it, is brought closely home to our daily needs by the assurance of grace sufficient.

2. *The Power of Holy Scripture.* Herein is another secret of power in the Christian life. Whatever grace is needed is found in Holy Scripture. It was intended for this very purpose, and it always accomplishes its end when properly used. It contains truth because it is a Divine revelation. It assures us of God's pardon as our consolation, God's presence as our cheer, God's power as our confidence. It reveals His will as our rule, His grace as our provision, and in its record of the life of God's people it shows that what has been done can be done again. Its promises elicit our faith, its experiences sustain us in difficulties. It is ever pointing onward to "that blessed hope," and this provides an "anchor" which keeps us from drifting (Heb. vi. 19), and an "helmet" which shields us from danger (1 Thess. v. 8). The more thoroughly, therefore, we become intellectually and spiritually acquainted with the Bible as the Word of God, the more deeply will it affect our character and transform our life. There is nothing in Christianity so potent for Christian living as a daily, definite, first-hand meditation of the Word of God. It is as impossible to exaggerate its power, as it is impossible to over-estimate the loss that accrues when our Christian life is not supported, sustained, and guided day by day by this close contact with Holy Scripture.

3. *The Provision of Prayer.* As the Apostle turns from Scripture to the Source of Scripture, so we in our daily life must resolve everything into prayer. Prayer means power, because it links us to the Fount of power, God Himself. Scripture and prayer are frequently associated in the New Testament, because in the one God speaks to us, and in the other we speak to God. With the channels of the spiritual life thus open at both ends and clear all the way through, we receive grace for daily living from "the God of all grace," and find ourselves enabled to fulfil the will of God, and live lives well-pleasing to Him.

LXI

CHRISTIAN BROTHERHOOD

Rom. xv. 8-13.

8. Now I say that Jesus Christ was a minister of the circumcision for the truth of God, to confirm the promises *made* unto the fathers:
9. And that the Gentiles might glorify God for *his* mercy; as it is written, For this cause I will confess to thee among the Gentiles, and sing unto thy name.
10. And again he saith, Rejoice, ye Gentiles, with his people.
11. And again, Praise the Lord, all ye Gentiles; and laud him, all ye people.
12. And again, Esaias saith, There shall be a root of Jesse, and he that shall rise to reign over the Gentiles; in him shall the Gentiles trust.
13. Now the God of hope fill you with all joy and peace in believing, that ye may abound in hope, through the power of the Holy Ghost.

At this stage we have a striking instance of the way in which the Apostle leads on from an ordinary subject into something deep and fundamental connected with it. We shall appreciate this thought if we review the preceding verses and observe how the transition is made. From the special case of the weak and the strong brethren in the Church at Rome he passes to the more general subject of the two classes, Jew and Gentile, in the Christian Church, and the need of union and fellowship in spite of all differences. First he pleads for mutual consideration by the example of Christ (vers. 1-3); then he depicts the union to be reached thereby (vers. 4-7); and from this he proceeds to indicate the special part attributed respectively to Jew and Gentile in this fellowship (vers. 8-13). And thus our present section is the explanatory proof of ver. 7, showing that Christ had received both Jews and Gentiles, and that therefore we as Christians should do likewise one with another. No conscientious differences are to be expressed in the form of sectionalism among Christians; for if God has vanquished that most notable of sectional differences, the one between Jew and Gentile, much more may His children follow His example and refuse to allow differences among themselves to pass into severances. This question of Jew and Gentile thus comes up once again, though it had necessarily been dropped since chapter xi. 32. The Apostle opens with his customary phrase of explanation, "Now I say," that is, "What I mean, is this." And then while the words, "meat," "weak," and "strong," are not again used, but the two nationalities are considered instead, it would almost seem that the Jew must have been the weak brother and the Gentile the strong, though there were pretty certainly exceptions in both cases.

I. *The Divine Plan* (vér. 8).—"Jesus Christ was a minister of the circumcision." This is a simple statement, and is only found here. It refers to the well-known fact that during our Lord's earthly ministry His work was restricted to the Jews. As He told the Canaanitish woman, He was only sent "to the lost sheep of the house of Israel." It was merely in very indirect ways that He came in contact with Gentiles, and it is quite a question whether even the Greeks who wished to see Him had their desire fulfilled (John xii. 21). At any rate there is no record of the fact, and the probabilities seem against it in the light of our Lord's definite attitude during His earthly life. It would have been premature, and even fatal, to have ministered to the Gentiles before offering the Gospel to Israel and making sure of the covenant people. At first sight this restriction of Christ's ministry to Israel is perplexing, and yet the more it is considered the more clearly the Divine plan becomes evident. It is often necessary to do less first in order to do more afterwards, and by concentrating His work on Israel, as the first Gospel indicates, it became possible for Him gradually to develop His purpose, until at length it reached "all nations."

II. *The Definite Purpose* (vers. 8, 9).—This concentration of Christ's ministry on the Jews was "for the truth of God," and had in view two distinct yet connected ideas. (*a*) First, "that He might confirm the promises given unto the fathers"; (*b*) Second, that "the Gentiles might glorify God for His mercy." In relation to the Jews it was necessary that God's truth should be manifested in faithfulness to His promises. In relation to the Gentiles it was essential to reveal His mercy, since they too were included in the Divine purpose of love and grace. And Jesus Christ performed this twofold task, fulfilling the promises on behalf of the Jew and revealing the love of God in relation to the Gentile. These two thoughts are respectively brought before us in the first and third Gospels, the one for the Jew and the other for the Gentile. And so the Apostle virtually makes his appeal to the strong (Gentiles) to deal forbearingly with the weak (Jews), by showing that Christ became a Jew in order to fulfil God's promises and purposes to Jews and Gentiles.

Thus Jews and Gentiles are urged to welcome one another, for both alike have been welcomed by God in Christ, even though there was a decided difference in the way in which they were received. The Jew was welcomed in connection with the promises made to his forefathers, and thereby God's fidelity to His word was made abundantly manifest. The Gentiles were welcomed not on account of any covenant position, for they had none, but because of the abundant and free mercy of God. But this difference in the method of receiving makes no difference whatever to the essential unity of Jew and Gentile when they are received. Unity has never meant unanimity of opinion, or uniformity of practice. On the contrary, there has always been an exquisite variety in the works of God in nature and in grace, and this is intended to produce that harmony which will glorify God far more than any mere uniformity could possibly do.

III. *The Scripture Proof* (vers. 9-12).—Four passages from the Old Testament are used in support of this position, proving that this Divine catholicity had been long pre-announced. If God himself, who separated Israel from all other nations, has in the Gospel cancelled this distinction as a dividing force, surely His children may follow His example and refuse to allow differences to become divisions. More especially must this be so if for centuries beforehand such an union was contemplated by God Himself (Deut. xxxii. 43; Psa. xviii. 49; Psa. cxvii. 1; Isa. xi. 10). It will be noticed that there is an emphasis on "Gentiles" in each verse, and this is the point of the Apostle's use of the passages. In the first one the Messiah is depicted as praising God among the "Gentiles," and thus the quotation suggests the conversion of those who are associated with Him in the praise. In the second one the Gentiles are exhorted to unite in praise with God's people, the Jews. In the third, which comes from the shortest of the Psalms, we see that God intended to introduce the Gentiles into His worship; and it is noteworthy that the little word "all" occurs twice. In the fourth passage the prophet declares that the Messiah, although coming from David's line, is to be King over the Gentiles, for "In Him shall the Gentiles hope." Thus once again, as in chapter xi., we have the Scriptural assurance that the Gentiles were intended to be brought to Christ. This scheme of Gentile salvation was as dear to the heart of the great Apostle as was the conversion of the Jew.

Looking over these verses, we can see what was in the Apostle's mind as he addressed himself both to Jews and Gentiles in regard to their duty of mutual considerateness and fellowship in the Church of God. "The Gentiles must remember that Christ became a Jew to save them; the Jews that Christ came among them in order that all the families of the earth might be blessed; both must realize that the aim of the whole is to promote God's glory" (Sanday and Headlam, *Romans*, p. 397).

IV. *The Special Prayer* (ver. 13).—Now comes a prayer, summing up and concluding the entire subject, and, indeed, the whole of the doctrinal part of the Epistle. After showing in the frankest and yet tenderest way the necessity for both parties, Jew and Gentile, weak and strong, to unite in their one Lord and Master, he lifts up his heart for them in this exquisite prayer, feeling sure that if these spiritual realities are experienced there will be no further difficulty or difference, still less division, in the Church. When problems involving possible severance of heart are brought before God in prayer, it is not difficult to see in this the guarantee of a right, complete, and lasting solution.

1. The Source of Blessing. "The God of hope." This is a title only used here, and is literally "the God of the hope," the preeminent hope of the Old Testament; the God Who gives hope,

sustains hope, crowns hope. The title is no doubt suggested by the words immediately preceding, wherein the Gentiles are to "hope in the God of Israel." When our souls are in direct fellowship with God as "the God of hope" we are most likely to realize His purpose and will.

2. The Character of Blessing. "All joy and peace." These are the active and passive sides of Christian experience. Joy is energetic, peace is restful. Scripture speaks much of the joy of salvation, and assures us that "the joy of the Lord is our strength." Peace is the great word of reconciliation, as we contemplate our relations to God and to our fellow-men. Still more, it is "all joy and peace," for everything that God has is to be ours in every way.

3. The Measure of Blessing. "Fill you." The Apostle frequently used this idea of fulness, for he was not content with any poor, narrow, or strained life. He knew that God was "the God of all grace," and he longed for himself and his friends that they might know the abundance that God was only too ready to provide.

4. The Purpose of Blessing. "That ye may abound in hope." Jew and Gentile were to look forward to a glorious future in their Lord. Hope is always connected with the coming of the Master, and in this spirit they were to face the future, and all the problems that might arise. This is the true Christian spirit of optimism and even buoyancy, because it is concentrated on the great event which is certain to happen; "the appearing of our great God and Savior." Pessimism is altogether alien from the true Christian spirit. A pessimist has been aptly described as "a man who with two evils chooses both," but the Christian will always be an optimist, not in a superficial, sentimental sense, but because of the great stronghold of hope which is his in Christ.

5. The Sphere of Blessing. "In the power of the Holy Ghost." This is where the life is to be lived. Not by any energy of self, nor by any possibilities of companionship in those around us, but in the constant, surrounding, pervading presence of the Holy Spirit, the Comforter, Who enables us to realize our union and communion with Christ and our fellow-Christians.

6. The Channel of Blessing. "In believing." This is the simple secret of everything. Our life must first of all be a life of faith, and from faith will come joy, peace, and hope. On the side of God it is the Holy Ghost Who works all this in us, and on our side the contact comes through simple trust. Faith links us to Christ, and in this union comes all power and grace.[1]

Thus the appeal is brought to an end, and the argument of the section, and, indeed, the argument of the Epistle, closes with the practical ideas associated with prayer, grace, hope, and praise. Every part of the Epistle from the very beginning has been leading up to this definite personal experience. No mere theological disquisition, no mere intellectual argument, but the contact of every Christian soul with his Lord, is the supreme thought of the Apostle's mind, and the constant aim of every line of his writing. "The harmonious glorification of the God and Father of our Lord Jesus Christ by the whole body of the redeemed, as it is the most exalted fruit of the scheme of redemption, so it is the last end of God in it."

For the moment it is difficult to realize that these verses close the subject discussed in the long section, ch. xiv. 1-xv. 13, and yet it is essential to remind ourselves of the Apostle's specific purpose in the earlier part. The pressure of the particular problem has altogether disappeared. Foods and festivals cease to trouble us today in the way that St. Paul's experiences indicate. And yet the value of the treatment is in some respects greater for us, because we find included in it some of the deepest principles connected with Christian brotherhood. Let us briefly sum up these thoughts as we contemplate once again the whole passage.

1. *The Great Law of Christian Brotherhood.* Each for the others and all for each. This is a vital and essential part of our Christianity. The fact that we are related to Christ necessarily carries with it a relation to our fellow-Christians, and in this relationship is involved that spirit of constant thought and unselfish love for our brethren which marks the true Christian life.

---

1 A most helpful treatment of this wonderful prayer of the Apostle will be found in Bishop Moule's *Romans,* "Expositor's Bible" (p. 403). Perhaps the writer may also refer to his own little book, *Royal and Loyal* (ch. v.) for yet another meditation on these words.

2. *The Definite Purpose of Christian Brotherhood.* "For his good to edification." There are few things more noteworthy in the New Testament than the Apostolic emphasis on "edification." It is the supreme purpose of God for the Church as inculcated by the Apostle (1 Cor. xiv. 4; Eph. ii. 21; iv. 12, 16). Passage after passage in St. Paul's writings has this thought of "edification" as the dominant idea in the Christian life of the individual and of the community. We are brothers in Christ for the one sole purpose of doing our share towards the upbuilding of character and conduct, so that thereby the Divine purpose may be fully realized, and the temple of God, the Church, which is His body, erected and brought to completion.

3. *The Perfect Standard of Christian Brotherhood.* Once more let us look at the three references in this brief section to the example of Christ. (*a*) "Christ pleased not Himself" (ver. 3); (*b*) "according to Christ Jesus" (ver. 5); (*c*) "as Christ also received you" (ver. 7). Nothing could be simpler and yet more searching than this requirement. We are indeed to "follow His steps," and "walk as He walked."

4. *The Divine Source of Christian Brotherhood.* Three titles of God in this passage indicate the graces that we need and the source from which we obtain them: (*a*) "The God of patience" (or endurance, or steadfastness); (*b*) "the God of consolation" (or encouragement, or comfort); (*c*) "the God of hope." With our hearts fixed upon God as the source of all grace Christian brotherhood becomes blessedly possible.

5. *The Glorious Results of Christian Brotherhood.* It is only necessary to mention once again, as suggested by the Apostle's prayer, the wonderful outcome of fellowship as it affects the Christian life. (*a*) The fulness of joy; (*b*) the fulness of peace; (*c*) the abundance of hope; (*d*) the constant and ever-increasing glory of God (vers. 6, 7, 9).

LXII

MOTIVES AND METHODS

Rom. xv. 14-16.

14. And I myself also am persuaded of you, my brethren, that ye also are full of goodness, filled with all knowledge, able also to admonish one another.

15. Nevertheless, brethren, I have written the more boldly unto you in some sort, as putting you in mind, because of the grace that is given to me of God,

16. That I should be the minister of Jesus Christ to the Gentiles, ministering the gospel of God, that the offering up of the Gentiles might be acceptable, being sanctified by the Holy Ghost.

The Epistle proper is now closed, and St. Paul passes from exhortations to explain his own motives and intentions in writing. He thus recurs to those personal elements with which the Epistle opened (ch. i. 1-16). The reference, in the form of a paragraph, to the Old Testament in regard to the actual call to Gentiles as well as to Jews, is the point of transition to this courteous and affectionate explanation which tells the Roman Christians why he had written, and also why he had not yet been able to visit them. The rest of the chapter is concerned with his personal explanations, and after a special reference to the Christians at Rome (ver. 14), and to himself as an Apostle (ver. 16), he proceeds in verses 16-33 to give four grounds of personal justification for writing to them. The spiritual truths of the entire passage are many, and each section in turn calls for close study and meditation.

I. *The Apostle's Courtesy* (ver. 14).—With remarkable wisdom and tact he approaches them, pointing out that although he admonishes and exhorts he is nevertheless convinced that they themselves, without any admonition from him, are full of those qualifications for helping others which are so essential in the Christian Church.

This noble courtesy is eminently noteworthy. In verse 13 he had prayed that the believers at Rome might be filled with all joy and peace and hope, and throughout the Epistle he had been teaching, guiding, and exhorting them. But he wishes them to know that all this does not mean any self-exaltation above them; they are his "brethren." Nor is he ignorant of their really remarkable Christian attainments, or merely echoing the almost universal report in their favor (ch. i. 8). He is perfectly aware of their capable Christian life which had impressed him with a personal conviction concerning their proficiency in all necessary service. This attitude of true spiritual delicacy is a fine illustration of the Spirit of Christ in the great Apostle. St. Peter shows a similar attitude when he tells those to whom he writes that he is not addressing them as though they were ignorant, but to stir up their pure minds in the way of remembrance, since they already knew the truth and were established in it (2 Pet. i. 12-14; iii. 1). In like manner, St. Paul tells his converts in so many words that he has no thought of being a spiritual dictator to them. And yet we all know that notwithstanding the fullest knowledge, or the highest goodness, we are in constant need of having the same things repeated again and again. To know our duty is not always to do it, and the Gospel provides for opportunities of reminder and methods of moral suasion. An inspired Apostle of Christ might well have been expected to write in a tone of great authority, but his constant thought was that he had no dominion over his converts' faith, but was only a helper of their joy (2 Cor. i. 24). True ministers of the Gospel will always adopt and maintain a similar attitude.

Mark the three qualifications here mentioned in connection with the Christians at Rome: "Full of goodness"; "filled with all knowledge"; "able also to admonish one another." (*a*) They were "full of goodness." Their Christian life had become thoroughly settled and grounded in character, and "goodness" is the highest possible proof of our religion. "He was a good man" is the word concerning Barnabas, and when people are "full of goodness," they have reached the highest point of Christian possibility. (*b*) They were "filled with all knowledge." This no doubt refers to spiritual perception rather than mere intellectual attainment. As such, it is the direct result of goodness. It is only the "good" who "know." Goodness invariably produces Christian insight, spiritual perception and a consciousness of Divine truths which cannot be obtained in any other way. It is well known that some of the humblest and most ignorant, unlettered people, so far as this world is concerned, are possessed of the profoundest spiritual experiences by reason of their fellowship with their Master. (*c*) They were "able also to admonish one another." This naturally followed from the two preceding qualities. Because they were good and had spiritual insight they were able to administer the necessary guidance or correction to their fellow-Christians, and thus help forward the life of the Church. The combination of "goodness' and "knowledge" was the secret of their power over others. The two should always go together, and neither of them alone is sufficient for the duty of "admonishing" our brethren. Happy the Christian community of which these three things are true; that they possess goodness, knowledge, and helpfulness.

II. *The Apostle's Courage* (ver. 15).—Having thus endeavored to remove from their minds anything that might have created an unfavorable influence on their attitude to him, he proceeds to say why he felt it necessary to address them at such length. He has dared the more boldly to write this Epistle on account of their possession of these spiritual gifts, though his boldness might seem greater than was warranted by his reference to the weak ones in ch. xv. 1. "In some sort" means "in some degree," referring to those parts of the Epistle which are more bold than others. It has been suggested that the following passages are specially applicable to this thought of frankness: ch. vi. 12-21; xi. 17, 18; xii. 3; xiii. 3, 4; and specially ch. xiv. 1-xv. 13. Godet, however, thinks that the phrase "in part" does not refer to the contents of the teaching, but to the *method* of giving instruction. St. Paul is writing to them, not with the view of teaching what was new, but reminding them of things known "in part," or "to a certain degree." He wished to treat them, not as learners, but as mature brethren in Christ. Whichever view we take of this expression we again notice St. Paul's courtesy and modesty. His boldness, as we shall see in a moment, is due to his position as the Apostle of the Gentiles, but he was fully aware that the discussion of truths already familiar was only part of his design. The Epistle records some of the profoundest thoughts ever expressed by the human mind, and this also was "in part" his aim in writing. Yet of this he says nothing, for he is more than content to let them discover for themselves that in writing as he has they have unwittingly, but really, obtained unfathomable treasures of Christian truth.

III. *The Apostle's Claim* (ver. 16).—It is his calling as the Apostle to the Gentiles that gives him the right to address them. "That I should be a minister of Christ Jesus unto the Gentiles, ministering the Gospel of God, that the offering up of the Gentiles might be made acceptable, being sanctified by the Holy Spirit." In these words he likens himself and his work to the priest of old. The preaching of the Gospel is his priestly function, and the believing Gentile constitute his offering to God. As a preacher, he is doing the work of a priest, and each time he preaches he performs an act of priestly consecration. It need hardly be said that this passage is no exception to the well-known fact that the Christian ministry is never described technically in the New Testament as a priesthood. The term "priest" (ἱερεύς) in the singular number is never applied to anyone in connection with Christianity but the Lord Jesus Christ Himself—not even to the individual Christian. The only reference to Christians in regard to priesthood is either the use of the plural (Rev. i. 6), or else a word implying the Church in its collective capacity (1 Pet. ii. 5, 9). The essential function of a priest is the representation of man to God (Heb. v. 1), and when this is clearly understood it is at once obvious that there is nothing in which the Christian minister, or layman, can be the representative of his fellows to God. Christianity provides for each man to enter and abide in the Divine presence for himself. In public worship the minister is often necessarily the mouthpiece of the congregation, but this is not a priestly, only a ministerial function. So the passage before us is altogether in line with the rest of the New Testament.

We should with these verses compare ch. xii. 1. In the latter the believer presents himself a living sacrifice to God. In the former the Gospel laborer is the offerer, his offering being the converts given him by God. But "the offering of the nations" is only acceptable to God as "sanctified in the Holy Ghost," and since we know that "they that are in the flesh cannot please God," we recall the Apostle's words that Christians are "not in the flesh, but in the Spirit" (ch. viii. 8, 9).

As we have already noticed, this short passage is a marvelous revelation of St. Paul's personal spiritual life. Let us concentrate attention on the aspects of Christian service here delineated (vers. 15, 16).

1. *The Source of Ministry.* "The grace that was given me of God." Only by the grace of God can our service be acceptable. It is God's work, and the power to do it must come from God. That is why the Apostle said, "Not I, but the grace of God" (1 Cor. xv. 10).

2. *The Purpose of Ministry.* "That I should be a minister of Christ Jesus." What a privilege it is to be a Temple servant, a public functionary belonging to Jesus Christ. "Such honor have all His saints." The word used here is that found in ch. xiii. 4 of civil rulers. Paul recognizes his work as having just as much authority and importance as the office of an Emperor or King.

3. *The Sphere of Ministry.* "Unto the Gentiles." This was the special place in which God had set the Apostle. He was commissioned to the whole Gentile world. He has already told us that he felt indebted to the Gentiles as well as to the Jew (ch. i. 14). To St. Paul in his day, and to us in ours, the evangelization of the world is our highest obligation and most pressing duty. We have no right whatever to limit salvation to home fields, and we should resolutely face this universal sphere as the one in which God's purposes of grace find their culmination.

4. *The Work of Ministry.* The second word used by the Apostle in this passage in connection with his service is, as we have seen, very suggestive: "Ministering the Gospel of God." Thus there are two ideas, the ambassador and the priest. Our work is at once kingly and priestly. We are to show the boldness of the public official and the tenderness of the personal priest. The Apostle's

conception of his work is sacrificial, and while he was in no sense a mediator his labor consisted in something more than mere teaching; his entire life of service was an act of consecration as he offered himself to God on behalf of his work. This is the spirit of true service, and the more we realize the *cost* of our work the more effective will it be.

5. *The End of Ministry.* "That the offering of the Gentiles may be acceptable." The purpose of his efforts was to bring about such changes in the lives of the people that they should be made an offering well-pleasing to God. The work would not be done at once, but would be ever growing and deepening as he was able to proclaim the Gospel, and the people were enabled to receive it and reproduce it in their lives. This thought of converts as an acceptable offering to God should impress itself upon the heart of every Christian worker as the end and object of all service.

6. *The Crown of Ministry.* "Sanctified." This was to be the result of the acceptable offering of the Gentiles. Their lives should be consecrated to God. Sin tends inevitably to separate man from God, and through the reconciliation of the Gospel the sinner is brought back, not merely to forgiveness, but that his life may be possessed and used by God for His service.

7. *The Guarantee of Ministry.* "In the Holy Ghost." This is the supreme thought in connection with all work for God, the presence and power of the Holy Spirit, and this it is that makes the difference between work that is real and work that is not. Only as we labor in the energy of the Divine grace shall we find our service of any effect either to God or to man. The mighty work of the world's evangelization must be in the power of the Holy Spirit if it is to be of any value.

LXIII

A WORKER'S VINDICATION

ROM. xv. 17-21.

17. I have therefore whereof I may glory through Jesus Christ in those things which pertain to God.

18. For I will not dare to speak of any of those things which Christ hath not wrought by me, to make the Gentiles obedient, by word and deed.

19. Through mighty signs and wonders, by the power of the Spirit of God; so that from Jerusalem, and round about unto Illyricum, I have fully preached the Gospel of Christ.

20. Yea, so have I strived to preach the Gospel, not where Christ was named, lest I should build upon another man's foundation:

21. But as it is written, To whom he was not spoken of, they shall see: and they that have not heard shall understand.

THE Apostle is still intent on putting himself on the best possible terms with readers who have not yet met him. He has pleaded his office as Apostle to the Gentiles in support of his action in addressing this letter to them. Now he takes a further step and states with exquisite simplicity and true Christian modesty that he is not only an Apostle, but an Apostle who has been used of God in his work. In this courteous and tender way he desires to commend himself to the believers in Rome.

I. *The Apostle's Boasting* (ver. 17).—Here again he uses the word "boasting" which, as we have seen (vol. i. p. 160), is capable of being separated from its unworthy associations. He has justification for boasting in Christ in relation to those things which God had used him to accomplish. He had no thought of magnifying himself, for his glorying was "in Christ Jesus," and the Gospel of which he was the instrument in preaching did not belong to him. His share was wholly ministerial; all that he desired to do was to glory in his Master in regard to the successful discharge of his work as a servant of the Gospel. He felt that he had this privilege of boasting; "I possess, therefore, the boasting in Christ Jesus," and yet with the privilege there was the immediate result of his subjection to the Master from Whom all grace had come.

II. *The Apostle's Humility* (ver. 18).—He will only speak of his own labors, and will not dare to refer to anything in which he had no personal share. It would be the highest presumption to mention anything outside his own sphere. This method of expression is probably due to his sensitiveness of anything like the idea of superiority over others. While his sphere was pre-eminently that of the Apostle to the Gentiles, yet he will carefully limit himself to those things in which Christ had used him, thus recognizing with becoming modesty that others have been laboring in the same sphere as himself. And even though he speaks of his own labors, yet he at once lays the emphasis on Christ rather than on himself, "those which Christ wrought through me." This combination of boasting and humility is particularly striking and indicates the true servant of Jesus Christ.

III. *The Apostle's Frankness* (vers. 18, 19).—Now he will speak in the plainest terms of the remarkable nature and extent of his service in the Gospel. Its character is evident from the description: "word and deed, in the power of signs and wonders in the power of the Holy Spirit" (R.V.). It was impossible to overlook the power and blessing of his labors in leading Gentiles to the foot of the Cross. In this plain statement we have the vindication of the Apostleship of St. Paul, and his appeal to the fact of "signs and wonders" shows conclusively that these things must have taken place, or he could have been answered by testimony and silenced for ever. Nothing short of deception on the part of a vast number of converts can explain their silence as to these claims to the working of miracles, and everything that we know of the Apostle and his life, surrounded as it was with virulent opposition, goes to show the reality of the claim here made.

IV. *The Apostle's Testimony* (ver. 19).—The scope and extent of the work were as remarkable as its nature, for he had been able to proclaim the Gospel from Jerusalem right to the north-west of

Macedonia. Illyricum may be the Roman province (also called Dalmatia), which was north of Macedonia and west of Thrace; or it may have been the Illyrican country in the Roman province of Macedonia. Dr. Beet thinks that it corresponds roughly to the present Turkish province of Albania. The remarkable width and extent of his labors are evident, and again we are faced with a claim which nothing but absolute fact could substantiate. His method of expressing what he had done is particularly significant: "I have fully preached the Gospel of Christ." The thought is not merely that of faithful, but of complete preaching. He had announced his message as fully as it was possible to do it, and had published the joyous tidings at the chief centers on his way from Jerusalem to Illyricum.

The history in the Acts reveals something of the strategy of the Apostle. His main thought was to concentrate on great centers, and by limiting his own evangelistic labors to these places the message of the Gospel could then be carried by the churches in the cities into the rural districts around. We know that although he was very near Colosse he never visited the place, which was evangelized by one of his own converts, Epaphras (Col. i. 6, 7; see ii. 1). This strategical method shows the true Christian statesman, and might almost warrant the assertion of the principle, "Take care of the cities and the villages will take care of themselves." This may not be as true today as in St. Paul's time, for conditions vary considerably, but there is a truth even for us in the constant insistence upon strengthening to the fullest extent our labors in great centers of population. The Apostle's prolonged stay at places like Corinth and Ephesus proved beyond question what he meant by "fully preaching" the Gospel of Christ. How marvelous were these efforts of the tireless, courageous, pioneer worker, more especially, as while writing this Epistle, he was contemplating a further extension of work in far-off Spain. If only the Church of God today had more men of this type the whole world could soon be evangelized.

V. *The Apostle's Aim* (vers. 20, 21).—In all this work he had one dominant thought; indeed, the expression he uses indicates something like "ambition." He endeavored to preach the Gospel only where Christ had not been named. He was particularly anxious not to build upon another man's foundation, and he made it a matter of personal honor to work on virgin soil. To confirm this he quotes from Isa. lii. 15, thus again supporting the reality of his Apostleship to the Gentiles by a reference to the Jewish Scriptures. This intense longing to let people know of Christ who had never before heard of Him is a special call to the churches today who are crowding workers into the home field and doing comparatively little for the "regions beyond." Happy is that Christian, and happy is that community, where the Apostle's aim is set first and foremost.

As we review this brief yet pregnant section we are impressed with the simple but significant way in which the Apostle reveals some of the essentials of Christian service.

1. *Work for God should be marked by Definite Results* (ver. 18). God does not intend any of us to labor in vain, or spend our strength for nought, and, though results may vary, we are justified in expecting them if only we are faithful to the Gospel and to the true methods of proclaiming it. Of course it is essential to distinguish between "having" results and "seeing" them, and it is the former rather than the latter that should be kept in mind. God may often grant results which are invisible to the worker. And yet if a man is working for God year after year without seeing some fruit of his labor, he may well ask himself whether he is serving God where or as his Master desires.

2. *The Worker as an Instrument, not an Agent* (ver. 18). The Apostle gloried in Christ, and spoke of those things that Christ had wrought through him. This is the true attitude of the Christian worker: God is the real worker and the Christian is the tool. We are sometimes inclined to think that we are to work and to call in God as our helper. The proper attitude is that of God as the Agent and the believer as His instrument. We do not overlook the fact that instruments or tools have no wills, but even this does not make a fundamental distinction, because, as Tennyson says, "Our wills are ours to make them Thine." As the Lord Himself always did the will of His Father, and the words that He spoke and the works that He performed were not His own but His Father's, so it is our privilege, as it ought to be our glory, to be as ready for the Master's use as

the pen or the chisel in the hand of a workman. When Joshua went up to the stranger before Jericho he asked whether He was for Israel or for their enemies. The significant answer came that He was neither "for" one or the other. He had not come to assist, but to take charge, to supercede Joshua, and to control the affairs of Israel. At once Joshua recognized the state of the case and said, "What saith my Lord unto His servant" (Josh. v. 14). It will make all the difference to our Christian work if we realize that it is "Not I, but Christ"; "Not I, but the grace of God."

3. *The Practical Purpose of Christian Work* (ver. 18). The one and all-embracing purpose stated by the Apostle is "the obedience of the Gentiles." It is identical with what he describes elsewhere as "the obedience of faith" (ch. i. 5; xvi. 26). Our work is nothing less, and it can be nothing more than this, to bring men into subjection to God, and to that obedience which is the expression of faith in Him. Everything is to converge to this end. All knowledge, all privileges, all experience, all blessings, are intended to express themselves in simple, loyal, constant obedience. It would simplify our work for God if we ever kept in view our one object of bringing God to man and man to God.

4. *Variety of Methods in Christian Work* (ver. 18). The Apostle was not confined to one plan of making known the Gospel of Christ. Sometimes it was done by word, sometimes by deed. But whatever was the method the object was the same. Christian workers will be well advised to make their methods as varied as possible. God has many ways of approaching men and there are many avenues of entrance into His kingdom. Be it ours to keep a sharp look out for every method new and old whereby men may be brought face to face with Christ.

5. *The Divine Demonstration of Christian Work* (ver. 19). The Apostle was able to speak of signs and wonders in the power of the Spirit of God, and although in one sense we do not experience today what was then regarded as miraculous, the Spirit of God is still at work and sets his seal on our ministry by working miracles of grace. God still shows His power, and difficulties are a challenge to His Divine working. The supreme need of every worker at home and

abroad is the possession and power of the Holy Spirit, and when He is manifested in heart and life the results are in demonstration of the grace and blessing of God. The mighty work here depicted is altogether beyond the power even of a mighty thinker and worker like St. Paul. It must be the work of the Holy Spirit, and only as this Divine energy possesses the worker can he expect the results to accrue.

6. *The Remarkable Thoroughness of Christian Work* (ver. 19). The more we ponder the Apostle's words the more deeply we are impressed with the reality of his service extending over so many years. There was a deep hunger for the souls of men that prompted him to preach fully the Gospel of Christ in such a remarkable way and to such a wide extent. He eagerly longed for everyone to know that which was everything to him. The need of this missionary spirit which prompts us to take the Gospel all over the world is becoming more and more widely felt among the churches, and we do well to pray that God will constantly put and keep this earnest desire and definite aim in the hearts of His people. It must be an exquisite joy to tell someone of Christ who has never before heard of Him: to be the first to narrate "the Sweet Story of Old" to some heart which without knowing it may have been longing for the satisfaction that Christ alone can give.

> "Let us go to the regions beyond,
> Where the Story has never been told;
> To the millions who never of Jesus have heard,
> Let us take the 'Sweet Story of Old.'"

7. *The Persistent Plan in Christian Work* (ver. 20). The Apostle had a definite aim, one of the three points of "honor," or "ambition," mentioned in the New Testament in connection with him. His first "ambition" was to be "acceptable" to his Lord and Master (2 Cor. v. 9). His second "ambition" was to be simple, quiet, consistent in ordinary Christian living (1 Thess. iv. 11). Here we notice his third "ambition," that of proclaiming Christ wherever He had not been named. This definite plan indicates one of the most important features of Christian work today. If only we observed the Apostle's rule how easy it would be to prevent overlapping in work for God.

It is a thousand pities when the whole world is practically open to the Churches of Christ that there should ever be an instance of more than one evangelical community working in any small or contracted sphere. Both at home and abroad there should be clear lines of delimitation, and particular churches should be left free to proclaim the Gospel within these borders, following such a definite plan as is here indicated. Christian work should always be marked by thought, consideration, wisdom and statesmanship. As it has been well put, "First plan your work, and then work your plan."

LXIV

A WORKER'S PLANS

Rom. xv. 22-29.

22. For which cause also I have been much hindered from coming to you.
23. But now having no more place in these parts, and having a great desire these many years to come unto you;
24. Whensoever I take my journey into Spain, I will come to you: for I trust to see you in my journey, and to be brought on my way thitherward by you, if first I be somewhat filled with your *company*.
25. But now I go unto Jerusalem to minister unto the saints.
26. For it hath pleased them of Macedonia and Achaia to make a certain contribution for the poor saints which are at Jerusalem.
27. It hath pleased them verily; and their debtors they are. For if the Gentiles have been made partakers of their spiritual things, their duty is also to minister unto them in carnal things.
28. When therefore I have performed this, and have sealed to them this fruit, I will come by you into Spain.
29. And I am sure that, when I come unto you, I shall come in the fulness of the blessing of the gospel of Christ.

St. Paul now gives the third proof of his interest in the Christians at Rome by referring to his plans for visiting them. Difficulties seemed to be clearing, and the way was apparently opening for his coming. We have in these simple statements another interesting and even remarkable revelation of the Apostle's character and life.

I. *Hindrances* (ver. 22).—His immense labors throughout the 1400 miles of territory mentioned in the former section had long prevented him from fulfilling his intense desire of visiting Rome. The way in which he states the difficulties should be noted. "Again and again I was hindered many times." Indeed, it was an almost constant succession of difficulties. All this shows that the Apostle's work was carefully arranged and not prosecuted on any haphazard plan.

II. *Openings* (ver. 23).—It is surprising that he is able to say he has "no more place in these parts." This can only mean that there was no locality still unevangelized; no place where he had not in one way or another proclaimed the Gospel. It cannot mean that he had been everywhere himself, for we know that it was his custom to concentrate on important strategical centers; but it certainly implies that by means of the efforts of those whom he had led to Christ all these regions had been thoroughly evangelized. The way was therefore open for him to proceed further west, taking Rome on his way to Spain. The tireless, eager Evangelist was ever on the alert for fresh fields to conquer for his Master.

III. *Longings* (ver. 23).—"Having a great desire these many years to come unto you." Here again he recurs to his intense longing to get to Rome (ch. i. 10, 11). It was legitimate that he should be influenced by this desire, for as Apostle to the Gentiles it was the most natural thing for him to wish to be at the center and heart of his great field. While he was of course ready to go to the place where God wished him to be, the Divine will was doubtless often indicated by the servant's personal desires, or by some natural yet providential circumstances. It was no mere wish to visit a great metropolis, but an intense longing to witness for his Master in the very heart of heathendom.

IV. *Intentions* (ver. 24).—The Apostle's purpose was to go to Spain, taking Rome by the way. He could have reached his goal direct by an easy voyage, though he did not wish to do this, but, instead, to make a stay in the metropolis. Whether his purpose of reaching Spain was ever accomplished is altogether unknown, and probably will never be settled by any historical discovery. So far as we can trace, no primitive tradition connects St. Paul with Spain. The fact that he here expresses his purpose does not of necessity imply its fulfilment. The Holy Spirit doubtless had been leading him to desire and endeavor to go to the "boundary of the West." But this in itself was no assurance that the hopes would be accomplished. It is impossible to avoid recalling the fact that the Pauline Gospel was remarkably powerful in Spain in the sixteenth century until it was utterly crushed by the horrors of the Inquisition. Once again Spain is becoming open to the Gospel, and St. Paul is visiting that country through his Epistles. Much remains to be done and hindrances are still mighty, but in spite of them all "the Gospel according to St. Paul" will penetrate into every part of that beautiful and as yet dark land.

V. *Hopes* (ver. 24).—The personal reference to his visit to Rome is a fine illustration of the Apostle's desire for Christian fellowship and the exquisite courtesy and tact with which he states his expectation of it. He hopes to see the Christians in Rome on his journey, and to be escorted by them after having had the enjoyment of their company. Let us notice the exact statement. "If first I be somewhat filled with your company." Quite literally we may render the words, "somewhat enjoyed you" (*cf.* ch. 1. 12). The "somewhat" means "not as much as I might wish, but as far as circumstances will allow." It indicates in a very beautfiul way that the Christians at Rome would have more to give than he would have time to receive. This expression of a desire and hope for Christian fellowship on the part of a strong, self-contained man like St. Paul is a striking testimony to the power of the new company of Christians and of the grace of Christ abiding among them.

VI. *Projects* (vers. 25-28).—Meanwhile the Apostle had a very important work immediately in front of him. He was on his way to Jerusalem, carrying with him contributions to the Christians in Macedonia and Achaia for the poor among the saints in the mother city. Persecution had doubtless led to poverty. The fact of a man's profession of Christianity would easily lead, as it has done since, to the loss of custom and the deprivation of employment. Hence the need of a wide appeal to Gentile Christians to support these poor believers in Jerusalem. This collection was one of St. Paul's great thoughts at that time (Acts xx. 4; 1 Cor. xvi. 1-4; 2 Cor. viii., ix; Gal. vi. 10). It was not merely an opportunity for the exercise of Christian benevolence, but something far more important; it was a splendid means of accomplishing one of the deepest purposes of the Apostle, the union of Jewish and Gentile Christians and the realization that they were one body in Christ. We know from other Epistles how heavily this burden was laid upon his heart, and how in every available way he endeavored to bring the two great sections of Christians together.

Here, however, he is concerned with the relationship of the two bodies of Christians, and he shows there was a sense in which the Gentiles were indebted to the Jews for their very Christianity (ver. 27). If spiritual blessings had accrued to the Gentiles from the Jews it was not surprising that some part of the debt should be repaid in things temporal. A similar distinction between the "carnal" and the "spiritual" is used by the Apostle in connection with the Christian ministry (1 Cor. ix. 11). This is one of the instances of the mutual relationship of Jew and Gentile on which he dwelt with such force in chapter xi.

The importance of the project is abundantly evident from the words, "When therefore I have performed this, and have sealed to them this fruit." The "fruit" was the product of his proper work, and the "sealing" was the official completion and consummation of the task. He felt that it was part of his duty as Apostle to the Gentiles, himself a Jew, to deliver this gift safely and to make sure that the project was accomplished. There were others who could have taken the money with as much safety as Paul himself, but his purpose in going on this mission was to do his utmost to disarm Jewish jealousy with regard to himself and the Gentiles. Nothing short of this could possibly have kept him from going westwards to Rome and Spain. This done he would be altogether free to realize his hopes of reaching the terminus of Gentile opportunity, as it was in his day.[1]

VII. *Convictions* (ver. 29).—Now the Apostle turns with evident relief to the contemplation of his westward journey, and without any hesitation he expresses his conviction that when he comes it will be "in the fulness of the blessing of the Gospel of Christ." This was the one thing of which he was absolutely sure. He had prayed for a prosperous journey (ch. i. 10); he had expressed his readiness if opportunity offered to preach the Gospel in Rome (ch. i. 15); he had also told them of his intense desire to go to Spain ((vers.

1 It is impossible to avoid calling attention to Paley's *Horae Paulinae,* in which the passages in Acts and the Epistles in regard to this collection for the saints at Jerusalem are brought together and carefully discussed. As a piece of New Testament evidence Paley's work is as original as it is permanently valuable.

23, 24). But all these were merely among possibilities and contingencies which might or might not be transformed into actualities. The one thing of which he was perfectly certain was that if the way opened and he had his desires realized it would be in close association with "the fulness of the blessing of Christ" (R.V.). Not only would he as an Apostle be enabled to bestow upon them the gifts of the Holy Spirit (ch. i. 11), but he himself would experience spiritual blessing at their hands (ch. i. 12). He was sure that God would give success to his Gospel, and that when he was present the fulness of the Divine blessing would be realized, and the visit fraught with the happiest results to him and to them.

In this section we have suggestions from one of the greatest of Christian workers in regard to the varied experiences of service for Christ.

1. *Difficulties in Daily Work* (ver. 22). The hindrances which the Apostle experienced are not different in kind from those that constantly arise in connection wtih Christian work. We must not be surprised by such hindrances. Satan does not easily relinquish any of his subjects, and when the Gospel of Christ is proclaimed it requires obedience (ver. 18), and thus is pretty certain to meet with opposition of various kinds. The boy's definition of difficulty as "a thing to be got over" may well be laid to heart by all Christian workers.

2. *Desire for Further Service* (ver. 23). The Apostle was never tired of serving Christ. He was doubtless often wearied *in* the work, but never *of* it, and when an opportunity for serving his Master came to an end in one place he was ready to turn eagerly to another. This is always the mark of a true laborer. "Something attempted, something done" is not intended to earn "repose," but to be the preparation and inspiration for something else to be accomplished. Let us heed the Apostle's example of being always occupied in some way in his Master's vineyard.

3. *Delight in Christian Fellowship* (ver. 24). How great was the pleasure the Apostle had in the society of his fellow-believers. Christians ought to rejoice in meeting one another, however much hitherto they may have been strangers according to the flesh. The

more Christian fellowship we can realize and cultivate the greater the power and blessing that will accrue to the Church as a whole and the particular community with which we are associated. Every Christian has some gift of God, and we ought to welcome every occasion of realizing our oneness in Christ, and at the same time of learning lessons that are being taught to others and of receiving blessings from God through them. A large-hearted fellowship that endeavors to see Christ in all those who name Him is one of the finest illustrations of the true spirit of the Gospel.

4. *Duty to Fellow-Christians* (vers. 25-27). Fellowship means something more than enjoyment; it calls for effort, and if necessary even self-sacrifice. The Apostle concentrated his attention on helping the poor saints in Jerusalem, and wherever we can find any member of "the household of faith" it is our bounden duty to do him "good" as one of the most signal proofs of our Christlikeness and our essential unity in Him. The New Testament makes very prominent this thought of practical fellowship, and it will be in every way spiritual uplifting if we do the same.

5. *Dependence upon God* (vers. 28, 29). In all our service for Christ we must never forget that God is to come first. Amidst all the hopes, desires, longings, intentions, aspirations, purposes, determinations, St. Paul never forgot that it was only as he lived in the fulness of blessing that blessing could accrue to others through him. It is a temptation on the part of workers to continue their service without due regard to the Source and Sphere of spiritual power. Our work will never rise higher than our character, and our character will never be stronger than the measure of our communion with Christ. Be it ours to live in union and communion with Him, and then our service will be inevitably and increasingly blessed.

LXV

A WORKER'S NEED

Rom. xv. 30-33.

30. Now I beseech you, brethren, for the Lord Jesus Christ's sake, and for the love of the Spirit, that ye strive together with me in *your* prayers to God for me;
31. That I may be delivered from them that do not believe in Judæa; and that my service which *I have* for Jerusalem may be accepted of the saints;
32. That I may come unto you with joy by the will of God, and may with you be refreshed.
33. Now the God of peace *be* with you all. Amen.

It was evident that St. Paul was full of deep anxiety, as he faced his journey to Jerusalem. His fear was twofold. On the one hand, he contemplated the possibility of opposition from unbelieving Jews who hated him, and persecuted him on every occasion. On the other hand, he was uncertain whether the gift from the Gentile Churches, of which he was the bearer, would be found acceptable by the narrow, bigoted, Jewish Christians at Jerusalem. We know from the history how well grounded the fear of opposition was (Acts xx. 3, 22; xxi. 11). Hence a great peril was before him, and he was clearly in doubt, indeed, was in great fear as to the result. He was suspected to such an extent by his enemies that he hoped the contribution he was bringing would be a means of producing peace.

I. *An Ernest Request for Prayer* (ver. 30).—The wording is particularly significant. "Now I beseech you, brethren." Paul had often prayed for them (ch. i. 9, 10), and now he beseeches them to pray for him. His anxiety for their prayers is a mark of his confidence in them. He knew them to be a praying Church.

II. *A Definite Motive for Prayer* (ver. 30).—The Apostle dwells upon a twofold motive, or, perhaps it would be more correct to say, two distinct though connected motives. This first is "for the Lord Jesus Christ's sake," that is, "by the feelings towards Christ that actuate you." The cause of Christ was undoubtedly involved in the Apostle's circumstances, and any failure in his mission would be taken to reflect upon the Master Himself. No wonder that he begs them to pray "by our Lord Jesus Christ." The other motive is "for the love of the Spirit." This seems to mean the love of God which the Holy Spirit sheds abroad in the hearts of all Christians (ch. v. 5). The reference would thus be to the love which Christians have one to another, and it is termed "the love of the Spirit" because it is produced in the heart by the Spirit of God. Other writers suggest that the interpretation is "the love which the Holy Spirit has to Christians," and while this is no doubt true in itself it may be questioned whether it is the meaning of the present passage. In another Epistle St. Paul speaks of "the fellowship of the Spirit" (Phil. ii. 1), which seems to mean the fellowship produced in Christian hearts by the Holy Spirit. Godet thinks that "the love of the Spirit" means "that love which is necessarily different from the love that exists between persons who know one another individually." In either case this twofold motive for prayer is very notable. By their feeling towards our Lord and also towards His Apostle, as expressed in the Holy Spirit's gift of love, they were to pray for him.

III. *A Striking Description of Prayer* (ver. 30).—"That ye strive together with me in your prayers to God for me." Prayer is here shown to be a struggle, for the word "strive" is used as of an athletic contest. More than once the Apostle employs this term, indicating that there are hostile powers to be faced whenever prayer is offered. He here associates the Roman Christians in his own prayers for himself. It would be well if we realized more frequently than we do the seriousness of prayer, that it is indeed "the Christian's vital breath." Instead of prayer being the easiest, it is the hardest work of the Christian, because principalities and powers of evil combine to oppose the progress of the soul in prayer, and thereby to hinder the Divine answers. St. Paul was anxious that his Colossian friends should know what his own prayers for them meant in the way of strife, struggle, and contest (Col. ii. 1), and in his description of Epaphras the same thought is found: "always striving for you in prayers" (Col. iv. 12).

IV. *A Threefold Petition in Prayer* (vers. 31, 32).—Three objects are specified, as to which the Apostle was keenly anxious: (*a*) To be delivered from the unbelieving Jews; (*b*) to have his ministration accepted by the Christians in Jerusalem; (*c*) to come to Rome with joy by the will of God, and to find rest in Christian fellowship there. The first of these petitions is a very natural one because the opposition of the vast majority of the Jews was a real force, especially as directed against St. Paul. His transformation from one of the ablest opponents of Christianity to one of its ablest advocates was particularly hateful to his fellow-countrymen, and he had nothing to expect but virulent hostility which might easily go to extreme lengths. We know indeed from the history how far the Jews were prepared to carry their opposition to St. Paul (Acts xxi.-xxvi.). It is almost incredible, did we not know it for fact, to read of the intensely bitter spirit with which they dogged his steps and used their utmost endeavors to get him within their power. But even the prospect of this danger could not deter him from going, because he felt that it was his Master's will, and more than once during his journey he expressed his readiness to suffer and to die if necessary (Acts xx. 22-24; xxi. 13).

The second petition was that the Apostle's service might be acceptable when he reached Jerusalem. In the ordinary course of events a gift like this could not have been other than welcome, but the prejudices and animosities against St. Paul on the subject of the uncircumcised Gentile Christians were so intense that he evidently feared that even a generous gift, especially with himself as the instrumentality, might fail of acceptance. That he had reason to fear rejection of his loving and large-hearted proposal seems to be pretty evident from the story of his reception in Jerusalem, and yet he was determined to make the attempt because of its far-reaching influence, if successful, in leading to the real union of Jewish and Gentile believers in Christ.

The third petition had reference to himself. He desired to come to Rome with joy instead of being weighted down with the sorrow of a failure at Jerusalem, and he wished this to take place "by the will of God," and not merely by reason of his own intense desire to see them. Further, he wished that in coming, there might be a mutual refreshment of rest, and enjoyment of spirit on both sides: on his, after his anxieties; on theirs, after their fears lest he should not come.

V. *A Definite Blessing through Prayer* (ver. 33).—Now the Apostle himself prays as he commends them to "the God of peace." This title of God is of special force in connection with the Apostle's anxieties and fears of trouble. Peace was the supreme object of all his prayers and efforts, and it could only come from the God of peace. It is the fourth title of God found in this chapter: "the God of patience" (ver. 5); "the God of consolation" (ver. 5); "the God of hope" (ver. 13); "the God of peace" (ver. 33). The last-named title is found very frequently in the Pauline writings, and seems invariably to unite the ideas of peace between God and man, issuing in peace between Christian brethren (Phil. iv. 9; 1 Thess. v. 23; Heb. xiii. 20).

In these verses we gain a clear insight into the Apostle's view of prayer in relation to service. It was to him the prime secret of blessing in Christian work.

1. *The Fellowship of Prayer.* The Apostle often sought the prayers of his Christian brethren. We might have thought of him as so strong in Christ as not to need the cheer derived from association in intercession with his fellow-believers. But his very strength led him to desire this oneness with his brethren. He had a profound consciousness of the manifold variety of grace in the Church and this led him to seek the prayers of those who knew how to approach the throne of God. It was no weakness that prompted him to pour out his anxieties to the Christians of Rome whom he had never seen. On the contrary he desires them to share with him the responsibility of facing these difficulties and finding in prayer the perfect victory over them. Let us never hesitate, therefore, to seek the loving assistance of brethren in prayer, and

let us feel assured that such prayer will be used of God to bring about great results.

2. *The Power of Prayer.* While prayer is mysterious in its methods it is undoubtedly mighty in its force. God has conditioned spiritual blessings on the exercise of prayer, and every Christian man in proportion as he knows the reality of spiritual things will rejoice in the consciousness that prayer means power. It is no mere poetic thought that suggests the world as "bound by gold chains about the feet of God," for prayer bridges all distances and overcomes all obstacles. The stronger our faith in prayer the more blessed and powerful will our life be.

> "The weary ones had rest, the sad had joy
> That day, and wondered 'how.'
> A ploughman, singing at his work, had prayed,
> 'Lord, help them now.'
>
> Away in foreign lands they wondered how
> Their simple word had power.
> At home, the Christians two or three had met
> To pray an hour.
>
> Yes, we are always wond'ring, wond'ring 'how':
> Because we do not see
> Someone, unknown perhaps, and far away,
> On bended knee!"[1]

3. *The Results of Prayer.* We naturally think of the way in which the Apostle's petitions were answered, and if we had this passage only, our impression would be very different from what was actually the case.

> "We think we see the Apostle, after happily finishing his mission in Palestine, embarking full of joy, and guided by the will of God; then arriving at Rome, there to rest his weary heart among his brethren in the joy of the common salvation, and to recover new strength for a new work" (Godet, *Romans*, vol. ii., p. 384).

While this was the glowing picture that the Apostle's expectation painted, the actual fact was altogether different. He was delivered out of the power of his enemies in Jerusalem, he did reach Rome, and so far, the desires of his heart were granted, but "the Lord took

[1] *How; And Other Poems,* by F. M. N. (Partridge & Co.).

His own way, a way they knew not, to answer Paul and his friends" (Moule, *Romans,* p. 417). A little child was once asked whether God answers every prayer. "Yes," said the child, "but sometimes He answers 'Yes' and sometimes 'No.'" The Apostle little realized when or how he would reach the city of Rome, but God had not forgotten him, and the Divine assurance given him in the midst of his troubles at Jerusalem, "Thou must also bear witness of Me in Rome," was the inspiration of those weary weeks and months until at last he landed in Italy and the brethren from Rome met him. Then he thanked God and took courage for all that still awaited him in the imperial city. "I will bring the blind by a way that they knew not; I will lead them in paths that they have not known: I will make darkness light before them, and crooked things straight. These things will I do unto them, and not forsake them" (Isa. xlii. 16).

LXVI

A SERVANT OF THE CHURCH

Rom. xvi. 1, 2.

1. I commended unto you Phebe our sister, which is a servant of the church which is at Cenchrea:

2. That ye receive her in the Lord, as becometh saints, and that ye assist her in whatever business she hath need of you: for she hath been a succorer of many, and of myself also.

The personal element of the previous section is here continued in reference mainly to the Apostle's readers. While he himself is about to journey to Jerusalem, he commends to the Church at Rome one who is coming there at once. This and the succeeding section afford a striking proof of the character and power of primitive Christianity.

I. *The Recommendation* (ver. 1).—Letters of commendation (2 Cor. iii. 1) between Christians in various churches were a primitive practice (Acts xviii. 27; 2 Cor. viii. 18-24; 3 John 9, 10), and were doubtless due to the fundamental principle of Christian fellowship. The believer who was a member of a church in one place might, and should be admitted to the communion of Christians elsewhere. The custom was also pretty certainly the means of cementing union and communion between the various churches. It would be well if this practice were more fully observed in the present day, for when Christians change their place of residence they ought to take with them recommendations from the church with which they have been associated. If ministers and people were careful to see that this was done there would be fewer lapses from membership, a very much larger increase in true association between churches and churches, and not least of all, a more thorough protection against unworthy profession. It ought to be made as difficult as possible to receive to church membership anyone coming from another locality without such "epistles of commendation."

The description of Phoebe is interesting, even though very little is actually told us. The name itself was one of the names of the goddess, Diana, and this would suggest that she was a convert from heathenism, not a Jewess. She is described as "our sister," an expression of that relationship between believers which comes from their oneness in God Who is their Father. We are all "children of God through faith in Jesus Christ," and as such there is a true relation of brotherhood and sisterhood among those who belong to Christ. But Phoebe is further described as "a servant of the Church which is at Cenchrea." The place was the port of Corinth, some nine miles away from the city, and the word rendered "servant" might also be translated "deaconess," though it is hardly possible that the term had a technical meaning so early as this date. That there were women and officebearers afterwards is evident (1 Tim. iii. 8), and of course it is possible that the necessity was found as early as the time now in question. There was much that a woman alone could do for women, especially in view of the Eastern separation of the sexes.

II. *The Request* (ver. 2).—This Christian woman is commended to the Christians at Rome for admission to fellowship with them while she is residing in the city. They are also asked to assist her in whatever matter she might have need. Some business was taking her to Rome, and St. Paul wishes that Phoebe may find herself surrounded with the life and love of Christ. They are asked to become her servants and to take her business to heart. This would mean willingness to spend time and effort on her behalf. Whatever the business was, and of this we know nothing, the special point is that our Christian life is intended to influence all our conduct, and to lead us to do our utmost to promote the interests of our fellow-believers. The wording of the Apostle's request is quite striking: "Receive her in the Lord, worthily of the saints." They were to do this in union with their Master, and in the spirit that should actuate those who belong to God. "As it becomes saints to receive a saint."

This title for Christians is again to be observed; it was evidently a favorite with St. Paul. He was deeply conscious of the fact that believers belong to God, and are dedicated, consecrated to His possession and service.

III. *The Reason* (ver. 2).—The Apostle explains why in particular he wishes this kindness to be shown to Phoebe. "She hath been a succorer of many, and of myself also." The word "succorer" is most striking, especially as applied here to a woman. It properly means "patroness," or "champion." A patron was one who in the Greek States took care of a stranger and was responsible for him to the civil authorities. Phoebe is here spoken of as one who had in things spiritual assumed this position on behalf of many, and even for the Apostle himself. She had "stood by" many, and now the Christians in Rome were asked to "stand by" her. The word, when translated into spiritual realities, means to "take protective charge," caring for interests as the patron did for those of his clients (see Greek of ch. xii. 8; 1 Thess. v. 12). All this seems to suggest that Phoebe must have been a person of position and influence, perhaps like one of the "honorable women" mentioned by St. Luke (Acts xvii. 12).

And thus we have in brief yet vivid outline the story of this unknown Christian woman. She is (*a*) a sister; (*b*) a servant; (*c*) a succorer of many; and in a place like Cenchrea with its utter wicknedness her testimony for Christ must have been exceptionally welcome. Nor can we overlook the beautiful introduction given of her by St. Paul. He does not stint his praise, for he took a pleasure in setting his fellow-believers before others in the most favorable light possible. Loving appreciation of others is altogether different from flattery. Christian courtesy could not be more delightfully presented than in these brief statements of St. Paul.

Special attention seems to be necessary to the phrase, "worthily of the saints." The thought of "worthiness" is frequent in the New Testament, and implies the idea of the estimate, or valuation which God places upon His people. The various words rendered "worthy," "worthily," and "to count worthy," indicate a profound truth of the New Testament. Thus the faithful followers of God are described as those "of whom the world was not worthy" (Heb. xi. 38), and the faithful ones in Sardis are to walk with Christ "for they are worthy" (Rev. iii. 4; *cf.* ch. xvi. 6). Six times we find the adverb "worthily" mentioned, and when they are all put together they constitute a vivid and striking testimony to the profound truth of that spiritual valuation which God makes of His people.

1. "*Worthily of the Gospel*" (Phil. i. 27). The Philippian Christians are urged to let their manner of life be worthy of the Gospel of Christ. They were to live in the constant thought of the essential value of that Gospel, and not to allow anything to come in to detract from it, so far as they were concerned. How helpful it would be if we had a similar estimate of the Gospel and endeavored to walk worthy of it.

2. "*Worthily of the Lord*" (Col. i. 10). This is even more important, for we are to let our conduct prove that we value Jesus Christ to such an extent that we shall seek to anticipate His will in everything "unto all well-pleasing." The more thoroughly we realize the value of Jesus Christ the more keenly we shall endeavor to behave ourselves in a manner befitting our relation to him.

3. "*Worthily of the Vocation*" (Eph. iv. 1). The New Testament makes much of the fact and purpose of the Divine calling. It is at once high (Phil. iii. 14), holy (2 Tim. i. 9), heavenly (Heb. iii. 1), and we are expected to live, and behave, and serve in the constant thought of what membership in the Christian community really means and involves. The Apostle himself tells us (Eph. iv. 2, 3) what "worthily" really implies, and the more highly we estimate what the calling is the more carefully we shall frame our lives in accordance with it.

4. "*Worthily of the Saints*" (Rom. xvi. 2). The distinctive character of a saint is separation from the world and its ways, and the consequent consecration of the life to God. In the midst of all that was earthly and sinful in the Christianity of Rome the little body of saints were living their lives, conscious of their position in the sight of God, and doing their utmost to live lives of dedicated service to their Redeemer and Lord. "Worthily of the saints" is a remarkable phrase, and shows what God thinks of his people. We

ought to have the same high estimate of our fellowship with one another in Him, and so to live, and so to serve others, as to show that we have a high value for those for whom God has such regard.

5. "*Worthily of God*" (3 John 6). The reference here is to certain messengers who were traveling with the Gospel from place to place, and the Apostle says that it would be a "beautiful" thing to show them hospitality, and to send them forward "worthily of God." This suggests what God thinks of His messengers, those who had gone out "on behalf of the Name, taking nothing from the Gentiles" (3 John 7). If we realize what God thinks of these workers in His vineyard we also shall feel our obligation to welcome such in order that we may be co-workers with the truth. In the Old Testament times the word was "Touch not Mine anointed, and do my prophets no harm," and this, in New Testament language, may be extended to mean that we are to take every opportunity of welcoming and helping those who are serving God in the Gospel.

6. "*Worthily of God*" (1 Thess. ii. 12). This is yet another aspect of our relation to God and concerns our daily walk. God is here depicted as having summoned us into His kingdom and glory, and in view of these wonderful prospects in the future we are to walk worthy of Him. This is only another way of saying with St. Peter, "What manner of persons ought ye to be in all holy conversation and godliness" (2 Pet. iii. 11).

The more we ponder this wonderful word "worthily," and enter into its depth and fulness of meaning, the more perfectly we shall understand and realize that Christian life which is depicted in the Apostle's prayer when he prays that God may "count us worthy of His calling" (2 Thess. i. 11).

LXVII

A GALAXY OF SAINTS

ROM. xvi. 3-16.

3. Greet Priscilla and Aquila my helpers in Christ Jesus:
4. Who have for my life laid down their own necks: unto whom not only I give thanks, but also all the churches of the Gentiles.
5. Likewise *greet* the church that is in their house. Salute my well-beloved Epænetus, who is the firstfruits of Achaia unto Christ.
6. Greet Mary, who bestowed much labor on us.
7. Salute Andronicus and Junia, my kinsmen, and my fellow-prisoners, who are of note among the apostles, who also were in Christ before me.
8. Greet Amplias my beloved in the Lord.
9. Salute Urbane, our helper in Christ, and Stachys my beloved.
10. Salute Apelles approved in Christ. Salute them which are of Aristobulus' *household.*
11. Salute Herodion my kinsman. Greet them that be of the *household* of Narcissus, which are in the Lord.
12. Salute Tryphena and Tryphosa, who labor in the Lord. Salute the beloved Persis, which labored much in the Lord.
13. Salute Rufus chosen in the Lord, and his mother and mine.
14. Salute Asyncritus, Phlegon, Hermas, Patrobas, Hermes, and the brethren which are with them.
15. Salute Philologus, and Julia, Nereus, and his sister, and Olympas, and all the saints which are with them.
16. Salute one another with an holy kiss. The churches of Christ salute you.

FROM his recommendation of Phoebe St. Paul passes to greet a number of Christians in Rome. It is very striking that this catalogue of obscure Christians should be included in a letter intended eventually for the whole Christian Church. It also affords a remarkable picture of the heart of the great Apostle, and of the real condition of Christianity in his day. Those who have opportunity should study all these personal references under the guidance of Paley's *Horæ Paulinæ,* and Bishop Lightfoot's article (*Philippians,* p. 171), and they will thereby see the remarkable testimony afforded to the truth and genuineness of the Epistle. No forger could have dealt so fully and freely with personal matters without betraying himself.

If it be asked how the Apostle knew so many in a church where he had not worked, it may be remarked that Rome was the center of the world, and there was a constant movement to and fro, so that in the course of over twenty years of service in various parts it would not be difficult for him to know some two dozen people there.

The entire section should be studied with all possible attention to details under the guidance of a good commentary and the descriptions noted and compared. The passage is full of important lessons for today.

I. *Life in the Church.*—We gain a very good idea from this section of various elements that made up the Christian Church of that day.

1. The number of women mentioned in this list shows the honor and prominence placed upon womanhood by Christianity. The majority of names are those of women, and this is all the more striking when we recall the restrictions of social life at that time. While the Apostle elsewhere limits woman's sphere in the Church, the restriction is only associated with her essential nature and place. Within these wide limits there are abundant opportunities for her service, and the history of centuries shows that only in connection with the Gospel of Christ can woman realize her true nature and fulfil her highest mission. In our own day the ministry of womanhood is being greatly honored both at home and abroad, and the more thoroughly woman enters into the essential spirit of the Gospel the more effective will be her life and work.

2. We also see the value of home life in relation to the Gospel by the various homes mentioned here. What beautiful glimpses we have of the work of the Gospel in hallowing home life. We read of several churches in homes, especially that of Aquila and Priscilla (ver. 5). For two or three centuries Christians met in private houses because they were not allowed to assemble in large numbers, and even if they had been permitted, they possessed no suitable buildings. There seems little doubt that these informal gatherings

of small groups of believers had great influence in preserving the simplicity and purity of early Christianity. The story is told of a Roman official asking Justin Martyr where Christians assembled. Justin replied: "Where each one can and will. You believe, no doubt, that we all meet together in one place; but it is not so, for the God of the Christians is not shut up in a room, but, being invisible, He fills both heaven and earth, and is honored everywhere by the faithful" (Quoted from Neander, by J. Brown, *Romans*, p. 592). We are accustomed to sing, "There's no place like home," but we are not always so accustomed to realize that it is only through the Gospel that home can become a reality. Aquila and Priscilla might not be able to preach, or take the lead in regard to church matters, but they could allow their house to be used for the Gospel, and in quiet ways help forward the cause of Christ in a spirit of keen interest and genuine devotion.

3. The element of service is also another item of early Christian life. Aquila and Priscilla are spoken of as fellow-workers (ver. 3). Mary is said to have bestowed "much labor" (ver. 6); Persis "labored much" (ver. 12). The Gospel inevitably expresses itself in practical work for God. In addition to this we may realize how even ordinary work can become hallowed and uplifted by the Gospel. We do not for a moment suppose that the tent-making of Priscilla, Aquila, and St. Paul suffered by their profession of Christianity; on the contrary, the humblest and the most (so-called) secular work becomes ennobled by the reception of the Gospel.

4. The experience of suffering must not be omitted from this record of the life of the Church. The words of the Apostle in regard to Aquila and Priscilla are very striking, whatever they mean: "Who for my life laid down their own necks." This must mean that they exposed their lives to some great danger for the purpose of protecting him. It made so deep an impression on him that he could not forget it, whatever it was (Acts xviii. 6, 12-17; 1 Cor. xv. 32; 2 Cor. i. 8). It is pretty certain that a long time had elapsed since the occurrence, and yet the Apostle's gratitude was as true as ever: "To whom not only I give thanks, but also all the churches of the Gentiles." Aquila and Priscilla served the whole

Church in protecting the life of so valuable a servant of God. In the same way the Apostle calls Andronicus and Junius "his fellow-prisoners," referring doubtless to some imprisonment in which they all suffered for Christ. The early Christians were not long without the experience of suffering. "All that will live godly in Christ Jesus shall suffer persecution" (2 Tim. iii. 12).

II. *Variety in the Church.*—How manifold is the expression of the Christian graces as here recorded. Some of the names are associated with *activity*. Their efforts were strenuous and persistent as they labored for Christ in the Gospel. Others were associated with *courage*. They did not hesitate to confront danger for the cause of Christ. The variety is seen both among the women and the men. There was opportunity for all. The women mentioned here are evidently of very different types, and as we look at the names of Phoebe, Priscilla, Junia, Mary, Tryphena, Tryphosa and Persis, we are struck with the variety of their life and service. So also with regard to men; Aquila, Andronicus, Urbanus, and others, expressed their Christianity in appropriate ways. Other Christians seem to have been noted for their beauty of *character*. Such terms as "approved" and "beloved" indicate this very plainly. All these features illustrate what St. Peter calls "the many-colored grace of God" (1 Pet. iv. 10), and we ought to rejoice in the infinite possibilities of the expression of Divine grace in Christ.

III. *Unity in the Church.*—And yet amid all this variety there is the most remarkable oneness, because there was one bond which united them all; the Lord Jesus Christ as their Savior, Master, and Friend. It is impossible to say too much about this twofold idea of variety amid the unity, and unity amid the variety. The grace of God comes along the line of individual temperament and circumstance, and yet it is the one grace of God throughout, coming from the one Savior, and ministered by the one Spirit. The unity of the Christian Church has never been, and can never be, a unity which means unanimity of opinion, or uniformity in modes of worship, still less, a unit of organization. It is something far different and infinitely more glorious than any of these things could be. It is a "unity of the Spirit" in the "one Lord, one faith, one baptism, one God and Father of all" (Eph. iv. 5, 6).

IV. *Honor in the Church.*—Here are people unknown to men, but known to Christ. A great many of them were doubtless slaves, and yet side by side are some of the most distinguished names in the metropolis. The great city of Rome knew nothing at all of most of these people, but in the sight of God they were "saints." It is encouraging to think that no one is too insignificant to be remembered in the Book of Life. "A book of remembrance was written before Him for them that feared the Lord, and that thought upon His Name. And they shall be Mine, saith the Lord of Hosts, in that day when I make up My jewels" (Mal. iii. 16, 17).

V. *Recognition in the Church.*—How beautifully the Apostle describes these various Christians. Let us ponder some of his words. "Epaenetus, my beloved, who is the firstfruits of Asia unto Christ" (ver. 5). Andronicus and Junius are said to be "of note among the Apostles" (ver. 7), and were in Christ before St. Paul himself. They must have belonged to the early Church in Jerusalem, and as such were of special interest to the Apostle whose conversion came later than theirs. Amplias is "my beloved in the Lord" (ver. 8). Apelles is "approved" (ver. 10). Rufus is "chosen" (ver. 13); perhaps he is to be identified with the Rufus of Mark xv. 21, and the reference to "his mother and mine" is very touching: the mother of Rufus by birth; the mother of St. Paul by Christian love (ver. 13). No one seems to have been forgotten by the Apostle.

VI. *Humility in the Church.*—Nearly all the names mentioned here are those of humble helpers rather than leaders. We do not know of anything marvelous or magnificent that they performed, but we are reminded in almost every verse of their subordinate, quiet simple service for the Master. As a modern teacher has well remarked:—

> "The Church of God is overrun with captains. She is in great need of a few more privates. A few rivers run into the sea, but a far larger number run into other rivers. We cannot all be pioneers, but we can all be helpers, and no man is fitted to go in the front until he has learned well how to go second" (A. B. Simpson, *Romans,* p. 291).

The Master's words are "To every man his work," and if only we realize that each has his proper place and sphere, and then seek to glorify God therein, the work of the Church will go forward increasingly to the glory of God and the salvation of man.

VII. *Fellowship in the Church.*—How personal and affectionate are these greetings. What a reality and breadth marked St. Paul's relationships. Although a profound thinker and a great leader, he is even still greater in the realm of the affections. Neither official position nor intellectual power dried up the streams of his intense devotion and self-sacrificing love. He carries in his heart this list of the saints, and with accurate memory, distinguishing detail, and intense affection, he greets them all. It must have been a precious thing to feel the love of this Greatheart. The Apostle has been beautifully described as "a distributing center of holy affection."

> Blest be the tie that binds
> Our hearts in Christian love;
> The fellowship of kindred minds
> Is like to that above.

But the love of St. Paul as here depicted was only an instance of that general mutual love that characterized the whole Church, for the greetings close with the general exhortation to "salute one another," and a message of salutation from "all the Churches of Christ" (ver. 16). The salutation by kissing was the ordinary way of expressing affiection in these countries, just as shaking hands is with us today, and we find similar exhortations elsewhere (1 Cor. xvi. 20; 2 Cor. xiii. 12; 1 Thess. v. 26; 1 Pet. v. 14). It was probably due to this simple, natural, and innocent custom among Christians that the baseless charges of the heathen took their rise, and it is not at all unlikely that owing to these slanders and calumnies the practice had to be discontinued. But whatever may be the precise mode of expression the reality and power of Christian love and fellowship remain unimpaired.

As we again look over this truly wonderful passage and try to extract from it its special meaning and message for our own hearts, we can hardly help noticing two great outstanding truths.

1. *The Glory of the Gospel.* Few passages in the New Testament reveal more hidden secrets of early Christianity than this apparently unimportant list of names. ((*a*) *How the Gospel penetrates.* Here we find men and women of all sorts led to Christ and used in His service in the great metropolis:—

> "See, in the very details of these short salutations, by what humble instruments, and yet how extensively, the Gospel had established itself in so short a time, in the mighty city of Rome. No Apostle had set his foot there, yet behold with wonder what progress had already been made by the Word of God, solely through the labors of artisans, merchants, women, slaves, and free men, who happened to be in Rome" (Gaussen, *"Theopneustia,"* p. 323).

Could anything be more striking as a testimony to that Gospel which the Apostle has already described as "the power of God unto salvation"? (*b*) *How the Gospel unites.* Here are masters and slaves, all one in Christ Jesus. We are sometimes inclined to feel surprised that the New Testament does not condemn slavery, especially as we know that the Gospel is absolutely opposed to this deplorable institution. The explanation lies in the fact that in the reception of the Gospel there came into the lives of masters and slaves such a new spirit and power as enabled each to realize true brotherhood in Christ, even amidst the social conditions of that day. The story of Philemon and Onesimus is a striking illustration of what must have happened continually on every hand. The Gospel is intended to deal separately with the rich and with the poor, and at the same time to unite both in one common fellowship in Christ Jesus. There is nothing on earth that tends to unite men and classes like the Gospel of peace. (*c*) *How the Gospel dignifies.* Life and labor become uplifted and transformed in proportion as the Gospel enters and dominates the soul. Aquila and Priscilla may be tentmakers, but they can do their work to the glory of God. William Carey can be a cobbler, and yet be the means of witnessing for Christ long before he is the missionary of India.

> "Teach me, my God and King,
> In all things Thee to see,
> And what I do in anything,
> To do it unto Thee.

A servant with this clause
Makes drudgery divine;
Who sweeps a room as for Thy laws
Makes that and the action fine."

(*d*) *How the Gospel enables.* The section is full of references to activity, to courage, to suffering, to character, and everything is due to the controlling and transforming power of the Gospel. Aquila and Priscilla little knew what was going to happen when they received the Apostle Paul into their house (Acts xviii. 1-3). Not only did it lead to their own conversion, but through them to the conversion of Apollos, the life-long friendship of St. Paul, and the entire revolution of all their interests. The Gospel comes into our life just as we are and where we are, and by its mighty power gives victory over all circumstances, makes us "more than conquerors through Him that loved us."

2. *The Secret of the Gospel.* We shall fail entirely to appreciate the true meaning of this passage if we overlook one small but significant part of the Apostle's statement. Ten times in sixteen verses he uses the little word "in," as expressive of the source and secret of all that he has described. "In the Lord" (ver. 2); "in Christ" (ver. 7). Whether for life, or brotherhood, or service, union with the Lord is the guarantee of true Christianity. There are other bonds of union mentioned in this passage, such as suffering, service, and gratitude, but they are all included and swallowed up in this supreme thought that St. Paul and his fellow-believers in Rome were all "in Christ," or "in the Lord." It is union with Him Who died and rose again, and is now alive for evermore, that alone can produce holiness of heart or earnestness of life. And while the Apostle is bold to say, "I can do all things," he is quick to add, "in Him Who is strengthening me" (Phil. iv. 13). We must never allow ourselves to forget for a single moment that our salvation, our holiness, our courage, our endurance, our service, are only possible as we are "in Christ"; "in the Lord."

LXVIII

A LAST LOOK OUTWARD

ROM. xvi. 17-24.

17. Now I beseech you, brethren, mark them which cause divisions and offenses contrary to the doctrine which ye have learned; and avoid them.
18. For they that are such serve not our Lord Jesus Christ, but their own belly; and by good words and fair speeches deceive the hearts of the simple.
19. For your obedience is come abroad unto all *men*. I am glad therefore on your behalf: but yet I would have you wise unto that which is good, and simple concerning evil.
20. And the God of peace shall bruise Satan under your feet shortly. The grace of our Lord Jesus Christ *be* with you. Amen.
21. Timotheus my workfellow, and Lucius, and Jason, and Sosipater, my kinsmen, salute you.
22. I Tertius, who wrote *this* epistle, salute you in the Lord.
23. Gaius mine host, and of the whole church, saluteth you. Erastus the chamberlain of the city saluteth you, and Quartus a brother.
24. The grace of our Lord Jesus Christ *be* with you all. Amen.

THE Apostle is drawing to a close, but he has still several things of prime importance to say. There are dangers and difficulties to which he must refer. Out of the fulness of his heart he has sent them affectionate greetings. All the while he is conscious that there were adverse influences at work in men of a very different attitude to Christ and His Gospel, and he feels it imperative to sound this warning note before he closes.

I. *An Urgent Appeal* (ver. 17).—"Now I beseech you, brethren." A tone of entreaty, not of command. The Apostle never uses the word signifying "order," or "command." He invariably carried out his own principle: "Not that we have lordship over your faith, but are helpers of your joy" (2 Cor. i. 24). The very fact that he appeals to them in this earnest loving way is a proof of the great necessity of his words.

II. *A Serious Trouble* (ver. 17).—"Them which cause divisions and offenses." The "divisions" represent ecclesiastical parties or factions. The "offenses" were the stumbling-blocks, or occasions of falling produced by the factions; one was ecclesiastical, the other moral. It seems pretty clear that the reference is to the Judaizers who were always following the Apostle and doing their utmost to oppose him and his Gospel (Phil. iii. 2; Tit. i. 10, 11). They were even then at work, and from the Epistle to the Philippians we see clearly that they were in Rome five years afterwards. Factions in the Church almost inevitably tend to moral troubles and disaster. In more than one sense, "Unity is strength."

III. *A Pressing Duty* (ver. 17).—"Mark them . . . and turn away from them." This means that the enemy was to be observed and avoided. The Roman Christians were to keep an eye on them, and, as the phrase is, "give them a wide berth." Enemies of this kind would probably prosecute their intentions in secret at first, and much trouble might easily accrue before any outward danger was seen. It was therefore essential that the danger should be noted in its earliest possible stages in order that every precaution might be taken later on to defeat their machinations. Chrysostom notes that the Apostle does not advise any debate with these men. Disputes and discussions would be ineffective and powerless, if not harmful, and the truest wisdom was to be found in utter avoidance.

IV. *A Simple Test* (ver. 17).—"Contrary to the doctrine which ye have learned." This was the one simple yet adequate way of testing the reality of these teachers. The Roman Christians had learned the doctrine of Jesus Christ in all its simplicity and purity, and as one of the immediate effects of that doctrine was to bind together in heart and soul all who belonged to Christ, it was evident that any teaching which caused division and trouble could not possibly be from God. It is well for us to have some such simple powerful means of putting to a test the things we hear from time to time. Are they in accordance with the truth which we have learned and received? If they are, let us accept them; if they are not, let us beware of them.

V. *A Solemn Warning* (ver. 18).—In the plainest possible language St. Paul says that these false teachers are serving their own appetites only, and are leading astray the immature and guileless Christians. "They that are such serve not our Lord Jesus Christ, but their own belly." False doctrine and vile living tend to go together, as we have already seen (ch. i. 21-25). These men were bold, hypocritical, and sensual, and were, in fact, making a living by false teaching. No thought of the glory of our Lord entered into the minds of these men. All that they considered was their own advantage and profit. Their methods, too, were admirably adapted to gain their ends. By good words and fair speeches they deceived the hearts of the simple. The "simple" are the innocent; those who are genuinely sincere, without possessing any special power of intellect or spiritual perception. By their benign speech and their beautiful benedictions they were liable to beguile and capture those who were not capable of distinguishing between the outward attractiveness and essential banefulness of the teaching. By the unwary and guileless such attractive utterances could not but be received as impressive and convincing. "How could they talk so seraphically if not saints?" (Stifler). Just at this point lay the deadliness of the danger.

It is very significant that all through the New Testament times there was this constant fear of intellectual and moral danger and disaster. Men were ready to take advantage of the Gospel for the sake of gain. By working on tender consciences and trading on fears, they easily captured and led astray simple, unwary souls. Nearly every section of the Epistles has something to say against these men. It is of such that St. Paul speaks when he describes them in the plainest of terms, "Whose god is their belly" (Phil. iii. 18, 19). The same class of false teachers is doubtless in view when reference is made to those who subvert houses and teach things which they ought not for filthy lucre's sake ((Tit. i. 10, 11). It is also more than probable that they were referred to in connection with leading captive silly women (2 Tim. iii. 6). St. Peter is equally clear about men of this type, who "beguile unstable souls," sporting themselves with their own deceivings, while feasting, and speaking great swelling words of vanity" (2 Pet. ii. 13-19). Doubtless, too, Jude is warning against the same men when he refers to those who "ran greedily after the error of Balaam for reward" (vers. 11-16). Nor has the Christian Church been without such dangers through the centuries since the Apostles' time. There are always those who are prepared to "turn the grace of God into lasciviousness," and trade upon the ignorance of simple, pious, earnest souls for the sake of financial and immoral gains.

VI. *A Splendid Testimony* (ver. 19).—"For your obedience is come abroad unto all men. I am glad therefore on your behalf." The Apostle here expresses his conviction that these false teachers cannot deceive the Christians at Rome, for their obedience is well known. They had so grown in grace as to have made for themselves a name among the Churches of Christ, and in all this St. Paul rejoices. He had spoken of their faith as known throughout the world (ch. i. 8). And it is as though he now remarked that his warning was due to the fact that the knowledge of their Christian life having already spread far and wide, the false teachers would not fail to hear of the Christians in Rome, and would therefore do their utmost to subvert them as they had others elsewhere.

VII. *An Earnest Desire* (ver. 19).—"But yet I would have you wise unto that which is good, and simple concerning evil." Although their obedience is well known, the Apostle with his usual delicate combination of confidence and warning, wants even them to be wise concerning good, and simple-minded concerning evil. Just as he warns he expresses his confidence in them first of all. They were not to be wise with regard to evil and simple with regard to good. This is the maxim of the world, but there is no need to practice evil in order to become wise in it. Purity of life which springs from purity of faith is the best possible safeguard against evil. "Be deep in the wisdom of humble faith; be contented to be unacquainted with a wisdom which at its root is evil" (Bishop Moule). Our Lord spoke in similar terms when He said to His disciples that they were to unite the wisdom of the serpent with the harmlessness (same word as rendered "simple") of the dove (Matt. x. 16).

"Human wisdom seeks to guard itself by a thorough knowledge of the world, and of all evil ways. This is not the wisdom that cometh down from above, but earthly, natural, devilish. The wisdom from above is first pure, then peaceful, gentle, yielding, full of mercy and good fruits, uncontentious and unfeigned. It needs not to cultivate acquaintance with evil; it knows good in Christ, it is satisfied, and adores. It hears and loves the Shepherd's voice; a stranger's voice it knows not, and will not follow. And this, as it suits the simplest soul brought to the knowledge of God, it may be today, so it alone becomes the wisest, because it alone glorifies the Lord, as indeed it is the only path of safety for us, being such as we are, and in such a world" (W. Kelly, *Romans,* p. 280).

The one question for all believers is whether a thing is right. If it is not, then we must get as far away from it as possible. Ability may easily become weakness in regard to evil. Our supreme need and our perfect safeguard is simplicity. "Darkness cannot reveal darkness" (Stifler).

VIII. *A Cheering Promise* (ver. 20).—"The God of peace will bruise Satan under your feet shortly." From the visible enemy the Apostle turns to the invisible foe and to the assurance of victory over him. Thus he encourages them to faithfulness by this promise of conquest. The reference is obviously to the story in Genesis (ch. iii. 15), and this seems to be the only place in the New Testament where it is mentioned. The word "shortly" does not mean "soon," but "swiftly." He did not mean them to understand that the victory might come at once, but that when God commenced to work, His conquest of Satan would be short and sharp. "Paul means not that the victory will be near, but that it will be speedily gained when once the conquest is begun. When the believer fights with the armor of God the conflict is never long" (Godet). It is also of interest to observe how the human and the Divine elements are blended in the promise that God shall bruise Satan, and yet that it shall come to pass "under our feet." God is the source of all power and grace, but we appropriate it and make it our own for use. The title, "the God of peace," should also be noted, especially as we had it in a different connection in the former chapter (xv. 33). God as the God of peace secures peace for us by overcoming Satan, and thus safeguarding us against his followers.

IX. *A Heartfelt Prayer* (ver. 20).—"The grace of our Lord Jesus Christ be with you." Thus with the benediction this solemn section closes, and in it is a renewed assurance of Divine "grace" which will issue in victory over all their foes.

X. *A Renewed Greeting* (vers. 21-24).—The warning over, St. Paul takes up again his loving salutations. The contrast is striking, as we contemplate the insertion of the solemn greeting. These salutations are from the Apostle's companions as he wrote his letter. It is more than probable that the Epistle was read out first at Corinth where it was written, and that these greetings from the Church were then added. Timothy is of course well known as the Apostle's "fellow-worker" (ver. 21), his beloved son in the faith. The three names that follow, Lucius, Jason, and Sosipater, are spoken of as St. Paul's own kinsmen (ver. 21), evidently showing (as in vers. 7, 11) that he had relatives united with him in the faith of Christ. The amanuensis of the Epistle, Tertius, then gives his own greeting (ver. 22), and, last of all, mention is made of three notable men, Gaius, Erastus, and Quartus (ver. 23). Gaius was the host of the Apostle and of the entire Church. The gatherings were doubtless held at his house. Erastus was none other than the treasurer of the city of Corinth, an important personage, one of the few "noble" among the saints in Corinth. Quartus is not "a" brother, but "the" brother, doubtless known to the Christians in Rome, and therefore able to be described in this way. How delightfully discriminating are these greetings from the Apostle's companions. The brotherliness and genuine appreciation are another proof both of the writer's large heart and also of the authenticity of his Epistle. The Revised Version omits the benediction in ver. 24, but some commentators (like Meyer) retain it. If it is to be accepted as genuine, we must consider it as the personal and fraternal benediction, just as that at ver. 20 was the official benediction, closing the Epistle.

Dangers similar to those mentioned here still threaten the Christian Church. The pathway of the Gospel through the countries is strewed with intellectual and moral disasters, and we therefore do well to concentrate attention and emphasize duty in the light of these solemn words.

1. *The Sensitiveness of Love.* Coming after the large-hearted and abundantly affectionate greetings of the earlier section, we can well understand the Apostle's concern in the face of these dangers. The very joy he felt in the faith and life of these Roman Christians made the thought of possible disaster still more terrible. His devotion to the Lord Jesus Christ, "our Lord Christ" (ver. 18) was an additional and weightier reason for his intense feeling against these enemies of the Cross of Christ. It is no narrowness to feel the pressure of danger and to warn against it. It is an utterly false charity to allow men of erroneous doctrine, charming speech, and selfish motive to make havoc of the Church of God. There is nothing in this world more sensitive than true love between man and wife, or friend and friend. Much more, therefore, will the love of Christ, when it fills the heart, possess the soul with a holy sensitiveness in the face of evil.

2. *The Safeguard of Truth.* The emphasis on knowledge of the truth in this section is particularly weighty. The errors were "contrary" to the doctrine (ver. 17). The danger was due to the deception of smooth and fair speaking (ver. 18), and for this reason the Apostle wishes them to have the true spiritual wisdom (ver. 19). It is one of the most impressive thoughts connected with the New Testament that spiritual perception is one of the marks of a ripe, mature Christianity. The young Christian is unable to distinguish things that differ, but the growing saint is able to understand, and in the light of spiritual experience is able to discern good and evil (Phil. i. 9, 10), and to distinguish between the beautiful and the base (Heb. v. 14). All this calls for a constant application of mind, heart, conscience, and will to the truth of God as revealed in His Word. The Christian who makes Bible study and meditation his daily portion and duty will never lack that spiritual enlightenment which will enable him to shrink from the first appearance of error and follow that which is good. The illuminated heart is able almost instinctively to say two things: "We are not

ignorant of his devices" (2 Cor. ii. 11); "We have the mind of Christ" (1 Cor. ii. 16).

3. *The Stronghold of Grace.* The Apostle leads his readers to contemplate "the God of peace" and "the grace of our Lord Jesus Christ." Thus an assurance of promise and prayer is expressed in connection with the danger from these false teachers. He would have them know that the God of peace and the grace of Christ would be their constant and sufficient shield from the assaults made upon them through false doctrine and unholy life. "They "that do know their God shall be strong, and do exploits" (Dan xi. 32). The God of truth is the God of grace, and the reason why we say "Truth is mighty" is because behind it is the personal revelation of Him Who is the truth. "Grace and truth came by Jesus Christ," and the soul that occupies itself with God in fellowship through His Word, and by His Spirit, will find himself surrounded by a complete safeguard in the armor of God.

LXIX

A LAST LOOK UPWARD

Rom. xvi. 25-27.

25. Now to him that is of power to stablish you according to my gospel, and the preaching of Jesus Christ, according to the revelation of the mystery, which was kept secret since the world began.

26. But now is made manifest, and by the scriptures of the prophets, according to the commandment of the everlasting God, made known to all nations for the obedience of faith:

27. To God only wise, *be* glory through Jesus Christ for ever. Amen.

At length the end of the Epistle is near. St. Paul has now done his utmost by letter, but as he closes he remembers that God alone can establish the Roman Christians in the faith. And so, as Godet remarks, we have in these verses "the look upwards." It is not usual for the Apostle to end an Epistle with a doxology, though there are doxologies in several of his Epistles. The normal method of closing his writing was seen in the benediction of verse 20, but the salutations (vers. 21-24) and this closing doxology are quite characteristic of his feelings at the time and under the circumstances of this Epistle. The doxology is very rich, deep, and full, and it is noteworthy for gathering up some of the fundamental thoughts of the Epistle, particularly those found in the opening section (ch. i. 1-17). Indeed, a closing study of these two parts reveals some quite striking points of agreement and contrast. Thus we have in the opening and closing sections references to Scriptures (ch. i. 2), our Lord Jesus Christ (ch. i. 3), the obedience of faith (ch. i. 5), the Gospel (ch. i. 15, 16), and revelation (ch. i. 17). Not that the subjects are all and wholly identical; on the contrary, as we shall see, there are both comparisons and contrasts. But the remarkable repetition at the opening and close of the Epistle, even with differences of the same words and ideas, deserves careful attention.

I. *Power* (ver. 25).—"Now to Him that is of power to stablish you." It was the desire and aim of the Apostle in the prospect of his visit to Rome to establish them by the impartation of some spiritual gift (ch. i. 11), and the entire Epistle was meanwhile intended for the same purpose. No doubt his teaching would do much, but after all he is conscious, and he wishes them to realize, that strength comes from God. A similar thought is found in his address to the elders at Miletus (Acts xx. 31, 32). He is naturally anxious that all the Christians in Rome should be included among those of whom he can speak as "we who are strong" (ch. xv. 1). In the face of the dangerous and deadly foes who were liable to enter into the Church, and also in view of the many and varied needs of their Christian profession and service, the supreme necessity for their life was strength.

II. *Provision* (vers. 25, 26).—Twice, or perhaps three times, the Apostle uses the phrase "according to," as indicating the provision made by God for this strength and establishment of the Christian life.

1. The first part of the provision was found in the Gospel proclaimed by the Apostle—"according to my gospel, and the preaching of Jesus Christ." We have already seen another reference to "my Gospel" (ch. ii. 16; *cf.* 2 Tim. ii. 8). And similarly the Apostle speaks elsewhere of "our Gospel" (2 Cor. iv. 3; 1 Thess. i. 5). This must mean the particular message which was characteristic of the Apostle's ministry, the free, complete, and universal Gospel of the righteousness and grace of God in Christ. This is further defined as "the preaching of Jesus Christ," which doubtless means that Jesus Christ was the constant theme and predominant subject of his message. We can see this in every Epistle that he wrote, and in particular in his own great statement of the Gospel, as it had been delivered to him and was being proclaimed far and wide (1 Cor. xv. 1-4). This is the first element of the great provision for Christian steadfastness. Power in daily life comes from the Gospel of which Jesus Christ in His Divine Person and Work is the substance and

theme. The more this Gospel enters into hearts and lives, the more fully will power and strength be experienced.

2. But the Apostle takes another step in speaking of the provision for Christian strength and firmness by showing that there is a further provision made by God—"According to the revelation of the mystery, which was kept secret since the world began; but now is made manifest, and by the scriptures of the prophets, according to the commandment of the everlasting God." Here again we have the Pauline word "mystery," which, as elsewhere (ch. xi. 25), invariably means something that was once secret but is now revealed. It should be carefully observed that "the revelation of the mystery" here mentioned was not that the Gospel was to be extended to the Gentiles, for this was no mystery at all, since it is clearly found in a number of passages in the Old Testament. The "mystery" was something that arose out of this extension to the Gentiles, namely, the union of Jew and Gentile on the same level as one body in Christ. This is the "mystery" of which nothing is said in the Old Testament. The first problem of the Apostle's life was to bring in the Gentiles, and this is the great theme of the Epistle to the Romans. But later on a second problem became acute, the question of the status of the Gentiles after they had been brought in. It is the latter with which the present statement is concerned, and it is spoken of as a "mystery" which had been "kept secret since the world began, but now is made manifest." This shows that whatever is in view, it is something that had not been known in earlier ages, but was only revealed at the time that the Apostle was writing. This is made still more evident when the phrase, "the scriptures of the prophets," is properly rendered. There are no articles in the original, and the term is simply "prophetic writings." The reference is not to the Old Testament prophets, but to the New, for, as we know, prophets as well as apostles were included in the gift of the exalted Christ (Eph. iv. 8-13). It was to the Apostle Paul in particular that this "mystery" was specially revealed (Eph. iii. 4-6). He does not elaborate this subject in the present Epistle, because it is the special message of that to the Ephesians, and those who would know what these verses really mean should read the latter Epistle

immediately after studying this doxology. St. Paul thus hints at the glorious thought that not only are Gentiles welcomed into the Christian Church on the same level of equality with Jews through simple faith, but that once they are in Christ they are to be united with the Jews as fellow-heirs of the same Body, both Jews and Gentiles forming the one Church of Christ. If only these truths are carefully observed there will be no difficulty whatever in understanding the Apostle's meaning, but if we interpret the passage of the Gospel and its extension to the Gentiles, we see at once how inappropriate and impossible it is in view of the full revelation of these latter truths in the Old Testament. When once we have entered by personal experience into the truths of Romans, we are then, and only then, ready for the still deeper truths of Ephesians. Romans shows how we come out of bondage into liberty; Ephesians continues the teaching by showing how we are raised up to the throne of God, and become "blessed with all spiritual blessings in the heavenlies in Christ."

III. *Purpose* (ver. 26).—The simple yet all-embracing object in what the Apostle had to say was "the obedience of faith." Just as he opened (ch. i. 5), so he closes. This means the obedience which springs from faith; that which faith causes, produces, guarantees. Faith in the New Testament is far more than any mere intellectual acceptance of truth. It is truth expressed in life; "faith that worketh by love." Obedience is the fruit of faith and shows itself in character and conduct. As the Anglican Article well teaches, good works "do spring out necessarily of a true and lively faith; insomuch that by them a lively faith may be as evidently known as a tree discerned by the fruit."

IV. *Praise* (ver. 27).—Everything is intended to lead up to this culminating point; the ascription of praise and glory to Him Who is "the only wise God." And so the Apostle ends with the highest of all thoughts, "the glory of God" (ch. iii. 23; v. 2).

"Thus this glorious epistle leaves us gazing into the endless succession of coming ages and listening to the song which throughout each successive age will rise with louder and sweeter note to Him Who, before the ages were, formed for us, whom He foresaw in sin and ruin, His wondrous and costly purpose of salvation and life, Who throughout the successive ages of the earlier covenants carried His purpose towards and to its historic completion in Jesus of Nazareth, and Who now day by day carries forward the same purpose by His Spirit in the hearts of us His children until that day when we and Paul and the whole family of earth and heaven shall join in that anthem of praise whose notes from afar, as the weary pen of the Apostle falls from his hand, are already ringing in his ears" (Beet, *Romans*, p. 363).

Let us pay special attention to the closing suggestions and hints here given by the Apostle for our spiritual life.

1. *The Supreme Need* (ver. 25). "Stablish you." In every age, under all circumstances, the Christian life should be one of spiritual consistency, for if there is firmness in the inner life there will be steadfastness in the outer conduct. A strong Christian is one who is saved, sanctified, and satisfied in Christ. His position as an established believer makes him at once happy, holy, and helpful. Weakness is perilous to the believer's own soul, and prejudicial to anything he endeavors to do for his Master. Strength, on the other hand, will give the heart and life confidence, comfort, and courage, and prove the means of usefulness on every hand. Let us, therefore, never fail to recall this last word of this important Epistle, the absolute necessity of strength and steadfastness in Christian living.

2. *The Sufficient Provision.* Two references to God indicate this: "Him that is of power" (ver. 25), or "Him that is able," and "God only wise" (ver. 27). God is both able and willing to guarantee strength and grace. His power and wisdom are the source of our stability. Again and again the Apostle dwells with loving confidence upon the ability of God (ch. iv. 21; xi. 23; xiv. 4; Eph. iii. 20; *cf.* Jude 24). Under all circumstances, in every emergency, amid every weakness, surrounded by the most pressing problems, let us take to our hearts these two inspiring truths: "God is able"; "God is wise." Resting on Divine wisdom and Divine power we shall be "strong in the Lord and in the power of His might."

3. *The Simple Method* (ver. 25). "According to my gospel." This is how God works to provide us with power. By means of the Gospel of Jesus Christ we become partakers of the Divine "ability" and "wisdom" which lead to personal steadfastness. Power through truth is the prime secret of Christian living. While we occupy our

minds with "Him that is of power" we know that He works through that Gospel, which is "the power of God." The more fully, therefore, we enter into the personal experience of the Gospel of Jesus Christ and allow it to dominate our lives, the more steadfast shall we become, as Christ is increasingly realized as "the power of God," and "the wisdom of God" (1 Cor. i. 24).

4. *The Sublime Object* (ver. 27). "To God . . . be glory through Jesus Christ for ever." This is the culminating point of the Christian life. The close of the Epistle suggests the course of Christian experience. God is to be glorified by our daily living, and if only we manifest that steadfastness which the Apostle desires, there can be no doubt that it will glorify God as perhaps nothing else can do. Men are impressed by strength, and when they realize that "our help cometh from the Lord" they too will be led to enter into personal relations with Him through the everlasting Gospel. Day by Day, hour by hour, and even moment by moment, may we never forget the supreme purpose of everything in life: "that God may be all in all."

LXX

A REVIEW

I. The Apostle Himself

It is impossible to leave this important Epistle without endeavoring to gather up some of the main threads of thought running through it. We are only too apt to lose sight of these in the abundance of suggestive detail, and we therefore fail to "see the wood for the trees." Amid very much that is in it from beginning to end it may be useful to consider four leading thoughts: what it reveals of St. Paul, of his Writing, of his Message, of his Master. And as we endeavor to make ourselves acquainted with the teaching of the Epistle along these lines we shall see its direct and constant application on our own lives.

Indirectly, but very really, the Epistle gives a revelation of St. Paul, and the various aspects of his character are worthy of the closest attention.

I. *His Courtesy.*—The Church in Rome was unknown to him, and we can see his anxiety not to appear to intrude upon what might be considered an unnecessary sphere of work. Even though he is conscious of being the Apostle to the Gentiles, and as such would have a perfect right to include Rome within the purview of his operations, he goes out of his way first to explain the reasons of the long delay in coming to them, and then to express his conviction that when he should arrive, it would be to receive, as much as to bestow blessing. In all this the fine gentlemanliness and courtesy of the Apostle shines out, and gives us a model of how to approach those who may be rightly regarded as quite capable of entering into spiritual experiences as ourselves. Although the Apostle wrote them this letter, he was persuaded that it was really unnecessary for him to say very much, in the light of their possession of a real Christian experience of life and work (ch. xv. 14). And he is sure that when he comes to them it will be in the fulness of the blessing of Christ and with mutual advantage (ch. xv. 24, 29).

II. *His Tenderness.*—The vigor, and sometimes the rigor, of the Apostle's thought might easily blind us to the fact that he was one of the most tender-hearted and considerate of men. We see this in his references to his fellow-countrymen, the Jews (ch. ix. 1-5), for in spite of the severity with which he was compelled to deal with their rejection of Christ, his heart overflowed in love and sympathy towards them, as he contemplated their profound spiritual loss in severance from the Messiah. Again, when he is dealing with the great question of conscience (ch. xiv. 1-xv. 7), his innate thoughtfulness and tenderness are manifest in almost every verse. He shrinks from anything that would cause a brother to stumble, and is especially concerned lest by a mere piece of food anyone should be destroyed for whom Christ died (ch. xiv. 15). Once again we can see his deep feeling as he refers to his projected visit to Jerusalem. He longs that his work there may be acceptable to the saints, and that it may be the means of bringing together the two great sections of the Christian Church. It is not often that we find a man of such force of character so exquisitely tender, thoughtful, and sympathetic in his dealings with others. Nothing was too small for the Apostle's thought if only thereby a fellow-Christian's feelings might be considered and his life helped.

III. *His Courage.*—This is the other side of Paul's character. He is face to face with resolute, and sometimes even virulent opposition, and yet he never dreams of modifying his Gospel in the slightest degree. In the face of all difficulties he goes straight ahead with his presentation of the truth as he received it. Jews might oppose, and Gentiles might scorn, but he is perfectly indifferent. He has a message from God, and come what may, he will deliver it everywhere. This unflinching courage is one of the finest characteristics of the Christian life. Like one of a still older day, the Apostle was ready to say in the prosecution of his task, "If I perish, I perish."

IV. *His Ability.*—It is in this Epistle in particular that we are made conscious of the intellectual power of St. Paul. His treatment of the Gospel is marked by a wonderfully wide range of thought, as well as a profound depth. There is a constant and irresistible logic about his presentation. He goes from point to point without any essential digression. He knows both his own mind, and also the truth that he has to present, and step by step from the opening words to the close of the doctrinal discussion we are impressed with the marvelous force, range and profundity of his teaching.

V. *His Spirituality.*—Intellectual teaching alone easily becomes dry, abstract, and remote from ordinary life. It must be permeated with spirituality if it is to become really powerful. This is the special feature of the Apostle's teaching, as seen in this and other Epistles. His life came out of his faith, and his faith expressed itself in life. As we read the great chapter on the power of the Holy Spirit over the flesh as the guarantee of holiness (ch. viii.), we are particularly conscious of the blending of thought and experience, of truth and spirituality. Phillips Brooks has defined preaching as "truth through personality," and this is pre-eminently illustrated by the Apostle Paul. Truth alone may easily be uninteresting and even hard, while personality alone might as easily be weak and sentimental, but when truth gives force to personality and personality gives warmth and life to truth, we have the perfect blend which recommends both. So in this Epistle we have a combination of profound intellectual ability and equally profound spirituality, and the consequence is that the teaching glows with life and recommends itself by its own inherent fragrance and charm. The Apostle's wonderful combination of thought for lowly things and sympathy with a narrow outlook, together with outstanding intellectual force and exceptional spirituality, show the essential Christianity of his character.

VI. *His Fairness.*—Although a man of strong convictions and intense feelings, it is remarkable how true he holds the balance between opposing views. There are no Jewish, or anti-Jewish prejudices, not withstanding the personal attacks made on him and his Gospel by his Jewish contemporaries. In the same way the treatment of the strong and the weak exhibits a striking fairness, which is all the more noteworthy because the Apostle quite clearly associates himself with the strong (ch. xv. 1), and realizes that the weakness to which he refers is no essential part of true Christianity. This attitude of fairness and balanced outlook commends the Apostle's teaching to all who desire to look at truth from different standpoints, and it gives us confidence in his convictions as we contemplate his wise and strong grasp of the matters in dispute.

VII. *His Earnestness.*—This feature of his character is seen at almost every stage. In the opening words (ch. i. 8-15) we are made conscious of his intense desire to reach Rome and to preach the Gospel in the great metropolis. His discussion of the Gospel is marked by the same earnestness, as he elaborates point by point the truth for which he has lived. When, too, he has to speak of his countrymen, the Jews, we observe at every stage of his discussion that he is keenly alive to their spiritual loss in the rejection of Christ, and this stirs his earnestness to the highest point. It is just the same when he is led to speak of the great work of his life as the Apostle to the Gentiles. His overmastering thought is the proclamation of the Gospel everywhere, and his supreme ambition is to make Christ known to all those who had never heard of Him (ch. xv. 18-21). As we contemplate this dominating earnestness of the great Apostle we cannot help feeling rebuked by our own puny efforts at soul-winning, and our own failure to respond to the call of the Gospel of Christ. If Simeon standing before the portrait of Henry Martyn was ever reminded to "Be in earnest," much more ought the consideration of an Epistle like this to stir our hearts to be in earnest "in season and out of season" on behalf of our Master and His work.

VIII. *His Patriotism.*—The fact that the Apostle had become a Christian did not make him any the less a Jew. On the contrary, he had an intensity of feeling for his fellow-countrymen which he never possessed in his unconverted days. The Christian should always be the truest patriot because of his possession of that Gospel which alone can make a country righteous, powerful, and strong. The strong feeling on behalf of the Jews is seen not only in the great section which deals with this problem (ch. ix.-xi.), but also in those references to the journey to Jerusalem which, as we know, had such a definite bearing on St. Paul's life and service for Israel. May we not once again contemplate amidst this thought of patriotism the great necessity for missions to Israel? If the Apostle felt so keenly the burden of sending the Gospel to the Jews, we too ought to have in mind the great principle that actuated him: "to the Jew first." Even as Apostle to the Gentiles St. Paul was ever anxious to move the Jews to emulation in order if possible to lead them to Christ.

IX. *His Certitude.*—We cannot fail to notice at every point of the Apostle's discussion the quiet, calm assurance of his presentation of the truth. He writes as a man who knows and is sure of his ground. There is no hitch, no hesitation, no difficulty, but, throughout, a perfect realization that the truth possesses him and that he possesses the truth. In particular the treatment in the closing section of his great doctrinal passage (ch. viii. 31-39) shows the buoyant confidence and absolute assurance of the Apostle's attitude to Christ. He knows Whom he believes, and he is perfectly certain of his ground as he contemplates past, present, and future, and bursts forth into rapturous adoration, "If God be for us who can be against us?" It makes all the difference to Christian life if it can go far beyond "I believe," or "I hope," and can look up to God in quiet faith and full assurance with, "I know."

As we contemplate these and other similar elements of the Apostle's life we cannot imagine anything finer than the type of Christian character here portrayed. And if we seek to know the cause of it all we are conpelled to attribute it to the Apostle's relation to Christ and His Gospel. Doubtless Saul of Tarsus was a man of fine temperament, great ability, and strong character in his unregenerate life. But it was the coming into contact with Christ that transformed him into what he was and gave him his Christlikeness of character and conduct. If we were permitted to ask him the secret of it all he would reply, and that with evident truth and ringing conviction, "By the grace of God I am what I am."

LXXI

A REVIEW

II. The Apostle's Letter

The importance of the Epistle to the Romans has long been recognized, and it is rightly regarded as in some respects the greatest of all the Apostle's writings. Among its elements of interest and value the following may be regarded as particularly noteworthy:—

I. *Doctrinal Value.*—More than any other Epistle, this gives a systematic treatment of some of the leading doctrines of the Apostolic message. While other Epistles, like Galatians, Ephesians, Colossians, and even Corinthians, have their doctrinal elements of supreme value, there is a system and a fulness in the treatment of Romans that marks it out from all the rest of St. Paul's works. No one can read its great sections on Justification, Sanctification, Consecration, to say nothing of its profound treatment of the Jewish problem, without becoming conversant with some of the leading doctrines of the Christian religion.

II. *Practical Value.*—Doctrine is always intended to be expressed in duty. Christian teaching is never merely speculative, but always intensely practical, and all that the Apostle has to say on such questions as Sin, Redemption, and Holiness, are related immediately and constantly to the life of the individual believer and of the Christian community. At every point his teaching is definitely personal and is intended for full and constant reproduction in character and conduct. Whether he speaks of the results of sin in Jew and Gentile, or of justification by faith, or of union with Christ in His death and resurrection, or of the gift of the Holy Spirit to the believer, or of Jewish rebellion, or of Gentile acceptance, or of the relation of the believer to the Christian community and the State, the doctrine inculcated is intended to be expressed in life. The ideal is to become realized, and following His Master St. Paul's supreme thought is this: "If ye know these things, happy are ye if ye do them."

III. *Historical Value.*—More than any other Epistle, Romans is concerned with the relation of the two periods of God's dealings with mankind, the Jewish and the Christian dispensations. The Apostle, as we have seen, shows that between the two there is at once an underlying harmony and an essential difference, and it is the discussion of these points that affords so much that is practically valuable to the student of history. In the same way the discussion turns on the religious differences between Jews and Gentiles, and thus provides another aspect of the historical problem. St. Paul was a great historical scholar, and yet underlying all his treatment of history is the religious idea and purpose. He would be the first to say what appears on almost every page of his discussion of history:—

> "There's a Divinity that shapes our ends,
> Rough hew them how we will."

IV. *Dispensational Value.*—History looks backward, but this Epistle looks forward as well, and it is in connection with a great future that part of its importance is seen. We have noticed something of this in our study of the great Jewish section. Romans should be constantly read in the light of the promise to Abraham (Gen. xii.). Israel failed to understand the full bearing of the Divine promise: "In thee and in thy seed shall all the nations of the earth be blessed." The opponents of the Apostle thought this meant that the Jews were to be blessed above and beyond all other nations, and while this was true in itself it was not the whole truth. God had chosen Israel not for itself, but for the sake of others, and the Apostle's discussion (ch. xi.) is to the effect that in the future the Jews are to be the means of blessing to the whole world in the fulfilment of God's purposes. It is this dispensational aspect, as it is rightly called, that makes this writing so important. And when, as we have seen, we view the Epistle in this light, it becomes luminous with new ideas and suggestions. Bishop Lightfoot and Dr. Hort were not far wrong when they regarded the great section about Israel (ch. ix.-xi.) as in some respects the very heart and core of the Epistle. And when we look at what the Apostle wrote in the light of this great truth we see that from the opening almost to the closing words the two dispensations, Jewish and Gentile, are in sight throughout. We must never allow the present possessions and privileges of the Church of God to shut our eyes to the Old Testament promises to the Jews. All the blessing that has come to the Church in the past and present is due to the Jews, from whom Christ came after the flesh, and it will be no different in the future; for all the blessing that is to come to the world when the Church of God has been taken away is to be through a Jewish channel. Well may the Apostle, as he contemplates all these glories of the future, burst forth into his doxology to "the depth of the wealth and of the wisdom and of the knowledge of God."

V. *Philosophical Value.*—The Apostle was a profound teacher as well as a practical evangelist, and in the course of his discussion he enables us to see some of the higher and more philosophical aspects and implications of the Gospel. He introduces us to his philosophy of religion, as Sir William Ramsay rightly calls it (ch. i.), showing us that there was a primitive revelation, followed by human degradation, and that moral corruption invariably follows religious debasement. He also gives us a philosophy of nature (ch. viii.) in his wonderful revelation that in some way or other nature and man are so connected that the ultimate victory over sin will issue in a new creation and a marvelous transformation of nature. So also we have the Apostle's philosophy of history, as he states and discusses the precise places of Jew and Gentile in the great unifying process of the future. The sweep of the Apostle's thought as he realizes first the place of Jew and Gentile, and then the unity of both that is to be consummated, is one of the most remarkable features of this remarkable Epistle. Not least of all is what may be called the Apostle's philosophy of law, as he states (ch. xiii.) the relation of the Christian to the country in which he happens to dwell. Submission to authority, and love to our fellowmen, is the simple yet sufficient principle that should dominate the Christian life. And thus quite apart from the purely theological and dogmatic elements of this Epistle we see its underlying philosophy as expressed by the great thinker.

VI. *Psychological Value.*—Students of human nature always find in this Epistle a wealth of information. The profound thought of the unity of the race (ch. v.) will be a starting point for much careful study. The way in which the results of sin in human action are depicted is another important topic (ch. i.). The possibilities of intellectual pride and moral self-deception amidst definite evil constitutes yet another aspect of thought (ch. ii.). The bondage of the will, and indeed the entire nature, to the power of evil is, however, the greatest problem in this connection. The more the great passages (ch. vi., vii.) are studied, the more clearly it will be seen that only in the results of sin on every part of our inner being can some of the deepest problems of life be met and explained. The conflict between good and evil, the defeat of good by evil, and the powerlessness of human nature to recommend itself to God and make itself holy, are among the great principles of life which led the Apostle to emphasize the need of that Gospel in which alone victory can be found.

VII. *Spiritual Value.*—The same writing that shows the powerlessness of our nature through the indwelling of sin reveals the Gospel as "the power of God," a power that is bestowed upon us by the indwelling presence of the Holy Spirit. After the one simple hint given to us in chapter v. about the Spirit of God, we are introduced to a chapter which may be called the *locus classicus* of the New Testament in regard to the work of the Holy Spirit on the soul. No other section has anything like the fulness, variety, and depth of teaching on this subject, and the more earnestly we ponder, and the more definitely we appropriate the fact of the Spirit's work, the more effective will our life and service be.

VIII. *Prophetical Value.*—There is one section (ch. xi.) where the Apostle leaves altogether the historical attitude, and occupies himself with that which is purely predictive. As already pointed out, there was nothing whatever in the circumstances of his time that should have prompted him to deal with this subject. Indeed, everything, humanly speaking, was against the thought of any glorious future for Jew and Gentile in which they would be united in Christ, but the Apostle does not hesitate to predict a wonderful time, and the result is that ch. xi. stands, and will stand, as one of the essentially prophetic parts of the New Testament. It is easy to think lightly of the old definition of prophecy as "history written beforehand," but it is impossible to ignore the predictive element as expressed in this chapter of the Epistle.

IX. *Evidential Value.*—It is impossible to overlook the real importance of Romans as an evidence of Christianity. St. Paul possessed the three essential requirements of a true witness: disinterestedness, sincerity, and ability. He had no personal interests to serve by becoming a Christian; on the contrary; humanly speaking, it was a change fatal to all his natural hopes. The honesty of the Apostle is equally evident, for no one has ever dreamed of charging him with any form of insincerity. As to his ability, it is patent on the face of everything he said and did, and all this makes his testimony to Christ and Christianity of the highest possible value.

> "No man ever forged this Epistle. It carries its own credentials on the face of it, and shows the broad seal of heaven stamped upon it, as clearly as the heavens and the earth declare that creation is the work of God, and not of an impostor" Haldane, *Romans,* p. 708).

In the face of these considerations we are justified in calling constant and close attention to the witness borne by St. Paul to the Christianity of his time.

LXXII

A REVIEW

III. The Apostle's Gospel

It is obvious that in the light of the Apostle's characteristic phrase twice used, "My Gospel (ch. ii. 16; xvi. 25), there must have been something distinctive about the message delivered by him. It seems essential, therefore, to look a little closely at his presentation of Christianity.

I. *Its Source.*—Why did the Apostle speak of the Gospel as his own? The inquiry is important. Does it mean that the way of salvation is, in Godet's words, "a creation of his powerful understanding, or a revelation of God's mind. . . . In the latter case we have a witness speaking; in the former a genius speculating. . . . In the first place the Epistle of Paul deserves our admiration; in the second our faith; it is clear that the difference is great and that the question cannot be declared idle" (*Romans,* vol. ii., pp. 431, 432). Now there can be no question that if we accept the Apostle's own testimony, his Gospel was a revelation from God. This keynote is struck in the opening words, and finds an echo at the close, while in other Epistles the same ringing testimony is given. "I certify you, that the Gospel which was preached of me is not after man. For I neither received it of man, neither was I taught it, but by the revelation of Jesus Christ" (Gal. i. 11, 12). The reason, therefore, why the Apostle speaks of "my Gospel" is that he had himself received the message direct from God, had appropriated it to himself for his own needs, and for years had preached it out of the fulness of his conviction and adhesion. It was the specific message intended for the whole world which could rightly be described by the Apostle of the Gentiles as his own Gospel. It is this that he means when he speaks of "the Gospel of the glory of the blessed God which was committed to my trust" (1 Tim. i. 11), and "Jesus Christ, risen from the dead, of the seed of David, according to my Gospel" (2 Tim. ii. 8). It was the same consciousness of a Divine revelation received into his heart and reproduced in his testimony that makes him speak to the Corinthians of "the Gospel which I preached unto you, which also ye have received, and wherein ye stand; by which also ye are saved. . . . For I delivered unto you first of all that which I also received" (1 Cor. xv. 1-3). This Divine source of the Pauline Gospel gives it its supreme authority, its distinctive character, and its unerring force.

II. *Its Nature.*—But what was the substance of this Gospel in which the Apostle gloried? As we recall the various sections of this great Epistle we are enabled to see the truths that filled the Apostle's heart and overflowed through his lips and life.

(*a*) It is the Gospel of Human Condemnation. But is not this an incongruity? Can the thought of condemnation be associated with "Good News"? It can, if we carefully remember that it is the first, and only the first, stage of a Divine message. It is the Gospel to the unsaved, the message of conviction, the declaration that man has sinned, and that judged by the standard of the Divine law he is guilty before God. It is the message that sin means lawlessness, and that in the sight of God there is no essential difference in the fact of human sinfulness. It means that God's revelations in nature, and even in the Old Testament, are not sufficient, that no natural theology can show how to put away sin, and that only as men measure themselves by the perfect law of God can they come to realize the true state of their souls through sin. It is recorded of a man under conviction of sin that on going to a clergyman with the burden of his trouble, the latter burst forth with an exclamation of praise to God. "What!" said the other, "do you praise God that I am a sinner?" "No," was the reply, "I praise God that you know that you are a sinner."

(*b*) It is the Gospel of Complete Justification. When the sinner becomes conscious of sin and condemnation the message of the Apostle assures him of the way of righteousness by faith in Christ.

Justification means acceptance with God, the gift of Christ as our righteousness, to be received by simple trust. No such Gospel as this ever came from man, for there is that in human nature which is utterly opposed to righteousness as a gift. Man always seeks to *attain,* while the Gospel urges men to *obtain* this righteousness by faith in Christ, for justification is "the glorious Gospel" which he preached far and wide. More perhaps than anything else this can be called his own Gospel.

(*c*) It is the Gospel of Continuous Sanctification. The soul that has been accepted must become acceptable. The removal of sins through justification does not carry with it the removal of sin as an inward principle. For this the Gospel of Sanctification is essential, which means holiness of heart and life, and victory over indwelling sin. In the three central chapters (vi.-viii.) the Apostle proclaims this aspect of his message, assuring the soul not only that the past has been forgiven and the sinner reinstated in his true position with God, not only that the future hereafter is all assured by virtue of the same Divine righteousness, but that the present time, be it long or short, between the past and the future, is met, and more than met by the presence of the Holy Spirit in the heart, Whose indwelling power gives complete and continuous victory, counteracting the evil principle and enabling the soul to walk in newness of life and to serve in newness of spirit.

(*d*) It is the Gospel of Divine Vindication. Face to face with the great and pressing Jewish problem the Apostle sets himself to "justify the ways of God to man." With unquestioned force and absolute fearlessness he drives home the two great truths: that God is righteous, and man is responsible. Not for an instant will he allow even the possibility of various objections raised against God; on the contrary, he carries the war into the enemy's country, and shows that so far from God being responsible for the state of the Jewish nation, it was due wholly and solely to their unwillingness to submit themselves to the righteousness of God. Then he goes on to depict in glowing terms that wonderful future when in the presence of Jewish and Gentile blessing God will be vindicated before the whole universe when He has mercy upon all.

(*e*) It is the Gospel of Practical Consecration. The Apostle was charged more than once with teaching in such a way as to give license to sin, but the taunt is absolutely unwarranted, as we see from various parts of this Epistle. In particular, the closing chapters show that "the mercies of God," as revealed in the Gospel, are the only and adequate motive power for personal devotedness of life. Whether in the Church or in the State, whether in individual or corporate life, whether among the vigorous or the halting in Christian experience, the life of the believer is to be wholly dedicated to his Master's service and glory. Everything, everywhere, and at all times, a life is to be lived which will reveal the beauty of holiness and the bounty of Divine love. The Apostle of righteousness by faith is the Apostle of reality by works, and the sanctification of the soul within is to express itself in the service of the life without. In matters of personal duty, Church requirements, State obligations, and conscientious scruples, the one principle that is to dominate everything is "the good, and perfect, and acceptable will of God."

III. *Its Characteristics.*—As we pass from the source and nature of the Apostolic Gospel we cannot help observing the features which marked his presentation of it.

(*a*) It was a Free Gospel. There were no conditions laid down, except the obvious and essential requirement of faith. This was man's simple, necessary, and adequate answer to the revelation of God. Faith received the gift from God, faith responded to the claim of God, faith rested on the promise of God, and in these three things the Apostle and his hearers found one of the glories of the Gospel of Christ.

(*b*) It was a Full Gospel. It covered all the needs of the soul, past, present, and future. Whether there was a sense of guilt, or a consciousness of condemnation, or a realization of separation, or an experience of bondage, or a feeling of powerlessness, or a loathing of defilement, the Gospel was ready with its complete provision. Towering above man's highest needs, rising high over man's sins, meeting man's greatest deserts, and soaring aloft over man's highest thoughts, the fulness of the Pauline Gospel was an inspiration to the preacher and a consolation to the recipient.

(*c*) It was a Universal Gospel. Wherever the Apostle went he preached it everywhere, and at all times. To Jew and Gentile, Greek and Barbarian, bond and free, wise and foolish, the Gospel was equally necessary, equally available, and equally adequate. Again and again the Apostle rejoiced to proclaim that "the same Lord over all is rich unto all that call upon Him."

(*d*) It was an Eternal Gospel. It lasted because it was permanent. It swept the whole horizon of human life. Looking back over the past, looking round upon the present, and looking on to the future, it proclaimed and provided the Lord our Righteousness."

And we must never forget that, as Godet well says, the experience of ages has set its seal to the conviction that the Apostle's Gospel was not his own, but God's.

LXXIII

A REVIEW

IV. The Apostle's Master

It is sometimes said that the Epistle to the Romans is not one of St. Paul's Christological Epistles. This is doubtless true in certain respects, especially when it is compared with Ephesians, and even Philippians. But there is more than enough in it to show what the Apostle believed and taught concerning the Person and Work of his Master. The Gospel which we have been considering had Christ for its theme and substance. Every blessing, every grace, every power, every privilege, every duty, was associated and inextricably bound up with the Pauline conception of Jesus Christ. What then may we learn concerning the Christ of the Epistle to the Romans?

I. *His Human Life.*—Very simply, and yet with perfect clearness the human nature and earthly life of Jesus Christ are stated and implied. He is "of the seed of David according to the flesh" (ch. i. 3). He was sent by God "in the likeness of sinful flesh" (ch. viii. 3). And He came from Jewish stock "concerning the flesh" (ch. ix. 5). Nothing could be more unequivocal than these references to the real humanity of Jesus Christ.

II. *His Divine Position.*—In the same way the Apostle bears abundant testimony to the Divine nature of Christ. Five times He is spoken of as "Son of God," and twice as "God's own Son." All through the Epistle He is depicted as the Source of salvation and the Object of faith in such a way as to prove beyond all question that these redemptive acts would have been impossible in anyone who is not "God, blessed for ever" (ch. ix. 5).

III *His Scriptural Relationships.*—At the outset the Apostle strikes the keynote of the Epistle, by speaking of the Gospel concerning

His Son as "promised afore through His prophets in the Holy Scriptures" (ch. i. 2), and it is not long before he elaborates this by showing that the righteousness of God provided in Christ is "witnessed by the law and the prophets" (ch. iii. 21). From the earliest words to the very last sentence the Old Testament bulks largely in the Apostle's thought and teaching. Everything concerning Christ is justified and vindicated from the Divine oracles, and thus both Jew and Gentile are given the Divine warrant and absolute assurance for all that the writer has to say. This connection of Jesus Christ with the Scriptures of the Old Covenant is one of the most striking features of Pauline thought in this Epistle, and calls for prolonged study as a testimony both to Christ and to the Old Testament.

IV. *His Redemptive Work.*—This Epistle is pre-eminently concerned with the message of the Cross. The death of Jesus Christ is shown to be a propitiation for the sin of man, and also a vindication of the righteousness of God (ch. iii. 25, 26). God gave His Son to die for the sin of the world, and thereby He commended His love toward us (ch. v. 8). The scarlet thread teaching of atoning sacrifice runs through all the Apostle's teaching, and whether it be for the righteousness of justification, or of sanctification, or of glorification, or of consecration, the sacrificial death of Christ is the Source and Spring of everything. We are justified by His blood; we are united with Him in His death for holiness; we are saved from wrath through Him; and we are so to live as not to hurt the conscience of anyone for whom Christ died. At all times, under all circumstances, the Apostle glories in the Cross.

V. *His Glorious Resurrection.*—This is the other side of the Apostolic message. The Christ Who died is the Christ Who lives, and as we are reconciled by His death, so we are kept safe in His life. His death was our redemption, and His resurrection our vindication. It provides newness of life, guarantees fulness of power, and assures us of immortality hereafter. The resurrection is the only explanation of Pauline Christianity.

VI. *His Racial Headship.*—In the great passage which deals with the two Adams the Apostle teaches that as we are united with the first Adam through sin, we are also one with the second Adam through grace and righteousness. Whatever we have lost in the one we have more than regained in the Other, for if trespasses abound through Adam, grace super-abounds in Christ. It is this racial unity that gives point to the Apostolic phrase, "in Christ," for it is in our union with Jesus Christ in death and life that we realize in personal, practical experience the preciousness of His death and the power of His resurrection. "In Christ" has been called "the monogram of St. Paul," and this is certainly true, for it is the seat and center of his thought concerning Jesus Christ.

VII. *His Divine Lordship.*—St. Paul's favorite title for his Master is "Jesus Christ our Lord," and this keynote is struck in the opening words (ch. i. 3), and carried on in almost every important section until the very close of this great writing. Every part of his doctrinal teaching is associated with the Lordship of Christ. "Being justified by faith, we have peace through our Lord Jesus Christ" (ch. v. 1). We rejoice in God "through our Lord Jesus Christ" (ch. v. 11). Grace reigns unto eternal life "through Jesus Christ our Lord" (ch. v. 21). "The gift of God is eternal life in Christ Jesus our Lord" (ch. vi. 23). He thanks God for deliverance "through Jesus Christ our Lord" (ch. vii. 25). And nothing shall be able to separate us from the love of God which is "in Christ Jesus our Lord" (ch. viii. 39). Not only so, but we are to confess "Jesus as Lord" (ch. x. 9), and never to forget that living or dying "we are the Lord's" (ch. xiv. 8). Indeed, it was for this very purpose that Christ died and rose from the dead, "that He might be Lord" (ch. xiv. 9). And every matter of conscience, every scruple, every difficulty is so to be faced that we may with one mind glorify the God and Father of "our Lord Jesus Christ" (ch. xv. 6). Nothing could be clearer or more unquestioned than this constant emphasis on the Lordship of Christ and the absolute necessity of our loyalty to Him.

As we review these aspects of the Person and Work of Jesus Christ and recall the fact that all this was taught and circulated within thirty years of the crucifixion of Christ on the Cross, we can understand at least a little of what the early Church thought of Christ, and of how He was regarded by Christians. The earliest message concerning Him was as high as our message today. Christ was never an example of Faith, but always its Object, and in these various aspects of what He was and did we have the essential substance and satisfying content of the Pauline Gospel.

And so we close our study of this marvelous Epistle. We have but touched the merest fringe of it; the study is for a life-time. As Luther said: "All wherein true Christianity consisteth . . . is to be found here in such perfection that it is impossible to wish anything more or better. So rich a treasure is it of spiritual wealth that even to him who has read a thousand times something new will ever be presenting itself." Practically the whole of Christianity is found here, and however much we may know of it already, there will still be always something fresh to discover in order to guide, cheer, and bless the longing, lowly, and loving soul. It will repay all the attention we can give it; the mind will be instructed, the heart uplifted, the imagination inspired, and the will directed. And those who come to it with an earnest desire to learn its truths will enter into its meaning, and will also experience that fulness of grace, rest, joy, and peace which it is absolutely certain to produce in the hearts and lives of all those who wish to know and possess of a truth the Pauline Gospel of the righteousness and grace of Jesus Christ our Lord.

BIBLIOGRAPHY

ALFORD, DEAN. *Greek Testament: Romans.*
BARMBY, J. *The Pulpit Commentary: Romans.*
BEET, J. A. *St. Paul's Epistle to the Romans.*
BROUGHTON, L. *Salvation and the Old Theology.*
BROWN, D. *Handbooks for Bible Classes: Romans.*
BROWN, J. *Exposition of the Epistle to the Romans.*
BRUCE, A. B. *St. Paul's Conception of Christianity.*
BULLINGER, E. W. *The Church Epistles: Romans.*
CHALMERS, T. *Lectures on the Romans.*
DARBY, J. N. *Synopsis of the Books of the Bible: Romans.*
DENNEY, J. *Expositor's Greek Testament: Romans.*
DU BOSE, W. P. *The Gospel according to St. Paul.*
FORBES, J. *Analytical Commentary on the Romans.*
FORT, J. *God's Salvation as set forth in the Epistle to the Romans.*
FOX, C. A. *The Spiritual Grasp of the Epistles.*
GAIRDNER, W. H. T. *Helps to the Study of the Epistle to the Romans,* Parts I. and II.
GARVIE, A. E. *Century Bible: Romans.*
GIFFORD, E. H. *The Speaker's Commentary: Romans.*
GODET, F. *Commentary on the Romans,* Vols. I. and II.
GORE, BISHOP. *St. Paul's Epistle to the Romans,* Vols. I. and II.
GOVETT, R. *The Righteousness of God.*
HALDANE, R. *Exposition of the Epistle to the Romans.*
HOARE, J. G. *Righteousness and Life.*
HODGE, C. *Commentary on the Epistle to the Romans.*
KELLY, W. *Notes on Romans.*
LIDDON, CANON H. P. *Explanatory Analysis on St. Paul's Epistle to the Romans.*
LIGHTFOOT, BISHOP J. B. *Notes on the Epistles of St. Paul;* Article on "Romans" in Smith's *Dictionary of the Bible.*

MABIE, H. C. *The Divine Reason of the Cross*, Ch. VII.
MACLAREN, A. *Expositions of Holy Scripture: The Epistle to the Romans.*
MAURO, P. *The "Wretched Man" and his Deliverance.*
MEYER, H. A. W. *Commentary on the New Testament: Romans*, Vols. I. and II.
MORGAN, G. CAMPBELL. *The Analyzed New Testament: The Epistle to the Romans.*
MOULE, BISHOP H. C. G. *The Expositor's Bible: The Epistle to the Romans. Cambridge Bible for Schools: The Epistle to the Romans.*
NEIL, C. *The Expositor's Commentary: Romans.*
NEWELL, W. R. *Bible Class Lessons on Romans.*
PHILIPPI, F. A. *Commentary on the Romans*, Vols. I. and II.
RAINSFORD, M. *Lectures on Romans v.; Lectures on Romans vi.; Lectures on Romans vii; No Condemnation—No Separation; Lectures on Romans viii.*
RUTHERFORD, W. G. *St. Paul's Epistle to the Romans.*
SABATIER, A. *The Apostle Paul.*
SANDAY, W. *Cassell's Commentary for Schools: Romans.*
SANDAY AND HEADLAM. *The International Critical Commentary: Romans.*
SIMPSON, A. B. *Christ in the Bible: Romans.*
STIFLER, J. M. *The Epistle to the Romans.*
VAUGHAN, C. J. *St. Paul's Epistle to the Romans.*
VENN, J. *St. Paul's Three Chapters on Holiness.*
WALFORD, W. *Curae Romanae.*
WENHAM, A. E. *Ruminations on the Epistle of Paul the Apostle to the Romans.*
Expository Times, Vols. II. and V.
Homiletic Review, Vols. VIII., IX., and X.